Colloquial
# Hindi

# The Colloquial Series

The following languages are available in the Colloquial series:

| | | |
|---|---|---|
| Afrikaans | German | Romanian |
| Albanian | Greek | Russian |
| Amharic | Gujarati | Scottish Gaelic |
| Arabic (Levantine) | Hebrew | Serbian |
| Arabic of Egypt | Hindi | Slovak |
| Arabic of the Gulf and | Hungarian | Slovene |
| Saudi Arabia | Icelandic | Somali |
| Basque | Indonesian | Spanish |
| Breton | Irish (forthcoming) | Spanish of Latin |
| Bulgarian | Italian | America |
| Cambodian | Japanese | Swahili |
| Cantonese | Korean | Swedish |
| Catalan | Latvian | Tamil |
| Chinese | Lithuanian | Thai |
| Croatian | Malay | Turkish |
| Czech | Mongolian | Ukrainian |
| Danish | Norwegian | Urdu |
| Dutch | Panjabi | Vietnamese |
| English | Persian | Welsh |
| Estonian | Polish | Yoruba |
| Finnish | Portuguese | |
| French | Portuguese of Brazil | |

## COLLOQUIAL 2s Series

*The Next Step in Language Learning*

| | | |
|---|---|---|
| Chinese | Italian | Spanish |
| Dutch | Portuguese of Brazil | Spanish of Latin |
| French | (forthcoming) | America |
| German (forthcoming) | Russian | |

Colloquials are now supported by FREE AUDIO available online. All audio tracks referenced within the text are free to stream or download from www.routledge.com/cw/colloquials. If you experience any difficulties accessing the audio on the companion website, or still wish to purchase a CD, please contact our customer services team through www.routledge.com/info/contact.

# Colloquial
# Hindi

## The Complete Course for Beginners

Tej K. Bhatia

Routledge
Taylor & Francis Group

LONDON AND NEW YORK

First published 1996
by Routledge
This edition first published 2008
by Routledge
2 Park Square, Milton Park, Abingdon, Oxon, OX14 4RN

Simultaneously published in the USA and Canada
by Routledge
711 Third Avenue, New York, NY 10017

*Routledge is an imprint of the Taylor & Francis Group, an informa business*

Typeset in 10/12 pt Times by Graphicraft Limited, Hong Kong

*British Library Cataloguing in Publication Data*
A catalogue record for this book is available from the
British Library

*Library of Congress Cataloging-in-Publication Data*
Bhatia, Tej K.
  Colloquial Hindi : a complete course for beginners /
Tej K. Bhatia. – [2nd, rev. ed.].
      p. cm.
    Previously published: 1996.
    Includes index.
  1. Hindi language – Textbooks for foreign speakers – English.   2. Hindi
language – Conversation and phrase books – English.   3. Hindi language
– Grammar.   I. Title.
PK1935.B525 2007
491′. 4382421–dc22                                         2007001478

ISBN13: 978-1-138-94972-0 (pbk)

Printed and bound in Great Britain by
TJ International Ltd, Padstow, Cornwall

**In memory of**
**my mother, Shrimati Krishna Wanti Bhatia**
**and**
**my father, Shri Parma Nand Bhatia**

# Contents

# Preface

Since the publication of this book over a decade ago, it has undergone several reprints. Nothing is more gratifying for an author than to hear from his/her readers. I consider myself privileged to be the beneficiary of my readers' reactions, suggestions, compliments and wish-lists which poured in from a highly diverse cross-section of readers around the globe. This encouraged me to create a revised and expanded version of the book. Based on the input that I have received, I know it is not the ideal solution to the multitudes of topics (ranging from the treatment of the Hindi script, grammatical details and cross-cultural insights) that one wishes to address; however, it is a modest step toward that goal.

Many changes have occurred since the first publication of the book. India is fast becoming a major global power. The dynamics of communicative situations further call for changes to reflect new situations and realities. Readers will find the following new changes and additions in this book:

* Facts and figures have been updated.
* The section dealing with the script has been beefed up considerably.
* Dialogues and prose texts integrate the Roman as well as the Devanagari in a way that reflects a mutually-feeding relationship between the two. As one of the anonymous reviewers of the book rightly noted, the execution of the Devanagari version of conversations and prose texts was cumbersome in the first edition. This limitation has been addressed.
* Roman is a non-syllabic script whereas Devanagari is syllabic. Whenever relevant, the complementary strengths of the two writing systems are exploited, particularly in explanations of grammar.
* While the new guidelines issued by the Government of India have been followed throughout the book (e.g. the letter jʰa; preference for *e* instead of *ye* in words such as **cāhie**; not separating the postpositions with the pronouns), readers are also exposed to

variation (e.g. two ways of writing the third person singular, polite imperative forms and the past tense).
- Whenever relevant, the content has been modernized.
- New topics of cross-cultural communication have been introduced in the cultural notes (e.g. how to say 'no' in socially sensitive situations, linguistic attitudes and hyper-politeness, etiquettes of gift-giving).
- Another innovation is the Online Resource Guide and the Internet links.
- Old errors and misprints have been corrected.

In spite of this, I am acutely aware that this work is not free from limitations. Therefore, I would be grateful for any comments, criticisms or suggestions that perceptive scholars may have on this book. Please send them to me at the following address: Linguistic Studies Program, 312 HBC, Syracuse University, Syracuse, New York-13244-1160, USA or send an email to: tkbhatia@syr.edu.

# Acknowledgements

I am especially indebted to Sophie Oliver, Senior Editor, Language Learning, for agreeing to consider and produce the new and revised version of this book and for her commendable patience and encouragement. I am equally indebted to three anonymous reviewers for their constructive and insightful input.

I have contracted many debts in the process of writing this book and its earlier edition. I am also grateful to my teachers and colleagues, Yamuna and Braj Kachru who have taught me and influenced me since my graduate school. I am also indebted to my friends and colleagues Rajeshwari Pandharipande, James W. Gair, Hans Hock, Meena and S.N. Sridhar, Rakesh Bhatt, Rajesh Kumar, William C. Ritchie, Jaklin Kornfilt, Jennifer L. Smith, Vasu Reganathan, Afroz Taj, Amer Bridger, Cassidy Perraeault and Dr Mangat R. Bhardwaj, the author of the companion volume on Punjabi, for their valuable discussions on matters of Hindi teaching and linguistics. Finally, I also owe my thanks to Dr P.R. Mehandiratta (Director General, American Institute of Indian Studies, New Delhi) and to my colleagues at the South Asia Center, Ann Gold, Jishnu Shankar and Susan Wadley, for their comments, support and encouragement.

My mother passed away before the first edition of this book became a reality. This has left a permanent vacuum in my life. My family migrated from the North West Frontier province close to the Pakistan and Afghanistan border, so Hindi was my mother's third language and according to the value system of that time she never had any formal schooling. During the writing of this book I remembered how at the insistence of her children she learned to sign her name in Hindi instead of using a thumb print as a signature. It is still a mystery to me how and when she learned to read the *Gita* in Hindi. I had thought there would still be a lot of time for us and that these questions were not urgent. I was wrong. This work is especially dedicated to her memory.

I owe special thanks to my wife, Shobha, for her encouragement and support and to my daughter, Kanika, and my son, Ankit, who first inspired me to write this book so that they could learn Hindi. My special thanks are also due to my niece, Nandita. No words can express my deepest appreciation of my brothers in India for their constant support during my entire career.

The pictures produced in this book were taken by the author as part of the ongoing collaborative project, Hindi OnLine, between Syracuse University and the University of Illinois at Urbana-Champaign and the University of Texas at Austin. The project is funded by a grant from the South Asia Research Center (SALRC), the University of Chicago and the US Department of Education. I gratefully acknowledge the support of Dr Steven M. Poulos, Director, SALRC, for making this work possible.

My heartfelt thanks are also due to: Professor Omkar Koul for his technical assistance in the preparation of the manuscript and his perceptive comments; and to the College of Arts and Sciences' Dean Cathryn R. Newton, Associate Dean Dr Gerold Greeenberg and Dr Ben Ware, Vice President, Research and Computing, for their support of this work.

# भूमिका
# b<sup>h</sup>umikā

## Introduction

## A word to the learner

Welcome to *Colloquial Hindi*. Very often at social get-togethers in the West, I am asked with utmost sincerity whether or not I speak Hindu. Although I have no difficulty in understanding the real intent of the question, unwittingly I find myself in an embarrassing situation. This is particularly true if this inquiry happens to come directly from my host. You see, *Hindu* is the name of the predominant religion in India and Nepal; *Hindi* is the name of the language that is the *lingua franca* of South Asia.

## About the language

Hindi is a modern Indo-Aryan language spoken in South Asian countries (India, Pakistan, Nepal) and also in other countries outside Asia (Mauritius, Trinidad, Fiji, Surinam, Guyana, South Africa and other countries). Approximately eight hundred million people speak Hindi, as either a first (480 million) or second language. It is the second most widely spoken language in the world. Along with English, it is the official language of India. In addition, it is the state language of Bihar, Chattisgarh, Delhi, Haryana, Himachal Pradesh, Jarkhand, Madhya Pradesh, Rajasthan and Uttar Pradesh. Also, I should point out that Hindi is the language of Agra (the city of the Taj Mahal).

Hindi, which is a descendant of the Sanskrit language, is not strictly the name of any chief dialect of the area but is an adjective, Persian in origin, meaning Indian. Historically, it was synonymous with Hindui, Hindawi, Rexta and Rexti. The terms Urdu and Hindustani are also used to refer to this language. All these labels denote a mixed speech spoken around the area of Delhi, North India, which gained currency during the twelfth and thirteenth century as a contact language between the Arabs, Afghans, Persian and Turks, and native residents.

Hindi is written in the Devanagari script which is ranked as the most scientific writing system among the existing writing systems of the world. The Devanagari script is written from left to right and is a descendant of the Brahmi script which was well established in India before 500 BC. The script is phonetic in nature and there is a fairly regular correspondence between the letters and their pronunciation. For more details see the section on the Hindi writing system and pronunciation.

The literary history of Hindi goes back to the twelfth century. Some notable literary figures of Hindi are Kabir, Surdas and Tulsidas. The two notable linguistic features of the language are as follows: (1) Hindi still retains the original Indo-European (1500 BC) distinction between aspirated and unaspirated consonants which results in a four-way contrast as shown by the following examples: *kāl*, 'time', *kʰāl*, 'skin', *gāl*, 'cheek' and *gʰāl*, 'to put into'; (2) it has the feature of retroflexion in its consonant inventory, cf. *Tāl*, 'to put off' and *tāl*, 'pond'. The retroflex consonant is transcribed as the capital **T**. For more details see the section on the Hindi writing system and pronunciation.

Hindi has an approximately three-century-old, well-attested and rich grammatical tradition of its own. It is a by-product of the colonial era and was born shortly after the arrival of Europeans in India. For a detailed treatment of this topic in general and the grammatical tradition in particular, see Bhatia (1987).

## About this book

This book is designed as a complete first-year language course, keeping in mind the proficiency guidelines of the American Council on the Teaching of Foreign Languages (ACTFL) and the European Language Community. Every attempt is made to optimize this goal by integrating the linguistic content with the culture of South Asia in general and India in particular. In fact, while teaching the language I have attempted to answer those questions that are often asked about the culture of India.

In my professional life I have often witnessed the fact that the teaching of non-Western languages, including Hindi, is more challenging in the West than the teaching of Western languages. If you have experienced any of the following problems, this book will enable you to achieve the goals described above:

- You sweat at the mere thought of learning a foreign language and/or foreign script.
- You think Hindi is a very difficult language to learn, so why try?
- You have some serious business, research interests or not-so-serious interests (such as travel) in India but you have been led to believe that everybody in India speaks English.
- You have learned Hindi from tools and settings which make native speakers laugh secretly or openly at your language use.
- India is culturally and linguistically so distant from the West that one cannot help but shy away from it.
- You haven't heard of Bollywood movies.
- You consider French the only language fit for romance.

If you subscribe to one or all of the above, you are in for a surprise. First, you might discover in the process of learning the language that learning about Hindi is learning about one's own roots. The only difference is that European migration to India is perhaps the oldest of all migrations from Europe, or vice versa as shown by recent DNA research. For this reason, you will still find some striking similarities between Hindi and English. For example, the Hindi word for English 'name' is **nām**. The list goes on and on. The important thing to know is that Hindi belongs to the Indo-European language family and is similar to English in a number of ways. Learning to note these similarities will make the process of learning this language full of pleasant surprises.

The book is grounded in the *current theories of language acquisition, learnability* and *language use*. Unlike other books (even some of the latest ones), it never loses sight of the social–psychological aspects of language use. In this book, I have not attempted to act like a protector or saviour of language by engaging in linguistic prescriptivism and puritanism. What you will find in this book is how Hindi speakers use Hindi and communicate with each other in meaningful ways. No attempt is made to translate the English word artificially into Hindi if Hindi speakers treat the English word like any other Hindi word. I was outraged when I noticed in a widely circulated course on Hindi in which the waiter asks his customers for their order, the word 'order' translated using the same verb as the English 'obey my order!' For more details see the section entitled 'English Prohibition?' in Unit 2.

## Beware . . .

These prescriptivist tendencies defeat the real goal of learning a language in order to communicate with native speakers. Even some of the latest books on Hindi suffer from such problems and un-wittingly do a disservice to their learners because of their authors' lack of familiarity with the social–psychological dimensions of language use. I came across some examples in one of the most recent books on Hindi which teaches learners how to introduce themselves to native speakers. The sentences are grammatically correct but the author(s) fail to take into account the invisible dimension of the phenomenon of 'turn taking'. For example, it is acceptable for English speakers to introduce themselves with a string of two clauses following the word 'Hi' (e.g. 'Hi, my name is John and what is yours?'). However, the Hindi speaker will pause after the Hindi equivalent of 'Hi' and wait for the listener to respond with a greet-ing, and only after that will the Hindi speaker perform the task of telling his name and asking about his listener's name. The failure to teach learners about 'turn taking' through naturalistic conversa-tions makes them run the risk of being seen as 'pushy' or 'impatient' by native speakers. This book is particularly aware of such 'non-linguistic' or invisible dimensions of language use. Therefore, this book never loses sight of *cross-cultural communication* while teaching *linguistic communication*.

This book deals with the four main linguistic skills:

|              | *receptive*             | *productive*            |
|--------------|-------------------------|-------------------------|
| *Aural–oral* | listening comprehension | speaking comprehension  |
| *Visual*     | reading comprehension   | writing comprehension   |

These skills are introduced in a manner consistent with the insights of modern Chomskyan linguistics. The learners are exposed to rules and discovery procedures, similar to those employed by native speakers, which enable them to generate an infinite number of sen-tences in their native language. Not only that, these rules enable native speakers to generate new sentences they have never encountered before (see Bhatia and Ritchie 2006 for details). This is the conceptual framework, combined with my twenty-five years of classroom experience, which has gone into the makeup of this book. Unlike other phrasebooks which emphasize parroting sentences without gaining insight into the linguistic system, this book emphasizes and serves as a catalyst to promote linguistic creativity and optimization. This goal is achieved in a simple and unpretentious way avoiding system overload.

## How this book is organized

This book attempts to accommodate two types of learners: (1) those who want to learn the language through the Hindi script called the Devanagari script; and (2) those who wish to learn the language in a relatively short period of time without the aid of the Devanagari writing system (henceforth, Hindi script). Such pragmatic considerations are an important feature of this book.

The book begins with Hindi script and pronunciation. The main body deals with ten conversational units which consist of the following parts: (1) vocabulary; (2) dialogues with English translation; (3) notes detailing pronunciation, grammar and usage relating to the unit; and (4) exercises. The dialogues with 'Tell me why?' and humour columns together with the notes explicitly deal with those aspects of Indian culture about which I am most often asked. The vocabulary or the new words used in the dialogues are given in English and Devanagari script. You may wish to consult the vocabulary sections while doing exercises.

The grammar summary gives an overview of the Hindi grammatical tradition with full paradigms. This section complements the section 'Notes and grammar' given in each lesson.

The vocabulary section gives all the Hindi words used in the dialogues. The words are listed alphabetically both in Hindi and English. The basic vocabulary section classifies Hindi words into different semantic groups.

## How to use this book

This book focuses on two types of track: (1) for those learners who want to adopt the English script path; and (2) for those who want to learn the Hindi script. Although learning Hindi script is highly recommended, if you decide to choose the first track, you can bypass the lessons on the writing system. For every learner, on both tracks, the lesson on the 'Hindi writing system and pronunciation' is a must and familiarity with the salient phonetic features of Hindi together with the 'Transcription table' is imperative. Please make sure that you learn the transcription of conversations, which differs from media convention. As shown in the transcription table, media convention is often broad and unsystematic. Examples of pronunciation are also recorded on the audio. The exercises with the audio icon are recorded on the audio. If you wish, you can refer to the listening exercises transcripts at the end of the book.

If you are on the Hindi script track, you should start from script unit 1: you will learn Devanagari script in its printed as well as its handwritten form. Conversations and keys are given in Roman as well as in Hindi script. While working on the script units, you can make a start on the conversation units. There is an added incentive to consult the script units: their exercise sections give some of the most common expressions any visitor to India may need. They deal with situations such as customs and immigration, baggage, reading weather charts, making reservations, sending mail, gift-giving, annoying and cautionary settings, shopping, food, entertainment and renting.

Naturally, you will need to memorize the vocabulary. The notes sections give you help on pronunciation, grammar and usage. Reading and learning these notes will stimulate your linguistic creativity.

The reference grammar goes hand in hand with the grammatical notes given at the end of each dialogue. Answers to the exercises can be found in the key to exercises, in both Hindi and English scripts.

## Icons used in this book

Icons are used throughout this book for several reasons, the most important of which is to draw attention to those sections that require careful reading.

Audio Symbol          This symbol means that the corresponding exer-
                      cise requires the use of the audio that accompanies
                      this course.

Magic Key

Information next to this icon is critical for creativity and is worth memorizing.

Sherlock Holmes

This icon appears next to important examples of regular usage, the understanding of which is a primary source of creativity for the native speakers.

Remember

This icon reminds you of material covered earlier.

Caution

The material marked by this icon deserves special attention. It warns you about common mistakes and sources of misunderstanding.

Web links

For additional practice or materials, web links are provided.

The other icons used in the book are thematic in nature and should prove self-explanatory.

## Where to go from here

Of course, I do not pretend to teach you everything that needs to be known about Hindi. Language learning can be a life-long venture if you set your goals very high. Your next step is to look for books offering the intermediate and advanced Hindi courses listed at the end of the book. I give this information to alleviate the misconception, quite widespread in the West, that there is a lack of intermediate and advanced-level courses in Asian and African languages. There is no shortage of material, in print or on the web, at these levels. The only difficulty you might face is that this material will invariably be in Hindi script. If that poses a problem for you, there are still many ways you can continue to sharpen your linguistic skills, the most important of which is Hindi films. India is the world's largest producer of films which are widely accessible in the East and the West on video and DVD. To develop a taste for Hindi films is most important in taking you to advanced Hindi language learning. Readers will find the following web resources useful. Please remember, however, that the links may not always be active and that the content may change. The following links were active at the time of writing:

> http://www.latrobe.edu.au/indiangallery/hin11.htm
> http://www.ncsu.edu/project/hindi_lessons/

Due to limitations of space, detailed descriptions of monuments such as the Taj Mahal could not be included in this book; for the sight and sounds of Indian monuments, lessons 2 and 9 from the www.ncsu.edu website are particularly recommended.

For intermediate and advance readings, the following sites deserve attention:

> http://ccat.sas.upenn.edu/plc/hindi/video/
> http://lrrc3.sas.upenn.edu/hindi_unicode/
> http://philae.sas.upenn.edu/Hindi/hindi.html
> http://munshi-premchand.blogspot.com/
> http://www.abhivyakti-hindi.org/
> http://www.anubhuti-hindi.org/

Newspaper and media sites:

> http://www.bbc.co.uk/hindi/
> http://www.naidunia.com/

Collection of Indian Newspaper sites:

> http://www.indiapress.org/index.php/Hindi/400x60

Best wishes.

## Reference

Bhatia, Tej K. 1987. *A History of the Hindi Grammatical Tradition*. Leiden: E.J. Brill.
Bhatia, Tej K. and William C. Ritchie. 2006. *Handbook of Bilingualism*. Oxford: Blackwell Publishing.

# हिन्दी लेखन और उच्चारण
# hindī lek<sup>h</sup>an aur uccāraN

## Hindi writing system and pronunciation

## Introduction 🎧 (Audio 1:2)

This chapter briefly outlines the salient properties of Devanagari script and Hindi pronunciation. Hindi is written in Devanagari script. Even if you are not learning the script, this chapter is indispensable because you need to know the pronunciation values of the Roman/ English letters used in the conversational units. Also, one or two unfamiliar symbols are drawn from the International Phonetic Alphabet (IPA). The transcription scheme followed here is widely used in the teaching of Hindi and in Hindi language, literature and linguistics. As I have said, the best way to learn Hindi is to learn the script as well. However, if this is not possible due to consideration of time, you will still need to refer to the transcription table until you have mastered the letters and their pronunciation value.

Listen to and repeat the pronunciation of Hindi vowels and consonants together with their minimal pairs, recorded on the audio accompanying this book.

## Devanagari script

A number of languages are written in Devanagari script. Besides Hindi, Nepali, Marathi and Sanskrit are also written in this script. Other languages such as Punjabi, Bengali, Gujarati use a slight variation of this script. This means that roughly *half of humanity* use either this script or its close variant which follows the same under-lying organizational system.

All scripts of Indic origin, including Devanagari script, are de-scendants of the Brahmi script which was well established some time before 500 BC in India. These scripts are considered the most scien-tific among the existing writing systems of the world for a number of reasons. (1) The arrangement and classification of the letters or symbols follow a system based on physiological or phonetic prin-ciples, namely the point and manner of articulation. Other writing systems, including the Roman system, employ arbitrary, random criteria to arrange and categorize the letters. (2) Each letter repres-ents one sound only (at least in most cases). For example, in English the [k] sound can be represented by the letters **k**, **q**, **c** and **ch**. This does not happen in Devanagari. Because of its scientific and pho-netic nature, this script has become the foundation of modern speech science and the International Phonetic Alphabet (IPA.) The IPA is basically the romanized version of Devanagari script. As a result there is fairly regular correspondence between script and pronuncia-tion. In other words, the words are pronounced as they are written, and that is good news for our learners.

Devanagari script is written from left to right and from the top of the page down, like Roman script. It does not distinguish between upper-case and the lower-case letters. It is syllabic in nature, i.e. every consonant letter/symbol represents the consonant plus the inherent vowel अ **a**. The pronunciation of the inherent vowel is the major exception to the rule of correspondence between script and pronunciation. These exceptions are detailed in script unit 1 and script unit 4. Other minor exceptions are indicated by angular brackets < > with the words listed in the vocabulary of each unit.

Below you will find Hindi vowel and consonant charts. In Devanagari vowels and consonants are listed separately because they involve distinct articulations.

## *Hindi vowels*

### Independent forms

| अ | आ | इ | ई | उ | ऊ | ए | ऐ | ओ | औ | ऋ |
|---|---|---|---|---|---|---|---|---|---|---|
| a | ā | i | ī | u | ū | e | ɛ | o | au | ri |

## Dependent forms: following a consonant

| ø | ा | ि | ी | ु | ू | े | ै | ो | ौ | ृ |
|---|---|---|---|---|---|---|---|---|---|---|
| a | ā | i | ī | u | ū | e | ɛ | o | au | ri |

## Notes on Hindi vowels

Hindi vowels do not distinguish between capital and non-capital. However, they do distinguish between independent and dependent forms. The independent forms are often called 'the main' or 'full' vowels, whereas the corresponding dependent forms are called 'matra' vowels and are connected to the preceding consonant.

## Nasalization

In the production of a nasal vowel, a vowel is pronounced through the mouth and the nose at the same time. Using either the symbol ˘ or ˙ with the vowel indicates nasalization in Hindi. Long vowels are usually nasalized in Hindi. In our transcription, the tilde symbol ˜ is used to indicate vowel nasalization, as in

आँ    ā̃    ऊँ    ū̃    एँ    ɛ̃

The symbol ˙ is used to indicate vowel nasalization when any stroke of the vowel crosses the top horizontal line, as in एँ.

## Diphthongs

ऐ **ɛ** and औ **au** are pronounced as *a + i* and *a + u* in the Eastern variety of Hindi, but are pronounced as single vowels in Standard Hindi. They receive dipthongal pronunciation only if they are followed by *y* and *w/v*, respectively.

ऋ **ri** does not occur in Hindi. It is used in the writing of a handful of words which are borrowed by Hindi from Sanskrit.

## *Hindi consonants*

| | Voiceless unaspirated | Voiceless aspirated | Voiced unaspirated | Voiced aspirated | Nasal |
|---|---|---|---|---|---|
| *k-group* | क | ख | ग | घ | ङ |
| | ka | kʰa | ga | gʰa | ŋa |
| *c-group* | च | छ | ज | झ | ञ |
| | ca | cʰa | ja | jʰa | ña |
| *T-group* | ट | ठ | ड | ढ | ण |
| | Ta | Tʰa | Da | Dʰa | Na |
| *t-group* | त | थ | द | ध | न |
| | ta | tʰa | da | dʰa | na |
| *p-group* | प | फ | ब | भ | म |
| | pa | Pʰa | ba | bʰa | ma |
| *Others* | य | र | ल | व | श |
| | ya | ra | la | wa/va | sha |
| | ष | स | ह | | |
| | SHa | sa | ha | | |
| | ड़ | ढ़ | | | |
| | Ra | Rʰa | | | |

Sanskrit letters used infrequently:   क्ष **ksha**   त्र **tra**   ज्ञ **gya**

## Notes on Hindi consonants

The first five groups of consonants are called stops because they are pronounced by stopping outgoing air from the mouth. The fifth column of these five groups of consonants is called nasal because the air is released through the nose while it is stopped from the mouth. The nasal consonants of the first two groups, i.e. ङ **ŋa** and ञ **ña** are *never* used in their syllabic form in Hindi, so you will not find them in this book. They are included here because they are part of the traditional Devanagari consonant chart.

## Place of articulation

All consonants arranged within each of the five groups share the same place of articulation, as described below:

## क-वर्ग *k-group*

These consonants are also called 'velar' because the back of the tongue touches the back of the soft palate, called the velum. They are similar to the English *k* and *g*.

| क | ख | ग | घ | ङ |
|---|---|---|---|---|
| ka | kʰa | ga | gʰa | ŋa |

## च-वर्ग *c-group*

These sounds are the closest equivalent to the English sound **ch** in 'church.' The main body of the tongue touches the hard palate in the articulation of these sounds.

| च | छ | ज | झ | ञ |
|---|---|---|---|---|
| ca | cʰa | ja | jʰa | ña |

## ट-वर्ग *T-group* (the 'capital T group')

| ट | ठ | ड | ढ | ण |
|---|---|---|---|---|
| Ta | Tʰa | Da | Dʰa | Na |

These consonants represent the most colourful features of the languages of the Indian subcontinent. They are also called 'retroflex' consonants. There is no equivalent of these sounds in English. In the articulation of these sounds, the tip of the tongue is curled back and the *underside* of the tongue touches the hard palate. The following diagram can help in the production of these sounds:

Note that ड़ *R* and ढ़ *Rʰ* are also pronounced with the same point of articulation.

## त-वर्ग *t-group*

The tip of the tongue touches the back of the teeth, and not the gum ridge behind the teeth as is the case in the pronunciation of the English **t** or **d**.

| त | थ | द | ध | न |
|----|----|----|----|----|
| ta | t$^h$a | da | d$^h$a | na |

Study the following diagrams carefully in order to distinguish Hindi *t*-group of sounds from the English *t*-group of sounds.

*English*                               *Hindi*

## प-वर्ग *p-group*

These sounds are similar to English **p** or **b** sounds. They are pronounced by closing or nearly closing the lips.

| प | फ | ब | भ | म |
|----|----|----|----|----|
| pa | p$^h$a | ba | b$^h$a | ma |

## Manner of articulation

All columns in the five groups involve the same *manner of articulation*.

## Voiceless unaspirated

| क | च | ट | त | प |
|----|----|----|----|----|
| ka | ca | Ta | ta | pa |

These sounds are like the English **k** (as in 'skin' but not as in 'kin'), **p** (as in 'spin' but not as in 'pin'). In 'kin' and 'pin', the English sounds **k** and **p** are slightly aspirated, i.e. they are followed by a slight 'puff of air'. In order to pronounce the corresponding Hindi **k** and **p**, you need to reduce the flow of breath.

## Voiceless aspirated

| ख | छ | ठ | थ | फ |
|---|---|---|---|---|
| $k^h$a | $c^h$a | $T^h$a | $t^h$a | $p^h$a |

The superscripted $^h$ means that these sounds are pronounced with a strong 'puff of air'. All you have to do is to increase the air flow slightly in the pronunciation of the English **k** and **p** sounds.

## Voiced unaspirated

| ग | ज | ड | द | ब |
|---|---|---|---|---|
| ga | ja | Da | da | ba |

In the production of these sounds the vocal cords vibrate and produce a buzzing sound, like that of a bee. You should have no difficulty producing these sounds as they are like English **g** and **b**.

## Voiced aspirated (breathy voiced)

If you pronounce voiced unaspirated consonants with a 'puff of air', you will produce voiced aspirated sounds. The superscripted $^h$ indicates the presence of the 'puff of air'. If this seems difficult, try pronouncing the voiced unaspirated consonants with an *h* (as in ho*g*-*h*og). If you pronounce the words fast enough, you will obtain the voiced aspirate $g^h$ at the end of the first break between the two words.

| घ | झ | ढ | ध | भ |
|---|---|---|---|---|
| $g^h$a | $j^h$a | $D^h$a | $d^h$a | $b^h$a |

## Nasal

| ङ | ञ | ण | न | म |
|---|---|---|---|---|
| ŋa | ña | Na | na | ma |

These sounds are similar to English nasal consonants such as **n** and **m**. The velar and palatal nasals are similar to the nasal consonants in the English words 'king' and 'bunch', respectively.

## य-ह वर्ग  Other consonants (miscellaneous)

The following consonants grouped together as 'others' are very similar to English sounds, so do not call for detailed phonetic description. The English transcription is sufficient to give you information about their pronunciation.

| य | र | ल | व | श | स | ह |
|----|----|----|-------|-----|----|----|
| ya | ra | la | wa/va | sha | sa | ha |

As mentioned above, the following two consonants are pronounced with a curled tongue. However, the underside of the tongue is flapped forward quickly, touching the hard palate slightly, instead of articulating the stop with the hard palate. ढ़ **R$^h$a** is the aspirated counterpart of ड़ **Ra**.

| ड़ | ढ़ |
|----|------|
| Ra | R$^h$a |

## Sanskrit letters

The following four consonants are from Sanskrit. They do not exist in Hindi except in the handful of words borrowed from Sanskrit.

षा SHa     क्ष ksha     त्र tra     ज्ञ gya

ष **SHa** is pronounced like श **sha**, and the other three letters represent consonant clusters in Hindi.

## Borrowed Perso-Arabic and English sounds

By placing a dot under the following five consonant symbols, the five Perso-Arabic sounds are represented:

| फ़ | ज़ | ख़ | क़ | ग़ |
|----|----|----|----|----|
| fa | za | xa | qa | Ga |

Out of these five, the first two are used quite frequently in Hindi. The reason for this is that **fa** and **za** are also found in English. The other three consonants are usually pronounced as **k$^h$a**, **ka** and **ga**, respectively. Even the first two sounds **fa** and **za** can be pronounced as **p$^h$a** and **ja**, respectively.

It should be noted that English alveolar sounds **t** and **d** are usually perceived and written as **T** and **D**, respectively. So the **t** and **d** in the proper name 'Todd' are written with the letters ट and ड, respectively.

# Pronunciation practice

## *Minimal pair practice* 🎧 (Audio 1:3)

### Vowels

### Oral vowels

| Vowel | | Pronunciation cue (English near-equivalent) | Hindi words | | |
|---|---|---|---|---|---|
| अ | a | *a*bout | कल | **kal** | yesterday/tomorrow |
| आ | ā | f*a*ther | काल | **kāl** | time, tense |
| इ | i | s*i*t | दिन | **din** | day |
| ई | ī | s*ea*t | दीन | **dīn** | poor |
| उ | u | b*oo*k | कुल | **kul** | total, family |
| ऊ | ū | b*oo*t, l*oo*t | कूल | **kūl** | shore |
| ए | e | l*a*te, d*a*te (without a glide) | हे | **he** | hey |
| ऐ | ɛ | b*e*t | है | **hɛ** | is |
| ओ | o | b*oa*t (without a glide) | ओर | **or** | side, towards |
| औ | au | b*ou*ght | और | **aur** | and |

### Nasalized vowels ˘ ˙

| Nasalized vowels (long) | | Hindi words | | |
|---|---|---|---|---|
| आँ | ā̃ | माँ | **mā̃** | mother |
| ईं | ī̃ | कहीं | **kahī̃** | somewhere |
| ऊँ | ū̃ | हूँ | **hū̃** | am |
| एँ | ẽ | में | **mẽ** | in |
| ऐं | ɛ̃ | मैं | **mɛ̃** | I |
| ओं | õ | गोंद | **gõd** | gum |
| औं | āũ | चौंक | **cāũk** | be alarmed, be startled |

## Minimal pair practice: words with oral and nasalized vowels

| Oral vowels | | | | Nasalized vowels | | | |
|---|---|---|---|---|---|---|---|
| आ | ā | कहा | kahā | said (m.sg) | आँ | ā̃ | कहाँ | kahā̃ | where |
| ई | ī | कही | kahī | said (f.sg) | ईं | ī̃ | कहीं | kahī̃ | somewhere |
| ऊ | ū | पूछ | pūchᵸ | ask | ऊँ | ū̃ | पूँछ | pū̃chᵸ | a tail |
| ए | e | ले | le | take | एँ | ẽ | लें | lẽ | take (optative) |
| ऐ | ɛ | है | hɛ | is | ऐं | ɛ̃ | हैं | hɛ̃ | are |
| ओ | o | गोद | god | the lap | ओं | õ | गोंद | gõd | gum |
| औ | au | चौक | cauk | a crossing | औं | ãũ | चौंक | cãũk | be alarmed, be startled |

## Consonants  (Audio 1:4)

Listen to the recording and repeat the words.

Remember, the contrasts shown below are very critical in Hindi. Failing to maintain such contrasts will result in a breakdown of communication. If you want to ask for food, खाना **kʰānā** failing to aspirate will result in saying काना **kānā** and you will end up asking for a one-eyed person. Similarly, if you do not distinguish the *T*-group of consonants from the *t*-group of consonants, rather than asking for रोटी **roTī**, 'bread', you will end up reporting that the girl is crying (i.e. रोती **rotī**).

## Minimal pair practice: words with unvoiced unaspirated stops and unvoiced aspirated stops

| Unvoiced unaspirated | | | | Unvoiced aspirated | | | |
|---|---|---|---|---|---|---|---|
| क | ka | काल | kāl | time | ख | kʰa | खाल | kʰāl | skin |
| च | ca | चल | cal | walk | छ | cʰa | छल | cʰal | cheat |
| ट | Ta | टाल | Tāl | postpone | ठ | Tʰa | ठाल | Tʰāl | sit idle |
| त | ta | तान | tān | tune | थ | tʰa | थाल | tʰāl | plate |
| प | pa | पल | pal | moment | फ | pʰa | फल | pʰal | fruit |

## Minimal pair practice: words with voiced unaspirated stops and voiced aspirated stops

| *Voiced unaspirated* | | | *Voiced aspirated* | | | |
|---|---|---|---|---|---|---|
| ग **ga** | गा **gā** | sing | घ **g$^h$a** | घा **g$^h$ā** | the fourth letter of the *k*-series |
| ज **ja** | जल **jal** | water | झ **j$^h$a** | झल **j$^h$al** | fan |
| ड **Da** | डाल **Dāl** | a branch | ढ **D$^h$a** | ढाल **D$^h$āl** | shield |
| द **da** | दान **dān** | charity | ध **d$^h$a** | धान **d$^h$ān** | paddy |
| ब **ba** | बाल **bāl** | hair | भ **b$^h$a** | भाल **b$^h$āl** | forehead |

## Minimal pair practice: words with unvoiced aspirated stops and voiced aspirated stops

| *Unvoiced aspirated* | | | *Voiced aspirated* | | | |
|---|---|---|---|---|---|---|
| ख **k$^h$a** | खाना **k$^h$ānā** | food | घ **g$^h$a** | घाना **g$^h$ānā** | Ghana, the name of a country |
| छ **c$^h$a** | छल **c$^h$al** | cheat | झ **j$^h$a** | झल **j$^h$al** | fan |
| ठ **T$^h$a** | ठक **T$^h$ak** | tapping sound | ढ **D$^h$a** | ढक **D$^h$ak** | cover |
| थ **t$^h$a** | थान **t$^h$ān** | roll of cloth | ध **d$^h$a** | धान **d$^h$ān** | paddy |
| फ **p$^h$a** | फूल **p$^h$ūl** | flower | भ **b$^h$a** | भूल **b$^h$ūl** | mistake |

## Minimal pair practice: words with the *T*-group (retroflex) stops and the *t*-group (dental) stops

| ट-वर्ग *T-group* | | | त-वर्ग *t-group* | | | |
|---|---|---|---|---|---|---|
| ट **Ta** | टाल **Tāl** | postpone | त **ta** | ताल **tāl** | pond |
| ठ **T$^h$a** | ठक **T$^h$ak** | tapping (sound) | थ **t$^h$a** | थक **t$^h$ak** | be tired |
| ड **Da** | डाल **Dāl** | branch | द **da** | दाल **dāl** | lentil |
| ढ **D$^h$a** | ढक **D$^h$ak** | cover | ध **d$^h$a** | धक **d$^h$ak** | palpitation, excitement |

Listen to the following:

## Nasal consonants

| Nasal consonant | Hindi word | |
|---|---|---|
| ङ ŋa | अंग **aŋg** | body, limb |
| ञ ña | अंजू **añjū** | female name |
| ण Na | बाण **bāN** | arrow |
| न na | नान **nān** | bread |
| म ma | मान **mān** | respect |

## Other consonants

Listen to the following words:

| Consonant | Hindi word | |
|---|---|---|
| य ya | यार **yār** | friend |
| र ma | राजा **rājā** | king |
| ल la | लाल **lāl** | red |
| व wa/va | वार **vār** | an attack |
| श sha | शाल **shāl** | shawl |
| स sa | साल **sāl** | year |
| ह ha | हाल **hāl** | condition, state |

## Minimal pair practice: words with r, R and Rʰ

| Consonant | Hindi word | |
|---|---|---|
| र ra | पर **par** | on, at |
| ड़ Ra | पड़ **paR** | lie, fall |
| ढ़ Rʰa | पढ़ **paRʰ** | read, study |

## Borrowed consonants

| फ़ | ज़ | ख़ | क़ | ग़ |
|---|---|---|---|---|
| **fa** | **za** | **xa** | **qa** | **Ga** |

As pointed out earlier, these consonants were not present in Hindi originally. Many speakers of Hindi still substitute the closest corresponding Hindi consonant for them, as shown below:

| | | | | | |
|---|---|---|---|---|---|
| फ़ | **fa** | becomes | फ | **p$^h$a** | |
| ज़ | **za** | becomes | ज | **ja** | |
| ख़ | **xa** | becomes | ख | **k$^h$a** | |
| क़ | **qa** | becomes | क | **ka** | |
| ग़ | **Ga** | becomes | ग | **ga** | |

In other words, the dots are added to the native symbols to represent the borrowed sounds.

Now listen to the two possible pronunciations of the following words.

| *Consonant* | *Word* | | | *Consonant* | *Word* | |
|---|---|---|---|---|---|---|
| फ़ **fa** | फ़ीस **fīs** | tuition, fee | | फ **p$^h$a** | फीस **p$^h$īs** | |
| ज़ **za** | ज़रा **zarā** | just, a little | | ज **ja** | जरा **jarā** | |
| ख़ **xa** | ख़रीद **xarīd** | buy | | ख **k$^h$a** | खरीद **k$^h$arīd** | |
| क़ **qa** | क़लम **qalam** | pen | | क **ka** | कलम **kalam** | |
| ग़ **Ga** | ग़रीब **Garīb** | poor | | ग **ga** | गरीब **garīb** | |

**Syllables**, **stress** and intonation: see Script Unit 5.

---

**Punctuation marks**

With the exception of the full stop, which is represented by the sign I, Hindi uses the same punctuation marks as English. For abbreviation purposes, a small circle • is used after the first syllable. For example, पं• stands for Pandit. Sometimes the sign ˘ is used over the vowel आ **ā** to represent the English sound **o**, as in जॉन 'John' and यॉर्क 'York'.

---

# Numerals

| १ | २ | ३ | ४ | ५ | ६ | ७ | ८ | ९ | ० |
|---|---|---|---|---|---|---|---|---|---|
| 1 | 2 | 3 | 4 | 5 | 6 | 7 | 8 | 9 | 0 |

If you do not have the recording, either skip the following section or seek the assistance of a native speaker.

## अभ्यास  **abʰyās**  **Exercises**

### Exercise 1 🎧 (Audio 1:5)

Listen to each group of three words and circle the word that is different.

|  | A | B | C |
|---|---|---|---|
|  | कर | खर | कर |
| *Example*: you hear | kar | kʰar | kar |
| Answer: |  | B |  |

| | A | B | C |
|---|---|---|---|
| 1 | A | B | C |
| 2 | A | B | C |
| 3 | A | B | C |
| 4 | A | B | C |
| 5 | A | B | C |

### Exercise 2 🎧 (Audio 1:6)

Listen to each group of four words and circle the aspirated words.

|  | A | B | C | D |
|---|---|---|---|---|
|  | कर | खर | गर | घर |
| *Example*: you hear: | kar | kʰar | gar | gʰar |
| Answer: |  | B, D |  |  |

| | A | B | C | D |
|---|---|---|---|---|
| 1 | A | B | C | D |
| 2 | A | B | C | D |
| 3 | A | B | C | D |
| 4 | A | B | C | D |
| 5 | A | B | C | D |

### Exercise 3 🎧 (Audio 1:7)

Listen to pairs of words contrasting the *T*-group (retroflex) and the *t*-group of consonants.

| A | | B | |
|---|---|---|---|
| टिक | **Tik** | तिक | **tik** |

After each pair has been pronounced, you will hear either 'A' or 'B' again. Underline the word that you hear this time.

*Example*: you hear टिक **Tik**, then underline **<u>Tik</u>**.

| | | | |
|---|---|---|---|
| 1 | ताक **tāk** | टाक | **Tāk** |
| 2 | थक **tʰak** | ठक | **Tʰak** |
| 3 | दाग **dāg** | डाग | **Dāg** |
| 4 | धक **dʰak** | ढक | **Dʰak** |
| 5 | पर **par** | पड़ | **paR** |
| 6 | सर **sar** | सड़ | **saR** |
| 7 | करी **karī** | कढ़ी | **kaRʰī** |
| 8 | थीक **tʰīk** | ठीक | **Tʰīk** |

## Exercise 4  (Audio 1:8)

Listen to pairs of words with constrasting vowel sounds.

| *A* | *B* |
|---|---|
| दिन **din** | दीन **dīn** |

After each pair has been pronounced, you will hear either 'A' or 'B' again. Underline the word that you hear this time.

*Example*: you hear दीन **dīn**, then underline **<u>dīn</u>**.

| | A | | B | |
|---|---|---|---|---|
| 1 | काल | **kāl** | कल | **kal** |
| 2 | दिन | **din** | दीन | **dīn** |
| 3 | मिल | **mil** | मील | **mīl** |
| 4 | चुक | **cuk** | चूक | **cūk** |
| 5 | मेल | **mel** | मैल | **mɛl** |
| 6 | सेर | **ser** | सैर | **sɛr** |
| 7 | बिन | **bin** | बीन | **bīn** |
| 8 | बाल | **bāl** | बल | **bal** |

# Transcription table

If you wish to learn Hindi principally via the Roman/English path or if you are used to seeing Hindi words in the English or Bollywood media, you might find the transcription of Hindi words a little odd or unfamiliar at first. However, a quick glance will reveal that media transcription is usually very broad, ambiguous and inconsistent. English–Hindi bilinguals/native speakers can cope with such transcription because they know the target word. Foreign learners do not have this advantage.

It is imperative that learners make themselves familiar with the scientific transcription used in this book – SALT, the transcription system widely used in South Asian language and literature. Such familiarity is critical to avoiding mishaps in communication and to increase learning efficiency: see the section entitled 'Hindi writing system and pronunciation' for details. The table below provides you with a convenient source of reference for Hindi sounds.

| Letter (Devanagari) | SALT (South Asian Language Transcription) | Media | As in English words |
|---|---|---|---|
| Vowels | | | |
| अ | a | uh/a | about |
| आ | ā | aa/ah/a | father |
| इ | i | i/e | sit |
| ई | ī | ee | seat |
| उ | u | u | book |
| ऊ | ū | oo/u | boot, loot |
| ए | e | ay/e | late, date (without a glide) |
| ऐ | ɛ (ai) | ai/aye | bet |
| ओ | o | o | boat (without a glide) |
| औ | au | au | bought |
| Nasal vowels | (e.g. ã, ĩ, ā̃, ī̃ . . . ); see 'Hindi writing system and pronunciation' | vowel + n/m | |

| *Letter (Devanagari)* | *SALT (South Asian Language Transcription)* | *Media* | *As in* English *words* |
|---|---|---|---|
| *Consonants* | | | |
| क | **ka** | **ka/ca** | ba*ck* |
| ख | **kʰa** | **kha/ka** | *c*at |
| ग | **ga** | **ga** | *g*ate |
| घ | **gʰa** | **gha** | ho*g-h*og |
| ङ | **ŋa** | **na** | ki*ng* |
| च | **ca** | **cha** | *ch*urch |
| छ | **cʰa** | **chha** | *ch*urch (with slight puff of air) |
| ज | **ja** | **ja** | *j*ug |
| झ | **jʰa** | **jha/ja** | hed*ge-h*og |
| ञ | **ña** | **na** | bu*n*ch |
| ट | **Ta** | **ta** | Not in English: see |
| ठ | **Tʰa** | **tʰa** | 'Hindi writing system |
| ड/ड़ | **Da/Ra** | **da/da** | and pronunciation' |
| ढ/ढ़ | **Dʰa/Rʰa** | **dha/da** | |
| ण | **Na** | **na** | |
| त | **ta** | **ta** | ca*t* |
| थ | **tʰa** | **tʰa** | *t*in |
| द | **da** | **da** | *d*og |
| ध | **dʰa** | **dha** | *dh*arma |
| न | **na** | **na** | *n*ab |
| प | **pa** | **pa** | zi*p* |
| फ/फ़ | **pʰa** | **pha** | *P*at |
| ब | **ba** | **ba** | *b*at |
| भ | **bʰa** | **bha** | ta*b-l*et |
| म | **ma** | **ma** | *m*at |
| य | **ya** | **ya** | *y*es |
| र | **ra** | **ra** | *r*at |
| ल | **la** | **la** | *l*ate |
| व | **wa/va** | **wa/va** | *v*at |
| श | **sha** | **sha** | *sh*e |
| ष | **SHa** | **SHa** | Like retroflex; not in English |
| स | **sa** | **sa** | *s*it |
| ह | **ha** | **ha** | *h*at |

*Source*: Adapted from Bhatia, Tej K. (2000). *Advertising in Rural India: Language, Marketing Communication and Consumerism*. Tokyo: Institute for the Study of Languages and Cultures of Asia and Africa, Tokyo University of Foreign Studies.

# 1 पहला पाठ – लिपि
# pɛhlā pāT<sup>h</sup> – lipi
## Script unit 1

The first letter of the Devanagari script is अ **a**.

When the preceding sound is a consonant, it is inherent in the consonant, so it is not written separately (as in the Hindi word पर **par** 'on/at'). In all other situations, however, it is written separately (e.g. अब **ab** 'now').

Look at the following combinations of consonants with the vowel अ **a** and try to read them aloud first. You may need to refer to the consonant chart in the transcription table.

| Letters | | | | Word | | Pronunciation |
|---------|---|----|---|------|---|---------------|
| प | + | र | = | पर | | |
| **pa** | + | **ra** | = | **para** | on/at | **par** |
| अ | + | ब | = | अब | | |
| **a** | + | **ba** | = | **aba** | now | **ab** |
| क | + | ल | = | कल | | |
| **ka** | + | **la** | = | **kala** | yesterday/tomorrow | **kal** |

Note that with a preceding **p, r, b, k** or **l** the independent shape of the vowel अ is not used. In such cases the vowel is absorbed into the consonant. It is for this reason that Hindi script is called a 'syllabic' script, i.e. a consonant letter such as क stands for **k + a**. Each consonant letter is not written separately, as is the case with the Roman script. So, **k + a** *cannot* be written as क + अ. Of course, there are ways to write a consonant without a vowel; we will learn to do this at a later stage.

If you thought that the vowel **-a** at the end of a word is absorbed into the preceding consonant, but is *not* pronounced (i.e. silent) in Standard Hindi speech, you would be right. So, a word written as

पर **para** 'on/at' is actually pronounced as **par**. Some dialects of Hindi do not drop the word-final **a** in pronunciation.

Combinations of three or more consonants follow the same pattern.

| Letters | | | | | | Word | | Pronunciation |
|---|---|---|---|---|---|---|---|---|
| स | + | ड़ | + | क | = | सड़क | | |
| **sa** | + | **Ra** | + | **ka** | = | **saRakx** | road | **saRak** |
| म | + | ग | + | र | = | मगर | | |
| **ma** | + | **ga** | + | **ra** | = | **magarx** | but | **magar** |
| अ | + | ग | + | र | = | अगर | | |
| **a** | + | **ga** | + | **ra** | = | **agarx** | if | **agar** |

## Handwriting

### Stroke order

| Letter/ Pronunciation | Stroke order | Head stroke/ Head bar | Handwriting |
|---|---|---|---|
| क – वर्ग | | | |
| क ka | च व क | क | क |
| ख kʰa | र रु रव ख | ख | रव |
| ग ga | ♪ ॻ | ग | ग |
| घ gʰa | ˈ ६ ध | घ | घ |
| च – वर्ग | | | |
| च ca | – ८ व | च | च |
| छ cʰa | ʻ छ | छ | छ |
| ज ja | ℧ ℧ ज | ज | ज |
| झ jʰa | ढ ड़ ड़ झ | झ | झ |

| Letter/ Pronunciation | Stroke order | Head stroke/ Head bar | Handwriting |
|---|---|---|---|

## ट – वर्ग

| | | | |
|---|---|---|---|
| ट Ta | ˊ ट | ट | ट |
| ठ Tʰa | ˊ ठ | ठ | ठ |
| ड Da | ˊ ड | ड | ड |
| ढ Dʰa | ˊ ढ | ढ | ढ |
| ण Na | ι υ ण | ण | ण |

## त – वर्ग

| | | | |
|---|---|---|---|
| त ta | ॱ त | त | त |
| थ tʰa | ॱ ॱ थ | थ | थ |
| द da | ˊ द द | द | द |
| ध dʰa | ॱ ॱ ध | ध | ध |
| न na | ॱ न | न | न |

## प – वर्ग

| | | | |
|---|---|---|---|
| प pa | ι प | प | प |
| फ pʰa | ι प फ | फ | फ |
| ब ba | c ब ब | ब | ब |
| भ bʰa | ॱ ॱ भ | भ | भ |
| म ma | ι ॱ म | म | म |

## य – ह वर्ग

| | | | |
|---|---|---|---|
| य ya | ॱ ॱ य | य | य |
| र ra | ॱ र | र | र |
| ल la | ॱ ॱ ल | ल | ल |
| व va | c व व | व | व |
| श sha | ॱ ॱ श | श | श |
| ष SHa | ι प ष | ष | ष |

| तु | तू | ते | तै |
|----|----|----|----|
| **tu** | **tū** | **te** | **tɛ** |

Read the following words. (In what follows the absence of the word-final short **a** is assumed.)

| चु | + | क | = | चुक | finish |
|----|---|---|---|------|--------|
| **cu** | + | **ka** | | **cuk** | |

| पू | + | छ | = | पूछ | ask |
|----|---|---|---|------|-----|
| **pū** | + | **cʰa** | = | **pūcʰ** | |

| जे | + | ल | = | जेल | jail |
|----|---|---|---|------|------|
| **je** | + | **la** | = | **jel** | |

| पै | + | सा | = | पैसा | money |
|----|---|----|---|------|-------|
| **pɛ** | + | **sā** | = | **pɛsā** | |

---

**Exceptions**

When ु and ू are joined to र ra, they are joined to the middle joint of the र, as shown below:

| r | + | u | | r | + | ū |
|---|---|---|---|---|---|---|
| र | + | ु | | र | + | ू |

रु               रू

---

It is incorrect to place ु and ू below the र as in रु **ru** and रू **rū**.

Also, notice the difference in the shape of ु. With र the symbol of the dependent vowel **u** becomes ऽ.

Now here are the last two dependent vowel forms:

| ो | ौ |
|----|----|
| **o** | **au** |

They are placed to the right of a consonant like **ā** and **ī**, as shown below:

| छो | + | टा | = | छोटा | small |
|----|---|----|---|------|-------|
| **cʰo** | + | **Tā** | | | |

चौ + क = चौक    crossing
cau + k

Observe some more examples of the vowels in question:

प + ड़ौ + सी = पड़ौसी    neighbour
**pa** + **rau** + **sī**

हौ + स + ला = हौसला    courage
**hau** + **sa** + **lā**

पौ + शा + क = पौशाक    dress
**pao** + **shā** + **k**

नि + चो + ड़ = निचोड़    squeeze, essence
**ni** + **co** + **R**

The use of मात्रा **mātrā** vowels with preceding consonants is shown below. The consonants that never occur with mātrā vowels are not listed here.

| क | का | कि | की | कु | कू | के | कै | को | कौ |
|---|---|---|---|---|---|---|---|---|---|
| **ka** | **kā** | **ki** | **kī** | **ku** | **kū** | **ke** | **kɛ** | **ko** | **kau** |
| ख | खा | खि | खी | खु | खू | खे | खै | खो | खौ |
| **kʰa** | **kʰā** | **kʰi** | **kʰī** | **kʰu** | **kʰū** | **kʰe** | **kʰɛ** | **kʰo** | **kʰau** |
| ग | गा | गि | गी | गु | गू | गे | गै | गो | गौ |
| **ga** | **gā** | **gi** | **gī** | **gu** | **gū** | **ge** | **gɛ** | **go** | **gau** |
| घ | घा | घि | घी | घु | घू | घे | घै | घो | घौ |
| **gʰa** | **gʰā** | **gʰi** | **gʰī** | **gʰu** | **gʰū** | **gʰe** | **gʰɛ** | **gʰo** | **gʰau** |
| च | चा | चि | ची | चु | चू | चे | चै | चो | चौ |
| **ca** | **cā** | **ci** | **cī** | **cu** | **cū** | **ce** | **cɛ** | **co** | **cau** |
| छ | छा | छि | छी | छु | छू | छे | छै | छो | छौ |
| **cʰa** | **cʰā** | **cʰi** | **cʰī** | **cʰu** | **cʰū** | **cʰe** | **cʰɛ** | **cʰo** | **cʰau** |
| ज | जा | जि | जी | जु | जू | जे | जै | जो | जौ |
| **ja** | **jā** | **ji** | **jī** | **ju** | **jū** | **je** | **jɛ** | **jo** | **jau** |
| झ | झा | झि | झी | झु | झू | झे | झै | झो | झौ |
| **jʰa** | **jʰā** | **jʰi** | **jʰī** | **jʰu** | **jʰū** | **jʰe** | **jʰɛ** | **jʰo** | **jʰau** |
| ट | टा | टि | टी | टु | टू | टे | टै | टो | टौ |
| **Ta** | **Tā** | **Ti** | **Tī** | **Tu** | **Tū** | **Te** | **Tɛ** | **To** | **Tau** |
| ठ | ठा | ठि | ठी | ठु | ठू | ठे | ठै | ठो | ठौ |
| **Tʰa** | **Tʰā** | **Tʰi** | **Tʰī** | **Tʰu** | **Tʰū** | **Tʰe** | **Tʰɛ** | **Tʰo** | **Tʰau** |

| ड | डा | डि | डी | डु | डू | डे | डै | डो | डौ |
|---|---|---|---|---|---|---|---|---|---|
| Da | Dā | Di | Dī | Du | Dū | De | Dɛ | Do | Dau |
| ढ | ढा | ढि | ढी | ढु | ढू | ढे | ढै | ढो | ढौ |
| Dʰa | Dʰā | Dʰi | Dʰī | Dʰu | Dʰū | Dʰe | Dʰɛ | Dʰo | Dʰau |
| ण | णा | णि | णी | णु | णू | णे | णै | णो | णौ |
| Na | Nā | Ni | Nī | Nu | Nū | Ne | Nɛ | No | Nau |
| त | ता | ति | ती | तु | तू | ते | तै | तो | तौ |
| ta | tā | ti | tī | tu | tū | te | tɛ | to | tau |
| थ | था | थि | थी | थु | थू | थे | थै | थो | थौ |
| tʰa | tʰā | tʰi | tʰī | tʰu | tʰū | tʰe | tʰɛ | tʰo | tʰau |
| द | दा | दि | दी | दु | दू | दे | दै | दो | दौ |
| da | dā | di | dī | du | dū | de | dɛ | do | dau |
| ध | धा | धि | धी | धु | धू | धे | धै | धो | धौ |
| dʰa | dʰā | dʰi | dʰī | dʰu | dʰū | dʰe | dʰɛ | dʰo | dʰau |
| न | ना | नि | नी | नु | नू | ने | नै | नो | नौ |
| na | nā | ni | nī | nu | nū | ne | nɛ | no | nau |
| प | पा | पि | पी | पु | पू | पे | पै | पो | पौ |
| pa | pā | pi | pī | pu | pū | pe | pɛ | po | pau |
| फ | फा | फि | फी | फु | फू | फे | फै | फो | फौ |
| pʰa | pʰā | pʰi | pʰī | pʰu | pʰū | pʰe | pʰɛ | pʰo | pʰau |
| ब | बा | बि | बी | बु | बू | बे | बै | बो | बौ |
| ba | bā | bi | bī | bu | bū | be | bɛ | bo | bau |
| भ | भा | भि | भी | भु | भू | भे | भै | भो | भौ |
| bʰa | bʰā | bʰi | bʰī | bʰu | bʰū | bʰe | bʰɛ | bʰo | bʰau |
| म | मा | मि | मी | मु | मू | मे | मै | मो | मौ |
| ma | mā | mi | mī | mu | mū | me | mɛ | mo | mau |
| य | या | यि | यी | यु | यू | ये | यै | यो | यौ |
| ya | yā | yi | yī | yu | yū | ye | yɛ | yo | yau |
| र | रा | रि | री | रु | रू | रे | रै | रो | रौ |
| ra | rā | ri | rī | ru | rū | re | rɛ | ro | rau |
| ल | ला | लि | ली | लु | लू | ले | लै | लो | लौ |
| la | lā | li | lī | lu | lū | le | lɛ | lo | lau |
| व | वा | वि | वी | वु | वू | वे | वै | वो | वौ |
| va | vā | vi | vī | vu | vū | ve | vɛ | vo | vau |
| श | शा | शि | शी | शु | शू | शे | शै | शो | शौ |
| sha | shā | shi | shī | shu | shū | she | shɛ | sho | shau |
| ष | षा | षि | षी | षु | षू | षे | षै | षो | षौ |
| SHa | SHā | SHi | SHī | SHu | SHū | She | SHɛ | SHo | SHau |
| स | सा | सि | सी | सु | सू | से | सै | सो | सौ |
| sa | sā | si | sī | su | sū | se | sɛ | so | sau |
| ह | हा | हि | ही | हु | हू | हे | है | हो | हौ |
| ha | hā | hi | hī | hu | hū | he | hɛ | ho | hau |

# The horizontal bar/head stroke and words

The horizontal bar is placed on a word. Thus **kām** क ा म = काम but not का म.

अभ्यास **ab^hyās Exercises**

## Exercise 1

Read the following Hindi words aloud and transcribe them. Note that your transcription should take into account the word-final absence of the short vowel अ **a**.

| | | | | | | |
|---|---|---|---|---|---|---|
| 1 भारी | 2 बड़ा | 3 कितना | 4 काला | 5 भारत | 6 गाड़ी | 7 किनारा |
| 8 गीत | 9 गायब | 10 चावल | 11 चाहना | 12 चिड़ियाघर | 13 ज़रा | 14 जीवन |
| 15 जापान | 16 चोर | 17 मोर | 18 फल | 19 भूत | 20 चौथा | 21 डौल |
| 22 पुलिस | 23 हाथी | 24 सितार | 25 शाम | | | |

## Exercise 2

Write the following words in Devanagari script:

| | | | | | |
|---|---|---|---|---|---|
| 1 jabki | 2 kī | 3 bāzār | 4 rājā | 5 rānī | 6 pahacān |
| 7 naī | 8 banāras | 9 kānapur | 10 mātā | 11 pitā | 12 kab^hī |
| 13 milan | 14 zamīn | 15 kār | 16 mahīnā | 17 sāl | 18 din |
| 19 cār | 20 sāt | 21 saverā | 22 cāy | 23 pānī | 24 pati |
| 25 b^hālū | 26 rāt | 27 dopahar | 28 k^hol | 29 sau | 30 sonā |

## Exercise 3

Practise writing the following names:

1 Richard   2 Bill   3 Sarah (seyra)   4 Jennifer   5 Don

## Exercise 4

The following words are written incorrectly in Hindi. Look at their transcription and write their correct form in Hindi:

| Correct | Incorrect | Correct | Correct | Incorrect | Correct |
|---------|-----------|---------|---------|-----------|---------|
| rupayā | रुपया | | Dar | दर | |
| rūkʰā | रूखा | | nām | नाभ | |
| kar | कअर | | tʰān | धान | |
| ki | कि | | gʰar | धर | |
| aur | आर | | Dāl | ड़ाल | |

# 3 तीसरा पाठ – लिपि
# tīsrā pāT$^h$ – lipi
## Script unit 3

## Independent vowels

In this unit we will learn how to use independent vowel forms and
nasalized vowels. In the last unit we showed that dependent counterparts are used with a preceding consonant. In all other cases, the
independent form is used. Here is the list of the independent vowels
again. These vowels are also called 'main' vowels.

| अ | आ | इ | ई | उ | ऊ | ए | ऐ | ओ | औ |
|----|----|----|----|----|----|----|----|----|----|
| a | ā | i | ī | u | ū | e | ɛ | o | au |

When the word begins with a vowel, the independent form of the
vowel is used, as in

आ + म = आम    mango, common
ā + m = ām

*but **not** the dependent form*

ा + म = म

Similarly:

इ + ध + र = इधर    in this direction, here
i + d$^h$a + r

*but **not***

ि + ध + र = धिर

Also, observe in the following example:

ओ  +  र  =  ओर      and
**au**  +  **r**

*but* **not**

ी  +  र  =  ीर

If the *preceding* sound is a vowel, the independent form of a vowel is used, e.g.:

**ā**  +  **i**  +  **e**
आ  +  इ  +  ए  =  आइए      please come

*but* **not** *any of the following ways:*

ा  +  ि  +  ए  =  ािए
ा  +  ि  +  ँ  =  ािँ
आ  +  ि  +  ँ  =  आिँ

Now you should be able to distinguish between the following two words:

**k**  +  **ī**          **ka**  +  **ī**

की of          कई several

Notice that the independent form of ई **ī** is used in कई **kaī** because its preceding sound is the vowel **a** अ.

## Nasalized vowels

In our transcription, vowel nasalization is indicated by a tilde ~ over the transliterated vowel.

In Hindi, the two symbols which are used to mark vowel nasal-ization are: **candrabindu** (moon dot) ँ and **bindu** (dot) ं. The former is used either over the head stroke of the vowel itself or over the head stroke of the consonant to which the vowel is attached. If any part of the vowel is written above the head stroke, then the dot is used rather than the moon dot. Note the following examples:

moon dot ँ      dot ं

| Nasalized vowel | Independent vowel | Dependent vowel (matra) |
|---|---|---|
| ã | आँ | ाँ |
| ĩ | —  | ीँ |
| ũ | ऊँ | —  |
| ẽ | —  | —  |
| ɛ̃ | —  | —  |
| õ | ओं | ाें |
| ãũ | औं | ाैं |

Now examine the usage of the nasalized vowels in the following words:

ह + ाँ = हाँ   yes      ह + ँ = हूँ   am
h + ã               h + ũ

आँ + ख = आँख   eye      म + ाँ = माँ   mother
ã + kʰ = ãkʰ       m + ã = mã

ऊँ + ट = ऊँट   camel      म + ँ = में   in
ũ + T = ũT        m + ẽ = mẽ

औं + धा = औंधा   overturned      म + ँ = मैं   I
ãũ + dʰā = ãũdʰā      m + ɛ̃ = mɛ̃

## लेखन   **lekʰan**   **Writing**

| Letter/ pronunciation | Stroke order | Head stroke/ Head bar | Handwriting |
|---|---|---|---|
| अ a | � 3 ᲟᲔ अ | अ | अ |
| आ ā | आ | आ | आ |
| इ i | Ო ᲜᲔ इ | इ | इ |
| ई ī | ᲜᲔ ई | ई | ई |
| उ u | Ე Ი | उ | उ |
| ऊ ū | ऊ | ऊ | ऊ |
| ए e | Ე Ი | ए | ए |

| Letter/ pronunciation | Stroke order | Head stroke/ Head bar | Handwriting |
|---|---|---|---|
| ऐ ɛ | ऐ | ऐ | ऐ |
| ओ o | आ ओ | ओ | ओ |
| औ au | औ | औ | औ |

## अभ्यास **ab<sup>h</sup>yās** Exercises

### Exercise 1

Write the following expressions in Devanagari script. Since they are useful, their English translation is also provided.

1 **t<sup>h</sup>ānā vahī̃ hɛ.**
   The police station is right there.

2 **āp merī madad kar sakte hɛ̃?**
   Can you help me?

3 **mɛ̃ vahā̃ kɛse jāū̃?**
   How shall I get there?

4 **ye merī galatī nahī̃.**
   This is not my mistake.

5 **yahā̃ xatrā hɛ.**
   There is danger here.

6 **bacāo!**
   Save! (or help!)

7 **ye** (written as **yah**) **bahut zarūrī hɛ.**
   This is very urgent.

8 **Dāk-k<sup>h</sup>ānā kahā̃ hɛ?**
   Where is the post office?

9 **kis k<sup>h</sup>iRkī par jāū̃?**
   Which window should I go to?

10 **TikaT** (ticket) **kitnā lagegā?**
   How much postage will (it) need?

11 **e-mail amrīkā** (America) **bʰejanā cāhatā hū̃.**
(I) want to send an e-mail to America.

12 **mujhe cintā/fikr hɛ.**
I am worried.

## Exercise 2

If you have the recording, listen to the above expressions while silently reading them.

## Exercise 3

Write the following words in Devanagari script:

1 **āie**   2 **āo**   3 **kʰāie**   4 **kʰāo**   5 **kʰā lo**   6 **māika** (Mike)

## Exercise 4

Oral vs nasal vowels

1 हा exclamatory sound   vs   हाँ yes
2 हू a sound                   हूँ am
3 है is                         हैं are
4 मे May                       में in

Now transcribe the above words into Roman.

# 4 चौथा पाठ – लिपि
# cautʰā pāTʰ – lipi
## Script unit 4

## Conjunct letters

In script unit 1 I mentioned that since Devanagari script is syllabic, every consonant symbol contains an invisible अ **a** in it. Now let us learn to write consonants without this vowel. Such consonants are also called 'half' consonants.

The simplest way to drop the अ **a** is to use the sign ॒ called 'hal' or 'halant'. For example, if you want to write the word **kyā**, just put the halant sign under क and then go on to write the next syllable. However, Hindi speakers, particularly in handwriting, tend to prefer special conjunct symbols over the halant sign. The halant is more prevalent in word processing and the Internet. These special conjuncts are described in this section.

If the consonant has a right vertical stroke ा, the vertical line is dropped, as in:

| Consonant | Conjunct form (half consonant) | Word with a conjunct | |
|-----------|-------------------------------|----------------------|---|
| ख **xa** | ख़ **x** | सख़्त **saxt** | hard |
| ग **ga** | ग **g** | अग्नि **agni** | fire |
| च **ca** | च **c** | अच्छा **accʰā** | good |
| ज **ja** | ज **j** | ज्यों **jyõ** | as |
| ण **Na** | ण **N** | ठण्डा **ThaNDā** | cold |
| त **ta** | त **t** | त्यौहार **tyauhār** | festival |
| न **na** | न **n** | अन्धा **andʰā** | blind |
| स **sa** | स **s** | सस्ता **sastā** | cheap |

Notice the placement of the dependent form of the vowel ि **i** which is placed before the conjunct letter ग **g** but is pronounced after the न **n**.

Consonants which contain the stroke ा in their *middle* have the following forms:

क ka    क्‍ k    क्या **kyā**    what
फ़ fa    फ़्‍ f    हफ़्ता **haftā**    week

For all other letters, either the halant sign is used or the conjunct letter sits on the top of the full consonant letter, as in:

| | | | | |
|---|---|---|---|---|
| ट् T + ट Ta | ट् + ट | **T + Ta** | *or* | ट्ट |
| | पट्टी | **paTTī** | *or* | पट्टी bandage |
| ड् D + ड Da | ड् + ड | **D + Da** | *or* | ड्ड |
| | अड्डा | **aDDā** | *or* | अड्डा station (bus) |

With the emergence of new printing technology, the halant form is gaining more prominence.

## Exceptions

Once again र **ra** is notorious and it needs special attention. The symbol for the conjunct र is ᷂ , as in

क + ᷂ + म = कर्म    *but not* कर्म
**ka** + **r** + **ma** = **karma**    fate

The conjunct **r** is placed at the very end of the syllable it precedes, e.g.

व + ᷂ + मा = वर्मा    *but not* वर्मा
**va** + **r** + **mā** = **Varma**    a last name

When र is the second member of the conjunct, it is realized as ⟍. Note the following clusters with **r**.

प + ⟍ = प्र
**p** + **ra** = **pra**

त + ⟍ = त्र
**t** + **ra** = **tra**

श + ्र = श्र
sh + ra = shra

With ट Ta and ड Da, ॒ is added rather than ्.

ट + ॒ = ट्र
T + ra = Tra

ड + ॒ = ड्र
D + ra = Dra

## Long consonants

With the exception of **tta**, the long consonants follow the conjunct formation rules described above.

त् + त = त्त *but not* त्त
t + ta = tta

## Nasal consonants

In Script Unit 3 we saw that the *moon dot* and the simple *dot* can express vowel nasalization. However, the dot has yet another function. When it appears over either a short vowel or a consonant, it shows the presence of a homorganic nasal consonant. 'Homorganic' means the sound is produced by the same speech organ. The consonants listed in each of the five groups in the consonant chart are homorganic. For example, the five consonant sounds listed in the fifth column – ङ **ŋ**, ञ **ñ**, ण **N**, न **n** and म **m** are homorganic to the rest of the velar, palatal, retroflex, dental and labial consonants, respectively.

When a dot is placed either over a short vowel or a consonant, it indicates the corresponding homorganic conjunct nasal consonant of the following consonant. So the dot can also be written with a conjunct nasal consonant, as in

| अंग | = | अङ्ग | **aŋg** | limb |
| पंच | = | पञ्च | **pañc** | juror |
| ठंड | = | ठण्ड | **TʰaND** | cold |
| हिंदी | = | हिन्दी | **hindī** | the Hindi language |
| खंबा | = | खम्बा | **kʰambā** | pole |

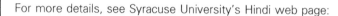

# The hide and seek game of अ **a**

I mentioned in the chapter on the Hindi writing system and pronunciation that the Devanagari script is a phonetic script and that
the words are primarily written in the way they are pronounced.
However, one should keep in mind that language is a living thing;
it keeps changing and even the most scientific script cannot keep
up with all the changes. We have already discussed the case of the
word-final silence of अ **a** in Script Units 1 and 2. Now do some detective work and see another situation in which अ **a** is *written but not
pronounced.*

| Word | Written | Pronounced | Word | Written | Pronounced |
|------|---------|------------|------|---------|------------|
| सड़क<br>road | **saRak** | **saR***a***k** | सड़कें<br>road | **saR***a***k+ē̃** | **saRkē̃** |
| औरत<br>woman | **aurat** | **aur***a***t** | औरतें<br>women | **aur***a***t+ē̃** | **aurtē̃** |
| लड़क<br>child (*not<br>used alone*) | **laRak** | **laR***a***k** | लड़का<br>boy | **laR***a***k+ā** | **laRkā** |
| लड़क<br>child (*not<br>used alone*) | **laRak** | **laR***a***k** | लड़की<br>girl | **laR***a***k+ī** | **laRkī** |
| समझ<br>understand | **samaj**ʰ | **sam***a***j**ʰ | समझा<br>understood | **samaj**ʰ**+ā** | **samj**ʰ**ā** |

## Exercise 3

Note that the presence or absence of the word-medial **a** in the following words. Take a lead from the Roman transcription and practise the pronunciation.

| | | | | |
|---|---|---|---|---|
| 1 | सड़क | saR*ak* | सड़कें | saRkẽ |
| 2 | औरत | aur*at* | औरतें | aurtẽ |
| 3 | लड़क | laR*ak* | लड़का | laRkā |
| 4 | लड़कपन | laR*ak*pan | लड़की | laRkī |
| 5 | समझ | sam*aj*ʰ | समझा | samjʰā |
| 6 | समझदार | sam*aj*ʰdār | समझी | samjʰī |

## Exercise 4

Read and transliterate the the following information about the functions of a Nokia cell phone into Roman text:

नोकिया फोन की दुनिया में आपका स्वागत है।
You are welcome in the Nokia world.

हिन्दी में टेक्ट सन्देश भेजिए
Send a text message in Hindi.

हटाएँ कुंजी clear key

नेवी कुंजी navigation key

स्काल कुंजियाँ scroll keys

नम्बर कुंजियाँ number keys

**Web resources**

For more details, see Syracuse University's Hindi web page:

http://faculty.maxwell.syr.edu/jishnu/101/alphabet/
default.asp?section=0

For more on consonant clusters:

http://www.avashy.com/hindiscripttutor.htm
http://acharya.iitm.ac.in/sanskrit/lessons/Devan/conj_1.html

# The hide and seek game of अ **a**

I mentioned in the chapter on the Hindi writing system and pronunciation that the Devanagari script is a phonetic script and that
the words are primarily written in the way they are pronounced.
However, one should keep in mind that language is a living thing;
it keeps changing and even the most scientific script cannot keep
up with all the changes. We have already discussed the case of the
word-final silence of अ **a** in Script Units 1 and 2. Now do some detective work and see another situation in which अ **a** is *written but not
pronounced*.

| Word | Written | Pronounced | Word | Written | Pronounced |
|------|---------|------------|------|---------|------------|
| सड़क<br>road | **saRak** | **saR*a*k** | सड़कें<br>road | **saR*a*k+ẽ** | **saRkẽ** |
| औरत<br>woman | **aurat** | **aur*a*t** | औरतें<br>women | **aur*a*t+ẽ** | **aurtẽ** |
| लड़क<br>child (*not<br>used alone*) | **laRak** | **laR*a*k** | लड़का<br>boy | **laR*a*k+ā** | **laRkā** |
| लड़क<br>child (*not<br>used alone*) | **laRak** | **laR*a*k** | लड़की<br>girl | **laR*a*k+ī** | **laRkī** |
| समझ<br>understand | **samaj^h** | **sam*a*j^h** | समझा<br>understood | **sam*a*j^h+ā** | **samj^hā** |

If you noticed that the penultimate (second to last) vowel **a** is dropped before a suffix, then your observation is correct. Now examine the following words:

| Word | Written | Pronounced | Word | Written | Pronounced |
|------|---------|-----------|------|---------|-----------|
| सड़क<br>road | **saRak** | **saRak** | सड़कपन<br>roadlike | **saRak+pan** | **saRakpan** |
| औरत<br>woman | **aurat** | **aurat** | औरतपन<br>womanhood | **aurat+pan** | **auratpan** |
| लड़क<br>child | **laRak** | **laRak** | लड़कपन<br>childhood | **laRak+pan** | **laRakpan** |
| समझ<br>understand | **samaj**ʰ | **samaj**ʰ | समझदार<br>intelligent | **samaj**ʰ**+dār** | **samaj**ʰ**dār** |

The data presented above show that the penultimate **a** is dropped in pronunciation if the suffix begins with a vowel. Othewise it is retained.

## अभ्यास  **abʰyās  Exercises**

### Exercise 1

Write the following expressions in Hindi. These are very useful expressions, so their meaning is also given.

1 **pūcʰ-tācʰ kā daftar**
   Inquiry office

2 **mɛ̃ rāstā bʰūl gayī hū̃.**
   I (f.) am lost. (lit. I have lost my way.)

3 **mɛ̃ rāstā bʰūl gayā hū̃.**
   I (m.) am lost. (lit. I have lost my way.)

4 **taŋg mat karo.**
   Do not bother me.

5 **mɛ̃ kuñjī Dʰū̃Rʰ rahā hū̃.**
   I am looking for my key.

6 **nahī̃ mil rahī.**
   (I) can't find (it).

7 **ciTTʰī havāī Dākse bʰejiye.**
   Please send (this) letter by air mail.

8 **kyā āp yah sāmān sīdʰe mumbaī bʰej sakte hɛ̃?**
   Can you send this baggage straight to Mumbai?

9 **sāmān ke liye rasīd dījiye.**
   Please give (me) a receipt for this baggage.

10 **merā sāmān nahī̃ āyā.**
   My baggage did not arrive (by this flight).

## Exercise 2

Transcribe the following sentences. Some words used in these expressions are from English but they have been written in the way they are pronounced by Hindi speakers. If you have the recording, listen to their pronunciation. Otherwise after transcribing the sentences, read the sentences and practise their pronunciation on your own.

1 हम एक हफ़्ता दिल्ली में रहेंगे।
   We will stay in Delhi for a week.

2 मैं यहाँ छुट्टी पर हूँ।
   I am here on holiday.

3 हम यहाँ काम से आये हैं।
   We (m.) came here on a business trip. (lit. We have come here with work.)

4 यह मेरा पासपोर्ट है।
   This is my passport.

5 क्या इस सामान पर ड्यूटी लगेगी?
   Will this baggage (*or* things) require duty?

6 ये चीज़ें मेरे अपने इस्तेमाल के लिए हैं।
   These things are for my own (personal) use.

7 मेरे पास ड्यूटी वाला सामान नहीं है।
   I have nothing to declare. (lit. I do not have anything that requires duty).

8 मेरे पास कुछ गिफ्ट्स हैं।
   I have some gifts.

9 इसमें सिर्फ कपड़े और किताबें हैं।
   There are only clothes and books in this (bag).

10 इस के अलावा और कोई चीज़ नहीं है।
   Besides this (I) have nothing else (to declare for duty.)

## Exercise 3

Note that the presence or absence of the word-medial **a** in the following words. Take a lead from the Roman transcription and practise the pronunciation.

| | | | | | |
|---|---|---|---|---|---|
| 1 | सड़क | saR*a*k | सड़कें | saRkẽ |
| 2 | औरत | aur*a*t | औरतें | aurtẽ |
| 3 | लड़क | laR*a*k | लड़का | laRkā |
| 4 | लड़कपन | laR*a*kpan | लड़की | laRkī |
| 5 | समझ | sam*a*jʰ | समझा | samjʰā |
| 6 | समझदार | sam*a*jʰdār | समझी | samjʰī |

## Exercise 4

Read and transliterate the the following information about the functions of a Nokia cell phone into Roman text:

नोकिया फोन की दुनिया में आपका स्वागत है ।
You are welcome in the Nokia world.

हिन्दी में टेक्ट सन्देश भेजिए
Send a text message in Hindi.

हटाएँ कुंजी clear key

नेवी कुंजी navigation key

स्काल कुंजियाँ scroll keys

नम्बर कुंजियाँ number keys

# 5 पाँचवाँ पाठ – लिपि
# pā̃cvā̃ pāT^h – lipi
## Script unit 5

You must have heard the expression 'It is not what you say that matters but how you say it.' In this chapter we will consider some 'how to' aspects of script and pronunciation together with some other questions, such as significant and insignificant variations.

## Syllables

The vowel and consonant segments can be combined into units which are called syllables. Syllables are the smaller units which make up a word. The syllable boundary is indicated by the symbol #, as follows:

### *Between successive vowels*

| Word | | Syllabification | |
|------|------|------|------|
| जाओ | jāo | जा # ओ | jā # o |
| आइए | āie | आ # इ # ए | ā # e # o |
| नई | naī | न # ई | na # ī |
| खाए | k^hāe | खा # ए | khā # e |

### *Between vowels and consonants*

| Word | | Syllabification | |
|------|------|------|------|
| जाता | jātā | जा # ता | jā # tā |
| सोना | nā | सो # ना | so # nā |
| पता | patā | प # ता | pa # tā |

## *Between consonants*

| Word | | Syllabification | |
|------|--|-----------------|--|
| इच्छा | icchā | इच् # छा | ic # chā |
| सड़कें | saRkē | सड़ # कें | saR # kē |
| आदमी | ādmī | आद # मी | ād # mī |

## Stress

Stress means loudness, a change in volume to express a wide variety of meanings such as emotions, contrast, focus and change in grammatical categories. This term is interchangeably used with 'accent' by some linguists. It refers to the most prominent part of a syllable or word. As in English, stress distinguishes some nouns from verbs in Hindi, as in

| *Noun* | | | *Verb* | | |
|--------|--|--|--------|--|--|
| गला | *gala* | neck | गला | **gala** | cause to melt |
| तला | *tala* | sole | तला | **tala** | cause to fry |

The stressed syllable is in italics. However, stress is usually indistinct in Hindi. So, whether one places stress on the first syllable or the second, the meaning will not be affected, nor will the quality of the pronunciation of the vowel:

सुना          सुना
*su*nā        su*nā*

This is different from English, where the vowel in the non-stressed syllable is reduced, such as in **Ala**ska, where one witnesses a difference between the pronunciation of the *a* in the middle position (i.e. stressed syllable) and in the word-initial and final position (i.e. unstressed syllables). This is why stress is not as distinctive and crucial in Hindi as in English. Therefore, Hindi is often characterized as a 'syllable-timed' language like French, where the syllables are pronounced in a steady flow, resulting in a 'machine-gun' effect.

   The predominant pattern in Hindi is to stress the penultimate syllable, as in

| किराया | **ki*r*āyā** | rent |
|---|---|---|
| जाना | ***jā*nā** | to go |
| चीता | **c*ī*tā** | leopard |
| इन्दु | ***in*du** | a name |
| रुचि | ***ru*ci** | interest |
| कनिका | **ka*ni*kā** | a female name |

Since short vowels are not stressed in English, chances are you will not hear stress on the Hindi syllables with short vowels.

The long vowel receives stress and thus takes precedence over the penultimate syllable rule, e.g.:

| तारिणी | ***tā*riNī** | a female name |
|---|---|---|
| सिरका | **sir*kā*** | vinegar |

Also, notice that if there is more than one long syllable, the stress falls on the first syllable. The other intricate aspects of the stress system in Hindi are beyond the scope of this introductory book. At the level of word-compounding, the stress is usually placed on the second word, as in

| बात-चीत | **bāt-*cīt*** | conversation |
|---|---|---|
| बोल-चाल | **bol-*cāl*** | colloquial |

In information-type questions, the question-word is usually stressed.

आप क्या करेंगे?
**āp *kyā* karẽge?**
you what do-will
What will you do?

आप ये क्यों करेंगे?
**āp ye *kyõ* karẽge?**
you this why do-will
Why would you do this?

आप कहाँ जायेंगे?
**āp *kahā̃* jāẽge?**
you where go-will
Where will you go?

## Intonation pattern

Take for example, the word अच्छा **acc<sup>h</sup>ā** 'good, ok'. It can be pronounced with different intonation in different contexts. When अच्छा **acc<sup>h</sup>ā** is uttered in the different contexts – in response to an inquiry, 'What kind of person is x?'; in a statement expressing surprise, 'Is that so?'; as an expression of agreement, disagreement or detachment – it will be produced with different intonation. Intonation is the rise and fall of the pitch of the voice. Hindi exhibits the following four main intonation patterns:

> rising ⤴
> falling ⤵
> rising, falling and rising ⤳
> neutral or level ──

## *Rising intonation*

As in English, the intonation rises towards the end of the sentence in a yes-no type of question.

| क्या | आप | वहाँ | जायेंगे? |
|------|-----|------|----------|
| **kyā** | **āp** | **vahā̃** | **jāẽge**? |
| what | you | there | go-will |

Will you go there?

In exclamatory sentences the intonation rises sharply:

| वो | पास | हो | गया! |
|-----|------|-----|-------|
| **vo** | **pās** | **ho** | **gayā**! |
| he | pass | be | went |

He passed (the exam!)

## *Falling intonation*

Statements, prohibitives and information questions show this intonation pattern:

| लड़का | अच्छा | है। |
|--------|--------|------|
| **laRkā** | **acc<sup>h</sup>ā** | **hε**. |
| boy | good | is |

The boy is good.

सिगरेट पीना मना है ।
**cigreT** **pīnā** **manā** **hɛ.**
cigarette drinking prohibited is
Smoking is prohibited.

आप कहाँ जायेंगे?
**āp** **kahā̃** **jāyẽge?**
you where go-will
Where will you go?

## Rising-falling and rising intonation

In tag-questions intonation rises at the beginning of the verb and falls at the end of the verb, and then rises slightly again while the tag marker is pronounced.

आप आयेंगे ना?
**āp** **āyẽge** **na?**
you come-will tag
You will come, won't you?

## Neutral or level intonation

Ordinary imperative sentences are uttered with a neutral or level intonation.

तुम जाओ
**tum** **jāo.**
You go.

## Linguistic variation

As mentioned in the section on the Hindi writing system and pronunciation, Hindi is spoken in a vast area both inside and outside South Asia. It is natural to expect linguistic variation in the regions. Some regional pronunciation differences have already been pointed out in the description of Hindi vowels and borrowed consonant sounds. One example of variation is the pronunciation of the word-final and medial **a**. In the eastern and southern varieties of Hindi, the vowel **a** is retained in both positions. However, the **a** is optional in many words of Perso-Arabic origin, even in Standard Hindi, as shown here:

| कुरसी | kur*a*sī | kursī | कुर्सी | chair |
|-------|----------|-------|--------|-------|
| सरदी | sar*a*dī | sardī | सर्दी | winter, cold |
| गरमी | gar*a*mī | garmī | गर्मी | summer, hot |
| नज़दीक | naz*a*dīk | nazdīk | नज़्दीक | near |
| कतल | qat*a*l | qatl | क़त्ल | murder |

Another important source of variation is the consonant **h**. The preceding stressed vowel **a** becomes ɛ if **h** is followed by a non-vowel sound. For example:

| कह | k*a*h | but pronounced | कैह | kɛh |
|-----|------|----------------|------|-----|
| रहना | r*a*hnā | but pronounced | रैह | rɛhnaa |
| वह | v*a*h | but pronounced | वो | vo |
| यह | y*a*h | but pronounced | ये | ye |

The stressed vowel is in italics. The only exceptions are the third-person singular pronouns which are pronounced as वो **vo** and ये **ye**, respectively.

When the preceding vowel is unstressed, the ह **h** is dropped but the vowel becomes long, as in

| वजह | vajah | but pronounced | वजा | vajā |
|------|-------|----------------|------|------|
| तरह | tarah | but pronounced | तरा | tarā |

If the **h** is preceded by **a** and followed by **u**, the **h** is dropped and the merger of the two vowels either results in **au** (as in 'caught') or **o**. For example, **bahut** is pronounced either as **baut** or **bot**.

In many dialects, the **h** follows the script pronunciation (i.e. is pronounced the way it is written).

# Verb forms: more than one spelling

Some verb forms ending in **aa** and **e** can be written with more than one spelling. For example, the subjunctive, past and imperative forms of the verb can be written using the following variations:

| Verb | Past | Subjunctive | Imperative |
|------|------|-------------|------------|
| जा **jā** to go | गए **gaye** <br> गये **gaye** | जाए **jāe** <br> जाये **jāye** <br> जाय **jāy** | जाओ **jāo** जाइए **jāiye** <br> जावो **jāvo** जाइये **jāiye** |

Phonetic considerations are primarily responsible for variations in traditional spellings.

## अभ्यास **ab<sup>h</sup>yās** Exercises

### Exercise 1

Mark the syllable boundary in the following words using the symbol #.

1 आइये **āiye**
2 औरतें **aurtẽ**
3 पढ़ता **paR<sup>h</sup>tā**
4 सुनो **suno**
5 नमस्ते **namaste**
6 मिलेंगे **milẽge**
7 सुनकर **sunkar**
8 आदमी **ādmī**

### Exercise 2

Read through the following question and answers, and try to imagine the intonation patterns involved. It would be helpful to seek the assistance of a native speaker.

1 Yes–no type
    *Q*:   क्या वो पास हो गया?
          **kyā vo *pās* ho gayā?**  Did he pass (the exam)?
    *Ans*:  हाँ
          **hā̃**

2 Information question
   *Q*:  कौन सा ग्रेड मिला?
        **kaun sā *grade* milā?**    What grade did he get?
   *Ans*:  A ग्रेड ।
          'A' grade

3 Statement
   वो अच्छा लड़का है।
   **vo acचhā laRkā hɛ.**
   He is a good boy.

4 Surprise
   *Statement*:  वो पास हो गया।
                 **vo pās ho gayā.**    He passed the exam.
   *reply*:  अच्छा!
            **accहā!**             (with surprised intonation)
                                   implying 'Is that so? I do not
                                   believe you.'

5 Agreement
                  आओ, फिल्म देखने चलें।
   *Suggestion*:  **āo, *film* dekहne calẽ.**   Come on, let's go and see
                                               a film.
   *Agreement*:   अच्छा।
                  **accहā.**                    Okay.

6 Detached
   *Suggestion*:  आओ, फिल्म देखने चलें।
                  **āo, *film* dekहne calẽ.**   Come on, let's go and see
                                               a film.
   *Agreement*:   अच्छा।
                  **accहā.**                    Okay.

7 Normal commands
   दरवाजा बंद करो।
   **darvāzā band karo.**    Close the door.

## Exercise 3

Read the following weather forecast for India and transcribe the
Hindi words into Roman. For numerals, consult the English–Hindi
vocabulary section. Assume that the word-final **a** is dropped.

| मौसम weather | दिल्ली Delhi | मुम्बई Mumbai | कोलकता Kolkata |
|---|---|---|---|
| तापमान temperature | 10 डिग्री सी 10°C | 15 डिग्री सी 15°C | 16 डिग्री सी 16°C |
| बरसात rain, precipitation | बारिश rain | बादल cloud | धूप sunny |
| हवा wind | तेज़ strong | हल्की light | मन्द light |

# पाठ
# pāT<sup>h</sup>
## Units

# 1 नमस्ते/नमस्कार ।
# namaste/ namaskār

## Greetings and social etiquette

**By the end of this unit you should be able to:**

- use simple greetings
- learn expressions of social etiquette
- use expressions for leave-taking
- ask simple questions
- make simple requests
- use personal pronouns (e.g., 'I', 'we', 'you', etc.)
- use some nouns and adjectives

## बातचीत   **bātcīt**   Dialogue 1 🎧 (Audio 1:9)

### नमस्ते   *namaste*   *greetings*

### Hindu–Sikh greetings and other social etiquette

Hindi greetings vary according to the religion of the speaker, but not according to the time of the day. In some cases, the speaker may choose to greet according to the religion of his/her listener. Such a choice is socially more appealing to the listener and you can easily win the hearts of your listeners by being sensitive to their way of greeting.

*Mohan goes to see Sarita in her office. They know each other but are not close friends.*

| | |
|---|---|
| मोहन: | नमस्ते जी । |
| MOHAN: | namaste jī. |
| सरिता: | नमस्ते । क्या हाल है? |
| SARITA: | namaste. kyā hāl hɛ? |
| मोहन: | ठीक है और आप? |
| MOHAN: | Tʰīk hɛ, aur āp? |
| सरिता: | मैं भी ठीक हूँ । हुकम कीजिये । |
| SARITA: | mɛ̃ bʰī Tʰīk hū̃. hukam kījie. |
| मोहन: | हुकम नहीं, विनती है । |
| MOHAN: | hukam nahī̃, vintī hɛ. |

*(The conversation continues for some time.)*

| | |
|---|---|
| मोहन: | अच्छा, नमस्ते । |
| MOHAN: | accʰā, namaste. |
| सरिता: | नमस्ते । |
| SARITA: | namaste. |

| | |
|---|---|
| MOHAN: | *Greetings.* |
| SARITA: | *Greetings. How are you?* |
| MOHAN: | *Fine. And you?* |
| SARITA: | *I am fine too. What can I do for you?* [lit. do order] |
| MOHAN: | *(It is) not an order, (but) a request.* |

(The conversation continues for some time.)

| | |
|---|---|
| MOHAN: | *Okay. Goodbye.* |
| SARITA: | *Goodbye.* |

## शब्दावली **shabdāvalī Vocabulary** 🎧 (Audio 1:10)

*(Note: It is standard convention to transliterate Hindi words in lower case and this convention is used here. Therefore, the first letter of the first word is not capitalized. The only exceptions are upper case T, D, N and R which represent the retroflex sounds.)*

| | | |
|---|---|---|
| नमस्ते | **namaste** | Hindu greeting and reply to the greeting; may be used by other religions too |
| जी | **jī** | honorific word (optional with greetings) |
| क्या | **kyā** | what |
| हाल | **hāl** (m.) | condition |
| है | **hɛ** | is |
| ठीक | **Tʰīk** | fine; okay |
| और | **aur** | and |
| आप | **āp** | you (honorific) |
| मैं | **mɛ̃** | I |
| भी | **bʰī** | also |
| हूँ | **hū̃** | am |
| हुकम | **hukam** (m.) | order |
| कीजिए | **kījie** | please do |
| नहीं | **nahī̃** | not |
| विनती | **vintī** (f.) | request |

## *Pronunciation*

In the eastern Hindi-speaking area (e.g. in the city of Banaras), the vowel ɛ in the words, मैं **mɛ̃** and है **hɛ**, is pronounced as a diphthong, a combination of two vowels, i.e. [ai = a + i]. However, in the western Hindi-speaking area (e.g. in Delhi), it is pronounced as a vowel ɛ, as in English words such as **cat**. Since this vowel pronunciation is considered to be the standard, this is given in the recordings. The word given in angular brackets < > shows that its pronunciation differs from that suggested by the script. This is shown only when the word is introduced for the first time.

The verb form कीजिए [kījie] can also be pronounced as [kījiye]. The semivowel [y] can intervene between the last two vowels. This word can be written with the semivowel too: कीजिये **kījiye**.

## *Notes*

### Hindu–Sikh greetings and their regional variants

नमस्ते **namaste** (lit. 'I bow in your respect'.) is the most common greeting used by Hindus and even by non-Hindus. It is expressed with the hands folded in front of the chest. It may be optionally followed by जी **jī** to show respect and politeness. A more formal alternative to नमस्ते **namaste** is नमस्कार **namaskār**. In the rural areas many other variants such as राम-राम **rām-rām** and जय **jɛ rām jī kī** (pronounced जै) राम जी की are found. Sikhs prefer सत श्री अकाल **sat srī akāl** instead of नमस्ते **namaste**. The gesture of folding hands, however, remains the same. Hindi greetings do not vary at different times of day.

**namaste** नमस्ते (or **sat srī akāl** सत श्री अकाल by Sikhs) and its variants are used for both 'hello' and 'goodbye'.

### Word-for-word translation

Where a Hindi expression differs literally from its English translational equivalent, we show this difference in the notes by giving a word-for-word translation. Observe the word-for-word translation of the Hindi equivalent of the English 'How are you?':

| क्या | हाल | है? |
|------|------|-----|
| **kyā** | **hāl** | **hɛ?** |
| what | condition | is? |

and its reply

| ठीक | है। |
|------|-----|
| **Tʰīk** | **hɛ** |
| fine | is |

### Honorific pronoun

The honorific pronoun आप **āp** 'you' is grammatically plural, even if it refers to one person. Grammatically, it is the same as the English 'you'. For example, in Standard English one will never say 'you is'.

### The politeness bug

Politeness can be quite infectious. If the speaker is being very polite in his/her speech, the listener is obligated either to match or out-perform the speaker. The expression

हुकम   कीजिए।
**hukam   kījie.**
order   please do
Please (give me) an order. = What can I do for you?

is a very formal and cultured way of asking 'What can I do for you?'
The listener appropriately uses an equally polite expression:

हुकम   नहीं   विनती   है।
**hukam   nahī̃   vintī   hε**
order   not   request   is
It is not an order (but) a request.

## Word order

Note the difference between the word order of Hindi and that of
English. In Hindi, the verb (e.g. 'is', 'am', 'are', etc.) usually appears
at the end of the sentence. The object (e.g. 'order') appears before
the verb.

बातचीत   **bātcīt**   **Dialogue 2** 🎧 (Audio 1:12)

सलाम   *salām*   *salam*

## Muslim greetings and social etiquette

Muslims tend to use more Persian and Arabic words and phrases.
They may refer to their language as 'Urdu' or 'Hindustani'. However, Hindi, Urdu and Hindustani are mutually intelligible (for
details see the Introduction).

*Tahsin Siddiqui and Razia Arif run into each other in a car park
(parking lot).*

| | |
|---|---|
| तहसीन: | सलाम, रजिया जी। |
| TAHSIN: | salām, raziā jī. |
| रजिया: | सलाम, सब ख़ैरियत है? |
| RAZIA: | salām. sab xεriyat hε? |
| तहसीन: | मेहरबानी है, और आपके मिज़ाज कैसे हैं? |
| TAHSIN: | meharbānī hε, aur āpke mizāj kεse hε̃? |
| रजिया: | अल्लाह का शुक्र है। |
| RAZIA: | allāh kā shukra hε. |

*(The conversation continues for some time.)*

तहसीन:    अच्छा, ख़ुदा हाफ़िज़ ।
TAHSIN:   acc^hā, xudā hāfiz.
रज़िया:   ख़ुदा हाफ़िज़ ।
RAZIA:    xudā hāfiz.

TAHSIN:   *Greetings Razia.*
RAZIA:    *Greetings. How are you?*
TAHSIN:   *Fine. And, how are you?*
(The conversation continues for some time.)
RAZIA:    *I am fine.*
TAHSIN:   *Okay. Goodbye.*
RAZIA:    *Goodbye.*

शब्दावली   **shabdāvalī   Vocabulary**

| सलाम | **salām** | Muslim greeting and reply to the greeting |
|---|---|---|
| सब | **sab** | all |
| ख़ैरियत | **xɛriyat** (f.) | safety, welfare |
| मेहरबानी | **meharbānī** (f.) | kindness |
| आपके | **āpke** | your |
| मिज़ाज | **mizāj** (m.) | temperament, nature |
| कैसे | **kɛse** | how |
| हैं | **hɛ̃** | are |
| अल्लाह का शुक्र | **allāh kā shukra** | fine |
| ख़ुदा हाफ़िज़ | **xudā hāfiz** | goodbye |

## *Pronunciation*

ख़ैरियत **xɛriyat** and ख़ुदा **xudā** are often pronounced as **k^hɛriyat** and **k^hudā** by non-Muslims, respectively. In short, **x** may be pronounced as [k^h]. (See Script Unit 1.)

मिज़ाज **mizāj** and हाफ़िज़ **hāfiz** are often pronounced as [**mijāj**] and [**hāp^hij**] respectively by non-Muslims. In other words, **z** may be pronounced as [**j**].

## *Notes*

## Muslim greeting and leave taking

सलाम **salām** (an abbreviated form of **salām alɛkum**) is used for 'hello' by Muslims instead of नमस्ते **namaste**. It is expressed by raising the right hand to the forehead. The word for 'goodbye' is खुदा हाफ़िज़ **xudā hāfiz**.

## Other ways of saying 'How are you?'

Another way of saying 'How are you?' is 'Is everything fine?' or 'Is all well (with you)?' The expression for this is

सब     ख़ैरियत   है?
**sab   xɛriyat   hɛ?**
all    welfare   is
How are you? (lit. 'Is everything fine [with you]?')

which is followed by an answer:

मेहरबानी      है।
**meharbānī   hɛ**
kindness     is
(It is your) kindness, i.e. because of your kindness, everything is fine with me.

Yet another interchangeable way of asking 'How are you?' is something like 'How are your habits?', as in the following sentence:

आपके    मिज़ाज    कैसे    हैं?
**āpke    mizāj    kɛse    hɛ̃?**
you-of   habits   how    are

This question is followed by the answer 'With God's grace, everything is fine.' The Hindi expression for this is:

अल्लाह    का    शुक्र    है।
**allāh    kā    shukra   hɛ**
God     of    thank    is

The above exchange is considered super-polite. Such an exchange is usually used more often by Muslims. Nevertheless, Hindus and others may also use it, depending upon their regional (e.g. in the city of Lucknow) and social background (e.g. inter-ethnic dealings).

## What to do when speakers of different religions meet

When speakers of different religions greet each other, it is considered polite for the person who speaks first to greet the listener according to his or her religion. Respecting the religious feelings of others is the rule of politeness. Nowadays the English word 'hello' can be used to stress neutrality and modernity at the same time. However, the English word 'hello' is usually followed by the respectful and polite denoting word जी **jī**.

# व्याकरण  **vyākaraNa  Grammar**

## *Word order in Hindi*

The order of words in a Hindi sentence is not as rigidly fixed as it is thought to be by prescriptive and traditional grammarians. Although a Hindi sentence usually (but not invariably) begins with a subject and ends with a verb, if the sentence has an object, this is sand-wiched between the subject and the verb. That is why Hindi is often called an SOV language (i.e. subject/object/verb language). However, Hindi speakers or writers enjoy considerable freedom in placing words to achieve stylistic effects. In dialogue 1 Sarita asks:

| क्या | हाल | है? |
|------|------|------|
| **kyā** | **hāl** | **hɛ?** |
| what | condition | is |

How are you?

Usually the question word क्या **kyā** 'what' does not appear in the sent-ence initial position. The ordinary form of the sentence is as follows:

| हाल | क्या | है? |
|------|------|------|
| **hāl** | **kyā** | **hɛ?** |
| condition | what | is |

How are you?

The question word क्या **kyā** 'what' is placed at the beginning of the sentence to give special emphasis to it. Also, you may have noticed the deletion of the implied element (i.e. the possessive pronoun 'your' modifying the subject noun 'condition') in the conversation. Such deletions also affect Hindi word order. For example, in the same dialogue, Mohan responds to Sarita's question in the following way:

| ठीक | है | |
|------|------|---|
| **Tʰīk** | **hɛ** | |
| fine | is | |

I am fine.

Mohan's reply has no subject because the subject phrase is implied. The full version of the sentence is as follows:

| मेरा | हाल | ठीक | है। |
|------|------|------|------|
| **merā** | **hāl** | **Tʰīk** | **hɛ** |
| my | condition | fine | is |

I am fine. (lit. 'My condition is fine.')

The implied subject (i.e. मेरा हाल **merā hāl**) is rarely spelled out in the reply.

## Yes–no questions

Yes–no questions involve either an affirmative or a negative answer. In spoken Hindi, yes–no questions are much simpler than in English. They are usually formed by changing *intonation*, i.e. with a rising tone of voice at the end of the sentence. You do not need to place any form of the verb before the subject, as you do in English. In dialogue 2 above, Razia asks

| सब | ख़ैरियत | है? |
|------|------|------|
| **sab** | **xɛriyat** | **hɛ?** |
| all | welfare | is |

Is all well? *or* Is everything fine?

simply by 'yes–no question intonation', i.e. by raising the pitch of voice at the end of the sentence. The same sentence with a 'statement intonation' (pitch falling at the end), as in English, would mean 'All is well' = 'I am fine.'

## Personal and demonstrative pronoun

The Hindi personal pronouns are

| **mɛ̃** | मैं | I |
|------|------|------|
| **tū** | तू | you (singular) |
| **<vo>** | वह | she, he, it; that |
| **<ye>** | यह | this |
| **ham** | हम | we |
| **tum** | तुम | you (plural) |
| **āp** | आप | you (honorific) |
| **ve** | वे | they; those |
| **ye** | ये | these |

absolute gender in the case of inanimate and abstract nouns. There follow some rules of thumb for you to navigate the unpredictable waters of gender.

Look at the following representative list of Hindi words and see if you can guess the gender rules.

| *Masculine* | | | *Feminine* | | |
|---|---|---|---|---|---|
| laRkā | लड़का | boy | laRkī | लड़की | girl |
| gʰoRā | घोड़ा | horse | gʰoRī | घोड़ी | mare |
| kamrā | कमरा | room | kursī | कुर्सी | chair |
| darvāzā | दरवाज़ा | door | kʰiRkī | खिड़की | window |
| landan | लन्दन | London | dillī | दिल्ली | Delhi |
| gʰar | घर | house | kitāb | किताब | book |
| hātʰ | हाथ | hand | nazar | नज़र | vision |
| namak | नमक | salt | mirc | मिर्च | pepper |
| ādmī | आदमी | man | aurat | औरत | woman |
| cʰātā | छाता | umbrella | mātā | माता | mother |

Most Hindi nouns ending in **ā** are masculine and those ending in **ī** are feminine. There are exceptions though: आदमी **ādmī** 'man' ends in **ī** and is masculine and माता **mātā** 'mother' ends in **ā** and is feminine. But you have probably guessed that the *logical gender* takes precedence over the word-final sound. After all, how could the word for 'mother' be other than feminine in gender and the word 'man' be other than masculine? These two criteria – logical gender and word-final sound – can solve the mystery of Hindi gender in nearly every case.

## Agreement: adjectives and possessive adjectives

You have already come across one very productive adjective: अच्छा **accʰā** 'good/fine' which ends in **ā**. It is a majority adjective. By substituting the suffixes given in the box, we can produce other forms. For example:

| | | | | | |
|---|---|---|---|---|---|
| **accʰā** | **laRkā** | अच्छा लड़का | **accʰe** | **laRke** | अच्छे लड़के |
| good | boy | | good | boys | |
| **accʰī** | **laRkī** | अच्छी लड़की | **accʰī** | **laRkiyā̃** | अच्छी लड़कियाँ |
| good | girl | | good | girls | |

The question word कैसा kɛsā 'how' also behaves like an adjective ending in ā.

| | | | |
|---|---|---|---|
| kɛsā laRkā | कैसा लड़का | kɛse laRke | कैसे लड़के |
| what kind of boy | | what kind of boys | |
| kɛsī laRkī | कैसी लड़की | kɛsī laRkiyā̃ | कैसी लड़कियाँ |
| what kind of girl | | what kind of girls | |

The Hindi equivalents of the English possessive pronouns ('my', 'our', etc.) are:

| | | |
|---|---|---|
| merā | मेरा | my |
| hamārā | हमारा | our |
| terā | तेरा | your (singular, most intimate/non-honorific) |
| tumhāra | तुम्हारा | your (plural, familiar) |
| āpkā | आपका | your (plural, honorific) |
| uskā | उसका | his/her (remote) |
| unkā | उनका | their (remote) |
| iskā | इसका | his/her (proximate) |
| inkā | इनका | their (proximate) |

Hindi possessive pronouns listed above follow the pattern of adjectives which end in ā.

| | | | | | |
|---|---|---|---|---|---|
| merā | laRkā | मेरा लड़का | mere | laRke | मेरे लड़के |
| my | boy | | my | boys | |
| merī | laRkī | मेरी लड़की | merī | laRkiyā̃ | मेरी लड़कियाँ |
| my | girl | | my | girls | |

From the above examples, it is clear that adjectives ending in ā agree with the nouns that follow them. Therefore, they behave like 'majority' adjectives.

In English, it is the gender of the *possessor* in third person singular pronouns (i.e. 'his girl', 'her girl') that is marked on possessive adjectives. Such a distinction is not made in Hindi. Notice, however, that because possessive adjectives agree with the nouns that follow them, the form of a possessive adjective can change in accordance with the gender and the number of the *possessed* noun. Thus, the following phrases are ambiguous in Hindi:

| | | | | | |
|---|---|---|---|---|---|
| uskā | laRkā | उसका लड़का | uske | laRke | उसके लड़के |
| his/her | boy | | his/her | boys | |
| uskī | laRkī | उसकी लड़की | uskī | laRkīyā̃ | उसकी लड़कियाँ |
| his/her | girl | | his/her | girls | |

उसका लड़का **uskā laRkā** means both 'his boy' and 'her boy'. Since लड़का **laRkā** 'boy' is masculine, the possessive adjective उसका **uskā** 'his/her' takes the masculine form, regardless of whether the boy in question belongs to a man or a woman. Similarly, उसकी लड़की **uskī laRkī** can mean both 'his girl' or 'her girl'. It is the feminine gender of the word लड़की **laRkī** 'girl' that assigns gender to the possessive pronoun.

## अभ्यास   **ab^hyās   Exercises**

## Exercise 1

How would you reply to someone who said this to you?

1  namaste.                      नमस्ते ।
2  kyā haal hɛ?             क्या हाल है?
3  salām.                          सलाम ।
4  mizāj kɛse hɛ̃?        मिज़ाज कैसे हैं?
5  acc^hā, namaste.      अच्छा, नमस्ते ।
6  sat srī akāl jī.          सत् सी अकाल जी ।
7  sab xɛriyat hɛ?        सब ख़ैरियत है?
8  namaste jī.                नमस्ते जी ।
9  hukam kījie.             हुकम कीजिये ।

## Exercise 2

Match the replies in column B with the greetings or questions in column A.

|   | A | B |
|---|---|---|
| 1 | नमस्ते । <br> namaste | ठीक है । <br> T^hīk hɛ |
| 2 | क्या हाल है? <br> kyā hāl hɛ? | अल्लाह का शुक्र है । <br> allāh kā shukra hɛ. |
| 3 | आपके मिज़ाज कैसे हैं? <br> āp ke mizāj kɛse hɛ̃ | नमस्ते । <br> namaste. |
| 4 | ख़ुदा हाफ़िज़ <br> xudā hāfiz. | ख़ुदा हाफ़िज़ । <br> xudā hāfiz. |
| 5 | सब ख़ैरियत है? <br> sab xɛriyat hɛ? | सलाम । <br> salām. |
| 6 | सलाम <br> salām. | मेहरबानी है । <br> meharbānī hɛ. |

## Exercise 3

Fill in the gaps in the two conversations given below:

## Conversation 1

A: सलाम |
   salām.

B: _____ |

B: सब ख़ैरियत है?
   sab xɛriyat hɛ?

A: _____है और आप के _____ कैसे हैं?
   _____hɛ, aur āp ke_____ kɛse hɛ̃?

B: अल्लाह का_____ _____ |
   allāh kā_____ _____ .

## Conversation 2

A: _____ |

B: सत स्री अकाल जी |
   sat srī akāl jī.

B: क्या_____ है?
   kyā_____ hɛ?

A: _____ है और _____?
   _____ hɛ, aur_____?

B: मैं भी _____ _____ |
   mɛ̃ bʰī_____ _____.

A: अच्छा _____ _____ _____ |
   accʰā,_____ _____ _____

B: सत स्री अकाल |
   sat srī akāl.

## Exercise 4

Answer the following questions:

1
   Question:  क्या हाल है?
              kyā hāl hɛ?
   Answer:
   Question:  और आप?
              aur āp?
   Answer:

English-speaking Indians tend to translate directly from English, this is not the natural tendency of native speakers. The expression 'Excuse me' is best paraphrased by the native Hindi speaker either as 'please say' कहिए **kahiye** or 'please listen' सुनिए **suniye**. In fact, this is true of many languages, for example Spanish.

*Do not use **māf kījiye** if you do not intend to apologize. Such an inappropriate choice could make a learner the easy target of unwanted jokes.*

## Social linguistic rituals

Every language employs some expressions which are often fixed and invariable. For instance, in greeting someone, one might use the expression 'Hi there'; but if one examines this expression, it is rather a strange one as there is no subject, no verb and no chance of changing the expression even slightly, for example to 'Hi here'. In some respects, Hindi expressions such as 'Pleased to see you' belong to this category. For the time being, you should memorize them without going further into their composition. Also, learn their appropriate usage. They are used usually in introductions. However, if a waiter is introducing himself, you do not need to use this expression in response.

The mystery of what the correct subject of 'Pleased to see you' is will become clear later when the concept of **ko** subjects (called 'dative subjects' or 'experiential subjects') is introduced. For the time being, use the expression as if it were a subject-less sentence.

## Word-for-word translation

The Hindi expression of 'I am pleased to meet you' is

| मिल के | बड़ी | खुशी | हुई। |
|---|---|---|---|
| **mil ke** | **baRī** | **xushī** | **huī** |
| met-having | big | happiness | happened |

In the above expression, the object 'you' is implied. However, for emphasis, the object can be inserted into the above expression:

| आपसे | मिल के | बड़ी | खुशी | हुई। |
|---|---|---|---|---|
| **āp se** | **mil ke** | **baRī** | **xushī** | **huī** |
| you-with | met-having | big | happiness | happened |

Notice the Hindi equivalent of the English 'I am pleased to meet you' is 'Having met you, I am pleased.'

## Word order of the question word 'what'

Observe the place of the question word क्या **kyā** 'what' in the following sentences:

| आपका | पूरा | नाम | क्या | है? |
|---|---|---|---|---|
| **āp kā** | **pūrā** | **nām** | **kyā** | **hɛ?** |
| your | full | name | what | is |

What is your full name?

| आप | क्या | काम | करते | हैं? |
|---|---|---|---|---|
| **āp** | **kyā** | **kām** | **karte** | **hɛ̃?** |
| you | what | work | do | are |

What do you do? = What is your job?

When one compares these sentences with the socially ritualistic expression क्या हाल है **kyā hāl hɛ**, one might be tempted to conclude that 'anything goes' regarding the placement of क्या **kyā** in a sentence. These examples strengthen this belief further because one can say the above two sentences in the following way:

| आपका | क्या | पूरा | नाम | है? |
|---|---|---|---|---|
| **āpkā** | **kyā** | **pūrā** | **nām** | **hɛ?** |
| your | what | full | name | is |

What is your full name?

| आप | काम | क्या | करते | हैं? |
|---|---|---|---|---|
| **āp** | **kām** | **kyā** | **karte** | **hɛ̃?** |
| you | work | what | do | are |

What do you do? = What is your job?

The placement of क्या **kyā** at the beginning or at the end of the sentence, or between the two verbal elements, causes some problems. It changes the meaning of the sentences and may even sound abrupt and impolite. Therefore, the rule of thumb is to keep the question word closer to the word that is the subject of the inquiry. क्या **kyā** is usually placed before the noun or the verb it modifies. If the noun phrase is modified, as the noun नाम **nām** is modified in the

## *Notes*

### Word-for-word translation: 'Where are you from?'

The Hindi equivalent of the English 'Where are you from?' is

| आप | कहाँ | की | हैं? |
|------|------|------|------|
| **āp** | **kahā̃** | **kī** | **hɛ̃?** |
| you | where | of | are |

The response to the English question in Hindi is

| मैं | दिल्ली | की | हूँ। |
|------|------|------|------|
| **mɛ̃** | **dillī** | **kī** | **hū̃.** |
| I | Delhi | of | am |

As we saw in the last chapter, like other possessive pronouns, की **kī** agrees with the number and the gender of its possessor. In the above two sentences the subject pronoun is the possessor. Since the subjects are feminine, the feminine form की **kī** is selected. It is not difficult to guess what would happen if the subjects were masculine. If these sentences are uttered by males, they are

| आप | कहाँ | के | हैं? |
|------|------|------|------|
| **āp** | **kahā̃** | **ke** | **hɛ̃?** |
| you | where | of | are |

| मैं | दिल्ली | का | हूँ। |
|------|------|------|------|
| **mɛ̃** | **dillī** | **kā** | **hū̃.** |
| I | Delhi | of | am |

Remember the honorific pronoun आप **āp** always takes the plural form.
    Don't be surprised if you hear someone using से **se** 'from' instead of का **kā**, का **ke** or की **kī**.

| आप | कहाँ | से | हैं? |
|------|------|------|------|
| **āp** | **kahā̃** | **se** | **hɛ̃?** |
| you | where | from | are |

| मैं | दिल्ली | से | हूँ। |
|------|------|------|------|
| **mɛ̃** | **dillī** | **se** | **hū̃.** |
| I | Delhi | from | am |

Usually, an educated Hindi–English bilingual would construct such a sentence. The important thing is to know that से **se** is invariable whereas का **kā** is variable. You will learn about the invariable elements such as से **se** later in the section on invariable postposition.

Notice also the placement of the English 'from' in the Hindi sentence.

## Postpositions

The Hindi equivalents of English 'in Banaras' and 'from Delhi' are

| बनारस | में | दिल्ली | से |
|-------|-----|--------|----|
| **banāras** | **mē** | **dillī** | **se** |
| Banaras | in | Delhi | from |

Notice the English prepositions placed after the noun of the prepositional phrase. In other words, the word order of the prepositional phrase is reversed in Hindi. Since the prepositional elements always follow the noun they modify, they are called *post*positions in Hindi grammar.

## Question words: 'where' and 'how many/much'

From the Hindi sentence 'Where are you from?' it should be obvious that the Hindi word for where is कहाँ **kahā̃**. Like the English question word, Hindi कहाँ **kahā̃** does not change its shape. It is also not placed at the beginning of the sentence. Its usual place is before the verb. However, this word is can be quite mobile within a sentence.

The Hindi equivalent of 'how many/much' is कितना **kitnā**. This question word agrees with its following noun in number and gender.

| कितना | काम | |
|-------|-----|---|
| **kitnā** | **kām** | how much work |
| कितने | भाई | |
| **kitne** | **bʰaī** | how many brothers |
| कितनी | बहनें | |
| **kitnī** | **bɛhɛnē̃** | how many sisters |

This question word is like a (an inflecting) possessive adjective.

## बातचीत  **bātcīt  Dialogue 3** 🎧 (Audio 1:21)

### *Where are you from?*

*During the train journey, Kanika and Sunita become friends; they are ready to exchange their addresses.*

| | |
|---|---|
| सुनीता: | यह मेरा पता है। |
| SUNITA: | ye merā patā hɛ. |
| कनिका: | यह पता बड़ा है। |
| KANIKA: | ye patā bahut baRā hɛ. |
| सुनीता: | हाँ, बड़ा शहर, बड़ा पता। |
| SUNITA: | hā̃ baRā shɛher, baRā patā. |
| कनिका: | लेकिन छोटा शहर, छोटा पता। |
| KANIKA: | lekin, cʰoTā shɛher, choTā patā. |
| *(both laugh)* | |
| सुनीता: | अच्छा, फिर मिलेंगे। |
| SUNITA: | accʰā, pʰir milẽge. |
| कनिका: | मिलेंगे। |
| KANIKA: | milẽge. |

| | |
|---|---|
| SUNITA: | *This is my address.* |
| KANIKA: | *This address is very big.* (i.e. long) |
| SUNITA: | *Yes, big city, big address.* |
| KANIKA: | *But small city, small address!* |
| (both laugh) | |
| SUNITA: | *Okay, (we) will meet again.* |
| KANIKA: | *Okay, (we) will meet.* |

## शब्दावली  **shabdāvalī  Vocabulary**

| | | |
|---|---|---|
| पता | **patā** (m.) | address |
| बहुत | **bahut** | very |
| बड़ा | **baRā** (m. adj.) | big |
| शहर | **<shɛher>** (m.) | city |
| लेकिन | **lekin** | but |
| छोटा | **cʰoTā** (m. adj.) | small |
| फिर | **pʰir** | again, then |
| अच्छा | **accʰā** (m. adj.) | good, okay |
| मिलना | **milnā** (–ne) | to meet |
| मिलेंगे | **milẽge** | will meet |

## Pronunciation

Like the word बहन **bahan**, the word for 'city' is written as शहर **shahar** but it is pronounced **shɛhɛr**. However, the pronunciation of बहुत **bahut** does not change because **h** is not surrounded by the vowel **a** on both sides.

## Notes

### Word-for-word translation

| यह | पता | बहुत | बड़ा | है। |
|------|---------|-------|-------|------|
| **ye** | **patā** | **bahut** | **baRā** | **hɛ.** |
| this | address | very | big | is |

Notice the sentence ends with a verb and not with an adjective as is the case with 'This address is very long.'

### Subject omission

The Hindi expression of 'we will meet again' is

| फिर | मिलेंगे। |
|------|---------|
| **pʰir** | **milɛ̃ge.** |
| again | will meet |

The subject 'we' is implied. It is rarely spelled out. Normally such subjectless expressions are considered ungrammatical in many languages including English; however, they are quite normal in Hindi. Many languages, such as Chinese, follow the tendency to drop subjects. Subject/pronoun dropping languages are called 'pro-drop' languages.

## व्याकरण **vyākaraNa  Grammar**

### Tag question

A tag question is usually tagged to a statement. The Hindi equivalent of 'You are Dr Anup Patel, aren't you?' is very simple – just add न **na** at the end of the statement. It will take care of both the

positive tags (e.g. 'is it?', 'will you?', 'do you?', etc.) and the negative
tags (e.g. 'isn't it?', 'won't you?', 'don't you?', etc.) attached to a
statement in English. The only difference is that whereas English
speakers will pause at the point where a comma is placed in the
English sentence Hindi speakers will not do so. Therefore, no comma
is placed between the statement and the tag. However, in both English and Hindi a tag question has a rising intonation.

## Verb 'to be'

This section will guarantee plain sailing into the sea of different
tenses. Once you have mastered the forms given below, your adven-
ture into different tenses becomes more rewarding and worthwhile.

There is a striking resemblance between the English and Hindi
verb 'to be'. In Hindi just as in English one cannot say 'you am', 'I
is', 'he am' or 'they is'. Different forms are used depending upon the
person and number of the subject. The Hindi counterparts of the
English verb 'to be' are given below in Magic Key 2.

### Magic Key 2

|              | Singular             | Plural                 | Honorific                      |
| ------------ | -------------------- | ---------------------- | ------------------------------ |
| *First person*  | हूँ **hū̃** (I) am      | हैं **hɛ̃** (we) are      | –                              |
| *Second person* | है **hɛ** (you sg.) are | हो **ho** (you pl.) are  | हैं **hɛ̃** (you honorific) are  |
| *Third person*  | है **hɛ** (he/she/it) is | हैं **hɛ̃** (they) are    | –                              |

Certainly there are some differences between Hindi and English. In
Hindi it is possible to say 'you is', provided the Hindi singular 'you'
तू **tū** is selected. Of course, the second person honorific pronoun
आप **āp** always takes a plural form. As we mentioned in the first unit,
be careful when using Hindi second person pronouns. Chances are
you will rarely get to use the pronoun तू **tū** and, thus, the singular
second person form of 'to be'.

## Present habitual actions = simple present tense

The Hindi sentences

| आप | क्या | करते | हैं? | |
|---|---|---|---|---|
| **āp** | **kyā** | **karte** | **hɛ̃?** | |
| you | what | do | are | |

| मैं | बनारस | में | रहती | हूँ। |
|---|---|---|---|---|
| **mɛ̃** | **banaras** | **mẽ** | **rɛhtī** | **hũ** |
| I | Banaras | in | live | am |

are equivalent to the English 'What do you do?' and 'I live in Banaras,' which refer to habitual or regularly repeated acts. Look at the verb form/phrase, and you will see that there are two main parts of the Hindi verb form. The first, usually called the 'main verb', is composed of three elements:

| कर | + त | + ी |
|---|---|---|
| **kar** | + **t** | + **e** |
| stem 'to do' | + aspect marker | + gender-number marker (m. pl.) |

| रह | + त | + � |
|---|---|---|
| **rɛh** | + **t** | + **ī** |
| stem 'to live' | + aspect marker | + gender-number marker (f. sg.) |

The first element of the first part is the verb stem. The second element is the aspect marker. The aspect marker simply shows whether the act is completed or ongoing. At this point it is important to understand the difference between tense and aspect. As mentioned just now, aspect is concerned about the ongoing, repeated or completed state of the action whereas tense (present, past or future) renders time information, i.e. as to what point in time the action took place. The third element of the main verb is the same masculine plural ending from Magic Key 1 discussed in the previous chapter.

The second part of the verb is called the 'auxiliary verb'. In our two sentences, the auxiliary verb is the same 'to be' verb form discussed above in Magic Key 2.

This verb form has various technical names. The most widely used forms are the following three: present imperfect tense, present habitual tense and simple present tense. Here we will call it the *simple present tense*. The full paradigm is given in the Grammatical Summary.

## Verb 'to have'

The Hindi expression for 'How many brothers and sisters do you have?' is

| आपके | कितने | भाई | बहनें | हैं? |
|-------|--------|------|---------|------|
| **āpke** | **kitne** | **bʰāī** | **bɛhɛnẽ** | **hɛ̃?** |
| your | how many | brothers-sisters | | are |

Notice that the Hindi sentence contains neither an equivalent to the English verb 'to have' nor the subject 'you'. In Hindi, the subject takes a possessive form and the verb 'to have' becomes the verb 'to be'. As we proceed further, it will become clear that many languages do not have the exact equivalent of English 'have'. This Hindi construction is used to express inseparable or non-transferable possessions (such as body parts, relationships or dearly held possessions such as a job, house or shop). Transferable possessions will be dealt with later on.

## Number and gender (plural formation of marked 'nerd' nouns)

Now do some detective work and discover Magic Key 3 for the following nouns:

**Masculine**

| *Singular* | | | *Plural* | | |
|---|---|---|---|---|---|
| भाई | **bʰāī** | brother | भाई | **bʰāī** | brothers |
| घर | **gʰar** | house | घर | **gʰar** | houses |
| हाथ | **hātʰ** | hand | हाथ | **hātʰ** | hands |
| मर्द | **mard** | man | मर्द | **mard** | men |
| आदमी | **ādmī** | man | आदमी | **ādmī** | men |

**Feminine**

| *Singular* | | | *Plural* | | |
|---|---|---|---|---|---|
| बहन | **bɛhɛn** | sister | बहनें | **bɛhɛnẽ** | sisters |
| किताब | **kitāb** | book | किताबें | **kitābẽ** | books |
| औरत | **aurat** | woman | औरतें | **auratẽ** | women |
| माता | **mātā** | mother | माताएँ | **mātāẽ** | mothers |

If you think that the masculine nouns that do not end in ā remain unchanged and the feminine nouns which do not end in ī take ẽ to form plurals, you are right. The masculine nouns which depart from the normal trend, i.e. those that do *not* end in ā and the feminine nouns that do *not* end in ī, are called 'marked' nouns. We affectionately call them 'nerd' nouns as an aid to memory.

## Magic Key 3

|  | *Singular* | *Plural* |
|---|---|---|
| *Masculine* | non-ā | 0 (zero = unchanged) |
| *Feminine* | non-ī | ẽ |

## अभ्यास ab<sup>h</sup>yās Exercises

### Exercise 1

Pac-man has swallowed either some parts of the words or whole words. Supply the missing part where you see the * sign:

मैं दिल्ली * हूँ । मे* चार भाई * । मेरा छोट* भाई शिकागो में काम कर* है । मे* दो बड़* भाई इंग्लैड़ में रहत* * । मेरा नाम अमर * । मैं स्कूल जा* हूँ । मेर* दो बहन* भी * । मेर* पिता जी भी काम करत* हैं । आप * रहते हैं? आप* कित* भाई-बहनें हैं । आप* माता जी क्या * कर* हैं?

mẽ dillī * hū̃. me* cār b<sup>h</sup>ai *. merā c<sup>h</sup>oT* b<sup>h</sup>āī *Chicago* mẽ kām kar* hε. mer* do baR* b<sup>h</sup>āī *England* mẽ rεht* *. merā nām amar *. mẽ *school* jā* hū̃. mer* do bεhεn* b<sup>h</sup>ī *. mer* pitā jī b<sup>h</sup>ī kām kart* hε̃. āp * rεhte hε̃? āp kit* b<sup>h</sup> āī-bεhεnẽ. āp* mātā jī kyā * kar* hε̃?.

### Exercise 2

Pair the words on the right with those on the left:

| अच्छा | छोटा |
|---|---|
| acc<sup>h</sup>ā | c<sup>h</sup>oTā |

| बड़ा | लड़की |
|---|---|
| baRā | laRkī |

| बहन | औरत |
|------|------|
| bεhεn | aurat |
| लड़का | बुरा |
| laRkā | burā |
| आदमी | नहीं |
| ādmī | nahī̃ |
| हाँ | भाई |
| hā̃ | bʰāī |

## Exercise 3

The software system of our computer has imposed some weird system on the following Hindi phrases. It's your job to correct them.

| से | बनारस |
|------|------|
| se | banāras |
| में | शहर |
| mε̃ | shεhεr |
| दस | बहन |
| das | bεhεn |
| चार | भाईयाँ |
| cār | bʰāīyā̃ |
| दो | आदमीयाँ |
| do | ādmīyā̃ |
| कितना | भाईयाँ |
| kitnā | bʰāīyā̃ |
| पीला | साड़ी |
| pīlā | sāRī |

## Exercise 4

Unscramble the following words/phrases and fill in the unscrambled expression in the blank spaces on the right:

| | | | |
|------|------|------|------|
| hiyeka | _____ | | |
| shīxu | _____ | | |
| bīRa xuīsh hīu | _____ | _____ | _____ |
| rūpā mnā | _____ | _____ | |
| dūrās | _____ | | |
| kinte bʰāī | _____ | _____ | |
| mε̃lieg | _____ | | |

## Exercise 5

In this puzzle there are four Hindi words from our dialogues. Find the words and circle them. They can be found horizontally and vertically.

```
a  d  g  a  b  a  d  z  x  s  u  n  i  y  e  z  y  x  u  f  g
l  l  k  j  a  z  x  c  v  b  n  m  a  s  p  q  w  e  r  t  y
z  x  c  v  R  a  d  g  a  r  t  y  f  g  h  a  s  g  h  j  o
r  t  y  f  i  b  g  t  x  u  s  h  i  i  z  q  t  s  k  x  p
c  v  b  n  i  w  s  x  e  d  v  r  a  t  g  h  t  a  h  z  c
q  a  z  w  c  w  s  v  f  r  y  h  n  m  h  u  i  k  a  u  c
```

## Exercise 6  (Audio 1:23)

If you have the recording, listen to it, and then play the role of Meenu Bharati. You can record your response.

*Setting: a crowded store*

अभिलाषा:　(*bumps into Meenu*) माफ़ कीजिये।
मीनू:　＿＿＿＿＿＿＿＿＿＿। बहुत भीड़ है।
अभिलाषा:　सच।
मीनू:　＿＿＿＿＿＿＿＿＿＿＿＿＿＿＿।
अभिलाषा:　और मेरा नाम अभिलाषा पाँडे है।
मीनू:　＿＿＿＿＿＿＿＿＿＿＿＿＿।
अभिलाषा:　आप दिल्ली की हैं, न?
मीनू:　＿＿＿＿＿＿＿＿＿＿＿।

ABHILASHA:　(*bumps into Meenu*) māf kījiye.
MEENU:　＿＿＿＿＿＿＿＿＿＿. bahut bʰīR hɛ.
ABHILASHA:　sac.
MEENU:　＿＿＿＿＿＿＿＿＿＿.
ABHILASHA:　aur merā nām Abhilasha Pande hɛ.
MEENU:　＿＿＿＿＿＿＿＿＿＿.
ABHILASHA:　āp dillī kī hɛ̃ na?
MEENU:　＿＿＿＿＿＿＿＿＿＿.

## शब्दावली  shabdāvalī  Vocabulary

| | | |
|---|---|---|
| माफ़ी | **māfī** (f.) | apology |
| भीड़ | **bhīR** (f.) | crowd |

(Rajinder shows a number of sarees. Anita asks Meghan about her choice.)

ANITA: *Meghan, which saree do you want?*

MEGHAN: *(I want) this yellow (one).*

(Turning to Rajinder to ask the price)

ANITA: *What is its price?*

RAJINDER: *Twelve hundred rupees.*

ANITA: *Please tell (me) the right (price); she is the visitor.* (lit. she has come from abroad)

RAJINDER: *This is the price nowadays . . . okay, eleven hundred (rupees).*

ANITA: *Okay, (that) is fine.*

## शब्दावली  shabdāvalī  Vocabulary

| | | |
|---|---|---|
| ज़रा | **zarā** | little, somewhat |
| नया | **nayā** (m. adj.) | new |
| नये | **naye** | new |
| साड़ी | **sāRī** | saree |
| दिखाना | **dikʰānā** [+ne] | to show |
| दिखाइये | **dikʰāiye** | please show |
| कौन सा | **kaun sā** (m. adj.) | which one |
| कौन सी | **kaun sī** | which one |
| चाहिये/चाहिए | **cāhiye** | desire, want |
| रेशम | **resham** (m.) | silk |
| रेशमी | **reshmī** | silken |
| या | **yā** | or |
| सूत | **sūt** (m.) | cotton |
| सूती | **sūtī** | cotton (adj.) |
| देखना | **dekʰnā** (+ne) | to see |
| देखिये/देखिए | **dekʰiye** | please see |
| आजकल | **āj-kal** | nowadays |
| रिवाज | **rivāj** (m.) | custom |
| आपको | **āp-ko** | to you |
| पसन्द | **pasand** (f.) | choice, liking |
| पीला | **pīlā** (m. adj.) | yellow |
| पीली | **pīlī** (f. adj.) | yellow |
| दाम | **dām** (m.) | price |
| बारह | **<bārā>** | twelve |
| सौ | **sau** | hundred |
| रुपये | **rupaye** (m.) | Rupees (Indian currency) |
| बताइये/बताइए | **batāiye** | please tell |

| बाहर | **bāhar** | outside |
|------|-----------|---------|
| आयी/आई | **āyī** | came |
| इतना | **itnā** (m. adj.) | this much |
| ग्यारह | **<gyārā>** | eleven |

# Pronunciation

The numerals eleven and twelve are written ग्यारह **gyārah** and बारह **bārah**, but are pronounced ग्यारा **gyārā** and बारा **bārā** in Standard Hindi. In the other varieties of Hindi, they are pronounced **gyārɛ** and **bārɛ**, respectively.

The Hindi word for 'silken' is written as रेशमी **reshamī** but the vowel अ **a** is dropped. Therefore, it is pronounced रेश्मी **reshmī**. For the time being, satisfy yourself with this observation. The rule for dropping अ **a** is given in Script Unit 4.

# Notes

## Rules of negotiation: direct and indirect strategies

The rules of bargaining or negotiating can be very complex indeed, and are beyond the scope of this book. However, one strategy deserves special mention. Towards the end of the conversation, the subject of visitors is brought up. Since Indian culture shows a great deal of sensitivity towards foreign visitors, this is a signal to request a discount. In this case, the shopkeeper appropriately obliges.

It is also quite common to ask the price indirectly by saying:

| *Asking the price (directly)* | | | | *Asking how much the total comes to (indirectly)* | | |
|---|---|---|---|---|---|---|
| इसका | दाम | क्या | है? | कितने | [पिसे] | हुए? |
| **iskā** | **dām** | **kyā** | **hɛ?** | **kitne** | **paise** | **hue?** |
| Its | price | what | is | how much | money | happened |
| ये | कितने | का | है? | कितना | हुआ/होगा? | |
| **ye** | **kitne** | **kā** | **hɛ?** | **kitnā** | **huā/hogā?** | |
| this | how much | of | is | how much | happened/will happen | |
| इसकी | कीमत | क्या | है? | | | |
| **iskī** | **kīmat** | **kyā** | **hɛ?** | | | |
| its | price | what | is | | | |

## Politeness bug

As we saw in the last unit, Hindi is a very rich language from the point of view of politeness.

When ज़रा **zarā** 'little', 'somewhat' is used at the beginning of a request, its main function is politeness. It is a little like the English 'I do not want to impose on you but . . .'. By adding ज़रा **zarā**, Hindi speakers convey the meaning 'I want to put as little burden as possible on you by my request'. ज़रा **zarā** remains invariable.

## चाहना cāhnā 'want' vs चाहिए cāhiye 'desire/want'

Just as the English expression 'What do you want?' would be considered less polite than 'What would you like to have?', similarly in Hindi

| आप | कौन | सी | साड़ी | चाहती | हैं? |
|-----|-----|-----|-----|-----|-----|
| **āp** | **kaun** | **sī** | **sāRī** | **cāhtī** | **hɛ̃** |
| you | what kind of | | saree | want | are |

would be considered less polite than

| आपको | कौन सी | साड़ी | चाहिए? |
|-----|-----|-----|-----|
| **āpko** | **kaun sī** | **sāRī** | **cāhiye?** |
| you-to | what kind of | saree | desire |

(lit. What kind of saree is desirable to you?)

In the first sentence the subject आप **āp** indicates a *deliberate* subject whereas in the second sentence the subject आपको **āpko** is an *experiencer* one. Sometimes politeness is achieved in Hindi by means of experiencer subjects. In other words, the verb चाहिए **cāhiye** is the relatively polite counterpart of English 'to want' (and Hindi चाहना **cāhnā** 'to want') because it always selects an experiencer subject. Experiencer subjects render polite reading in some contexts. Hereafter the Hindi verb चाहिए **cāhiye** will be glossed as 'want' because 'desire' is not its best translation.

For more information, see the discussion of the experiencer subject in the next unit.

## Word-for-word translation

The Hindi equivalent of English 'It is very much in fashion' is

| इसका | बहुत | रिवाज | है। |
|------|------|-------|-----|
| **iskā** | **bahut** | **rivāj** | **hɛ.** |
| its | very | custom | is |

Similarly, the English expression 'This (she) is a visitor' is realized in Hindi as

| ये | बाहर | से | आई | हैं। |
|----|------|-----|-----|-----|
| **ye** | **bāhar** | **se** | **āyī** | **hɛ̃.** |
| this (hon.) | outside | from | came | are |

In other words, the Hindi expression is literally 'She has come from outside.' The past tense will be dealt with later on; for the time being memorize this sentence and learn to make number and gender changes in आई **āyī** (आया **āyā** for masculine singular subjects, आए/आये **āye** for masculine plural and आईं/आयीं **āyī̃** for feminine plural) and person and number changes in the 'to be' form.

## Polite commands

The Hindi equivalent of English 'please show' and 'please see' are

| दिखाइए | देखिए |
|--------|-------|
| **dikʰā-iye** | **dekʰ-iye** |
| show-imperative (polite) | see-imperative (polite) |

The other examples of polite commands you have encountered earlier are:

| कहिए | सुनिए |
|------|-------|
| **kah-iye** | **sun-iye** |
| say-imperative (polite) | listen-imperative (polite) |

In short, **iye** is added to a verbal stem to form polite commands. It is called the 'polite imperative' in grammatical literature.

## No word for 'please'

There is really no *exact* equivalent of the English word 'please'. The most important way of expressing polite requests is by means of the polite verb form, i.e. by adding -**iye** to a verb stem. If one looks for word-for-word Hindi equivalents of 'please', there are two: कृपया **kripyā** or मेहरबानी करके **meharbānī karke**; even then the verbal form with -iye must be retained. कृपया **kripyā** and मेहरबानी करके **meharbānī karke** mean 'kindly' in Hindi.

## Context

Note the use of the change in meaning of Hindi कौन सा **kaun sā** 'which one' in the following two contexts: when a saree has yet to be shown by the shopkeeper

| कौन सी | साड़ी | चाहिए? |
|--------|-------|--------|
| **kaun sī** | **sāRī** | **cāhiye?** |
| what kind of | saree | want |

What kind of saree do (you) want?

and in the context of choosing a saree from a set of sarees which are being shown to the customer

| आपको | कौन | सी | साड़ी | पसंद | है? |
|------|-----|-----|-------|------|-----|
| **āpko** | **kaun** | **sī** | **sāRī** | **pasand** | **hɛ?** |
| you-to | which | one | saree | choice/liking | is |

Which saree do (you) like?

## Subject omission

| कौन | सी | साड़ी | चाहिए? |
|-----|-----|-------|--------|
| **kaun** | **sī** | **sāRī** | **cāhiye?** |
| what | kind of | saree | want |

What kind of saree do (you) want?

## बातचीत    **bātcīt**    Dialogue 2    🎧 (Audio 1:26)

## *Booking a flight*

*John Smith goes to the airline booking office to make an airline reservation for Jaipur (the Pink City). He talks with the agent.*

| जान: | जयपुर की एक टिकट चाहिए। |
|------|------------------------|
| JOHN: | jaipur kī ek TikaT (*ticket*) cāhiye. |
| एजेंट: | कौन से दिन के लिये? |
| AGENT: | kaun se din ke liye? |
| जान: | कल के लिए। |
| JOHN | kal ke liye. |

| | |
|---|---|
| एजेंट: | कम्प्यूटर पर देखता हूँ, है या नहीं। |
| AGENT: | kampuTar (*computer*) par dek<sup>h</sup>tā hū̃, hɛ yā nahī̃. |
| जान: | सुबह की फ़्लाइट चाहिये। |
| JOHN: | subā kī flāiT (*flight*) cāhiye. |
| एजेंट | टिकट है। |
| AGENT: | Ticket (*ticket*) hɛ. |
| जान: | तो दीजिए। फ़्लाइट कब चलती है? |
| JOHN | to dījiye. flight (*flight*) kab caltī hɛ? |
| एजेंट: | सुबह दस बजे । |
| AGENT: | subā das baje. |
| जान: | मेरे पास कैश नहीं है। |
| JOHN: | mere pās *cash* nahī̃ hɛ. |
| एजेंट: | तो कैडिट कार्ड दीजिए। |
| AGENT: | to krɛDiT kārDa (*credit card*) dījiye. |

| | |
|---|---|
| JOHN: | *(I) want one ticket for Jaipur* |
| AGENT: | *For which day?* |
| JOHN: | *For tomorrow.* |
| AGENT: | *(I) must look at the computer (to see), whether or not (I have it). (lit. [it] is or not).* |
| JOHN: | *(I) need a morning flight.* |
| AGENT: | *(I) have a ticket.* |
| JOHN: | *Then (please) give (it to me). When does the flight leave?* |
| AGENT: | *10 o'clock (in the) morning.* |
| JOHN: | *I do not have cash.* |
| AGENT: | *Then use a credit card. (lit. give a credit card)* |

## शब्दावली   shabdāvalī   Vocabulary

| | | |
|---|---|---|
| दिन | **din** (m.) | day |
| के लिये | **ke liye** | for |
| कल | **kal** | yesterday, tomorrow |
| पर | **par** | on, at |
| देखना | **dek<sup>h</sup>nā** (+ne) | to see |
| सुबह | **&lt;subā&gt;** | morning |
| तो | **to** | then |
| देना | **denā** (+ne) | to give |
| दीजिए | **dījiye** | please give |
| कब | **kab** | when (question word) |
| चलना | **calnā** (–ne) | to leave, to walk |
| दस | **das** | ten |
| बजे | **baje** | o'clock |
| पास | **pās** | near, possession (have) |

## *Pronunciation*

The word for morning is written as सुबह **subah**, but is pronounced
**subā** सुबा.

In the borrowed words from English such as *computer* and *ticket*,
the English *t* is pronounced with the retroflex ट **T** (see chapter on
Hindi writing system and pronunciation for the pronunciation of
Hindi retroflex sounds).

## *Notes*

### Word-for-word translation

| जयपुर | की | टिकट |
|-------|-----|------|
| **jaipur** | **kī** | **TikaT** |
| Jaipur | of (f.) | ticket (f.) |

A ticket for Jaipur. (lit. Jaipur's ticket)

The borrowed English words 'ticket' and 'computer' have been
assimilated into Hindi and assigned feminine and masculine gender,
respectively.

The equivalent Hindi expression for 'morning flight' is

| सुबह | की | फ़्लाइट |
|-------|-----|---------|
| **subā** | **kī** (f.) | **flāiT** |
| morning | of | flight |

Guess the gender of 'flight' in Hindi. Of course, it is feminine (clue:
the feminine form **kī**).

### Short form of तब **tab** 'then'

The short form of तब **tab** 'then' is तो **to**, as in

| तो | दीजिए |
|-----|--------|
| **to** | **dījiye** |
| then | please give |

### Compound and oblique (peer pressure) postpositions

Observe the structure of the English preposition in Hindi:

| *(noun)* | *postposition* | *postposition* |
|---|---|---|
| कल | के | लिए |
| **kal** | **ke** | **liye** |
| tomorrow | of | for |

As we proceed further we will introduce the concept of the 'oblique' case in Hindi, which I affectionately call the 'peer pressure' case. Languages do show the effects of peer pressure! You will notice, as we go on, that the compound postpositions will either begin with के **ke** or की **kī**, but never with का **kā**. The reason is that का **kā** and की **kī** have to be followed by another postposition in the compound postposition, and the succeeding postposition influences the preceding one. In the above expression लिए **liye** changes का **kā** to के **ke**. That is, the postposition ending **ā** becomes **e**.

The oblique effect does not last to the preceding postposition but to the phrase as a whole.

| कौन | सा | दिन |
|---|---|---|
| **kaun** | **sā** | **din** |
| which | | day (m.) |

Notice that the सा **sā** part of the question word 'which' agrees in number and gender with the following noun, i.e. दिन **din** 'day', which is masculine singular. Now let us expand this phrase by adding the Hindi compound postposition के लिए **ke liye**

| कौन | से | दिन | के | लिए |
|---|---|---|---|---|
| **kaun** | **se** | **din** | **ke** | **liye** |
| which | | day (m.) | of | for |

Now the peer pressure of लिए **liye** not only extends to के **ke** but all the way to से **se**. The way का **kā** gives in to the peer pressure of लिए **liye** is similar to the way सा **sā** gives in to से **se**. As a matter of fact, even the noun दिन **din** is affected too. The only exceptions are the marked nouns (or nerd nouns: remember this distinction from the last chapter), where the effect does not surface. However, if we replace the marked noun with an unmarked noun, लड़का **laRkā** 'boy', you can see a clear change.

| कौन | से | लड़के | के | लिए |
|---|---|---|---|---|
| **kaun** | **se** | **laRke** | **ke** | **liye** |
| which | | boy (m.) | of | for |
| For which boy | | | | |

Although लड़का **laRkā** 'boy' changes to लड़के **laRke** under peer pressure, its meaning does not change. It still keeps its singular identity. Remember, people usually give in to peer pressure only superficially!

## Separable or transferable possessions

In the last unit we dealt with non-transferable and inseparable possessions, i.e. expressions such as 'I have four brothers.' Let us turn our attention to separable possessions, as in

| मेरे | पास | कैश | नहीं | है। |
|------|-----|-----|------|-----|
| mere | pās | *cash* | nahī̃ | hɛ |
| my | near | cash | not | is |

I do not have cash.

Similarly, in Hindi the expression 'You have a ticket' is

| आपके | पास | टिकट | है। |
|-------|-----|------|-----|
| āpke | pās | TikaT | hɛ. |
| your | near | ticket | is |

You have a ticket.

In other words, in the case of separable possession the subject receives के पास **ke pās** compound postposition and, subsequently, the following changes take place. Notice के **ke** makes the subject oblique masculine possessive.

| मैं | | के पास | | मेरे पास | |
|-----|---|--------|---|----------|---|
| **mɛ̃** | + | **ke pās** | ⇒ | **mere pās** | I have |

| आप | | के पास | | आपके पास | |
|-----|---|--------|---|----------|---|
| **āp** | + | **ke pās** | ⇒ | **āp ke pās** | You have |

## बातचीत **bātcīt** Dialogue 3 🎧 (Audio 1:28)

## डॉक्टर के पास जाना *DākTar ke pās jānā*
## *A visit to the doctor*

*Kushwant Singh is under the spell of cold weather. He has a fever and headache. He goes to his doctor, Charan Chaturvedi. After exchanging greetings, Kushwant tells Charan the purpose of his visit.*

| | | |
|---|---|---|
| कुशवंत: | डॉक्टर साहिब, मुझको कुछ बुख़ार है। | |
| KUSHWANT: | DākTar sāhib, muj<sup>h</sup>ko kuc<sup>h</sup> buxār hε. | |
| चरन: | कब से है? | |
| CHARAN: | kab se hε? | |
| कुशवंत: | कल रात से। | |
| KUSHWANT: | kal rāt se. | |
| चरन: | सिर–दर्द भी है। | |
| CHARAN: | sir-dard b<sup>h</sup>ī hε? | |
| कुशवंत: | जी हाँ। | |
| KUSHWANT: | jī hā̃. | |

*(putting the thermometer in Kushwant's mouth)*

| | |
|---|---|
| चरन: | थरमामीटर लगाइए। |
| CHARAN: | thermometer lagāiye. |

*(after taking the thermometer from Kushwant's mouth)*

| | |
|---|---|
| चरन: | थोड़ा बुख़ार है . . . यह दवाई दिन में दो बार लीजिये . . . जल्दी ठीक हो जायेंगे। |
| CHARAN: | t<sup>h</sup>oRā buxār hε . . . ye davāī din mẽ do bār lījiye . . . jaldī Thīk ho jāẽge. |

| | |
|---|---|
| KUSHWANT: | *Doctor sir, I have some fever.* |
| CHARAN: | *Since when (i.e. is it)?* |
| KUSHWANT: | *Since last night.* |
| CHARAN: | *(Do you have) a headache too?* |
| KUSHWANT: | *Yes.* |
| CHARAN: | *Put the thermometer (into your mouth)* |

*(putting the thermometer into Kushwant's mouth)*

| | |
|---|---|
| CHARAN: | *(You have) a little fever . . . please take this medicine twice a day. (You) will be fine.* |

## शब्दावली shabdāvalī Vocabulary

| | | |
|---|---|---|
| डॉक्टर | **DākTar** | Doctor |
| साहिब | **<sāhib>** | sir |
| मुझको | **muj<sup>h</sup> ko** | to me |
| कुछ | **kuc<sup>h</sup>** | some |
| बुख़ार | **buxār** (m.) | fever |
| कब | **kab** | when |
| कल | **kal** | yesterday/tomorrow |
| रात | **rāt** (f.) | night |
| सिर | **sir** (m.) | head |
| दर्द | **dard** (m.) | pain |
| लगाना | **lagānā** (+ne) | to fix, to put into, to stick |

| | | |
|---|---|---|
| लगाइए/लगाइये | lagāiye | please fix, put into, stick |
| थोड़ा | thoRā (m. adj.) | little |
| दवाई | davāī (f.) | medicine |
| दो | do | two |
| बार | bār (f.) | time, turn |
| लेना | lenā (+ne) | to take |
| लीजिए/लीजिये | lījiye | please take |
| जल्दी | jaldī | soon, quickly |
| हो जाएँगे/जायेंगे | ho jāẽge | will become |

## Pronunciation

The word साहिब **sāhib** also has other variants: **sāhab** साहब and more colloquial साब **sāb**.

## Notes

### साहिब **sāhib**

The original meaning of Hindi साहिब **sāhib** is 'master' or 'lord'. This word is more formal than the English 'sir'. In highly formal addresses, साहिब **sāhib** can be substituted for the Hindi जी **jī**. Usually it is used with last names and titles (e.g. जज **jaj** 'judge'; **sāhib**). The other two variants are: **sāhab** साहब and **sāb** साब.

### 'Since'

The Hindi equivalent of 'since' is the postposition से **se** 'from', e.g.

| कब | से | कल | रात | से |
|---|---|---|---|---|
| **kab** | **se** | **kal** | **rāt** | **se** |
| when | from | yesterday | night | from |
| Since when | | Since last night | | |

### 'Tell me why' column

| | |
|---|---|
| सवाल: | हिन्दुस्तानी औरतें बिन्दी क्यों लगाती हैं? |
| **savāl**: | **hindustānī auratẽ bindī kyõ lagātī hẽ?** |
| Question: | Why do Indian women put a dot (on their foreheads)? |

Circle the correct response:

| | | |
|---|---|---|
| 1 **singār** | सिंगार | (for) make up |
| 2 **shādī-shudā hɛ** | शादी–शुदा है | (to show she) is married |
| 3 **donō** | दोनों | (for) both (reasons) |

दोनों

> **javāb:**    3 **donō** दोनों
> Answer:    3 both

## शब्दावली    **shabdāvalī**    **Vocabulary**

| | | |
|---|---|---|
| भारत | **bʰārat** (m.) | India |
| हिन्दुस्तान | **hindustān** (m.) | India |
| भारतीय | **bʰāratīya** | Indian |
| हिन्दुस्तानी | **hindustānī** | Indian |
| सवाल | **savāl** (m.) | question |
| बिन्दी | **bindī** (f.) | dot |
| क्यों | **kyō** | why |
| लगाना | **lagānā** (+ne) | to attach, to fix |
| जवाब | **javāb** (m.) | answer |
| सिंगार | **singār** (m.) | make up |
| शादीशुदा | **shādī-shudā** | married |
| दोनों | **donō** | both |

## बातचीत    **bātcīt**    **Dialogue 4** 🎧 (Audio 1:30)

## मज़ाक    *mazāk*    *Humour column*

*Two thieves are being interrogated in a Delhi Police Station. The inspector is interrogating the thieves and his assistant is taking notes.*

| | |
|---|---|
| इंस्पैक्टर: | तुम्हारा नाम? |
| INSPECTOR: | tumhāra nām? |
| चोर: | बैनरजी। |
| THIEF: | Banerjī. |

*(inspector now turns to the other)*

| | |
|---|---|
| इंस्पैक्टर : | तुम्हारा नाम? |
| INSPECTOR: | tumhāra nām? |
| चोर: | चैटरजी। |
| THIEF: | Chatterjī. |

*(inspector talks to both thieves)*

इंस्पैक्टर:   चोरी करते हो और नाम के साथ 'जी' लगाते हो।
INSPECTOR:  corī karte ho aur nām ke sāt<sup>h</sup> 'jī' lagāte ho.
*(turning to his assistant)*
इंस्पैक्टर:   इनका नाम लिखिये, बैनर और चैटर।
INSPECTOR:  inkā nām lik<sup>h</sup>iye, Baner aur Chatter.

| | |
|---|---|
| INSPECTOR: | *Your name?* |
| THIEF: | *Banerjī.* |

*(inspector now turns to the other)*

| | |
|---|---|
| INSPECTOR: | *Your name?* |
| THIEF: | *Chatterjī.* |

*(inspector talks to both thieves)*

INSPECTOR:  *(You) steal and use 'jī' with your name.*
*(turning to his assistant)*
INSPECTOR:  *Write their names, Baner and Chatter.*

शब्दावली  **shabdāvalī  Vocabulary**

| चोरी करना | corī karnā (+**ne**) | to steal |
|---|---|---|
| लिखना | lik<sup>h</sup>nā (+**ne**) | to write |
| के साथ | ke sāth | with |
| लगाना | lagānā (+**ne**) | to attach, to fix |
| लिखिये/लिखिए | lik<sup>h</sup>iye | please write |

## Note (cultural)

Some common last names in the state of Bengal end in जी –**jī**. However, this जी **jī** is not an honorific as in Hindi.

व्याकरण  **vyākaraNa  Grammar**

## चाहिए *cāhiye and verb agreement*

The verb चाहिए **cāhiye** is a frozen verb. It agrees neither with a subject nor with an object in Standard Hindi.

## Simple present tense: subject–verb agreement

As pointed out earlier, the verb agrees with the subject in person, number and gender. The first part of the verb (called the 'main verb') agrees in number and gender, and the second part of the verb (called the 'auxiliary verb') agrees in person and number with the subject.

| फ्लाइट | कब | चलती | है? |
|---|---|---|---|
| **flight** | **kab** | **caltī** | **hɛ?** |
| flight (f.) | when | move/walk | is |

When does the flight leave?
(lit. when does the flight walk/move?)

## Object–verb agreement (postposition syndrome)

| आपको | साड़ी | पसन्द | है? |
|---|---|---|---|
| **āpko** | **sāRī** | **pasand** | **hɛ?** |
| you-to | saree (f.) | choice/liking | is |

Do you like the saree?

Note that, unlike in English, the Hindi verb does not agree with the subject. Instead, it agrees with the object. The rule of thumb is that whenever the subject is followed by any postposition, the verb does not agree with it. Recall the 'have' construction:

| मेरे | चार | भाई | हैं। |
|---|---|---|---|
| **mere** | **cār** | **bʰāī** | **hɛ̃** |
| my | four | brothers (m. pl.) | are |

I have four brothers.

In the above sentence, the verb form is not हूँ **hū̃**, indicating that the verb does not agree with the subject. The verb agrees with भाई **bʰāī** 'brothers' and takes the plural ending.

| मेरे | पास | साड़ियाँ | हैं। |
|---|---|---|---|
| **mere** | **pās** | **sāRiā̃yā̃** | **hɛ̃** |
| my | near | sarees | are |

I have sarees.

Similarly, the verb agrees with साड़ियाँ **sāRiā̃**, which is plural.
How about the expression 'I have some fever'?

| मुझको | कुछ | बुखार | है। |
|---|---|---|---|
| **mujʰko** | **kucʰ** | **buxār** | **hɛ** |
| me-to | some | fever | is |

I have some fever.

Once again the verb does not agree with the subject because it is followed by the postposition को **ko**. Instead, it agrees with 'fever'.

In fact, if both the subject and the verb are followed by a postposition, the verb never agrees with either. In this case, it stays masculine singular (called 'default agreement').

## When does the subject take a postposition?

Hindi verbs such as पसंद होना **pasand honā** 'to like' and चाहिए **cāhiye** 'to want' select the को **ko** postposition with their subject. You will need to remember which verb takes which postposition with the subject. For example, you will need to know that the English verb 'to have' takes three different postpositions in the Hindi subject:

| Subject postposition | | Possession |
|---|---|---|
| के पास | **ke pās** | separable, transferable |
| का, के, की | **kā, ke, kī** | inseparable |
| को | **ko** | physical states (such as fever, headache) |

## अभ्यास **ab<sup>h</sup>yās** Exercises

### Exercise 1

Translate the following sentences into Hindi according to the model example. (Remember that Hindi does not have articles so the articles 'a', 'an' and 'the' cannot be translated into Hindi.)

*Model*
आपको    किताब    चाहिए
**āpko    kitāb    cāhiye.**    You want a book.

मुझको    किताब    चाहिए
**muj<sup>h</sup>ko    kitāb    cāhiye.**    I want a book.

1  I want a ticket for Jaipur.
2  Do you want medicine?
3  I want two houses.
4  I want a car in my garage.    (garage: use the English word)
5  You want this beautiful saree. (beautiful: सुन्दर **sundar**)

## Exercise 2

Fill in the blanks by making an appropriate choice from the following Hindi subjects.

| मेरा | मेरे | मेरी | मेरे पास | मुझको |
|------|------|------|----------|-------|
| merā | mere | merī | mere pās | muj$^h$ko |

1 _____ एक बहन है।
_____ek bɛhɛn hɛ.
2 _____दो भाई हैं।
_____do b$^h$āī hɛ̃.
3 _____ एक कम्प्यूटर है।
_____ ek *computer* hɛ.
4 _____हाल ठीक है।
_____hāl T$^h$īk hɛ.
5 _____ सिर–दर्द है।
_____ sir-dard hɛ.
6 _____ काम चाहिए।
_____kām cāhiye.
7 _____ लड़का घर लेता है।
_____laRkā g$^h$ar letā hɛ.

## Exercise 3

Match the parts of the sentences given on the right with those on the left to make a complete sentence.

| मुझको | घर में कितने आदमी हैं? |
|-------|------------------------|
| muj$^h$ko | g$^h$ar mẽ kinte ādmī hɛ̃? |
| मेरे पास | क्या है? |
| mere pās | kyā hɛ? |
| आपके | बुखार है। |
| āpke | buxār hɛ. |
| मेरा शहर | आपके लिये है। |
| merā shɛhɛr | āpke liye hɛ. |
| ये फ़्लाइट | बहुत सुंदर है। |
| ye *flight* | bahut sundar hɛ. |

## वातचीत  **bātcīt**  **Dialogue 1** 🎧 (Audio 1:32)

### *आपके शौक क्या हैं?*  *āpke shauk kyā hɛ̃?*
### What are your hobbies?

*Professor James Jones, an internationally acclaimed expert on international adverstising, is being profiled in an ethnic Indian newspaper from California. After talking about his research, the interviewer, Y. Malik, wants to report Professor Jones' interests to his readers*

मलिक:   क्या आप भारत जाते हैं?
MALIK:   kyā āp bʰārat jāte hɛ̃?

जोन्ज़:   जी हाँ, कई बार।
JONES:   jī hā̃ kaī bār.

मलिक:   आपको हिन्दुस्तानी खाना पसन्द है?
MALIK:   āpko hindustānī kʰānā pasand hɛ?

जोन्ज़:   जी हाँ, तन्दूरी चिकन, डोसा . . . वैसे समोसा भी पसन्द है।
JONES:   jī hā̃, tandūrī cikan (*tandoori chicken*), Dosā (*dosa*) . . .
         vɛse samosā bʰī bahut pasand hɛ.

मलिक:   आपके शौक क्या–क्या हैं?
MALIK:   āpke shauk kyā-kyā hɛ̃?

जोन्ज़:   मुझको तैरने का शौक है, इसके अलावा भारतीय संगीत का भी शौक है।
JONES:   mujʰ ko tɛrne kā shauk hɛ, iske alāvā bʰāratīya saŋgīt kā
         bʰī shauk hɛ.

मलिक:   गाने का भी?
MALIK:   gāne kā bʰ ī?

जोन्ज़:   ज़रूर, मेरे गाने पर मेरे बच्चे हैड फ़ोन लगाते हैं।
JONES:   zarūr, mere gāne se mere bacce hɛD fon (*head phone*)
         lagāte hɛ̃.

मलिक:   वाह वाह।
MALIK:   vāh, vāh.

MALIK:   *Do you visit India (quite frequently)?*
JONES:   *Yes, quite often. (lit. several times)*
MALIK:   *Do you like Indian food?*
JONES:   *Yes, tandoori chicken, dosa . . . in addition (I) like samosas very much.*
MALIK:   *What are your hobbies?*
JONES:   *I am fond of swimming; besides this, (I) am fond of Indian music.*
MALIK:   *(Fond) of singing too?*

JONES:     *Of course, my children put on headphones (because of) my singing.*

            (lit. (my) children put on head phones from my singing)

MALIK:     *Excellent!* (i.e. what an excellent sense of humour!)

## शब्दावली    shabdāvalī    Vocabulary

| | | |
|---|---|---|
| जाना | **jānā (–ne)** | to go |
| कई | **kaī** | several |
| खाना | **kʰānā (m.), v (+ne)** | food (n.), to eat (v.) |
| वैसे | **vɛse** | otherwise, in addition |
| शौक | **shauk (m.)** | hobby, fondness, interest |
| तैरना | **tɛrnā (–ne)** | to swim |
| संगीत | **saŋgīt (m.)** | music |
| के अलावा | **ke <alāvā>** | beside, in addition to |
| गाना | **gānā (m.); v. (+ne)** | song (n.); to sing (v.) |
| ज़रूर | **zarūr** | of course, certainly |
| पर | **par** | on, at |
| वाह | **vāh** | ah!, excellent!, bravo! |

## Pronunciation

अलावा **alāvā** is also pronounced as इलावा **ilāvā**.

## Notes

### The experiential (dative) subject: (को ko-subjects)

The Hindi equivalent of the English 'I am fond of swimming' is

| मुझको | तैरने | का | शौक | है। |
|---|---|---|---|---|
| **mujʰko** | **tɛrne** | **kā** | **shauk** | **hɛ** |
| me-to | swimming | of | fondness | is |

In English 'I' is the subject of the sentence. However, in Hindi the equivalent of the English 'I' is मुझको **mujʰko** 'to me'. Such a distinction is very important in South Asian languages. The nominative subjects (e.g. 'I') denote volitional/deliberate subjects, as in the English 'I met him.' The experiential (**ko** को) subjects are non-volitional/non-deliberate, as in the English 'I ran into him.' को **ko** subjects emphasize something happening without any deliberate effort being made. In other words, expressions such as the following are expressed in a slightly different fashion:

| English | Hindi |
|---------|-------|
| I am fond of swimming | The fondness of swimming is to me. |
| You want a ticket | The desire of a ticket is to you. |
| I have some fever. | Some fever is to me. |
| She likes this book. | The choice of this book is (i.e. experienced by) to her. |

The experiencer subjects receive the को **ko** postposition in Hindi. Recall the postposition syndrome of Hindi verbs which refuse to agree with any element that contains a postposition. As a result, the verb 'to be' in Hindi does not agree with the को **ko** subject. Instead, शौक **shauk** 'fondness' becomes the element of agreement.

There are two other terms for experiential subjects – dative subjects and को **ko** subjects. We will call them experiential subjects in this book.

## Verbal nouns (infinitive verbs)

Now note the status of the word 'swimming' in the English sentence: 'I am fond of swimming.' The word 'swimming' functions like a noun in the sentence. As a matter of fact, one could replace it with a noun, e.g. 'I am fond of chocolate.' The only difference is that 'chocolate' is a noun to begin with and 'swimming' is derived from the verb 'swim' by adding '-ing' to it. Such derived nouns are called verbal nouns or gerunds. We will call them verbal nouns throughout this book.

Hindi does not distinguish verbal nouns and infinitive forms, e.g. 'to swim'. You get two for one. Examples of Hindi verbal nouns or infinitive forms are given below:

| Verb stems | | | Verbal nouns/infinitive verbs | | |
|---|---|---|---|---|---|
| कर | **kar** | do | करना | **karnā** | to do/doing |
| आ | **ā** | come | आना | **ānā** | to come/coming |
| जा | **jā** | go | जाना | **jānā** | to go/going |
| देख | **dekʰ** | see | देखना | **dekʰnā** | to see/seeing |
| बता | **batā** | tell | बताना | **batānā** | to tell/telling |
| तैर | **tɛr** | swim | तैरना | **tɛrnā** | to swim/swimming |
| खा | **kʰā** | eat | खाना | **kʰānā** | to eat/eating |
| गा | **gā** | sing | गाना | **gānā** | to sing/singing |
| लिख | **likʰ** | write | लिखना | **likʰnā** | to write/writing |

You must have discovered by now that the only counterpart of the English infinitive 'to' (as in 'to leave') and the verbal noun marker '-ing' (as in 'leaving') in Hindi is ना **nā**. It is like English '-ing' in the sense that it follows a verbal stem rather than the English infinitive marker 'to', which precedes a verbal stem rather than following it.

## Oblique verbal nouns

Remember the peer-pressure influence of postposition on the words in a phrase? See the section on 'compound and oblique postposition' in case you have forgotten it.

Now consider the Hindi counterpart of the English 'of swimming', as in 'I am fond of swimming':

| तैरने | का |
|-------|-----|
| **tɛrne** | **kā** |
| swimming | of |

Under peer pressure from the postposition का **kā**, the Hindi verbal noun तैरना **tɛrnā** 'swimming' undergoes a change exactly like the noun लड़का **laRkā**: it becomes तैरने **tɛrne**. Study the following sentences carefully. Do you see the same change?

| मुझको | गाने | का | शौक | है | |
|-------|------|-----|------|------|---|
| **muj<sup>h</sup>ko** | **gāne** | **kā** | **shauk** | **hɛ.** | |
| me-to | singing | of | fondness | is | |

I am fond of singing.

| मुझको | खाने | का | शौक | है | |
|-------|------|-----|------|------|---|
| **muj<sup>h</sup>ko** | **k<sup>h</sup>āne** | **kā** | **shauk** | **hɛ.** | |
| me-to | eating | of | fondness | is | |

I am fond of eating.

| आपको | मूवी | देखने | का | शौक | है | |
|-------|------|-------|-----|------|------|---|
| **āpko** | **movie** | **dek<sup>h</sup>ne** | **kā** | **shauk** | **hɛ.** | |
| you-to | movie | seeing | of | fondness | is | |

You are fond of watching movies.

| आपको | खाने | का | शौक | है | |
|-------|------|-----|------|------|---|
| **āpko** | **k<sup>h</sup>āne** | **kā** | **shauk** | **hɛ.** | |
| you-to | eating | of | fondness | is | |

You are fond of eating.

## Yes–no questions with क्या kyā

In Unit 1, we showed you how to change a statement into a yes–no question with a mere change of intonation. One can also place क्या kyā in front of a statement and form a yes–no question from it. (Yes, this is the same word क्या kyā that means 'what'!) Even if क्या kyā is placed at the beginning of a sentence, the rising question intonation is imperative. Since it is difficult to show intonation in writing, क्या kyā is more prevalent in written Hindi, and its omission is common in speech.

The statement

आप    भारत    जाते    हैं।
**āp**    **bʰārat**    **jāte**    **hɛ̃.**
you    India    go    are
You go to India.

becomes a yes–no question with the addition of क्या kyā to its front:

क्या    आप    भारत    जाते    हैं?
**kyā**    **āp**    **bʰārat**    **jāte**    **hɛ̃?**
(Q)    you    India    go    are
Do you go to India [often/regularly]?

You do not need any verb forms at the beginning of a yes–no question in Hindi.

## Reduplication of question words

The repetition of a question word is quite common in Hindi. In many languages of South East Asia repetition indicates plurality. Much the same is true of Hindi.

आपके    शौक              क्या    क्या    हैं?
**āpke**    **shauk**              **kyā**    **kyā**    **hɛ̃?**
your    interests/hobbies    what    what    are
What are your interests/hobbies?

In English you cannot repeat the question word 'what' even if you know that the person in question has many interests. However, the repetition of क्या kyā has a 'listing' function, and thus asks the person to give a list of more than one interest from the viewpoint of the speaker.

Similarly, if someone asks in Hindi

| आप | कहाँ | कहाँ | जाते | हैं? |
|----|------|------|------|------|
| **āp** | **kahā̃** | **kahā̃** | **jāte** | **hɛ̃?** |
| you | where | where | go | are |

What places do you go to?

the speaker has reason to believe that the listener goes (often/ regularly) to more than one place.

## बातचीत   **bātcīt   Dialogue 2** 🎧 (Audio 1:34)

### भारतीय फ़िल्में   *bʰārtīya* **filmẽ**   *Indian films*

*India is the largest producer of films in the world. More movies are produced by the Bombay film industry (Bollywood) than by Hollywood. It is no wonder, therefore, that Hindi films dictate social conversation and are an excellent mode of expressing agreement–disagreement, likes–dislikes, and social and political thoughts. In this dialogue, the topic of discussion is Hindi films. The participants are Akbar Ali and Suhas Ranjan. Suhas saw the movie* Black *and he is ready to express his delight over it.*

| सुहास: | 'ब्लैक' मेरी मन–पसन्द फ़िल्म है। |
|--------|------|
| SUHAS: | *Black* merī man-pasand film hɛ. |
| अकबर: | वह कैसे? |
| AKBAR: | vo kɛse? |
| सुहास: | गाने बहुत अच्छे हैं, कहानी और ऐकटिंग भी शानदार है। |
| SUHAS: | gāne bahut accʰe hɛ̃, kahānī aur *acting* bʰī shāndār hɛ. |
| अकबर: | हिन्दी फ़िल्में तो मुझको बिल्कुल पसन्द नहीं। सिर्फ फ़ार्मूला। |
| AKBAR: | Hindi *filmẽ* to mujʰko bilkul pasand nahī̃. sirf formula. |
| सुहास: | लेकिन यह फ़ार्मूला फ़िल्म नहीं, इसका अन्दाज़ और है। |
| SUHAS: | lekin ye *formula film* nahī̃, iskā andāz aur hɛ. |
| अकबर: | सब हिन्दी फ़िल्में एक–सी होती हैं, लड़का लड़की से मिलता है, दोनों में प्यार होता है, फिर खलनायक आता है। |
| AKBAR: | sab Hindi *filmẽ* ek-sī hotī hɛ̃, laRkā laRkī se miltā hɛ, donõ mẽ pyār hotā hɛ, pʰir kʰalnāyak ātā hɛ. |

*(Suhas interrupts)*

| सुहास: | और दोनों की शादी होती है। जी नहीं, यह ऐसी फिल्म नहीं। |
|---|---|
| SUHAS: | aur donõ kī shādī hotī hɛ. jī nahĩ, ye ɛsī *film* nahĩ. |
| अकबर: | तो पश्चिम की नकल होगी। |
| AKBAR: | to pashcim kī nakal hogī. |
| सुहास : | तो आप के ख्याल से सिर्फ पश्चिमी फिल्में अच्छी होती हैं? |
| SUHAS: | to āp ke xayāl se sirf pashcimī *filmẽ* acchī hotī hɛ̃? |
| अकबर: | मैं यह नहीं कहता, पुरानी हिन्दी फिल्में अच्छी होती हैं। |
| AKBAR: | mɛ̃ ye nahĩ kɛhtā, purānī hindī filmẽ accʰī hotī hɛ̃. |

*(Ajit Singh patiently listens to this discussion and intervenes:)*

| अजीत: | फिल्म की बात पर महाभारत क्यों? |
|---|---|
| AJIT: | film kī bāt par mahābʰārat kyõ? |

| SUHAS: | *'Black' is my favourite movie.* |
|---|---|
| AKBAR: | *How come?* |
| SUHAS: | *(The) songs are very good; (the) plot and acting are great too.* |
| AKBAR: | *I dislike Hindi films – (they are) only formula (films).* |
| SUHAS: | *But this (one is) not a formula film. Its style is different.* |
| AKBAR: | *All Hindi films are alike – a boy meets a girl, both fall in love, then a villain comes . . .* |

*(Suhas interrupts)*

| SUHAS: | *And both get married. No, this is not such a film.* |
|---|---|
| AKBAR: | *Then it must be an imitation of the West.* |
| SUHAS: | *(Do) you think only Western films are (generally) good?* (lit. in your opinion only Western films are (generally) good) |
| AKBAR: | *I do not say this: the old Hindi films are good.* |

*(Ajit Singh listens patiently to this discussion and intervenes:)*

| AJIT: | *Why (wage a) fierce battle over the topic of films?* (implying that the topic of films is not worthy of such a serious discussion) |
|---|---|

## शब्दावली  shabdāvalī  Vocabulary

| 'ब्लैक' | *Black* | black |
|---|---|---|
| मन-पसन्द | **man-pasand** | favourite |
| वह कैसे | **vo kɛse** | how come? |
| कहानी | **kahānī** (f.) | story |
| शानदार | **shāndār** | splendid, great |
| बिल्कुल | **bilkul** | absolutely |
| नापसन्द | **pasand** (f.) | like |
| और | **aur** | and, more, other, else |
| अन्दाज़ | **andāz** (m.) | style |

| एक–सा | **ek-sā** | alike |
|---|---|---|
| नायक | **nāyak** | hero |
| खलनायक | **kʰalnāyak** | villain |
| नायिका | **nāyikā** | heroine |
| प्यार | **pyār** (m.) | love |
| शादी | **shādī** (f.) | marriage |
| होना | **honā** (–ne) | to be/happen |
| होती हैं | **hotī hɛ̃** | generally happen, generally take place (pl.) |
| होती है | **hotī hɛ** | generally happens, generally takes place (sg.) |
| होगी | **hogī** | will be |
| ऐसा | **ɛsā** | such |
| पश्चिम | **pashcim** (m.) | West |
| पश्चिमी | **pashcimī** | Western |
| नकल | **nakal** (f.) | copy, fake, imitation |
| ख़्याल | **<xayāl>** (m.) | opinion, view |
| सिर्फ़ | **sirf** | only |
| कहना | **<kɛhnā>** (+ne) | to say |
| पुराना | **purānā** (adj. m.) | old (inanimate) |
| बात | **bāt** (f.) | matter, conversation, topic |
| महा | **mahā** | great |
| महाभारत | **mahābʰārat** | one of the two greatest epics from Sanskrit; fierce battle (non-literal context) |
| क्यों | **kyõ** | why |

## Pronunciation

The Hindi word for 'opinion' can be pronounced and written in two ways: ख़याल **xayāl** and ख़्याल **xyāl**. The latter form is more frequent among the educated; we will use this form here.

The verb 'to say' is pronounced **kɛh** but is written कह **kah**.

## Notes

### फ़िल्में *filmẽ*

The English word 'film' has been assimilated into Hindi. It is no longer treated as a foreign word in the language; therefore, it has gender. From the plural ending ँ **ẽ**, you can predict its gender. It is, of course, feminine. (It is treated as a feminine of the nerd category, i.e. marked.)

## Negative markers: नहीं **nahī̃**, न **na**

The short version of नहीं **nahī̃** 'not' is न **na**. It is written न **na** but in pronunciation the vowel **a** often becomes long, i.e. **ā**.

In polite orders न **na** is used instead of नहीं **nahī̃**. It is also used with subjunctives. Do not worry about subjunctives for now. However, observe the use of न **na** in polite orders ('polite imperatives').

| न | दीजिए |
|---|---|
| **na** | **dījiye** |
| not | please give |

Please do not give.

It is also used with the word नापसन्द **nāpasand** 'dislike'. However, with nouns it is not as productive as with polite commands. For example, you cannot make the word 'dissatisfaction' using न **nā** with the Hindi equivalent of 'satisfaction'.

## और **aur** as an adjective or adverb

| इसका | अन्दाज़ | और | है। |
|---|---|---|---|
| **iskā** | **andāz** | **aur** | **hɛ.** |
| its | style | different | is |

The conjunction 'and' in Hindi expresses a range of meanings when used either as a predicate, as in the above sentence, or as an adjective, as below:

| और | चाय | दीजिए। |
|---|---|---|
| **aur** | **cāy** | **dījiye.** |
| more | tea | please give |

Please give me (some) more tea.

| और | साड़ी | दिखाइए। |
|---|---|---|
| **aur** | **sāRī** | **dikʰāiye.** |
| other | saree | please show |

Please show (me some) other saree.

और **aur** is equivalent to the English 'different', 'more', 'else.' Observe another frequent expression with और **aur**.

और    कुछ    चाहिए?
**aur    kuc<sup>h</sup>    cāhiye?**
else    some    want
Do you want something else?

Note the difference in word order.

## एक-सा ek-sā: 'same', 'alike'

| सब | हिन्दी | फ़िल्में | एक | सी | होती | | हैं। |
|----|--------|----------|-----|-----|------|---|------|
| **sab** | **Hindi** | **filmē** | **ek** | **sī** | **hotī** | | **hɛ̃** |
| all | Hindi | films | one | -ish | generic Be | | are |

Generally all Hindi films are alike.

The सा **-sā** is like the English '-ish' (e.g. 'boyish'). So the Hindi sentence in English is literally 'Generally all Hindi films are one-ish.'

## Generic होता होना 'be'

The sentence above gives the generic meaning. There is no separate word exactly equivalent to the English 'generally' in the sentence. It is the verb होती **hotī** that contributes to this meaning. Compare this sentence with the following:

| सब | हिन्दी | फ़िल्में | एक | सी | हैं। |
|----|--------|----------|-----|-----|------|
| **sab** | **Hindi** | **filmē** | **ek** | **sī** | **hɛ̃** |
| all | Hindi | films | one | -ish | are |

All Hindi films are alike.

which expresses the universal truth, i.e. without exception, Hindi films are alike.

Note the slight difference in the *two conjugations* of होना **honā** 'to be':

| Generic | | | Non-generic |
|---------|---|---|-------------|
| ho + t      + ī | | hɛ̃ | hɛ̃ |
| be + aspect + number, gender | are | | |

It is the generic conjugation which contains the English word 'generally' in Hindi. The verb agrees with the subject. Now observe the two other examples of the generic Be in Hindi:

*Circle the correct answer.*

| | | |
|---|---|---|
| ठीक जवाब: | (b) | |
| **Tʰīk javāb:** | (b) | |
| Correct answer: | (b) | कभी कभी। kabʰī kabʰī. |

| ३ | सवाल: | हिन्दुस्तानी शब्दों से कैसे कहते हैं 'I love you.'? |
|---|---|---|
| 3 | **savāl:** | **hindustānī shabdō se kɛse kɛhte hɛ̃ 'I love you.'** |
| | Question: | How do Indians say in words: 'I love you'? |

| • | जवाब: | (a) | मैं तुम से प्यार करता हूँ। |
|---|---|---|---|
| | | (b) | मुझ को तुम से प्यार है। |
| | **javāb:** | (a) | **mɛ̃ tum se pyār kartā hū̃.** |
| | | (b) | **mujʰko tum se pyār hɛ.** |
| | Answer: | (a) | I love you. |
| | | (b) | Love with you is to me. |

*Circle the correct answer.*

| | | |
|---|---|---|
| ठीक जवाब: | (b) | |
| **Tʰīk javāb:** | (b) | |
| Correct answer: | (b) | मुझ को तुम से प्यार है। mujʰko tum se pyār hɛ |

## शब्दावली  **shabdāvalī   Vocabulary**

| लोग | **log** (m.) | people |
|---|---|---|
| आँख | **ā̃kʰ** (f.) | eye |
| आँखों | **ā̃kʰõ** (f. oblique) | eyes |
| से | **se** | from, with, by |
| शब्द | **shabda** (m.) | word |
| शब्दों | **shabdō** (m. oblique) | words |
| सिर्फ़ | **sirf** | only |
| कभी | **kabʰī** | ever |
| कभी नहीं | **kabʰī nahī̃** | never |
| कभी–कभी | **kabʰī kabʰī** | sometimes |

## Note

### 'I love you' prohibition

The name for 'Cupid' is काम देव **kāma Dev** ('the God Kāma'). काम देव **kāma Dev** carried bows and arrows exactly the same way as 'Cupid' in the West. Did you notice the similarity between the two words – 'Cupid' and काम **kāma**? Although काम **kāma** has delighted Indians  since approximately 3000 BC, Indians do not like to express 'I love you' in exactly the same way as in English. Some expressions are better made non-verbally than verbally. Such is the preference of Indians. If one has to say 'I love you' in words, it is better to express it by means of *experiential subject* construction rather than using the *non-experiential deliberate subject*. The following expression is almost vulgar. (Although such expressions are now common in Bollywood films. The language is changing!)

| मैं | तुमसे | प्यार | करता | हूँ। |
|----|-------|-------|-------|------|
| **mɛ̃** | **tumse** | **pyār** | **kartā** | **hū̃** |
| I | you-with | love | do | am |

Therefore, the expression 'I love you' is best expressed in the following words:

| मुझको | तुमसे | प्यार | है। |
|-------|-------|-------|------|
| **mujʰko** | **tum-se** | **pyār** | **hɛ.** |
| me-to | you with | love | is |

However, nowadays among the educated and the younger generation the English expression 'I love you' is becoming quite popular.

## Reduplication and pluralization

The reduplication of the adverb कभी **kabʰī** 'ever' gives the plural meaning 'sometimes'.

## Oblique plural nouns

Remember peer pressure. Notice the influence of a postposition on plural nouns.

|  | Masculine | | | Feminine | | |
|---|---|---|---|---|---|---|
| *Singular* | **shabda** | शब्द | word | **ā̃kh** | आँख | eye |
| *Plural* | **shabda** | शब्द | words | **ā̃kʰɛ̃** | आँखें | eyes |

Plural nouns yield to the pressure of postposition and take the ending ō̃.

| | | | |
|---|---|---|---|
| shabdõ | se | शब्दों से | by words |
| ā̃khõ | se | आँखों से | by eyes |

## बातचीत  **bātcīt**  Dialogue 3  🎧 (Audio 1:36)

### नाश्ते में आप क्या खाते हैं?  *nāshte mẽ āp kyā kʰāte hẽ? What do you eat for breakfast?*

*Rakesh Seth visits his doctor and complains about his stomach problems. Apparently, he suffers from gas. The doctor begins by inquiring about his eating habits.*

| | |
|---|---|
| डॉक्टर: | राकेश जी, नाश्ते में आप क्या खाते हैं? |
| DOCTOR: | Rakesh jī, nāshte mẽ āp kyā kʰāte hẽ? |
| राकेश: | दस समोसे। |
| RAKESH: | das samose. |
| डाक्टर: | और क्या पीते हैं? |
| DOCTOR: | aur, kyā pīte hẽ? |
| राकेश: | मुझे चाय बहुत अच्छी लगती है। सवेरे बहुत चाय पीता हूँ। |
| RAKESH: | mujʰe cāy bahut acchī lagtī hɛ. savere bahut cāy pītā hū̃. |
| डाक्टर: | आपको शरीर की बिमारी नहीं। दिमाग की बिमारी है इसलिये आप किसी साकिऐट्रिसट के पास जाइये। |
| DOCTOR: | āpko sharīr kī bimārī nahī̃. dimāg kī bimārī hɛ. is liye āp *psychiatrist* ke pās jāiye. |

| | |
|---|---|
| DOCTOR: | *Rakesh jī, what do you eat for breakfast?* |
| RAKESH: | *Ten samosas.* |
| DOCTOR: | *And, what (do you) drink?* |
| RAKESH: | *I like tea a lot. (In the) morning (I) drink a lot of tea.* |
| DOCTOR: | *You do not have (any) physical illness. (You) have a mental illness. Therefore, you (should) go to the psychiatrist.* |

## शब्दावली  **shabdāvalī**  Vocabulary

| | | |
|---|---|---|
| नाश्ता | **nāshtā** (m.) | breakfast |
| पीना | **pīnā** (+ne) | to drink |
| चाय | **cāy** (f.) | tea |
| मुझे, मुझको | **mujʰe, mujʰko** | (to) me |
| लगना | **lagnā** (+ko) | to seem, to be applied |
| अच्छा लगना | **accʰā lagnā** (+ko) | to like |

| | | |
|---|---|---|
| सवेरा | **saverā** (m.) | morning |
| शरीर | **sharīr** (m.) | body |
| बिमारी | **bimārī** (f.) | illness |
| दिमाग़ | **dimāG** (m.) | brain |
| इसलिए | **isliye** | therefore, so, thus, because of this |

## Notes

### अच्छा लगना **acc^hā lagnā** 'to like'

You have already learned expressions (with experiential subjects) such as

| | | | |
|---|---|---|---|
| मुझको | चाय | पसन्द | है। |
| **muj^hko** | **cāy** | **pasand** | **hε.** |
| me-to | tea | liking | is |

I like tea.

Another common way of saying the same expression is

| | | | |
|---|---|---|---|
| मुझको | चाय | अच्छी | लगती | है। |
| **muj^hko** | **cāy** | **acc^hī** | **lagtī** | **hε.** |
| me-to | tea (f.) | good | feel | is |

I like tea. (lit. Tea feels good to me.)

### 'Ghost' postposition

The Hindi equivalents of 'breakfast' and 'morning' are नाश्ता **nāshtā** and सवेरा **saverā** respectively.

If we attach the postposition **mε** 'in' to these nouns, the peer pressure exerted by the postposition makes the nouns oblique.

| Unmarked masculine nouns | | | Oblique singular (unmarked nouns) | | |
|---|---|---|---|---|---|
| नाश्ता | **nāsht*a*** | breakfast | नाश्ते में | **nāsht*e* mε** | for (in) breakfast |
| सवेरा | **saver*a*** | morning | सवेरे में | **saver*e* mε** | in the morning |

However, the English expression of time 'in the morning' is सवेरे **savere** in Hindi. Although the effect of the Hindi postposition (peer pressure) is quite apparent, the postposition में **mε** is dropped. The oblique form indicates its presence. Therefore, this is the 'ghost' postposition.

## Word-formation: derived adjectives

Do some detective work and see how English adjectives such as 'silken' are formed in Hindi:

| Nouns | | | Adjectives | | |
|---|---|---|---|---|---|
| रेशम | **resham** | silk | रेशमी | **reshamī** | silken |
| सूत | **sūt** | cotton | सूती | **sūtī** | cotton (as in cotton clothes) |
| नकल | **nakal** | copy | नकली | **nakalī** | fake |
| असल | **asal** | fact | असली | **asalī** | real, genuine |
| हिन्दुस्तान | **hindustan** | India | हिन्दुस्तानी | **hindustanī** | Indian |
| बनारस | **banāras** | Banaras | बनारसी | **banārasī** | from Banaras (lit. Banarasian) |

If you think that the addition of ī at the end of the word makes it an adjective, you are right. Note that all the nouns (and place names) given above end in a consonant. You cannot derive an adjective by adding ī to the nouns ending in a vowel. For example, the expressions 'from Delhi' or 'from Agra' cannot be reduced to one-word adjectives by the addition of ī. Only the postposition से **se** can rescue these expressions.

Now, observe how words such as 'physical' and 'mental' are formed in Hindi:

| शरीर | की | बीमारी | | दिमाग | की | बिमारी |
|---|---|---|---|---|---|---|
| **sharīr** | **kī** | **bimārī** | | **dimāg** | **kī** | **bimārī** |
| body | of | illness (f.) | | brain | of | illness (f.) |
| Physical/bodily illness | | | | Mental illness | | |

The possessive construction is used instead. Is it possible to reduce शरीर की **sharīr kī** and दिमाग की **dimāg kī** to the ī- type adjectives? Yes, of course.

| शरीरी | बीमारी | | दिमागी | बिमारी |
|---|---|---|---|---|
| **sharīrī** | **bimārī** | | **dimāgī** | **bimārī** |
| Physical/bodily illness | | | Mental illness | |

Always remember, though, that word-formation can sometimes be quite tricky in languages.

## Go to the doctor

You have observed that the English 'to' is usually को **ko** in Hindi. However, the English expression 'go to the psychiatrist' is

| साकिऐट्रिसट | के | पास | जाइये। |
|---|---|---|---|
| *psychiatrist* | **ke** | **pās** | **jāiye** |
| Psychiatrist | of | near | please go |

In other words, the English expression is phrased in Hindi as 'Please go near the psychiatrist.' The compound postposition के पास **ke pās** is used instead of को **ko**. Similarly, the Hindi version of 'Please go to the doctor' is

| डाक्टर | के | पास | जाइये। |
|---|---|---|---|
| **dākTar** | **ke** | **pās** | **jāiye** |

## Contractive e pronoun forms

मुझे **mujʰe** is the short form of मुझको **mujʰko**.

## अभ्यास   abʰyās   Exercises

## Exercise 1

Choose any word from the following four columns and form at least seven sentences. You can use a word from the columns as many times as you like.

| मुझको | पढ़ने | का | शौक | है। |
|---|---|---|---|---|
| mujʰko | paRʰne | kā | shauk | hɛ |
| आपको | गाने | पसन्द | | हैं। |
| āpko | gāne | pasand | | hɛ̃ |
| | क्या/kyā | | | hɛ̃ |
| | तैरने/tɛrne | | | |
| | खाने/kʰāne | | | |
| | क्या-क्या/kyā–kyā | | | |

## Exercise 2

Read the following statements and then answer the question about each statement. Your answer should be in Hindi.

1 Statement: John is fond of dancing and singing. (Hint: dancing
= नाचना **nācnā**)

   Question: गाने के अलावा जॉन को क्या पसन्द है?
   **gāne ke alāvā John ko kyā pasand hɛ?**

   Answer: ............

2 Statement: Judy loves to write stories and poems? (Hint: poem
= कविता **kavitā** (f.))

   Question: जूडी को क्या क्या शौक हैं?
   **Judy ko kyā kyā shauk hɛ̃?**

   Answer: ............

3 Statement: Ramesh's likes and dislikes are given below:

| Likes | Dislikes |
|---|---|
| समोसा खाना **samosā kʰānā** | चिकन खाना **cikan kʰānā** |
| to eat samosa | to eat chicken |
| शाकाहारी खाना **shākāhārī kʰānā** | माँसाहारी खाना **mãsāhārī kʰānā** |
| vegetarian food | non-vegetarian food |
| कहानियाँ **kahāniyā̃** | कविताएँ **kavitāyẽ** |
| stories | poems |
| भारतीय संगीत **bʰārtīya saŋgīt** | देसी संगीत **desī saŋgīt** |
| Indian music | Country music |

   Question: रमेश को क्या क्या नापसन्द है/हैं?
   **Ramesh ko kyā kyā nāpasand hɛ/hɛ̃?**

   Answer:

   Question: रमेश को क्या क्या पसन्द है/हैं?
   **Ramesh ko kyā kyā pasand hɛ/hɛ̃?**

   Answer:

## Exercise 3

There are two possible interpretations of the following sentences.
Uncover their ambiguity by translating them into English.

1 जॉन को खाना पसन्द है।
   John ko kʰānā pasand hɛ.

2 जॉन को गाना पसन्द है।
   John ko gānā pasand hɛ.

## Exercise 4

Write two things children do not like about their parents.

## Exercise 5

How many ways can you find to say 'I like swimming' in Hindi?

## Exercise 6   (Audio 1:38)

If you have the recording, circle the items which the speaker's daughter likes:

1 cats बिल्ली **billī**
2 dogs कुत्ता **kuttā**
3 spicy foods मसालेदार खाना **masāledār kʰānā**
4 cricket (game) क्रिकेट **krikeT**
5 a classical Indian dance भरतनाट्यम् **bʰaratnāTyam**
6 rock music रॉक म्यूज़िक **rāk myuzik**

# 5 छुट्टियों में क्या करेंगे?
# c<sup>h</sup>uTTiyõ mẽ kyā karẽge?

## What will you do during the break?

By the end of this unit you should be able to:

- talk about your own and others' plans
- compare people and objects
- develop paraphrasing skills
- express desires (use desiratives)
- use the future tense
- use capabilitatives
- use progressive tense forms

## बातचीत  **bātcīt**  **Dialogue 1** 🎧 (Audio 2:1)

### मैं भारत जाना चाहता हूँ /  *mɛ̃ bʰārat jānā cāhtā hū̃*
### I want to go to India

*Suman Kumar is planning to spend his Christmas vacation in India.*
*He knows that December and January are excellent months to visit*
*India. Summers are hot and they are followed by monsoons. So he*
*goes to an ethnic travel agent in Toronto to make his travel plans.*

| | |
|---|---|
| एजेन्ट: | क्या सेवा कर सकती हूँ? |
| AGENT: | kyā sevā kar saktī hū̃? |
| सुमन: | हिन्दुस्तान के लिये टिकट चाहिये। |
| SUMAN: | hindustān ke liye TikaT (*ticket*) cāhiye? |
| एजेन्ट: | सिर्फ अपने लिये? |
| AGENT: | sirf apne liye? |
| सुमन: | परिवार के लिये। |
| SUMAN: | parivār ke liye. |
| एजेन्ट: | कितने लोग हैं? |
| AGENT: | kitne log hɛ̃? |
| सुमन: | चार– दो बड़े और दो बच्चे। |
| SUMAN: | cār – do baRe aur do bacce. |
| एजेन्ट: | बच्चों की उमर बारह से कम है? |
| AGENT: | baccõ kī umar bārā se kam hɛ? |
| सुमन: | लड़की की उमर बारह है और लड़के की छह। |
| SUMAN: | laRkī kī umar bārā hɛ aur laRke kī cʰe. |
| एजेन्ट: | कब जाना चाहते हैं? |
| AGENT: | kab jānā cāhte hɛ̃? |
| सुमन: | क्रिसमस में। |
| SUMAN: | *Christmas* mɛ̃. |
| एजेन्ट: | पीक सीज़न है, टिकट महँगी होगी। |
| AGENT: | *peak season* hɛ TikaT (*ticket*) mɛhɛ̃gī hogī. |
| सुमन: | कोई बात नहीं। |
| SUMAN: | koī bāt nahī̃. |

| | |
|---|---|
| AGENT: | *What can I do (for you)* (lit. what service can I do)? |
| SUMAN: | *I need a ticket for India.* |
| AGENT: | *Only for yourself?* |
| SUMAN: | *For the family.* |
| AGENT: | *How many people are (there in the family)?* |
| SUMAN: | *Four – two adults and two children.* |

AGENT:    *Is the age of the children less than twelve?*
SUMAN:    *The girl is twelve and the boy (is) six.*
AGENT:    *When do (you) want to go?*
SUMAN:    *During Christmas.*
AGENT:    *(It) is (the) peak season. The ticket will be expensive.*
SUMAN:    *It does not matter* (lit. none matter).

## शब्दावली  shabdāvalī  Vocabulary

| | | |
|---|---|---|
| सेवा | **sevā** (f.) | service |
| सकना | **saknā** | can, be able to |
| अपना | **apnā** | one's own |
| परिवार | **parivār** (m.) | family |
| उमर | **<umar>** (f.) | age |
| से | **se** | than, from, by |
| कम | **kam** | less |
| चाहना | **cāhnā** (+**ne**) | to want |
| में | **mẽ** | in, during |
| छुट्टियों में | **chuTTiyõ mẽ** | during break/vacation |
| महँगा | **<mɛhẽgā>** (m. adj.) | expensive |
| कोई | **koī** | some, any, someone, anyone |

## *Pronunciation*

The word for 'age' is pronounced and written in two ways: उमर **umar** and उम्र **umra**.

The Hindi word **mɛhẽgā** is written **mahãgā** महँगा.

## *Notes*

### सकना **saknā** 'can'

The expression 'What can I do (for you)' is expressed as

| मैं | क्या | सेवा | कर | सकती | हूँ? |
|---|---|---|---|---|---|
| **mẽ** | **kyā** | **sevā** | **kar** | **saktī** | **hū̃?** |
| I (f. sg.) | what | service | do | can | am |

Notice the placement of सकना **saknā** 'can/to be able to', which is like any other verb in Hindi. It is conjugated in different tenses.

Consider one more example.

| मैं | बोल | सकता | हूँ । |
|------|------|------|------|
| **mɛ̃** | **bol** | **saktā** | **hū̃.** |
| I (m. sg.) | talk | can | am |

I can talk.

The form सकता हूँ **saktā hū̃** agrees with the subject and the real verb बोल **bol** 'talk' precedes सकता हूँ **saktā hū̃**.

## अपना **apnā** 'one's own'

अपना **apnā** is a possessive pronoun which means 'one's own'. The English possessive pronouns can either be translated as regular possessives or using the अपना **apnā** form. Observe the distinction Hindi makes in this regard.

| मेरा | नाम | जान | है । |
|------|------|------|------|
| **merā** | **nām** | **John** | **hɛ** |
| my | name | John | is |

My name is John.

and

| मैं | अपना | नाम | लिखता | हूँ । |
|------|------|------|------|------|
| **mɛ̃** | **apnā** | **nām** | **likʰtā** | **hū̃.** |
| I | own | name | write | am |

I write my name.

In other words, the English phrase 'my' can be said in two ways in Hindi: मेरा **merā** or अपना **apnā**. The possessive pronoun does not show any relationship to the subject of the sentence whereas अपना **apnā** shows this relationship. In the second sentence, the possessed thing मेरा नाम **merā nām** belongs to the subject of the sentence; therefore, मेरा **merā** changes to अपना **apnā**. In the first sentence, however, the subject नाम **nām** *is* part of the possessed element. The rule-of-thumb is that if in a simple clause you come across the following situation in *the same clause*, the possessive pronoun becomes अपना **apnā**.

| Subject | Possessive | Possessive changes to | |
|---------|-----------|----------------------|---|
| मैं mɛ̃ | मेरा merā | अपना apnā | |
| हम ham | हमारा hamārā | अपना apnā | |
| तू tū | तेरा terā | अपना apnā | |
| तुम tum | तुम्हारा tumhāra | अपना apnā | |
| आप āp | आपका āpkā | अपना apnā | |
| वह vo | उसका uskā | अपना apnā | (वह vo . . . उसका uskā must refer to the same person) |
| वे ve | उनका unkā | अपना apnā | (वे ve . . . उनका unkā must have the same referent) |

## Prediction

In Hindi मैं . . . मेरा **mɛ̃ . . . merā** type combinations cannot be found in a simple sentence. In the third person, the वह . . . उसका **vo . . . uskā** (वे . . . उनका **ve . . . unkā**) combination cannot occur if the possessed thing and the possessor subject refer to the same person.

| वह | अपना | काम | करता | है | |
|----|------|-----|------|----|----|
| **vo** | **apnā** | **kām** | **kartā** | **hɛ** |
| he | own | job | do | is |

He (John) does his (John's) work.

However, if in the English sentence 'he' refers to John and 'his' refers to Bill, then अपना **apnā** will not be used. When the subject possessor and the possessed thing are not identical, possessive pronouns will be used.

| वह | उसका | काम | करता | है | |
|----|------|-----|------|----|----|
| **vo** | **uskā** | **kām** | **kartā** | **hɛ** |
| he | his | job | do | is |

He (i.e. John) does his (i.e. Bill's) work.

अपना **apnā** is the masculine singular form. Its two other number gender variants are अपने **apne** (m. pl.) and अपनी **apnī** (f.). In Dialogue 1, in

| सिर्फ़ | अपने | लिए |
|-------|------|-----|
| **sirf** | **apne** | **liye** |
| only | own | for |

the subject आप **āp** is implied. Because of the following postposition, अपना **apnā** becomes oblique.

## Comparative/Superlative से se 'than'

When learning Hindi, you do not need to memorize different forms such as 'good, better, best'. Only the से **se** postposition is used with the standard of comparison.

| बच्चों | की | उम्र | बारह | से | कम | है। |
|--------|-----|------|------|-----|------|------|
| baccõ | kī | umar | bārā | se | kam | hɛ. |
| children | of | age (f.) | twelve | than | less | is |

The children's age is less than twelve.

The से **se** is used after the standard/object of comparison, which is 'twelve'. Also, the adjective follows the postposition. Similarly,

| जॉन | राम | से | अच्छा | है। |
|------|------|-----|--------|------|
| John | rām | se | acc$^h$ā | hɛ. |
| John | Ram | than | good | is |

John is better than Ram.

Thus, the word of the comparative phrase 'better than Ram' is reversed in Hindi, i.e. 'Ram than good'.

The superlative degree is expressed by choosing सब **sab** 'all' as the object of comparison. The English sentence 'John is best' is expressed as 'John is good than all', as in

| जॉन | सब | से | अच्छा | है। |
|------|-----|-----|--------|------|
| John | sab | se | acc$^h$ā | hɛ. |
| John | all | than | good | is |

John is the best.

Again notice the Hindi word order – all than good.

The adjective can be further modified by words indicating degree, such as ज़्यादा **zyādā** 'more':

| जॉन | राम | से | ज़्यादा | अच्छा | है। |
|------|------|-----|---------|--------|------|
| John | rām | se | zyādā | acc$^h$ā | hɛ. |
| John | Ram | than | more | good | is |

John is much better than Ram.

## चाहना **cāhnā 'to want'**

Note the word order of the English sentence 'You want to go.'

| आप | जाना | चाहते | हैं। |
|----|------|-------|------|
| **āp** | **jānā** | **cāhte** | **hɛ̃.** |
| you | to go | want | are |

You want to go.

The infinitive form 'to go' precedes the verb चाहना **cāhnā** 'to want'. The verb चाहना **cāhnā** receives tense conjugation. Study one more example:

| वह | नाचना | चाहती | है। |
|----|-------|-------|-----|
| **vo** | **nācnā** | **cāhtī** | **hɛ.** |
| she | to dance | want | is |

She wants to dance.

## बातचीत **bātcīt  Dialogue 2**  (Audio 2:3)

### भारत के बारे में सोचना *bʰārat ke bāre mẽ socnā* **Thinking about India**

*On the same day Suman Kumar runs into his colleague Al Nasiri. They start talking about the Christmas break. Al catches him off-guard, lost in his own world. He attracts Suman's attention by saying:*

अल:  भई, किस दुनिया में हो? क्या सोच रहे हो?
AL:  bʰaī, kis duniyā mẽ ho? kyā soc rahe ho?

सुमन:  हिन्दुस्तान के बारे में सोच रहा था।
SUMAN:  hindustān ke bāre mẽ soc rahā tʰā.

अल:  क्यों, सब ठीक है न?
AL:  kyõ, sab Tʰīk hɛ na?

सुमन:  हाँ, किसमस बेक में हिन्दुस्तान जा रहे हैं।
SUMAN:  hã̄, *Christmas Break* mẽ hindustān jā rahe hɛ̃.

अल:  अकेले या परिवार के साथ।
AL:  akele yā parivār ke sātʰ?

सुमन:  बीबी बच्चे यानी कि पूरे कुटुम्ब के साथ।
SUMAN:  bībī bacce yānī ki pūre kutumba ke sātʰ.

अल:  हाँ भाई, नहीं तो बीबी तलाक के लिये कहेगी। कहाँ जाओगे?
AL:  hã̄ bʰāī, nahī̃ to bībī talāk ke liye kahegī. kahã̄ jāoge?

| | |
|---|---|
| सुमन: | दिल्ली, आगरा और जयपुर। |
| SUMAN: | dillī, āgrā aur jaipur. |
| अल: | आगरा, कैसे जाओगे? |
| AL: | āgrā kɛse jāoge? |
| सुमन: | हवाई जहाज़ से। |
| SUMAN: | havāī jahāz se. |
| अल: | हवाई जहाज़ से जाना बेकार है। |
| AL: | havāī jahāz se jānā bekār hɛ. |
| सुमन: | क्यों? |
| SUMAN: | kyõ? |
| अल: | हवाई जहाज़ से गाड़ी में कम समय लगता है। |
| AL: | havāī jahāz se gāRī mẽ kam samaya lagtā hɛ. |

| | |
|---|---|
| AL: | *Well, in what world are you? What are you thinking?* |
| SUMAN: | *I was thinking about India.* |
| AL: | *Why, everything is all right, isn't it?* |
| SUMAN: | *Yes (everything is fine); (we) are going to India during the Christmas break.* |
| AL: | *Alone or with the family?* |
| SUMAN: | *Wife, children, that is, with the whole family.* |
| AL: | *Yes, brother; otherwise (your) wife will ask for a divorce. Where will (you) go?* |
| SUMAN: | *Delhi, Agra and Jaipur.* |
| AL: | *How will (you) go to Agra?* |
| SUMAN: | *By plane.* |
| AL: | *(It is) useless to go (to Agra) by plane.* |
| SUMAN: | *Why?* |
| AL: | *(It) takes less time (to go to Agra) on the train than by plane.* |

## शब्दावली shabdāvalī Vocabulary

| | | |
|---|---|---|
| भई | b$^h$aī | hey, well (excl.) |
| किस | kis | which |
| दुनिया | duniyā (f.) | world |
| सोचना | socnā (+ne) | to think |
| के बारे में | ke bāre mẽ | about, concerning |
| था | t$^h$ā | was |
| सब | sab | all |
| अकेला | akelā (m. adj.) | alone |
| परिवार | parivār (m.) | family |
| के साथ | ke sāt$^h$ | with, together |

The Hindi equivalent of English 'was thinking' is सोच रहा था **soc rahā tʰā**. The Hindi verb is broken into three units: 'verb stem' (सोच **soc**), 'ing' (रहा **rahā**), 'was' (था **tʰā**). The only difference between Hindi and English is that in Hindi '-ing' is a separate word and the auxiliary 'was' ends the verbal string. Sentences such as the above are called either 'past progressives' or 'past continuous'. We will call them *past progressive*.

Like an adjective ending in **ā**, **rahā** has three variants: रहा **rahā** (masculine, singular), रहे **rahe** (masculine, plural) and रही **rahī** (feminine).

In order to form the present progressive as in English the auxiliary 'was' is replaced by present forms such as 'am', 'is', 'are'. The same is true in Hindi. Just substitute the present 'to be' forms and you will get the present progressive verb form. For instance:

| मैं | हिन्दुस्तान | के बारे में | सोच | रहा | हूँ। |
|------|------------|-------------|------|------|------|
| **mē** | **hindustān** | **ke bāre mē** | **soc** | **rahā** | **hū̃** |
| I | India | about | think | ing | am |

I am thinking about India.

## Future

The English future tense consists of two verbal units, whereas in Hindi it is only one. You came across an example of a Hindi future tense in Unit 3:

| हम | फिर | मिलेंगे। |
|------|------|---------|
| **ham** | **pʰir** | **milēge** |
| we | again | meet-will |

We will meet again.

| तुम | कहाँ | जाओगे? |
|------|------|--------|
| **tum** | **kahā̃** | **jāoge?** |
| you | where | go-will |

Where will you go?

The Hindi verb forms can be broken up in the following manner.

| मिल | + एँ | | + ग | | + ए |
|------|------|---|------|---|------|
| **mil** | + **ẽ** | | + **g** | | + **e** |

stem + person (आप **āp**) + future 'will' + number-gender (m. pl.)

| जा | + ओ | | + ग | | + ए |
|---|---|---|---|---|---|
| **jā** | + **o** | | + **g** | | + **e** |

stem + person (तुम **tum**) + future 'will' + number-gender (m. pl.)

| जा | + ऊँ | | + ग | | + ईं |
|---|---|---|---|---|---|
| **jā** | + **ū̃** | | + **g** | | + **ī̃** |

stem + person (मैं **mɛ̃**) + future 'will' + number-gender (f. sg./pl.)

## The ghost postposition को **ko** 'to' with locations

| आप | क्रिसमस | बेक | में | हिन्दुस्तान | जा | रहे | हैं। |
|---|---|---|---|---|---|---|---|
| **āp** | **Christmas** | **break** | **mɛ̃** | **hindustān** | **jā** | **rahe** | **hɛ̃.** |
| you | Christmas | Break | in | India | go | ing | are |

You are going to India during the Christmas break.

Although the postposition को **ko** is dropped in Hindi, this is the ghost postposition we referred to in the previous chapter. Recall the discussion of the phrase 'in the morning' सवेरे **savere**. If we place, say, अपना **apnā** 'own' before India, the ghost postposition will change it to its oblique form – अपने **apne**.

## बातचीत **bātcīt** Dialogue 3 🎧 (Audio 2:5)

## आगरा की गाड़ी **āgrā kī gāRī** *The train to Agra*

*Al Nasiri and Suman Kumar continue to discuss the best ways of getting to Agra. Finally, Al Nasiri convinces Suman Kumar to take a train to Agra.*

अल: आगरा के लिये सब से अच्छी गाड़ी ताज ऐक्सप्रेस है।
AL: āgrā ke liye sab se acc^hī gāRī Taj Express hɛ.
सुमन: ताज ऐक्सप्रेस कहाँ से चलती है?
SUMAN: Taj Express kahā̃ se caltī hɛ?
अल: नयी दिल्ली से, सवेरे सात बजे।
AL: nayī dillī se, savere sāt baje.
सुमन: और आने के लिए?
SUMAN: aur āne ke liye?
अल: वही गाड़ी शाम को वापस आती है।
AL: vahī gāRī shām ko vāpas ātī hɛ.
सुमन: लेकिन हम लोग रात को ताजमहल देखना चाहते हैं।
SUMAN: lekin ham log rāt ko tāj mɛhɛl dek^hnā cāhte hɛ̃.

| | |
|---|---|
| अल: | हाँ, ताज रात को और भी सुन्दर लगता है। |
| AL: | hā̃, tāj rāt ko aur bʰī sundar lagtā hɛ. |
| सुमन: | तो एक रात आगरा रुकेंगे, अगले दिन दिल्ली लौटेंगे। |
| SUMAN: | to ek rāt āgrā rukẽge, agle din dillī lauTẽge. |
| अल: | चाँदनी रात, ताज महल और बीबी साथ. . . . मज़ा कीजिये। |
| AL: | cā̃dnī rāt, tāj mɛhɛl aur bībī sātʰ . . . mazā kījiye. |

| | |
|---|---|
| AL: | *The best train for Agra is the Taj Express.* |
| SUMAN: | *Where does the Taj Express leave from?* |
| AL: | *From New Delhi, (at) seven o'clock in the morning.* |
| SUMAN: | *And to come (back)?* |
| AL: | *The same train comes back (to New Delhi) in the evening.* |
| SUMAN: | *But we people want to see the Taj Mahal at night.* |
| AL: | *Yes, Taj looks even more beautiful at night.* |
| SUMAN: | *Then, we will stay (for a) night (in) Agra; the next day (we) will return to Delhi.* |
| AL: | *The moonlit night, Taj Mahal and with (your) wife . . . (you) enjoy (both).* |

## शब्दावली  shabdāvalī  Vocabulary

| | | |
|---|---|---|
| नया | **nayā** (m. adj.) | new |
| सात बजे | **sāt baje** | seven o'clock |
| आना | **ānā** (–ne) | to come |
| वह | **vah** <vo> | that, he, she |
| वही | **vahī** (vah+hī) | same, that very |
| शाम | **shām** (f.) | evening |
| वापस | **vāpas** | back |
| वापस आना | **vāpas ānā** (–ne) | to come back |
| रात | **rāt** (f.) | night |
| ताज | **tāj** (m.) | crown |
| महल | **mɛhɛl** (m.) | palace |
| ताजमहल | **tāj mɛhɛl** | the Taj Mahal |
| और भी | **aur bʰī** | even more |
| लगना | **lagnā** (+ko) | to seem, to appear |
| रुकना | **ruknā** (–ne) | to stop |
| अगला | **aglā** (adj.) | next |
| दिन | **din** (m.) | day |
| लौटना | **lauTnā** (–ne) | to return, to come back |
| चाँद | **cā̃d** (m.) | moon |
| चाँदनी | **cā̃dnī** (f.) | moonlit |
| मज़ा करना | **mazā karnā** (+ne) | to enjoy |

## *Pronunciation*

mɛhɛl is written as **mahal** महल.

## *Notes*

### Time expressions

| | | |
|---|---|---|
| सवेरे | **savere** | in the morning |
| दोपहर को | **dopɛhɛr ko** | at noon |
| शाम को | **shām ko** | in the evening |
| रात को | **rāt ko** | at night |

With the exception of सवेरे **savere**, the को **ko** postposition is uniformly used with other time adverbs. सवेरे **savere** takes the ghost postposition को **ko**.

### Emphatic particle ही **hī** 'only, right, very'

The particle of exclusion is ही **hī** 'only.' The English word 'same' is equivalent to 'that very' in Hindi. It can be used with nouns, pronouns and adverbs. It is usually used as a separate word except with those pronouns and adverbs which end in -h. It undergoes contraction with -h ending pronouns and adverbs.

| *Pronouns* | | | *Particle* | | *Emphatic pronoun* | |
|---|---|---|---|---|---|---|
| वह | | + | ही | = | वही | |
| **vo** | he/she/that | + | **hī** | = | **vahī** | that very, same |
| यह | | + | ही | = | यही | |
| **ye** | this | + | **hī** | = | **yahī** | this very |

| *Adverbs* | | | *Particle* | | *Emphatic adverb* | |
|---|---|---|---|---|---|---|
| वहाँ | | + | ही | = | वहीं | |
| **vahā̃** | there | + | **hī** | = | **vahī̃** | right there |
| यहाँ | | + | ही | = | यहीं | |
| **yahā̃** | here | + | **hī** | = | **yahī̃** | right here |

## अभ्यास  ab^hyās  Exercises

### Exercise 1

You land at New Delhi airport and, on arrival at immigration, the officer asks you the following questions in Hindi. First, translate the questions into English in the space given next to the question, and then answer the questions in Hindi.

OFFICER: आपका नाम?  _____
 āpkā nām?

YOU: _____

OFFICER: आप भारत में कितने दिन रहेंगे?  _____
āp b^hārat mẽ kitne din rahẽge?

YOU: _____

OFFICER: कहाँ-कहाँ जायेंगे?  _____
kahā̃-kahā̃ jāẽge?

YOU: _____

OFFICER: हिन्दुस्तान में पता क्या है?  _____
hindustān mẽ patā kyā hɛ?

YOU: _____

OFFICER: वापस कब जायेंगे?  _____
vāpas kab jāẽge?

YOU: _____

OFFICER: कोई *illegal* सामान है?  _____
koī *illegal* sāmān hɛ?

YOU: _____

### Exercise 2

There are a few incorrect verbs in the following passage. Pick them out and replace them with the right verbs.

मैं आप के लिए क्या करना सकता है? हम आगरा जा चाहता है। आगरा कितनी दूर हैं? बहुत दूर नहीं, लेकिन आप कब जा रहा है? हम कल जायेगा। गाड़ी सुबह दिल्ली से चलते है। आप गाड़ी से जा चाहता हैं।

mẽ āp ke liye kyā karnā saktā hɛ? ham āgrā jā cāhtā hɛ. āgrā kitnī dūr hɛ̃? bahut dūr nahī̃, lekin āp kab jā rahā hɛ? ham kal jāegā. gāRī subā dillī se calte hɛ. āp gāRī se jā cāhtā hɛ̃?

### Exercise 3

The sentences in the following letter are in the wrong order. Rearrange them in the right order.

प्रिय राकेश

तुम्हारा मिला खत। पढ़ कर खुशी हुई। तुम रहे कब आ हो? कल मैं शिकागो हूँ जा रहा। शिकागो बहुत शहर है बड़ा । मैं शिकागो से हवाई जहाज़ जाऊँगा। लेकिन मैं जाना चाहता हवाई जहाज़ से नहीं हूँ। गाड़ी मुझे पसन्द है से ज्यादा हवाई जहाज़। बाकी सब है ठीक।

तुम्हारा दोस्त,
राजीव

Priya Rakesh:

tumhārā milā xat. paR$^h$ kar xushī huī. tum rahe kab ā ho? kal mɛ̃ *Chicago* hū̃ jā rahā. *Chicago* bahut shɛher hɛ baRā. mɛ̃ *Chicago* se hawāī jahāz (airplane) jāū̃gā. lekin mɛ̃ jānā cāhtā hawāī jahāz se nahī̃ hū̃. gāRī muj$^h$e pasand hɛ se zyāda hawāī jahāz. bākī sab hɛ T$^h$īk.

tumhārā dost,
Rājīv.

## Exercise 4

Here are the answers. What were the questions? (Wherever needed, the object of the inquiry is underlined.)

Q: _____
A: मैं शिकागो जा रही हूँ।
   mɛ̃ <u>Chicago</u> jā rahī hū̃.

Q: _____
A: मैं यहाँ सात दिन रहूँगी।
   mɛ̃ yahā̃ <u>sāt din</u> rahū̃gī.

Q: _____
A: मैं अपना काम कर रही हूँ।
   mɛ̃ <u>apnā kām</u> kar rahī hū̃.

Q: _____
A: जी हाँ, चाय बहुत पसन्द है।
   jī hā̃, <u>cāy</u> bahut pasand hɛ.

Q: _____
A: मेरे चार भाई हैं।
   mere <u>cār b$^h$āī</u> hɛ̃.

## Exercise 5

If you won a million dollars, what would you do? Use the following
words or phrases:

| | |
|---|---|
| king | become crazy with happiness |
| queen | buy diamonds for my wife/girlfriend |
| buy a yacht, Rolls Royce | return to work |
| travel around the world | |

## Exercise 6

This fast-talking robot is programmed for the 'me' generation. Could
you change his speech to suit the 'we' generation? Note the gender
of 'robot' is masculine in Hindi.

मैं *रोबाट* हूँ। मैं *कालिफ़ोनिया* से हूँ। मैं हिन्दी बोल सकता हूँ। मैं हिन्दी समझ भी सकता
हूँ। मैं हिन्दी गाने गा सकता हूँ । मेरी *मैमोरी* बहुत बड़ी है। मैं हर सवाल पूछ सकता
हूँ और हर जवाब दे सकता हूँ। यानी हर काम कर सकता हूँ। मैं हमेशा काम कर
सकता हूँ। मैं कभी नहीं थकता हूँ। मेरे पास हर सवाल का ज़वाब है। लेकिन मसालेदार
खाना नहीं खा सकता।

mɛ̃ *robot* hū̃. mɛ̃ *California* se hū̃. mɛ̃ hindī bol saktā hū̃. mɛ̃ hindī
samaj^h b^hī saktā hū̃. mɛ̃ hindī gāne gā saktā hū̃. merī *memory*
bahut baRī hɛ. mɛ̃ har savāl puc^h saktā hū̃ aur har javāb de saktā
hū̃. yānī har kām kar saktā hū̃. mɛ̃ hameshā kām kar saktā hū̃.
mɛ̃ kab^hī nahī̃ t^haktā hū̃. mere pās har savāl kā javāb hɛ. lekin
masāledār k^hānā nahī̃ k^hā saktā.

## Exercise 7

Listen to Mr Smith's comments about a forthcoming visit to North
America and then answer the following questions in Hindi:

1 मि॰ स्मिथ *अमरीका* कब जायेंगे?
   Mr Smith *America* kab jāẽge?

2 वे कौन सी एयरलाइन से *न्यू यार्क* जायेंगे?
   ve kaun sī *airline* se *New York* jāẽge?

3 क्या वे अपने परिवार के साथ *न्यू यार्क* पहुँचेंगे?
   kyā ve apne parivār ke sāt^h *New York* pahũcẽge?

4 वे *डिज़्नी वर्ड* क्यों जाना चाहते हैं?
   ve *Disney World* kyõ jānā cāhte hɛ̃?

5 वे *डिज़्नी वर्ड* में कितने दिन रहेंगे?
   ve *Disney World* mɛ̃ kitne din rahẽge?

# 6 कल क्या किया?
## kal kyā kiyā?
### What did you do yesterday?

By the end of this unit you should be able to:

- talk about past events/actions
- use time adverbials with full clauses
- talk about topics dealing with 'lost and found'
- learn to express sequential actions
- learn more about paraphrasing devices
- employ some more very common expressions

## बातचीत  **bātcīt   Dialogue 1** 🎧 (Audio 2:9)
## क्या बात है? *kyā bāt hɛ? What is the matter?*

*Aditi Chatterjī is coming to America for graduate study. She lands at Kennedy Airport. As she is cleared through customs and is ready to take her flight to Chicago, she makes the horrifying discovery that her passport and traveller's cheques have been stolen. She calls her family in Calcutta (now Kolkatta), reversing the charges. She gets in touch with her father, Suman Chatterjī, who is anxiously waiting for news of her arrival in the USA.*

सुमन:     हैलो।
SUMAN:    hɛllo.

अदिति:    हैलो, डैड, मैं अदिति बोल रही हूँ।
ADITI:    hɛllo, DɛD, mɛ̃ Aditi bol rahī hũ.

सुमन:     कहाँ से बोल रही हो?
SUMAN:    kahā̃ se bol rahī ho?

अदिति:    न्यू यॉर्क से।
ADITI:    New York se.

सुमन:     क्यों, अभी शिकागो नहीं पहुँची।
SUMAN:    kyõ, abʰī Chicago nahī̃ pahũcī?

अदिति:    नहीं।
ADITI:    nahī̃.

सुमन:     क्या बात है? परेशान लग रही हो। सब ठीक-ठाक है न?
SUMAN:    kyā bāt hɛ? pareshān lag rahī ho. sab Tʰīk-Tʰāk hɛ na?

अदिति:    मैं तो ठीक हूँ, लेकिन मेरा पासपोर्ट, मेरे पैसे और (ट्रैवलर्ज़) चैक्स गुम हो गये।
ADITI:    mɛ̃ to Tʰīk hũ, lekin merā *passport*, mere pɛse aur Trɛvlars
          (*traveller's*) *cheques* gum ho gaye.

सुमन:     क्या!
SUMAN:    kyā!

अदिति:    किसी ने मेरी जेब काटी – ऐसा लगता है।
ADITI:    kisī ne merī jeb kāTī – ɛsā lagtā hɛ.

सुमन:     सच!
SUMAN:    sac!

अदिति:    हाँ।
ADITI:    hã̃.

ADITI:    *Hello, Dad, this is Aditi calling.* (lit. I am Aditi speaking)
SUMAN:   *Where are you calling from?*
ADITI:   *From New York.*
SUMAN:   *Hey, haven't you reached Chicago yet?* (lit. why, you did
         not reach Chicago yet?)

ADITI:    *No.*

SUMAN:    *What is the matter? (You) seem to be upset. Everything is fine, isn't it?*

ADITI:    *As regards me, I am fine, but my passport, money and traveller's cheques are lost.*

SUMAN:    *What! (lit. What! I do not believe it!)*

ADITI:    *Someone picked my pocket – it seems.*

SUMAN:    *Is that right! (lit. Truth!)*

ADITI:    *Yes.*

## शब्दावली    shabdāvalī    Vocabulary

| | | |
|---|---|---|
| हैलो | hɛllo | hello |
| अभी | abʰī | right now |
| पहुँचना | pahū̃cnā (–ne) | to reach, arrive |
| बात | bāt (f.) | matter |
| क्या बात है? | kyā bāt hɛ? | what is the matter? |
| परेशान | pareshān (adj.) | troubled |
| सब | sab | all |
| ठीक–ठाक | Tʰīk-Tʰāk | fine, hale and hearty |
| तो | to (particle) | then, as regards |
| गुमना | gumnā (–ne) | to be lost |
| गए/गये | gaye (m. pl) | went |
| क्या | kyā! | what! I do not believe it! |
| किसी | kisī | someone |
| ने | ne | agent marker in the past tense |
| जेब | jeb (f.) | pocket |
| काटना | kāTnā (+ne) | to cut |
| जेब काटना | jeb kāTnā | to pickpocket |
| ऐसा | ɛsā | such, it |
| सच | sac! | Truth! It can't be true! |

## Notes

### The perfective form (the simple past)

We introduced the simple past tense forms of the verb 'to be'. Now, note the Hindi equivalent of the English 'Didn't (you) reach Chicago?':

| तुम | अभी | शिकागो | नहीं | पहुँचीं? |
|---|---|---|---|---|
| **(tum)** | **abʰī** | **Chicago** | **nahī̃** | **pahū̃cī̃?** |
| you | right now | Chicago | not | reached (f. pl.) |

Although the Hindi verb पहुँचीं **pahŭcĩ** is translated as 'reached', it has no intrinsic tense reference like words such as है **hε** 'is' and था **t<sup>h</sup>ā** 'was'. It simply shows that the action or situation is completed. The act may be completed in the present, past or future tense. Usually adverbs such as 'yesterday' and 'tomorrow' and the form of the verb 'to be' provide the tense information.

Now recall the suffixes given in Magic Key 1 and do some detective work regarding the feminine forms.

| *Verb stem* | | *Perfective form* | |
|---|---|---|---|
| पहुँच **pahŭc** | reach | पहुँचा **pahŭcā** | masculine singular |
| | | पहुँचे **pahŭce** | masculine plural |
| | | पहुँची **pahŭcī** | feminine singular |
| | | पहुँचीं **pahŭcĩ** | feminine plural |

Yes, for the first time feminine plural forms compete with masculine forms and have their own distinct plural identity. The Hindi pronoun तुम **tum** always takes the plural form.

Now note another perfective form from the above dialogue:

| किसीने | मेरी | जेब | काटी । |
|---|---|---|---|
| **kisī-ne** | **merī** | **jeb** | **kāTī** |
| someone-agent | my | pocket (f.) | cut (f. sg.) |

Someone picked my pocket. (lit. someone cut my pocket)

You will notice two things different that are from the previous sentence: (1) the use of the postposition ने **ne**, and (2) the verb agreement. The postposition ने **ne** occurs with those subjects that have transitive verbs in the perfective form. Notice verbs such as 'come', 'go', and 'reach' are intransitive, whereas verbs such as 'cut', 'write', 'do', and 'buy' are transitive. The Hindi word for the English 'someone' is कोई **koī**. Because of the postposition ने **ne**, the subject pronoun कोई **koī** becomes किसी **kisī**. In other words, peer pressure makes it oblique. Also, remember that the verb does not agree with those subjects followed by a postposition. Therefore, the verb does not agree with the subject; instead it agrees with the object जेब **jeb** 'pocket', which is feminine singular in Hindi. For details about perfective forms see the Reference grammar section.

Because the perfectives mark a situation or action as completed, they are usually associated with the past tense.

## गया 'Went' – an exception in verb form

The English verb 'to go' is an exception in the past tense form – 'went' rather than 'goed'. Similarly, it is also irregular in Hindi in the perfective form. Here are the Hindi equivalents of the English verb form 'went':

| *Verb stem* | *Perfective form* | | | |
|---|---|---|---|---|
| जा **jā** *go* | गया | **gayā** | went | (masculine singular) |
| | गये/गए | **gaye** | went | (masculine plural) |
| | गयी/गई | **gayī** | went | (feminine singular) |
| | गयीं/गईं | **gayī̃** | went | (feminine plural) |

Because Hindi and English belong to the same language family, what is remarkable is that the English 'g' of the verb stem 'go' shows up in the Hindi irregular form and then takes the Hindi perfective suffixes. The sound 'y' intervenes in the two vowels which is quite common, occurring in many languages.

The other three important verbs that are irregular in the past tense are the following: लेना **lenā** 'to take', देना **denā** 'to give' and पीना **pīnā** 'to drink'.

| *Stem* | *Masculine* | | *Feminine* | |
|---|---|---|---|---|
| | *Singular* | *Plural* | *Singular* | *Plural* |
| ले **le** take | लिया **liyā** | लिये/लिए **liye** | ली **lī** | लीं **lī̃** |
| दे **de** give | दिया **diyā** | दिये/दिए **diye** | दी **dī** | दीं **dī̃** |
| पी **pī** drink | पिया **piyā** | पिये/पिए **piye** | पी **pī** | पीं **pī̃** |

## Compound verbs: word-for-word translation

| मेरे | पैसे | और | ट्रैवलरज़ | चैक्स | गुम | गये। |
|---|---|---|---|---|---|---|
| **mere** | **pɛse** | **aur** | *traveller's* | *cheques* | **gum** | **gaye.** |
| my | money | and | traveller's | cheques | lost | went |

My money and traveller's cheques (are) lost.

Notice the clustering of the two verbs गुम **gum** 'be lost' and गये **gaye** 'went' (m. pl.). This clustering of the real verbs is a special property of Hindi and other South Asian languages. They are called 'compound verbs'. We will deal with this class of verbs later on in this book. For the time being note this verb clustering and memorize the sentence given above.

## Echo-words

You have already come across the word ठीक **Tʰīk** 'fine, correct'. In the phrase ठीक–ठाक **Tʰīk Tʰāk**, the second word ठाक **Tʰāk** does not have any meaning of its own. It just echoes the first word by making a slight vowel change. The meaning added by the echo word is 'etc.', 'and all that' or 'other related things/properties'. Therefore, ठीक–ठाक **Tʰīk Tʰāk** means 'fine, etc.'. Very often the first consonant sound is changed in Hindi echo words, e.g. काम-वाम **kām vām** 'work, etc.', नाम-वाम **nām vām** 'name etc.'. The preferred consonant change is by means of व **v**.

## बातचीत   **bātcīt**   Dialogue 2 🎧 (Audio 2:11)

### मेरा पासपोर्ट गुम गया है   *mera pāsporT gum gayā hɛ*
### My passport is lost

*Aditi Chatterjii continues to talk with her father, Suman Chatterjii about the incident. She informs her father that she filed a report at the airport and that American Express will issue her new traveller's cheques but not without her passport. So, she needs some money by telegram, and in the meanwhile she needs to go to the Indian Consulate Office in New York. At the consulate, she talks with an officer.*

| | |
|---|---|
| अदिति: | मेरा पासपोर्ट गुम गया है। नया पासपोर्ट चाहिये। |
| ADITI: | mera pāsporT (*passport*) gum gayā hɛ. nayā pāsporT (*passport*) cāhiye. |
| अफ़सर: | कब गुमा? |
| OFFICER: | kab gumā? |
| अदिति: | आज, करीब पाँच घंटे पहले। |
| ADITI: | āj, karīb pā̃c gʰanTe pɛhle. |
| अफ़सर: | आपको मालूम है कि कहाँ गुमा? |
| OFFICER: | āpko mālūm hɛ ki kahā̃ gumā? |
| अदिति: | जी हाँ, कैनेडी हवाई अड्डे में। |
| ADITI: | jī hā̃, *Kennedy* havāī aDDe mẽ. |
| अफ़सर: | कैसे? |
| OFFICER: | kɛse? |
| अदिति: | जब इम्मिगेशन से बाहर आई, तो मेरे पास था। फिर, शिकागो की फ़्लाइट के लिये दूसरे टर्मिनल गयी, तब भी था। जब काउन्टर पर पहुँची, तो देखा, पासपोर्ट, टिकट, पैसे, और ट्रैवलर्ज़ चैक्स पर्स में नहीं थे। |

ADITI: jab *immigration* se bāhar āyī, to mere pās tʰā. pʰir, Chicago kī *flight* ke liye dūsre Tarminal (*terminal*) gayī, tab bʰī thā. jab kāunTar (*counter*) par pahũcī, to dekʰā, pāsporT, *ticket*, pɛse, aur *traveller's cheques* purse mẽ nahĩ tʰe.

अफ़सर: पुलिस में रिपोर्ट की।

OFFICER: police mẽ riporT (report) kī?

अदिति: जी हाँ, ये देखिए।

ADITI: jī hã̄, ye dekʰiye.

अफ़सर: अच्छा ये फ़ार्म भरिये, एक–दो महीने में नया पासपोर्ट आपको मिल जायेगा।

OFFICER: accʰā ye *form* bʰariye, ek-do mahīne mẽ nayā pāsporT āpko milegā.

अदिति: इससे जल्दी नहीं मिल सकता?

ADITI: isse jaldī nahĩ mil saktā?

अफ़सर: जी नहीं, पहले रिपोर्ट हिन्दुस्तान जायेगी और क्लियरैंस के बाद ही पासपोर्ट मिल सकता है।

OFFICER: jī nahĩ, pɛhɛle *report* hindustān jayegī aur *clearance* ke bād hī pāsporT mil saktā hɛ.

अदिति: शुक्रिया।

ADITI: shukriyā

अफ़सर: कोई बात नहीं।

OFFICER: koī bāt nahĩ.


ADITI: *My passport is lost? (I) need a new passport.*

OFFICER: *When was (it) lost?*

ADITI: *About five hours ago today.*

OFFICER: *Do you know where (it) was lost?*

ADITI: *Yes, at Kennedy Airport.*

OFFICER: *How?*

ADITI: *When I came out of Immigration, I had (it). (lit. then (it) was near me) Then (I) went to the other terminal for the flight to Chicago; even then I had (it).*
*When I reached the counter, then (I) noticed the passport, ticket, money and the traveller's cheques were not in (my) handbag.*

OFFICER: *(Did you) report (this) to (lit. in) the police?*

ADITI: *Yes, look at this (referring to the police report).*

OFFICER: *Okay. Fill out this form. In one or two months you will get a new passport.*

ADITI: *Can't (I) get (it) earlier than that?*

OFFICER: *No, first the report will go to India and only after clearance (you) can get (it).*

ADITI:     *Thanks.*
OFFICER:   *You are welcome* (or do not mention it).

## शब्दावली  shabdāvalī   Vocabulary

| | | |
|---|---|---|
| नया | **nayā** (m. adj.) | new |
| करीब | **karīb** | about, approximately |
| घंटा | **gʰanTā** (m.) | hour |
| पहला | **pɛhɛlā** (m. adj.) | first |
| पहले | **pɛhɛle** | (at) first, ago, previously |
| मालूम होना | **mālūm honā** (+ko) | to know, to be known |
| हवाई अड्डा | **havāī aDDā** (m.) | airport |
| जब | **jab** (relative pronoun) | when |
| बाहर | **bāhar** | out, outside |
| आना | **ānā** (–ne) | to come |
| आयी/आई | **āyī** (f. sg.) | came |
| दूसरा | **dūsrā** (m. adj.) | second, other, another |
| तो | **to** | then |
| देखना | **dekʰnā** (+ne) | to see, to look at, to notice |
| देखिये/देखिए | **dekʰiye** | please see, look at, notice |
| भरना | **bʰarnā** (+ne) | to fill |
| भरिये/भरिए | **bʰariye** | please fill, please fill out |
| एक–दो | **ek-do** | one or two |
| महीना | **mahīnā** | month |
| मिलना | **milnā** (–ne, +ko) | to meet, to get, to be available |
| मिलेगा | **milegā** (m. sg.) | will get |
| जल्दी | **jaldī** | quickly |
| के बाद | **(ke) bād** | after, later |
| शुक्रिया | **shukriyā** | thanks |

## Pronunciation

**dūsre** is written as **dūsare** दूसरा. The vowel **a** is dropped in colloquial pronunciation (see Script Unit 4).

## Notes

### मालूम होना **mālūm honā** vs जानना **jānnā** 'to know'

Consider the word-for-word translation of the Hindi equivalent of the English expression 'Do you know . . . ?' in our dialogue.

| आपको | मालूम | है? |
|------|-------|-----|
| **āpko** | **mālūm** | **hɛ?** |
| you-to | known | is |

Do you know . . . ?

The Hindi sentence is similar to the English 'Is it known to you . . . ?'
The only difference is that in Hindi आपको **āpko** is still the subject
but the non-volitional subject. Remember the discussion of dative/
experiential subjects in Unit 3: in Hindi there is a distinction between non-volitional and volitional verbs. The verb मालूम होना **mālūm
honā** suggests the type of knowing or knowledge which is non-
volitional or unintentional in nature. The verb जानना **jānnā** can also
be translated as 'to know' but the difference is that जानना **jānnā** refers
to an act of knowing that is volitional and where some effort or
research has gone into that knowledge. As I pointed out earlier, the
volitional verbs do not take dative को **ko** marking with their subjects.
Observe the following volitional counterpart of मालूम होना **mālūm honā**.

| आप | जानती | हैं? |
|-----|-------|-----|
| **āp** | **jāntī** | **hɛ̃ . . . ?** |
| you (f.) | know | are |

Do you know . . . ?

Notice that the verb agrees with the subject आप **āp** which is feminine
in our dialogue. In the former sentence आपको **āpko** is the subject and
the verb does not agree with it. We will detail the question of agreement again in this chapter. In the former sentence the verb agrees
with the implied object यह **ye** 'this', which is masculine singular, and
that is why the verb takes the singular form है **hɛ**.

Similarly, you have already come across two different usages of
the verb मिलना **milnā** 'to meet' and मिलना **milnā** 'to get, to obtain.'

| हम | मिलेंगे | |
|-----|---------|--|
| **ham** | **milɛ̃ge** | |
| we | meet-will | |

We will meet.

The understood subject in the Hindi expression of the English 'you
will get the passport' is supplied below:

| आपको | पासपोर्ट | मिलेगा | |
|------|----------|--------|--|
| **āpko** | **passport** | **milegā** | |
| you-to | passport | get-will | |

You will get the passport.

English verbs such as 'to get' or 'to obtain' are treated as unintentional acts in Hindi and many other South Asian languages. That explains why the Hindi subject is followed by the postposition को **ko**. Can you predict the element which the verb मिलेगा **milegā** agrees with? No more suspense: it agrees with the object passport which is masculine singular in Hindi.

## The ने **ne construction**

If we fill in the understood subjects in the following two expressions from the above dialogue –

| तो | देखा। |
|----|------|
| **to** | **dekʰā** |
| then | saw |

and

| पुलिस | को | रिपोर्ट | की? |
|-------|-----|---------|------|
| **police** | **ko** | **reporT** | **kī?** |
| police | to | report | did |

the complete sentences will be

| तो | मैंने | देखा। |
|----|-------|-------|
| **to** | **mɛ̃ne** | **dekʰā** |
| then | I-agent | saw |
| Then I saw. | | |

and

| आपने | पुलिस | को | रिपोर्ट | की? |
|-------|-------|-----|---------|------|
| **āpne** | **police** | **ko** | **reporT** | **kī?** |
| you agent | police | to | report (f.) | did (f. sg.) |
| Did you report to the police? | | | | |

The ने **ne** postposition is attached to the subject. Without the postposition the sentences would be ungrammatical. However, observe the following sentences:

| जब | मैं | इम्मिग्रेशन | से | बाहर | आई। |
|----|-----|-------------|-----|------|------|
| **jab** | **mɛ̃** | **immigration** | **se** | **bāhar** | **āyī.** |
| when | I (f. sg.) | immigration | from | out | came (f. sg.) |
| When I came out of immigration. | | | | | |

and

| मैं | दूसरे | टर्मिनल | गयी | |
|---|---|---|---|
| **mɛ̃** | **dūsre** | **Tarminal** | **gayī.** |
| I (f. sg.) | other | terminal | went (f. sg.) |

I went to the other terminal.

The above two sentences do not require the ने **ne** postposition. But why not? The difference is that verbs such as 'come' and 'go' are intransitive. The ने **ne** postposition is restricted to the transitive verbs in the perfective form. Verbs such as 'to see' and 'to report' are transitive and are used in the perfective form; so the postposition ने **ne** with the subject is required. This type of construction is called 'the ergative' construction in linguistic literature. Many languages of the world, such as Basque and some Australian Aboriginal languages, have this property.

The pronominal forms with the ने **ne** postposition are as follows:

| *Nominative pronouns* | | *The* ने *ne pronouns* | | |
|---|---|---|---|---|
| मैं | **mɛ̃** | मैंने | **mɛ̃ne** | I |
| हम | **ham** | हमने | **hamne** | we |
| तू | **tū** | तूने | **tūne** | you (singular) |
| तुम | **tum** | तुमने | **tumne** | you (plural) |
| आप | **āp** | आपने | **āpne** | you (honorific) |
| वह | **vo** | उसने | **usne** | she, he, it, that |
| वे | **ve** | उन्होंने | **unhõne** | they, those |
| यह | **ye** | इसने | **isne** | this |
| ये | **ye** | इन्होंने | **inhõne** | these |

Note that the third person pronouns show peer group pressure as a result of ने **ne**. If you are learning the script, it is written as one word with the third person plural pronoun.

The ने **ne** forms of the question pronoun are: किसने **kisne** 'who' (singular) and किन्होंने **kinhõne** 'who' (plural).

## Complex verbs

As in English, in Hindi a noun can be turned into a verb. The only difference is that the noun has to be anchored in verbs such as करना **karnā** 'to do' and होना **honā** 'to be'. This is a very productive process which allows Hindi to take nouns from languages such as Sanskrit and Persian and turn them into verbs. English has not been spared

either. So you can take English nouns such as the following and turn
them into verbs:

| English noun | Hindi verb | Complex verb | | | |
|---|---|---|---|---|---|
| report | **karnā** करना | रिपोर्ट करना | report | **karnā** | 'to report' |
| telephone | **karnā** करना | टेलीफोन करना | telephone | **karnā** | 'to telephone' |
| pay | **karnā** करना | पे करना | pay | **karnā** | 'to pay' |
| complain | **karnā** करना | कम्पलेन करना | complain | **karnā** | 'to complain' |

As a matter of fact, even English adjectives and verbs can be used to
generate Hindi complex verbs:

| English adjective/verb | Hindi verb | Complex verb | | |
|---|---|---|---|---|
| better | **honā** होना | better | **honā** | 'to recover' |
| choose | **karnā** करना | choose | **karnā** | 'to choose' |

This construction can be extremely useful in those situations where
one fails to recall the Hindi verb. For example, if you fail to recall
the Hindi verb पढ़ना **paRʰnā** 'to read/study', do not give up the idea:
you can custom-make the verb **study karnā** from the English word
'study'. We will nickname Hindi anchor verbs such as **karnā** and
**honā** 'transformer'.

## The omission of 'to'

We pointed out earlier the use of the preposition in English in
expressions such as 'I went to the other terminal.' In Hindi no
postposition is used with the target; therefore, it is not appropriate
to substitute Hindi को **ko** for English 'to'.

## Approximation by compounding

एक–दो      महीने      में
**ek-do**  **mahīne**  **mẽ**
one-two    month      in
In one or two months.

दो–एक      महीने      में
**do-ek**  **mahīne**  **mẽ**
is also fine.

## बातचीत  **bātcīt**   Dialogue 3  🎧 (Audio 2:13)

### ज्योतिषी के पास जाना  *jyotishi ke pās jānā*
### Visiting an astrologer

*John Kearney has visited India several times and he loves Indian philosophy. The concept of reincarnation fascinates him, and therefore he never misses a chance to visit an astrologer or a fortune-teller. An international fair is being held in London. John visits the Indian pavilion and there he finds an astrologer and palmist. He shows the palmist his hand in order to learn about his past. The palmist looks at his hand and makes some general remarks about him, and finally asks about the purpose of John's visit.*

| | |
|---|---|
| जॉन | मैं अपने भूत के बारे में जानना चाहता हूँ। |
| JOHN: | mɛ apne bʰūt ke bāre mẽ jānnā cāhtā hũ. |
| ज्योतिषी | अपने फ़रिश्ते के बारे में पूछिये, भूत के बारे में क्यों? |
| PALMIST: | apane farishte ke bāre mẽ pūcʰiye, bʰūt ke bāre mẽ kyõ? |
| जॉन | मेरा मतलब है कि पिछले जन्म के बारे में। |
| JOHN: | merā matlab hɛ ki picʰle janma ke bāre mẽ. |
| ज्योतिषी | पत्रे के बिना मुश्किल है। |
| PALMIST: | patre ke binā mushkil hɛ. |
| जॉन | तो मेरे बचपन के बारे में बताइये। |
| JOHN: | to mere bacpan ke bāre mẽ batāiye. |
| ज्योतिषी | ये लाइनें बताती हैं कि आपका बचपन बहुत अच्छा था . . . सुन्दर परिवार . . . बड़ा घर . . . ये ठीक है? |
| PALMIST: | ye lāinẽ batātī hɛ̃ ki āpkā bacpan bahut accʰā tʰā . . . sundar parivār . . . baRā gʰar . . . ye Tʰīk hɛ? |
| जॉन | जी हाँ, . . . लेकिन. . . . |
| JOHN: | jī hã̄, . . . lekin . . . |
| ज्योतिषी | लेकिन पिछले पाँच साल अच्छे नहीं थे। |
| PALMIST: | lekin picʰle pã̄c sāl accʰe nahī̃ tʰe. |
| जॉन | पिता जी के मरने के बाद परिवार पर बहुत मुश्किलें आईं। |
| JOHN: | pitā jī ke marne ke bād parivār par bahut mushkilẽ āyī̃. |
| ज्योतिषी | यह बड़े अफ़सोस की बात है। |
| PALMIST: | ye baRe afsos kī bāt hɛ. |

| | |
|---|---|
| JOHN: | *I want to know about my past/ghost.** |
| PALMIST: | *Please ask about your angels; why ask about (your) ghost?* |
| JOHN: | *I mean about my last birth.* |
| PALMIST: | *It is difficult (to tell) without the astrological chart.* |

JOHN:       *Then, tell me about my childhood.*

PALMIST:    *These lines (on your hand) tell me that your childhood was
            very good . . . beautiful family . . . a big house . . . is this
            right?*

JOHN:       *Yes, . . . but . . .*

PALMIST:    *But (your) last five years were not good.*

JOHN:       *After the death of (my) father, (our) family faced a lot of
            difficulties.* (lit. very many difficulties came on the family)

PALMIST:    *I am sorry (to hear) this.* (lit. this is a matter of great
            sorrow)

(*The word **bʰūt** is ambiguous. The palmist interprets it as 'ghost'
just for fun.)

## शब्दावली  **shabdāvalī**  Vocabulary

| | | |
|---|---|---|
| भूत | **bʰūt** (m.) | ghost, past |
| फ़रिश्ता | **farishtā** (m.) | angel |
| पूछना | **pūcʰnā** (–ne) | to ask |
| पूछिये/पूछिए | **pūcʰiye** | please ask |
| मतलब | **matlab** (m.) | meaning |
| जन्म | **janma** (m.) | birth |
| पत्रा | **patrā** (m.) | astrological chart |
| के बिना | **(ke) binā** | without |
| मुश्किल | **mushkil** (f.) | difficult, difficulty |
| बचपन | **bacpan** (m.) | childhood |
| बताना | **batānā** (+ne) | to tell |
| बताइये/बताइए | **batāiye** | please tell |
| साल | **sāl** (m.) | year |
| मरना | **marnā** (–ne) | to die |
| के बाद | **(ke) bād** | after |
| आना | **ānā** (–ne) | to come |
| अफ़सोस | **afsos** (m.) | sorrow |

## *Notes*

### Very frequent expressions: word-for-word translation

Consider how the following three very frequent English expressions
are phrased in Hindi:

| English | Hindi | | | | |
|---|---|---|---|---|---|
| 1  I mean. | मेरा<br>**merā**<br>my | मतलब<br>**matlab**<br>meaning | है।<br>**hɛ**<br>is | | |
| 2  I am glad to hear this. | ये<br>**ye**<br>this | खुशी<br>**xushī**<br>happiness | की<br>**kī**<br>of | बात<br>**bāt**<br>matter (f.) | है।<br>**hɛ.**<br>is |
| | This is a matter of happiness. | | | | |
| 3  I am sorry to hear this. | ये<br>**ye**<br>this | अफ़सोस<br>**afsos**<br>sorrow | की<br>**kī**<br>of | बात<br>**bāt**<br>matter (f.) | है।<br>**hɛ.**<br>is |
| | This is a matter of sorrow. | | | | |

## लाइनें **lāinẽ** 'lines'

| आपकी | लाइनें | बताती | हैं। |
|---|---|---|---|
| **āpkī** | **lāinẽ** | **batātī** | **hẽ.** |
| you of | lines | tell | are |

Your lines tell (me).

Note that the English word 'line' takes the feminine gender in Hindi.

## अभ्यास    **ab$^h$yās**    Exercises

### Exercise 1

Rearrange the following words to make correct sentences in Hindi.

मेरे दोस्त, वे थे अच्छे कितने दिन! मैं सोचा ने वे रहेंगे दिन हमेशा। वे बचपन दिन के
थे। मैं था हमेशा खेलता और नाचता था हर सुन्दर चीज़ थी। हर था दिन नया और
हर रात अन्दाज़ का था। दिन वे अब नहीं रहे।

mere dost, ve t$^h$e acc$^h$e kitne din! mẽ socā ne ve rahẽge din hameshā.
ve bacpan din ke t$^h$e. mẽ t$^h$ā hameshā k$^h$eltā aur nāctā t$^h$ā. har
sundar cīz t$^h$ī. har t$^h$ā din nayā aur har rāt andāz kā t$^h$ā. din ve ab
nahī̃ rahe.

## Exercise 2

Underline the correct form of the subject and the verb in the following sentences. (Hint: the gender of the English word 'report' is feminine.):

1  (मैंने/मैं) वहाँ (गये/गयी) ।
   (mẽne/mẽ) vahā̃ (gaye/gayī).

2  (वह/उसने) मुझको (बताया/बताये) ।
   (vo/usne) mujhko (batāyā/batāye).

3  (हम/हमने) घर (आया/आये) ।
   (ham/hamne) ghar (āyā/āye).

4  (तुम/तुमने) घर देर से (पहुँचे/पहुँचा) ।
   (tum/tumne) ghar der se (pahũce/pahũcā).

5  (वे/वेने /उन्होंने) पुलिस को रिपोर्ट (की/किया/किये) ।
   (ve/vene/unhõne ) *police* ko *reporT* (kī/kiyā/kiye).

6  (आप/आपको/आपने) ये किताब कब (मिला/मिले/मिली) ।
   (āp/āpko/āpne) ye kitāb kab (milā/mile/milī).

## Exercise 3

Activity: asking about your family histories
First talk about your family history making use of the cues to make questions. Use the same method to ask your friends or partners questions about their family.

*Examples:*  परिवार/कहाँ से/आ **parivār** 'family'/**kahā̃ se/ā** 'come'
आपका परिवार कहाँ से आया?
**āpkā parivār kahā̃ se āyā?**

माता–पिता/जन्म/हो **mātā-pitā** 'mother-father'/**janma** 'birth'/**ho** 'be, happen'
आपके माता-पिता का जन्म कहाँ हुआ?
**āp ke mātā- pitā kā janma kahā̃ huā?**

Hint: use the English word for 'arranged marriage'.
The verb 'to be married' = marriage to take place/happen.
younger/older = small/big

1  parents/where/ born
2  parents/when/ born
3  rich or poor
4  marriage/when/happen

5  how old
6  arranged marriage /love marriage
7  mother younger than your father.

## Exercise 4

Make questions from the following statements. The object of an inquiry is indicated by the underlined words in the statements:

*Examples:* शादी के बाद मेरे माता-पिता इंग्लैंड गये।
shādī ke bād mere mātā-pitā <u>England</u> gaye.

शादी के बाद मेरे माता-पिता कहाँ गये?
shādī ke bād mere mātā-pitā kahā̃ gaye?

मेरा परिवार दस साल पहले यहाँ आया।
merā parivār <u>das</u> sāl pɛhɛle yahā̃ āyā

आपका परिवार कितने साल पहले यहाँ आया?
āpkā parivār kitne sāl pɛhɛle yahā̃ āyā?

1 कल <u>जॉन</u> का जन्म दिन था।
  kal John kā janma din tʰā.
2 <u>जॉन</u> कके परिवार ने एक पार्टी की।
  <u>John</u> ke parivār ne ek party kī.
3 वो पार्टी <u>शाम को</u> हुई।
  vo *party* <u>shām ko</u> huī.
4 जॉन को <u>पार्टी</u> के बारे में मालूम नहीं था?
  John ko *party* ke bāre mẽ mālūm nahī̃ tʰā?
5 ये <u>सरप्राइस</u> पार्टी थी।
  ye <u>*surprise*</u> *party* tʰī.
6 <u>कल</u> जॉन का जन्म दिन था।
  <u>kal</u> John kā janma din tʰā.

## Exercise 5: पुराना ज़माना
## purānā zamānā 'Old days' 🎧 (Audio 2:15)

Indians, like most of us, have nostalgic feelings about the past. The past is good and glorious. But the present . . . If you have the recording, listen to the passage. After the beep, answer each statement either by saying सच **sac** (true) or झूठ **jʰūTʰ** (false).

Circle true (सच **sac**) or false (झूठ **jʰūTʰ**) for each statement:

| | | |
|---|---|---|
| 1 आजकल लोग लव मैरिज करते हैं। | स (सच) | झू (झूठ) |
| āj-kal log *love marrige* karte hɛ̃. | s (true) | jʰ (false) |

2 पुराने ज़माने में आदमी घर में काम करते थे।    स (सच)    झू (झूठ)
   purāne zamāne mẽ ādmī gʰar mẽ    **s** (true)    **jʰ** (false)
   kām karte tʰe.

3 आज–कल सिर्फ़ आदमी टीवी देखते हैं।    स (सच)    झू (झूठ)
   āj-kal sirf ādmī TV dekʰte hẽ.    **s** (true)    **jʰ** (false)

4 आज–कल सिर्फ़ आदमी खाना बनाते हैं।    स (सच)    झू (झूठ)
   āj-kal sirf ādmī kʰānā banāte hẽ.    **s** (true)    **jʰ** (false)

5 पुराने ज़माने में परिवार अच्छा था।    स (सच)    झू (झूठ)
   purāne zamāne mẽ parivār accʰā tʰā.    **s** (true)    **jʰ** (false)

6 पुराने ज़माने में टीवी नहीं था।    स (सच)    झू (झूठ)
   purāne zamāne mẽ TV nahī̃ tʰā.    **s** (true)    **jʰ** (false)

7 और आज–कल समय नहीं है।    स (सच)    झू (झूठ)
   aur āj-kal samay nahī̃ hɛ.    **s** (true)    **jʰ** (false)

Now write sentence corrections of the false statements.

# 7 क्या आप हिन्दी बोल सकते हैं?
# kyā āp hindī bol sakte hɛ̃?

## Can you speak Hindi?

By the end of this unit you should be able to:

- talk about your skills
- give advice
- use obligatives
- form purpose clauses
- observe compound verbs
- use emphatic and persuasive forms

## बातचीत **bātcīt   Dialogue 1**  🎧 (Audio 2:16)

### क्या आप हिन्दी बोल सकते हैं? *kyā āp hindī bol sakte*
### *hɛ̃?   Can you speak Hindi?*

*Vijay Mishra lives in Vancouver, Canada and he takes a bus from the*
*University of British Columbia to downtown Vancouver. The bus is*
*not crowded. He puts his money into the fare box slot. The bus driver,*
*who is a white blue-eyed Canadian, utters something and Vijay Mishra*
*understands it as 'downtown eh', and he replies 'yes' and sits down. As*
*he settles down, he thinks that what he heard was not English but*
*Hindi. A bit puzzled, he does not want to rule out that what he actually*
*heard was the Hindi language. In fact, the driver had asked, 'down-*
*town **jānā hɛ**'. So Vijay Mishra asks:*

| | |
|---|---|
| विजय: | माफ कीजिये, आपने क्या कहा? |
| VIJAY: | māf kījiye, āpne kayā kahā? |
| ड्राइवर: | मैंने पूछा कि डाउनटाउन जाना है। |
| DRIVER: | mɛ̃ne pūchā ki *downtown* jānā hɛ. |
| विजय: | अरे आप तो बहुत अच्छी हिन्दी बोल सकते हैं। |
| VIJAY: | are! āp to bahut acchī hindī bol sakte hɛ̃. |
| ड्राइवर: | हाँ, थोड़ी–थोड़ी हिन्दी बोल लेता हूँ। |
| DRIVER: | hā̃, thoRī thoRī hindī bol letā hū̃. |
| विजय: | हिन्दी आपने कहाँ सीखी? |
| VIJAY: | hindī āpne kahā̃ sīkhī? |
| ड्राइवर: | दूसरी वर्ल्ड वार के समय मैं ब्रिटिश आर्मी में सैनिक था। उस समय हिन्दुस्तान में सीखी। |
| DRIVER: | dūsrī *World War* ke samaya mɛ̃ *British Army* mɛ̃ sɛnik thā. us samaya hindustān mɛ̃ sīkhī. |
| विजय | अभी भी अच्छी हिन्दी आती है। |
| VIJAY: | abhī bhī acchī hindī ātī hɛ. |
| ड्राइवर: | काफी समय से योग और मैडीटेशन सीख रहा हूँ इसलिये हिन्दी नहीं भूली। |
| DRIVER: | kāfī samaya se yoga aur *meditation* sīkh rahā hū̃ isliye hindī nahī̃ bhūlī. |
| विजय | ये तो बहुत अच्छा है, नहीं तो यहाँ हिन्दुस्तानी भी हिन्दी भूल जाते हैं। |
| VIJAY: | ye to bahut acchā hɛ nahī̃ to yahā̃ hindustānī bhī hindī bhūl jāte hɛ̃. |
| ड्राइवर: | यह बात तो सच है। |
| DRIVER: | ye bāt to sac hɛ. |

| | |
|---|---|
| VIJAY: | *Excuse me, what did you say?* |
| DRIVER: | *I asked if you need to go downtown.* |

VIJAY:      *Hey, you can speak Hindi very well.*
DRIVER:     *Yes, (I) can speak a little Hindi.*
VIJAY:      *Where did you learn Hindi?*
DRIVER:     *At the time of World War II, I was a soldier in the British Army. During that time (I) learned (it) in India.*
VIJAY:      *Even now you know Hindi well.*
DRIVER:     *For a long time I have been learning yoga and meditation; therefore, (I) did not forgot Hindi.*
VIJAY:      *This is very good; otherwise even Indians forget Hindi here.*
DRIVER:     *This is true.*

## शब्दावली  shabdāvalī   Vocabulary

| तो | to | as regards (particle) |
|---|---|---|
| थोड़ा | tʰoRā | little, few |
| बोलना | bolnā (+/−ne) | to speak |
| बोल लेना | bol lenā (+ne) | to speak for one's benefit |
| बोल लेता हूँ | bol letā hū̃ | (I can) speak |
| सीखना | sīkʰnā (+ne) | to learn |
| समय | samaya (m.) | time |
| सैनिक | sɛnik (m.) | soldier |
| अभी भी | abʰī bʰī | even now |
| काफ़ी | kāfī | enough, sufficient |
| भूलना | bʰūlnā (+/−ne) | to forget |
| नहीं तो | nahī̃ to | otherwise |
| यहाँ | yahā̃ | here |

# Notes

## Linguistic attitudes and hyper-politeness

The linguistic attitudes of Indians are very interesting. A foreigner with minimal linguistic competence (even limited to just a few words) in Indian languages will be showered with compliments such as 'you speak excellent Hindi' and 'you speak beautiful Hindi'. This is more of a welcome gesture than a faithful reflection of one's linguistic competence. So try to understand the main intention behind such compliments. Also, do not be quick to judge your complimenter with suspicion. They are not mocking your linguistic competence.

## Formulaic expression: माफ़ कीजिये **māf kījiye** 'forgive me/excuse me'

The English expression 'excuse me' ('I beg your pardon' in British English) is ambiguous in a number of ways. We pointed out earlier, in Unit 2, that when the main function of 'excuse me' is to get attention, then it is paraphrased as 'please say' or 'please listen'. In this dialogue, Vijay did not hear the driver at first and then asked him to repeat his statement; this calls for an apology. Thus Vijay appropriately uses माफ़ कीजिये **māf kījiye**. The first part of the expression माफ़ **māf**, 'pardoned' is the short adjectival form of the noun माफ़ी **māfī** 'forgiveness', which is used with the verb करना **karnā** 'to do'. (Remember the 'transformer' verbs outlined in the last unit.) Thus, this expression is like other conjunct verbs you have encountered in earlier dialogues:

| *Noun* | *Verb* |
|--------|--------|
| माफ़ | करना |
| māf | karnā |
| पसन्द | करना |
| pasand | karnā |
| रिपोर्ट | करना |
| riporT | karnā |

The polite imperative form of माफ़ करना **māf karnā** is माफ़ कीजिये **māf kījiye**. You guessed it right; the subject आप **āp** and the object मुझको **mujʰ ko** 'me' are implied.

## The internal obligative (one's inner need): मुझको जाना है **mujʰko jānā hɛ** 'I need to go'

The Hindi counterpart of the English expression 'you need to go downtown' is

| आपको | डाउनटाउन | जाना | है। |
|------|----------|------|-----|
| **āpko** | **downtown** | **jānā** | **hɛ** |
| you-to | downtown | to go | is |
| You need to go downtown. | | | |

The internal obligation is expressed by the infinitive form followed by the 'to be' verb form. The subject is always the experiencer subject with the को **ko** postposition. In the above sentence the 'to be'

verb is in the present tense form. In short, the internal obligatives
have the following structure:

| subject | infinitive verb | 'to be' verb | |
|---------|-----------------|--------------|------|
| + को **ko** | जाना **jānā** | है **hɛ** | is |
| | | था **tʰā** | was |
| | | होगा **hogā** | will be |

*Examples:* आपको डाउनटाउन जाना है।
**āpko downtown jānā hɛ.**
You need to go downtown.

आपको डाउनटाउन जाना था।
**āpko downtown jānā tʰā.**
You needed to go downtown.

आपको डाउनटाउन जाना होगा।
**āpko downtown jānā hogā.**
You will need to go downtown.

In the case of an intransitive verb, the verb always stays masculine
singular. This is because the verb cannot agree with a subject
because it has to be followed by the postposition को **ko** and there is
no object to agree with either.

## Three types of capabilitatives

In the dialogue, you will have noticed the three different ways of
saying 'one can speak Hindi'. This is the first:

| आप | हिन्दी | अच्छी | बोल | सकते | हैं। |
|-----|--------|--------|------|-------|------|
| **āp** | **hindī** | **accʰī** | **bol** | **sakte** | **hɛ̃** |
| you | Hindi | good | speak | can-present | are |

You can speak Hindi well.

Notice the placement of सकना **saknā** in the Hindi sentence. The subject is just plain nominative as in English. The verb agrees with the
subject. It is सकना **saknā** which receives the tense conjugation and it
is preceded by the plain stem form of the verb.

The second way is:

| मैं | थोड़ी | थोड़ी | हिन्दी | बोल | लेता | हूँ। |
|------|-------|-------|--------|------|------|------|
| mɛ̃ | tʰoRī | tʰoRī | hindī | bol | letā | hū̃. |
| I | little | little | Hindi | speak | take-present | am |

I can speak Hindi a little.

When one does not have native-like or full competence in a skill, this construction is used. In other words, this type of expression is used to express 'partial competence' and it usually has quantifiers such as थोड़ा **tʰoRā** 'a little/few' with it. Notice the clustering of the two verbs – **bol** बोल 'to speak' and लेना **lenā** 'to take'. It is the second verb which carries the tense/aspect form. These types of verb are called 'compound' verbs. We will discuss this class of verbs in detail later on. For the time being just memorize this expression.

The third way is like saying 'Hindi comes to you' as in

| आपको | अभी भी | हिन्दी | आती | है। |
|-------|---------|--------|------|------|
| āpko | abʰī bʰī | hindī | ātī | hɛ |
| you-to | now even | Hindi | come-present | is |

You even now know Hindi, or You even now know (how to) speak) Hindi. (lit. Hindi even now comes to you)

In this construction the verb is आना **ānā** 'to come' and the subject is an experiential/dative subject. Remember that dative subjects are marked with the postposition को **ko**. The verb agrees with 'Hindi', which is feminine singular. Unless otherwise modified with a quantifier denoting meagreness, this construction expresses 'full' or 'near complete' competence in a skill, to the extent that a skill comes to a person without any conscious effort.

*This construction – 'Hindi comes to you' – is restricted to skills such as swimming, playing the sitar or any other musical instrument. It cannot be used in expressions such as 'I know John.'*

Compare the following two sentences:

| उसको | तैरना | आता | है। |
|-------|-------|------|------|
| usko | tɛrnā | ātā | hɛ |
| he/she-to | to swim | come-present | is |

(S)he knows (how to) swim. (lit. Swimming/to swim comes to him/her)

The verb agrees with the infinitive form तैरना **tɛrnā** which is masculine singular.

| मैं | जॉन | को | जानता | हूँ। |
|---|---|---|---|---|
| **mɛ̃** | **John** | **ko** | **jāntā** | **hū̃.** |
| I | John | object | know-present | am |

I know John.

However, one cannot say 'John comes to me.'

## Focus, emphasis and word order

In the dialogue, Vijay asks the driver

| हिन्दी | आपने | कहाँ | सीखी? |
|---|---|---|---|
| **hindī** | **āpne** | **kahā̃** | **sīkʰī?** |
| Hindi | you agent | where | learned |

Where did you learn Hindi?

Normal word order is as follows:

| आपने | हिन्दी | कहाँ | सीखी? |
|---|---|---|---|
| **āpne** | **hindī** | **kahā̃** | **sīkʰī?** |
| you agent | Hindi | where | learned |

Where did you learn Hindi?

Since Hindi is the subject of the discussion, 'Hindi', which is the object of the sentence, is moved to the beginning of the sentence. If you have the recording, you will hear a slight emphasis on the word, 'Hindi'. In other words, an element of a sentence can be pulled out of its normal place in a sentence and placed at its beginning to express focus or emphasis.

## The particle तो to 'as regards'

We came across the use of तो **to** in the sense of 'then'. However, observe that in the following two examples तो **to** follows a constituent rather than appearing in the clause-initial position in a 'when–then' type of sentence.

| आप | तो | बहुत | अच्छी | हिन्दी | बोल | सकते | हैं। |
|---|---|---|---|---|---|---|---|
| **āp** | **to**-particle | **bahut** | **accʰī** | **hindī** | **bol** | **sakte** | **hɛ̃.** |
| you | as regards | very | good | Hindi | speak | can-present | are |

As regards you, you can speak very good Hindi.

| ये | तो | बहुत | अच्छा | है। |
|----|-----|------|-------|-----|
| ye | to-particle | bahut | acc<sup>h</sup>ā | hɛ |
| this | as regards | very | good | is |

As regards this, this is very good.

The particle तो **to** is another way of expressing emphasis but implies some sense of exclusion. The first sentence says 'As regards you, you can speak very good Hindi' and implies that 'others (from your group) cannot speak very good Hindi'.

## Compound verb भूल जाना b<sup>h</sup>ūl jānā 'to forget'

Observe another example of a compound verb in dialogue:

| यहाँ | हिन्दुस्तानी | भी | हिन्दी | भूल | जाते | हैं। |
|------|-------------|-----|--------|-----|------|------|
| yahā̃ | hindustānī | b<sup>h</sup>ī | hindī | b<sup>h</sup>ūl | jāte | hɛ̃. |
| here | Indians | also | Hindi | forget | go-present | are |

Here even Indians forget Hindi.

The two verbs are clustered together – भूल b<sup>h</sup>ūl and जाना jānā. They share the chore of expressing meaning. भूल b<sup>h</sup>ūl, the first verb, is in the form of a stem and conveys the main meaning, whereas जाना jānā carries the tense form but does not convey its literal meaning of 'going'. As promised, we will detail this class of verb later. For the time being satisfy yourself with the 'sharing' nature of Hindi compound verbs.

## बातचीत  bātcīt  Dialogue 2 🎧 (Audio 2:18)

### *क्या आपको हिन्दी लिखनी आती है? kyā āpko hindī lik<sup>h</sup>nī ātī hɛ? Can you write Hindi?*

*Vijay and the driver continue to talk to each other. The topic of discussion continues to be the Hindi language.*

| विजय: | क्या आपको हिन्दी लिखनी आती है? |
|--------|-------------------------------|
| VIJAY: | kyā āpko hindī lik<sup>h</sup>nī ātī hɛ? |
| ड्राइवर: | ज़्यादा नहीं। आर्मी में कभी-कभी लिखनी पड़ती थी लेकिन अब कोई ज़रूरत नहीं। |

DRIVER: zyādā nahī̃. *army* mẽ kab<sup>h</sup>ī-kab<sup>h</sup>ī lik<sup>h</sup>nī paRtī t<sup>h</sup>ī lekin ab koī zarūrat nahī̃.

विजय: हिन्दी में क्यों लिखना पड़ता था?

VIJAY: hindī mẽ kyõ lik<sup>h</sup>nā paRtā t<sup>h</sup>ā?

ड्राइवर: सन्देश कोड और सन्देशों के लिये – ख़ासकर यूरोप जाने वाले सन्देशों के लिये। डाउनटाउन में कुछ काम है?

DRIVER: *secret codes* aur sandeshõ ke liye – xāskar Europe jāne vāle sandeshõ ke liye. Downtown mẽ kuc<sup>h</sup> kām hɛ?

विजय: बिजली का बिल देना था। आज फ़ुरसत मिली, तो सोचा कि ख़ुद वहाँ जाऊँ।

VIJAY: bijlī kā bill denā t<sup>h</sup>ā. āj fursat milī, to socā ki xud vahā̃ jāū̃.

ड्राइवर: तो वह दफ़्तर आने वाला है ... असल में अगला स्टाप है।

DRIVER: to vo daftar āne vālā hɛ . . . asal mẽ aglā *stop* hɛ.

विजय: अच्छा, नमस्कार।

VIJAY: acc<sup>h</sup>ā, namaskār.

ड्राइवर: नमस्कार।

DRIVER: namaskār.

VIJAY: *Do you know (how to) write Hindi? (lit. does to write Hindi come to you?)*

DRIVER: *Not much. In the army I had to write sometimes but now (there) is no need (to write in Hindi).*

VIJAY: *Why did (you) have to write in Hindi?*

DRIVER: *For secret codes and messages, especially for messages going to Europe. Do (you) have some work downtown?*

VIJAY: *(I) needed to pay the electric bill (lit. I need to give the electricity bill). Today (I) had (some) free time so I thought I would go myself (i.e. in person).*

DRIVER: *Then (in that case), that office is about to come up . . . in fact, (it) is the next stop.*

VIJAY: *Okay. Goodbye.*

DRIVER: *Bye.*

## शब्दावली shabdāvalī Vocabulary

| लिखना | lik<sup>h</sup>nā (+ne) | to write |
|---|---|---|
| ज़्यादा | zyādā (invariable) | more |
| कभी | kab<sup>h</sup>ī | ever |
| कभी–कभी | kab<sup>h</sup>ī-kab<sup>h</sup>ī | sometimes |
| पड़ना | paRnā | to fall, to lie down; in compound verbs 'to have to' |
| ज़रूरत | zarūrat (f.) | need, necessity |
| संदेश | sandesh (m.) | message |

| ख़ासकर | **xāskar** | especially, particularly |
|---|---|---|
| जाने वाले | **jāne vāle** | going |
| काम होना | **kām honā** (+ko) | to have work |
| बिजली | **bijlī** (f.) | electricity, lightning |
| फ़ुरसत | **fursat** (f.) | free time, spare time, leisure |
| ख़ुद | **xud** | oneself |
| जाना | **jānā** (–ne) | to go |
| जाऊँ | **jāū̃** | should go (subjunctive) |
| दफ़्तर | **daftar** (m.) | office |
| आने वाला | **āne vālā** | about to come |
| असल में | **asal mẽ** | in fact, in reality |
| अगला | **aglā** (m. adj.) | next |

## *Notes*

## Variation: हिन्दी लिखनी आती है Hindi likʰnī āti hɛ or हिन्दी लिखना आता है Hindi likʰnā ātā hɛ

In the Standard-Hindi-speaking area, the verb and the preceding infinitive form agree with the object in number and gender, whereas in the Eastern-Hindi-speaking area both remain invariable, i.e. masculine singular.

| *Standard Hindi* | *Eastern Hindi* |
|---|---|
| आपको <u>हिन्दी</u>     लिख<u>नी</u> आ<u>ती</u> है। | आपको <u>हिन्दी</u> लिख<u>ना</u> आ<u>ता</u> है। |
| **āpko <u>hindī</u>** (f.) **likʰ<u>nī</u> ā<u>tī</u> hɛ.** | **āpko <u>hindī</u> likʰ<u>nā</u> ā<u>tā</u> hɛ.** |
| you know how to write Hindi. | you know how to write Hindi. |
| आपको <u>ख़त</u>     लिख<u>ने</u>   हैं। | आपको <u>ख़त</u>     लिख<u>ना</u>    है। |
| **āpko <u>xat</u>     likʰ<u>ne</u>   hɛ̃.** | **āpko <u>xat</u>     likʰ<u>nā</u>    hɛ.** |
| you-to letters to write are (m. pl.) | you-to letters to write is (m. sg.) |

However, the following sentence in our dialogue

| बिजली | का | बिल | देना | था। |
|---|---|---|---|---|
| **bijlī** | **kā** | *bill* | **denā** | **tʰā.** |
| electricity | of | bill (m. sg.) | to give | was |
| (I) needed to pay the electric bill. | | | | |

remains the same in both dialects because in Standard Hindi the agreement is with *bill* which is masculine singular.

## The external obligative (compulsion): मुझको जाना पड़ता है muj<sup>h</sup>ko jānā paRtā hɛ 'I have to go'

The only difference between the internal and the external obligative is that in the latter the infinitive is followed by the verb पड़ना **paRnā** 'to lie down' instead of the verb होना **honā** 'to be'. The external obligative expresses 'an external pressure/compulsion to do something' rather than 'one's own internal need to do something'. Compare the two types of obligatives:

### Internal obligative (inner need)

| आपको | हिन्दी | लिखनी | है। |
|------|--------|--------|-----|
| **āpko** | **hindī** | **lik<sup>h</sup>nī** | **hɛ.** |
| you-to | Hindi (f. sg.) | write (f. sg.) | is |

You need to write Hindi.

### External obligative (compulsion)

| आपको | हिन्दी | लिखनी | पड़ती | है। |
|------|--------|--------|--------|-----|
| **āpko** | **hindī** | **lik<sup>h</sup>nī** | **paRtī** | **hɛ.** |
| you-to | Hindi (f. sg.) | to write (f. sg.) | lie down (f. sg.) | is |

You have to write Hindi.

In Eastern Hindi the infinitive and the verb form are in the masculine singular form, i.e. लिखना है **lik<sup>h</sup>nā hɛ** and लिखना पड़ता है **lik<sup>h</sup>nā paRtā hɛ**, respectively.

Now, take a look at the use of the external obligative in our dialogue:

| आर्मी | में | कभी-कभी | लिखनी | पड़ती | थी। |
|-------|-----|----------|--------|--------|------|
| **army** | **mẽ** | **kab<sup>h</sup>ī-kab<sup>h</sup>ī** | **lik<sup>h</sup>nī** | **paRtī** | **t<sup>h</sup>ī.** |
| Army | in | sometimes | to write (f. sg.) | lie down (f. sg.) | was |

I had to write sometimes in the Army. (lit. I used to have to write sometimes in the Army)

The omitted subject मुझको **muj<sup>h</sup>ko** 'to me' is experiential and the object is Hindi. The tense form chosen is the past habitual. If the act of compelled writing was carried out only once, the verb पड़ना **paRnā** would have to be in the simple past form, i.e. पड़ी. **paRī** and the adverb कभी-कभी **kab<sup>h</sup>ī-kab<sup>h</sup>ī** would have to be dropped.

There is a striking similarity between the verb पड़ना **paRnā** 'to lie down' and पढ़ना **paR<sup>h</sup>nā** 'to read/study'.

## Negative-incorporated words: 'nobody', 'nowhere', 'never', etc.

Have a look at the Hindi expression 'now (I have) no need of Hindi writing':

| अब | कोई | जरूरत | नहीं । |
|------|------|---------|--------|
| **ab** | **koī** | **zarūrat** | **nahī̃.** |
| now | some | need | not |

Now (I have) no need.

Negative words such as 'nobody', 'nowhere', 'never' are simply derived from their positive Hindi counterparts and the negative particle नहीं **nahī̃** is placed in its original position, i.e. right before the verb.

| कोई **koī** | someone | नहीं **nahī̃** | = | no one, nobody |
|-------------|-----------|-----------------|----|----------------|
| कहीं **kahī̃** | somewhere | नहीं **nahī̃** | = | nowhere |
| कभी **kabʰī** | ever | नहीं **nahī̃** | = | never |

## The immediate future: the वाला **vālā** construction

वाला **vālā** is quite notorious for the meaning it renders and the behaviour it exhibits. It has many facets. Here, we will examine the cases in which वाला **vālā** follows an infinitive verbal form and thus marks the 'immediate future' tense.

| वह | दफ़्तर | आने | वाला | है । |
|------|---------|-------|--------|------|
| **vo** | **daftar** | **āne** | **vālā** | **hɛ** |
| that | office (m. sg.) | to come | about | is |

That office is about to come up (i.e. the next stop is that office).

The many facets of वाला **vālā** become evident from the following two facts: (1) it acts like a postposition and exercises peer pressure on the preceding infinitive form, and consequently the infinitive form becomes oblique; and (2) it agrees with the subject in number and gender in the way that is typical of an adjective ending in -ā. Now, observe one more example of such usage:

| गाड़ी | जाने | वाली | थी । |
|--------|-------|--------|------|
| **gāRī** | **jāne** | **vālī** | **tʰī.** |
| train (f. sg.) | to go | about (f. sg.) | was (f. sg.) |

The train was about to go/leave.

It might be puzzling to see how वाला **vālā** can still be considered an example of the 'immediate future'. However, in this example, वाला **vālā** still renders the 'immediate future' with reference to the past. In short, the structure of the 'immediate future' construction in Hindi is as follows:

subject (nominative)   stem + ने **ne**   वाला **vālā**   verb 'to be'
वाली **vālī**
वाले **vāle**

## The agentive वाला **vālā** construction

In comparison with the above examples, observe the position of वाला **vālā** in the following phrase. Here, its best literal translation is the English agentive suffix '-er'.

| यूरोप | जाने | वाले | सन्देशों | के लिये |
|---|---|---|---|---|
| **Europe** | **jāne** | **vāle** | **sandeshõ** | **ke liye** |
| Europe | to go | -er | messages | for |

For the Europe-going messages. (lit. for the Europe go-er messages)

Can you guess the meaning of the following the phrases?

खेलने वाला k**ʰelne vālā** and पढ़ने वाली **paRʰne vālī**

The meaning is 'player' and 'reader', respectively. In the former a masculine singular head (e.g. 'boy') is implied whereas the feminine singular head (e.g. 'girl') is implied in the latter.

The meaning of the वाला **vālā** phrase is often contextually governed. For example, the phrase

| दिल्ली | वाला |
|---|---|
| **dillī** | **vālā** |
| Delhi | -er |

means 'the person who lives in Delhi'. However, if the phrase is used in the context of a train or vehicle, it can mean either 'the train which goes/is going to Delhi' or 'a vehicle which is made in Delhi'.

## Formulaic expressions: 'I have some work' and 'Are you free?'

| क्या | आपको | डाउन टाउन | में | कुछ | काम | है? |
|------|------|-----------|-----|-----|-----|-----|
| **kyā** | **āpko** | *downtown* | **mẽ** | **kuc^h** | **kām** | **hɛ?** |
| what | you-to | downtown | in | some | work | is |

Do you have some work downtown?

| आज | मुझको | फुरसत | मिली | |
|-----|-------|-------|------|---|
| **āj** | **muj^hko** | **fursat** | | **milī.** |
| today | me-to | free/spare time (f.) | | got |

Today I was free.

The English expressions such as 'I am busy' and 'I am free' are paraphrased as 'to me the work is' and 'to me the free/leisure/spare time is'. Similarly, the best way to ask 'Are you free?' is

| आपको | फुरसत | है? |
|------|-------|-----|
| **āpko** | **fursat** | **hɛ?** |

and 'are you busy?' is

| आपको | काम | है? |
|------|-----|-----|
| **āpko** | **kām** | **hɛ?** |

## The subjunctive

The subjunctive expresses the idea of a possibility. Expressions with words such as 'perhaps' and suggestion (e.g. 'Shall we go?'), or permission (e.g. 'May I come in?') usually employ the subjunctive.

| मैंने | सोचा | कि | खुद | वहाँ | जाऊँ | |
|-------|------|-----|-----|------|------|---|
| **mɛ̃ne** | **socā** | **ki** | **xud** | **vahā̃** | **jāū̃** | |
| I-agent | thought | that | self | there | go (subjunctive) | |

I thought that (I) myself would go there.

Verbs such as चाहना **cāhnā** 'to want', सोचना **socnā** 'to think' (which are called non-factive verbs) and जानना **jānnā** 'to know' (which belongs to the class of factive verbs) select a subjunctive verb form in their subordinate clause, i.e. जाऊँ **jāū̃**.

The subjunctives are very simple to form. The magic trick is to take any future form and just drop the future ending, i.e. गा **gā**, गे **ge** and गी **gī**. For instance, the corresponding subjunctive forms of हम मिलेंगे **ham milẽge** 'we will meet', तुम जाओगे **tum jāoge** 'you will go' and मैं जाऊँगी **mẽ jāū̃gī** 'I will go' are: हम मिलें **ham milẽ** 'we shall meet', तुम जाओ **tum jāo** 'you would go', and मैं जाऊँ **mẽ jāū̃** (with rising intonation) 'may I go?', respectively.

## The emphatic reflexive: खुद xud 'oneself'

The emphatic pronoun खुद **xud** is very similar to English emphatic pronouns, with the difference that the Hindi form खुद **xud** remains invariable whereas the English emphatic pronouns vary according to their subject. In

| मैंने | सोचा | कि | मैं | खुद | वहाँ | जाऊँ । |
|-------|------|-----|-----|-----|------|--------|
| **mẽne** | **socā** | **ki** | **mẽ** | **xud** | **vahā̃** | **jāū̃** |

the emphatic form will always remain unchanged even if the subject of the (subordinate) clause changes.

## बातचीत  **bātcīt**  Dialogue 3  🎧 (Audio 2:20)

### मेरी तबीयत बहुत खराब है। *merī tabīyat bahut xarāb hɛ I am very sick*

*Professor John Ryder is on his first research trip to rural India. He reached his village at the beginning of the Monsoon season. Although he took all precautions and vaccinations before leaving for India, he awakens one night with a high fever and diarrhoea. He calls Dr Naim's residence. Dr Naim's wife picks up the phone.*

| जॉन: | हैलो, क्या डा॰ नाइम हैं? |
|------|------------------------|
| JOHN: | hello, kyā Dr. Naim hɛ̃? |
| नाइम की पत्नी: | जी नहीं, कोई ज़रूरी बात है? |
| NAIM'S WIFE: | jī nahī̃, koī zarūrī bāt hɛ? |
| जॉन: | मेरी तबीयत बहुत खराब है। |
| JOHN: | merī tabīyat bahut xarāb hɛ. |
| नाइम की पत्नी: | एक मरीज को देखने गये हैं। |
| NAIM'S WIFE: | ek marīz ko dekʰne gaye hɛ̃. |
| जॉन: | कितनी देर में लौटेंगे? |
| JOHN: | kitnī der mẽ lauTẽge? |

नाइम की पत्नी: मेरे ख़्याल से जल्दी आ जायेंगे । मुझे अपना टैलिफ़ोन नम्बर और पता दे दीजिये । आते ही उन्हें भेज दूँगी ।

NAIM'S WIFE: mere xyāl se jaldī ā jāyẽge. mujʰe apnā Telīfon (*telephone*) *number* aur patā de dījiye. āte hī unhẽ bʰej dū̃gī.

जॉन: बहुत-बहुत धन्यवाद ।

JOHN: bahut-bahut dʰanyavād.

JOHN: *Hello, is Dr Naim (there)?*

NAIM'S WIFE: *No, is (there) something urgent?*

JOHN: *(I) am very sick.* (lit. my condition/health is very bad)

NAIM'S WIFE: *He went to see a patient.*

JOHN: *When will he return?* (lit. in how much period of time will he return?)

NAIM'S WIFE: *I think (he) will come (back) soon.* (lit. with my opinion [he] will come soon)
*Please give me your phone number and address. As soon as (he) returns, (I) will send him (to your place).*

JOHN: *Thanks a lot.*

## शब्दावली  shabdāvalī  Vocabulary

| | | |
|---|---|---|
| ज़रूरी | **zarūrī** | important, urgent, necessary |
| तबीयत | **tabīyat** (f.) | health, disposition |
| ख़राब | **xarāb** | bad |
| मरीज़ | **marīz** (m.) | patient |
| देर | **der** (f.) | delay, time (period of, slot of) |
| लौटना | **lauTanā** (–ne) | to return |
| लौटेंगे | **lauTẽge** | will return |
| ख़्याल | **xyāl** (m.) | opinion, thought |
| जल्दी | **jaldī** | quickly |
| आ जाना | **ā jānā** (–ne) | to come (compound verb) |
| आ जायेंगे | **ā jāyẽge** | will come (compound verb) |
| मुझे | **mujʰe** | to me |
| पता | **patā** (m.) | address |
| दे देना | **de denā** (+ne) | to give (compound verb) |
| दे दीजिये | **de dījiye** | please give (compound verb) |
| आते ही | **āte hī** | as soon as (he) comes |
| उन्हें | **unhẽ** | him (honorific) |
| भेजना | **bʰejnā** (+ne) | to send |
| भेज देना | **bʰej denā** (+ne) | to send (compound verb) |
| भेज दूँगी | **bʰej dū̃gī** | will send (compound verb) |
| धन्यवाद | **dʰanyavād** | thanks |

## *Notes*

### Variation

**tabīyat** can also be spelled with a short **i** (i.e. **tabiyat** तबियत).

### Present and past perfective forms

| वे | एक | मरीज़ | को | देखने | गये | हैं । |
|---|---|---|---|---|---|---|
| **ve** | **ek** | **marīz** | **ko** | **dekʰne** | **gaye** | **hɛ̃.** |
| he (hon.) | one | patient | obj. | to see (obl.) | gone | are |

He went to see a patient. (lit. he has gone to see a patient)

| क्या | आप | कभी | आगरा | गये | हैं? |
|---|---|---|---|---|---|
| **kyā** | **āp** | **kabʰī** | **āgrā** | **gaye** | **hɛ̃?** |
| what | you | ever | Agra | went | are |

Have you ever been (lit. gone) to Agra?

| हाँ, | मैं | गया | हूँ । |
|---|---|---|---|
| **hā̃,** | **mɛ̃** | **gayā** | **hū̃.** |
| yes | I | went | am |

Yes, I have been (there). (lit. Yes, I have gone there.)

| हाँ, | दो | साल | पहले | मैं | गया | था । |
|---|---|---|---|---|---|---|
| **hā̃,** | **do** | **sāl** | **peɦele** | **mɛ̃** | **gayā** | **tʰā.** |
| yes | two | years | ago | I | went | was |

Yes, two years ago I went (there). (lit. Yes, two years ago, I had gone (there).)

By adding the present forms (हूँ **hū̃** 'am', है **hɛ** 'is', हैं **hɛ̃** 'are' and हो **ho** 'are' (you)) and past forms (था **tʰā** 'was', थे **tʰe** 'were', थी **tʰī** 'was' and थीं **tʰī̃** 'were') of the verb 'to be' to the perfective form, one can get present and past perfective forms, respectively. The present perfect indicates the completed action which has relevance for the present situation and the past perfective shows relevance to the past. That is why the present perfective and past perfective are called 'recent past' and 'remote past'. What is notable is that in the first sentence and the last sentence English will use the simple perfective form but Hindi will use the present and the past perfective, respectively. The past perfect in English is viewed with reference to an event in the past, as in 'When I was in Agra, he had already come.'

## Compound verbs

We have already mentioned compound verbs in Hindi. Observe another example from our dialogue:

| मेरे | ख्याल | से | वे | जल्दी | आ | जायेंगे । |
|------|-------|-----|-----|-------|-----|-----------|
| **mere** | **xyāl** | **se** | **ve** | **jaldī** | **ā** | **jāyẽge** |
| my | opinion | with | he (hon.) | soon | come | go-will |

I think he will come (back) soon.

Note the two verbs आ **ā** 'come' and जा **jā** 'go' are clustered in the verb phrase. The meaning of the sentence is not merely an accumulative or conjunctive meaning rendered by the verbs. In other words, the sentence does not mean 'he will come and go'. On the contrary, the action of coming is being described and the verb जाना **jānā** 'to go' is only a responsible carrier of the tense information. It also loses its literal meaning and adds some related but new overtone or emphasis to the first verb. In the case of capabilitative construction with सकना **saknā**, the helping verb adds a clear (literal) meaning; however, as you will see below, this is usually not the case with helping verbs such as आना **ānā** and जाना **jānā**.

You can view compound verbs as people married to each other or romantically in love with one another, with both willing to cooperate to the extent of being dependent on each other in some ways. The compound verb

| आ | जायेंगे । |
|---|-----------|
| **ā** | **jāyẽge** |

is composed of two units: (1) the main verb आ **ā** 'come', which is in its stem form and is totally dependent on the second unit, i.e. (2) the helping verb – जा **jā** 'go' – for tense information. In addition to supplying tense information, the other roles played by the helping verb are described below:

## जाना **jānā** as a helping verb

As we already know, the literal meaning of **jānā** जाना is 'to go'. As a helping verb, it refers to the 'transformation of a state or action, completeness or finality'.

| Simple verbs | | | Compound verbs | | |
|---|---|---|---|---|---|
| आना | **ānā** | to come | आ जाना | **ā jānā** | to come back, arrive |
| खाना | **kʰānā** | to eat | खा जाना | **kʰā jānā** | to eat up |
| पीना | **pīnā** | to drink | पी जाना | **pī jānā** | to drink up |
| समझना | **samajʰnā** | to understand | समझ जाना | **samajʰ jānā** | to understand fully |
| होना | **honā** | to be | हो जाना | **ho jānā** | to become |
| भूलना | **bʰūlnā** | to forget | भूल जाना | **bʰūl jānā** | to forget completely |

## देना **denā** as a helping verb

The literal meaning of देना **denā** is 'to give'. When one gives something, the beneficiary of the action is someone other than the subject. That is exactly what is added to the main verb by the helping verb देना **denā**, i.e. to do an action for others. In Dialogue 3, the doctor's wife first asks for John's address and telephone number. The expression she uses is as follows:

| मुझे | अपना | टेलीफोन | नम्बर | और | पता | दे | दीजिये। |
|---|---|---|---|---|---|---|---|
| **mujʰe** | **apnā** | *telephone* | *number* | **aur** | **patā** | **de** | **dījiye.** |

Give me your telephone number and address.

She then says:

| आते | ही | उन्हें | भेज | दूँगी। |
|---|---|---|---|---|
| **āte** | **hī** | **unhē** | **bʰej** | **dū̃gī.** |

As soon as he comes, I will send him.

The compound verbs दे देना **de denā** and भेज देना **bʰej denā** are used to highlight the beneficiary of the actions. The simple corresponding verbs देना **denā** 'to give' and भेजना **bʰejnā** 'to send' are unable to emphasize the beneficiary. In the first sentence, the direct beneficiary of the action is the wife herself and in the second sentence John is the beneficiary of the wife's action of sending Dr Naim to his house.

## लेना **lenā** as a helping verb

The verb लेना **lenā** means 'to take'. You can now predict its meaning as a helping verb. It conveys 'doing for oneself', i.e. for the benefit of the subject. For example, in answer to the request for the telephone number and address, John could have answered as follows:

अच्छा    लिख    लीजिए।
**accʰā,    likʰ    lījiye**
OK      write   take-imp.
Please, write (it) down for your benefit.

The compound verb लिख लेना **likʰ lenā** stresses that Dr Naim's wife is the direct beneficiary of the action of writing down the address and telephone number.

In the previous dialogue, we saw the other meaning (i.e. partial competence) of लेना **lenā** when used as a helping verb with skill verbs.

## -ते ही -te hī 'as soon as'

The addition of -ते ही -**te hī** to the verbal stem renders the meaning of 'as soon as', as in

आते ही                उन्हें            भेज   दूँगी।
**āte hī**             **unhẽ**        **bʰej   dū̃gī.**
come-as soon as    him (hon.)   send  give-will
(I) will send him as soon as (he) comes (back).

## The pitfalls:

### 'I think'

Compare and contrast the Hindi phrase with its English translation.

मेरे ख्याल से       **mere xyāl se** . . .      I think . . .

The Hindi equivalent is either मेरे ख्याल से **mere xyāl se** 'with my opinion' or मेरे ख्याल में **mere xyāl mẽ** 'in my opinion'. The Hindi verb सोचना **socnā** 'to think' is not acceptable in this context, as in the following sentence:

मैं        सोचता              हूँ।
**mẽ**    **soctā**          **hū̃**
I        think-present     am

The English verb 'to think' is ambiguous: (1) it refers to the process of thinking, as in 'I will think of something', and (2) it expresses an opinion, as in 'I think he is a nice man.' In the latter sense, it is paraphrased as 'In my opinion he is a nice man.' The failure to distinguish between the two types of 'think' is the most common source of errors on the part of English learners of Hindi as a second language.

## Compound verbs

Failure to understand the shades in meaning conveyed by compound verbs can take a toll on communication. For example, if a student goes to a professor and requests a letter of recommendation, it makes a significant difference whether the student uses

| recommendation letter | लिखिये | **likʰiye** |
| recommendation letter | लिख दीजिये | **likʰ dījiye** |
| recommendation letter | लिख लीजिये | **likʰ līrjiye** |

Even though the polite forms are used in all three expressions, the only appropriate choice is the second. The first and last have the potential to offend the professor. The first is polite, but still a command, and the last claims the professor to be the direct beneficiary of the act of writing a letter of recommendation.

Similarly, be gentle and sensitive with the use of obligatives and capabilitatives.

## Coping skills

If you are unsure which form to use, compound or simple verb, the best thing you can do is to spell out the beneficiary मेरे लिए **mere liye** 'for me' with simple verbs. By doing this, you cannot totally eliminate the ill-effects of making a bad choice, but you can reduce the damage considerably.

## अभ्यास **abʰyās** Exercises

## Exercise 1

Underline the appropriate choice of subject in the following sentences and then translate the sentences into English:

1 (मैं/मुझको/मैंने) सितार आती है।
   (mɛ̃/mujʰko/mɛ̃ne) sitār ātī hɛ.
2 क्या (आप/आपको/आपने) तैर सकते हैं?
   kyā (āp/āpko/āpne) tɛr sakte hɛ̃?

3 (उसको/वह/उसने) कहाँ जाना है?
  (usko/vo/usne) kahā̃ jānā hε?
4 (वे/उन्होंने/उनको) संगीत कब सीखा?
  (ve/unhõne/unko) saŋgīt kab sīkʰā?
5 वह सेल्समैन है। (उसको/उसने/वहे) बाहर जाना पड़ता है।
  vo *salesman* hε. (usko/usne/vo) bāhar jānā paRtā hε.
6 जॉन को बहुत काम है। इसलिए (वे/उसको/उसने) कुछ फुरसत नहीं है।
  John ko bahut kām hε. isliye (ve/usko/usne) kucʰ fursat nahī̃ hε.

## Exercise 2

Complete the following sentences by supplying the missing parts of
the verb:

1 बिल को जल्दी है क्योंकि उसकी गाड़ी दस मिनट में जा ____ _____ है।
  Bill ko jaldī hε kyõki uskī gāRī das minute mē̃ jā ___ ____ hε.
2 ड्राइवर जल्दी करो, मेरे दोस्त की फ़्लाइट आ ___ ___ है।
  Driver jaldī karo, mere dost kī *flight* ā ____ ___ hε.
3 सर्दी का मौसम था, जल्दी बर्फ गिर ___ ____ थी।
  sardī kā mausam tʰā, jaldī barf gir___ ____ tʰī.
4 पार्टी के लिए मेहमान पहुँच ____ _____ हैं।
  party ke liye mεhmān pahũc _____ _____ hε̃.
5 शाम का समय था, अंधेरा हो ____ _____ था।
  shām kā samay tʰā, andʰerā ho ___ _____ tʰā.
6 आप कभी हिन्दुस्तान ग ___ हैं।
  āp kabʰī hindustān ga __ hε̃.

## Exercise 3

Match the duties given on the left with the professions given on the
right:

| | |
|---|---|
| 1 अध्यापक | उसको कार चलानी है। |
| adʰyāpak | usko kār calānī hε. |
| 2 डॉक्टर | उसको कपड़े धोने हैं। |
| *doctor* | usko kapRe dʰone hε̃. |
| 3 गायक | उसको पढ़ाना है। |
| gāyak | usko paRʰānā hε. |
| 4 ड्राइवर | उसको लिखना है। |
| *driver* | usko likʰnā hε. |
| 5 धोबी | उसको मरीज को देखना है। |
| dʰobī | usko marīz ko dekʰnā hε. |

6 लेखक      उसको गाना है।
   lek<sup>h</sup>ak      usko gānā hɛ.

## Exercise 4

Underline the appropriate helping verb(s) in the following sentences:

1 क्या आप मेरे लिए *रिकॉमेंडेशन लैटर* लिख लेंगे/देंगे?
   kyā āp mere liye *recommendation letter* lik<sup>h</sup> (lẽge/dẽge)?
2 रात आयी और अंधेरा हो (गया/आया) था।
   rāt āyī aur and<sup>h</sup>erā ho (gayā/āyā) t<sup>h</sup>ā.
3 मैं हिन्दी नहीं पढ़ सकता, आप ये खत पढ़ (लीजिये/दीजिये)
   mɛ̃ hindī nahī̃ paR<sup>h</sup> saktā, āp ye xat paR<sup>h</sup> (lījiye/dījiye).
4 वो थोड़ा थोड़ा तैर (सकता/लेता/आता) है।
   vo t<sup>h</sup>oRā t<sup>h</sup>oRā tɛr (saktā/letā/ātā) hɛ.
5 उसको बहुत अच्छा नाचना (सकता/लेता/आता) है।
   usko bahut acc<sup>h</sup>ā nācnā (saktā/letā/ātā) hɛ.
6 मैं आपकी बात बिल्कुल भूल (आया/गया)।
   mɛ̃ āpkī bāt bilkul b<sup>h</sup>ūl (āyā/gayā).

## Exercise 5

Write five sentences about the things you hated but had to do during your childhood. The following sentence can serve as a model for your answers.

| बचपन | में | मुझे | पालक | खानी | पड़ती | थी। |
|---|---|---|---|---|---|---|
| **bacpan** | **mẽ** | **muj<sup>h</sup>e** | **pālak** | **k<sup>h</sup>ānī** | **paRtī** | **t<sup>h</sup>ī.** |
| childhood | in | to me | spinach (f.) | eat-to | lay-present | was |

During childhood, I had (lit. used) to eat spinach.

## Exercise 6 🎧 (Audio 2:22)

If you have the recording, listen to the recorded passage. After the beep, answer each statement either by saying सच **sac** (true) or झूठ **j<sup>h</sup>ūT<sup>h</sup>** (false).

Now circle either सच **sac** (true) or झूठ **j<sup>h</sup>ūTh** (false) for each statement.

1 सोमवार को मैंने काम किया।
   somvār ko mɛ̃ ne kām kiyā.
                 स (सच)    झू (झूठ)
                 s (true)    j<sup>h</sup> (false)
2 मंगलवार को मैं अपने दोस्त से मिला।
   maŋgalvār ko mɛ̃ apne dostõ se milā.
                 स (सच)    झू (झूठ)
                 s (true)    j<sup>h</sup> (false)

3 बुधवार को घर से बाहर नहीं गया।

बुध<sup>h</sup>vār ko g<sup>h</sup>ar se bāhar nahĩ gayā.

स (सच) झू (झूठ)

s (true) j<sup>h</sup> (false)

4 गुरुवार को लन्दन में ही रहा।

guruvār ko Londan mẽ hī rahā.

स (सच) झू (झूठ)

s (true) j<sup>h</sup> (false)

5 शुक्रवार को मेरी तबीयत ठीक नहीं थी।

shukravār ko merī tabīyat T<sup>h</sup>īk nahĩ t<sup>h</sup>ī.

स (सच) झू (झूठ)

s (true) j<sup>h</sup> (false)

6 शनिवार को मैंने काम किया।

shanivār ko mẽne kām kiyā.

स (सच) झू (झूठ)

s (true) j<sup>h</sup> (false)

7 रविवार को मैंने आराम किया।

ravivār ko mẽne ārām kiyā.

स (सच) झू (झूठ)

s (true) j<sup>h</sup> (false)

# 8 मुझे चैक कैश करवाने हैं।
# mujʰe *cheque cash* karvāne hɛ̃

## I need to get cheques cashed

By the end of this unit you should be able to:

- understand causatives
- use the present participial forms
- understand more about compound verbs, subjunctives and obligatives
- understand about auxiliary verb deletion with negation
- use conditionals
- highlight contrast
- persuade someone
- advise and caution someone

## बातचीत　**bātcīt**　Dialogue 1 🎧 (Audio 2:23)

*कुछ परहेज़ कीजिये*　**kuc<sup>h</sup> parhez kījiye**　*Be careful what you eat*

*Finally, Dr Naim reaches John Ryder's house. It is about eleven o'clock at night. Indian doctors still make house calls!*

| | |
|---|---|
| जॉन: | आदाब अर्ज़, डाक्टर नाइम। |
| JOHN: | ādād arz, Dr Naim. |
| डॉक्टर: | आदाब, रायडर साहिब। इस बार कई साल के बाद मुलाकत हुई। |
| DR NAIM: | ādāb, Ryder sāhib. is bār kaī sāl ke bād mulākāt huī. |
| जॉन: | जी हाँ, कोई पाँच साल बाद। |
| JOHN: | jī hā̃, koī pā̃c sāl bād. |
| डॉक्टर: | तशरीफ़ रखिए . . . अच्छा, पहले बताइये, तबीयत कैसी है? |
| DR NAIM: | tashrīf rak<sup>h</sup>iye . . . acc<sup>h</sup>ā, pɛhle batāiye, tabīyat kɛsī hɛ? |
| जॉन: | तबीयत तो अच्छी नहीं, नहीं तो इतनी रात को आपको तकलीफ़ न देता। |
| JOHN: | tabīyat to acc<sup>h</sup>ī nahī̃, nahī̃ to itnī rāt ko āpko taklīf na detā. |
| डॉक्टर: | तकलीफ़ की बात क्या है? ये तो मेरा फ़र्ज़ है। ख़ैर बुख़ार कितना है? |
| DR NAIM: | taklīf kī bāt kyā hɛ? ye to merā farz hɛ. xɛr, buxār kitnā hɛ? |
| जॉन: | जब एक घंटे पहले मैंने थर्मामीटर लगाया, तो एक सौ दो डिग्री था अब शायद कुछ ज़्यादा हो। |
| JOHN: | jab ek g<sup>h</sup>anTe pɛhle mɛ̃ne *t<sup>h</sup>ermometer* lagāyā, to ek sau do *degree* t<sup>h</sup>ā ab shāyad kuc<sup>h</sup> zyādā ho. |
| डॉक्टर: | अच्छा, ज़रा फिर थर्मामीटर लगाइये। |
| DR NAIM: | acc<sup>h</sup>ā, zarā p<sup>h</sup>ir *t<sup>h</sup>ermometer* lagāiye. |

*(Dr Naim takes John's pulse and temperature)*

| | |
|---|---|
| डॉक्टर: | बुख़ार थोड़ा बढ़ गया है। दस्त भी हैं? |
| DR NAIM: | buxār t<sup>h</sup>oRā baR gayā hɛ. dast b<sup>h</sup>ī hɛ̃? |
| जॉन: | जी हाँ, दो घंटे में सात-आठ बार बाथरूम गया। |
| JOHN: | jī hā̃, do g<sup>h</sup>anTe mẽ sāt-āT<sup>h</sup> bār bathroom gayā. |
| डॉक्टर: | पिछली बार आपने बहुत समोसे खाये थे, और इस बार? |
| DR NAIM: | pic<sup>h</sup>lī bār āpne bahut samose k<sup>h</sup>āye t<sup>h</sup>e, aur is bār? |
| जॉन: | शाम को कुछ आम खाये। |
| JOHN: | shām ko kuc<sup>h</sup> ām k<sup>h</sup>āye. |
| डॉक्टर: | मेरी सलाह मानिये . . . एक–दो महीने तक आप कुछ परहेज़ कीजिये, समोसे और आम बन्द। मैं एक टीका लगाता हूँ और यह दवाई लीजिये। दो गोलियाँ हर दो घंटे। तो कल सुबह अपनी तबीयत के बारे में बताइये। अच्छा, अब आराम कीजिये। मैं आपके टेलिफ़ोन का इंतज़ार करूँगा। ख़ुदा हाफ़िज़। |

| | |
|---|---|
| DR NAIM: | merī salāh māniye . . . ek-do mahīne tak āp kuc$^h$ parhez kījiye, samose aur ām banda. mẽ ek Tīkā lagātā hū̃ aur ye davāī lījiye. do goliyā̃ har do g$^h$anTe. to kal subā apnī tabīyat ke bāre mẽ batāiye. acc$^h$ā ab ārām kījiye. mẽ āpke Telifon kā intzār karū̃gā. xudā hāfiz. |
| जॉन: | बहुत बहुत शुक्रिया, डाक्टर साहिब, ख़ुदा हाफ़िज़ । |
| JOHN: | bahut bahut shukriyā, Doctor sāhib, xudā hāfiz. |

| | |
|---|---|
| JOHN: | *Greetings, Dr Naim.* |
| DR NAIM: | *Greetings, Ryder sir, (we) meet again after several years.* |
| JOHN: | *Yes, after about five years.* |
| DR NAIM: | *Please be seated . . . OK. First, tell (me), how you are feeling?* (lit. how is (your) disposition?) |
| JOHN: | *As regards my disposition, I am not feeling well; otherwise I would not have bothered you so late at night.* |
| DR NAIM: | *Why talk about trouble. This is my duty. Well, how high is the fever?* |
| JOHN: | *An hour ago when I took my temperature, it was one hundred and two degrees. Now it might be slightly higher.* |
| DR NAIM: | *Okay, again (let's) take (your) temperature.* |
| (Dr Naim takes John's pulse and temperature) | |
| DR NAIM: | *The fever has increased slightly; (do you) have diarrhoea too?* |
| JOHN: | *Yes, (I) went to the bathroom about seven or eight times in the past two hours.* |
| DR NAIM: | *The last time you ate many samosas and this time?* |
| JOHN: | *In the evening (I) ate some mangoes.* |
| DR NAIM: | *Please take my advice. For about one or two months exercise some caution* (lit. do some abstinence). *No more samosas and mangoes* (lit. samosas and mangoes closed). *I (will) give you an injection and (you) take this medicine Two pills every two hours. Then tell me tomorrow morning how you feel. I will wait for your call. Okay. Now get some rest. Goodbye.* |
| JOHN: | *Many many thanks, doctor. Goodbye.* |

## शब्दावली  shabdāvalī  Vocabulary

| आदाब | **ādāb** (m.) | salutation, greetings |
|---|---|---|
| अर्ज़ | **arz** (f.) | request |
| इस बार | **is bār** | this time |
| साल | **sāl** (m.) | year |

| के बाद | ke bād | after |
|---|---|---|
| मुलाकात | mulākāt (f.) | meeting |
| मुलाकात होना | mulākāt honā (–ne) | to meet |
| तशरीफ़ | tashrīf (f.) | (a term signifying respect) |
| तशरीफ़ रखना | tashrīf rakʰnā (+ne) | to be seated |
| तशरीफ़ लाना | tashrīf lānā (–ne) | to grace one's place, welcome, come |
| पहले | pɛhle | first |
| इतना | itnā (m. adj.) | so much/many, this much/many |
| रात | rāt (f.) | night |
| तकलीफ | taklīf (f.) | trouble, bother |
| तकलीफ़ देना | taklīf denā (+ne) | to bother |
| फ़र्ज़ | farz (m.) | duty |
| लगाना | lagānā (+ne) | to fix, apply |
| शायद | shāyad | perhaps |
| बढ़ना | baRʰnā (–ne) | to increase, advance |
| दस्त | dasta (m.) | diarrhoea |
| आम | ām | mango; as adj. common, general |
| सलाह | salāh (f.) | advice |
| सलाह मानना | salāh mānnā (+ne) | to accept/take advice |
| सलाह लेना | salāh lenā (+ne) | to seek/take advice |
| महीना | mahīnā (m.) | month |
| परहेज़ | parhez (m.) | abstinence |
| x से परहेज़ करना | x se parhez karnā (+ne) | to abstain, avoid |
| बन्द | banda | to be closed |
| बन्द करना | banda karnā (+ne) | closed |
| बन्द होना | banda honā (–ne) | to close |
| टीका लगाना | Tīkā lagānā (+ne) | to give an injection/a shot |
| दवाई/दवा | davāī/davā (f.) | medicine |
| गोली | golī (f.) | tablet, pill; bullet |
| इंतज़ार | intzār (m./f.) | wait |
| x (का/की) इंतज़ार करना | x (kā/kī) intzār karnā (+ne) | to wait for x |
| आराम | ārām (m.) | comfort, rest |
| आराम करना | ārām karnā (+ne) | to rest |
| ख़ुदा हाफ़िज़ | xudā hāfiz | goodbye |

## *Notes*

### 'We meet again after several years'

Another way of saying 'we meet again after several years' in Hindi is
something like 'our meeting took place after several years'.

| कई | साल | (के) बाद | हमारी | मुलाकात | हुई । |
|---|---|---|---|---|---|
| **kaī** | **sāl** | **(ke) bād** | **hamārī** | **mulākāt** | **huī.** |
| several | years | after | our | meeting (f.) | happened. |

### The politeness bug

Note the use of तशरीफ़ रखिए **tashrīf rak<sup>h</sup>iye** instead of बैठिए **bɛT<sup>h</sup>iye**
'please sit'. As in English, when receiving a guest, we will usually say
'Please have a seat', or 'Please be seated', rather than 'please sit'.
Similarly, it is more polite and much friendlier to use तशरीफ़ रखिए
**tashrīf rak<sup>h</sup>iye** than बैठिए **bɛT<sup>h</sup>iye**, particularly if the listener is a
Muslim. In English if the verb 'sit' is used, it is modified in some
form, e.g. 'Please sit down for a while'; the same is true of the Hindi
verb बैठ **bɛT<sup>h</sup>** 'sit'. If it is used, it needs to precede the polite form of
the verb आ **ā** 'to come' (e.g. आइए, बैठिए **āiye, bɛT<sup>h</sup>iye** 'Please come
(and) sit') or be followed by a question tag (e.g. बैठिए न **bɛT<sup>h</sup>iye na**
'Please sit down, won't you?').

### x का इंतज़ार करना  'To wait for x'

The Hindi equivalent of the English 'I was waiting for you' turns
out to be

| मैं | आपका | इंतज़ार | कर | रहा | था । |
|---|---|---|---|---|---|
| **mɛ̃** | **āpkā** | **intzār** | **kar** | **rahā** | **t<sup>h</sup>ā.** |
| I | your | wait (m.) | do | ing | was |

i.e. I was doing your wait

### The conditional: counter-factive

The Hindi sentence in our dialogue is as follows:

| इतनी | रात | को | मैं | आपको | तकलीफ़ | न | देता । |
|---|---|---|---|---|---|---|---|
| **itnī** | **rāt** | **ko** | **mɛ̃** | **āp-ko** | **taklīf** | **na** | **detā.** |
| so much | night | at | I | you-to | bother | not | give-would have |

The previous sentence is a part of the 'if' clause which is implied.

| अगर | तबीयत | ठीक | होती | तो ... |
|------|---------|------|------|--------|
| **agar** | **tabīyat** | **Tʰīk** | **hotī** | **to** ... |
| if | disposition | fine | were | then ... |

If my condition were fine ...

Note that the simple present form without the auxiliary verb is used in such counter-factive sentences. The 'if' clause implies that the condition has not been fulfilled; therefore, the action expressed by the 'then' clause did not take place. Consider another example of counter-factives:

| अगर | वह | आता | तो | मैं | जाता। |
|------|------|------|------|------|--------|
| **agar** | **vo** | **ātā,** | **to** | **mɛ̃** | **jātā** |
| if | he | come-pres. | then | I | go-pres. |

If he had come, I would have come.

| अगर | वह | किताबें | लिखती | तो | हम | बहुत | खुश | होते। |
|------|------|----------|--------|------|------|-------|------|--------|
| **agar** | **vo** | **kitābɛ̃** | **likʰtī,** | **to** | **ham** | **bahut** | **xush** | **hote.** |
| if | she | books | write-present | then | we | very | happy | be-pres. |

Had she written books, we would have been very happy.

Thus, the English verb forms such as 'had come' and 'would have gone' are translated, not as a past tense form, but with the present imperfective without an auxiliary verb.

## Formulaic expression

The Hindi expression

| तकलीफ | की | बात | क्या | है? |
|--------|------|------|------|------|
| **taklīf** | **kī** | **bāt** | **kyā** | **hɛ** |
| bother | of | matter | what | is |

is not a question sentence. It is equivalent to the English expressions 'do not bother' and 'do not mention'. Thus, the Hindi question word क्या **kyā** is like 'not' in the expression in question. The verb form is always in the simple present rather than in the imperative form as in English.

## Negative particle: न na

We have already come across नहीं **nahī̃** 'not'. Another Hindi negative particle is न **na**, which occurs in constructions such as 'neither . . . nor', counter-factives and polite imperatives. (See the Grammar section for more details.)

## The subjunctive

| अब | बुखार | कुछ | ज्यादा | हो। |
|------|-----------|-----------|--------|------------------|
| **ab** | **buxār** | **kuc**ʰ | **zyādā** | **ho** |
| now | fever (m.s.) | some | more | be-subjunctive |

The fever might be slightly more.

Since the context is the probable increase in fever, the Hindi verb 'to be' is in the subjunctive form. The verb agrees with बुखार **buxār** 'fever'. Although the verb हो **ho** might appear to be in the simple present tense form, it is not because तुम **tum** is not the subject in the above sentence.

## Compound verb with the helping verb: जाना jānā

In the expression

| बुखार | थोड़ा | बढ़ | गया | है। |
|----------|----------|-----------|--------|------|
| **buxār** | **t**ʰ**oRā** | **baR**ʰ | **gayā** | **hε** |
| fever | little | increase | went | is |

The fever has shot up a little.

the compound verb बढ़ जाना **baR**ʰ **jānā** is employed for the reasons explained in the previous unit.

## मेरी सलाह मानिये   meri salāh māniye   'Accept my advice'

Hindi paraphrases the English expression 'Take my advice' as 'Accept my advice'.

| मेरी | सलाह | मानिये। |
|--------|----------|-------------------|
| **merī** | **salāh** | **māniye.** |
| my | advice (f.) | accept-imperative |

Please accept my advice.

The substitution of the verb लेना **lenā** 'take' produces an odd sentence in Hindi.

## बातचीत **bātcīt**  Dialogue 2  🎧 (Audio 2:25)

### दिल्ली में गुम जाना  *dillī mẽ gum jānā*   *Lost in Delhi*

*Philip Rosenberg is lost in downtown Delhi. He knows that somewhere in the vicinity there is an American Express office where he could cash some traveller's cheques. In fact, he visited that office just two days ago. He does not remember its address either. He inquires from a stranger about its location:*

फ़िलिप: यहाँ पास कोई अमरीकन ऐक्सप्रेस का दफ़्तर है। मैं दो दिन पहले वहाँ गया था, लेकिन आज नहीं मिल रहा।

PHILIP: yahā̃ pās koī *American Express* kā daftar hɛ. mɛ̃ do din pɛhele vahā̃ gayā tʰā, lekin āj nahī̃ mil rahā.

अजनबी: आपको पता मालूम है?

STRANGER: āpko patā mālūm hɛ?

फ़िलिप: मैं पता तो भूल गया।

PHILIP: mɛ̃ patā to bʰūl gayā.

अजनबी: मेरे ख़्याल से अगली सड़क पर अमरीकन ऐक्सप्रेस का दफ़्तर है।

STRANGER: mere xyāl se aglī saRak par *Amercian Express* kā daftar hɛ.

*(pointing to the street)*

फ़िलिप: *(seemingly puzzled)* वह सड़क तो सुन्दर है, लोग उसे अगली सड़क क्यों कहते हैं?

PHILIP: *(seemingly puzzled)* vo saRak to sundar hɛ, log use aglī saRak kyõ kɛhte hɛ̃?

अजनबी: अगली हिन्दी का शब्द है अंगेज़ी का नहीं। 'अगली' का मतलब अंगेज़ी में 'next' है।

STRANGER: aglī hindī kā shadba hɛ angrezī kā nahī̃. 'aglī' kā matlab angrezī mẽ 'next' hɛ.

फ़िलिप: बहुत ख़ूब।

PHILIP: bahut xūb.

*(Philip goes to the cashier's window at the American Express office)*

फ़िलिप: मुझे कुछ ट्रैवलरज़ चैक कैश करवाने हैं।

PHILIP: mujʰe kucʰ *traveller's cheque cash* karvāne hɛ̃.

कैशियर: कौन-सी करन्सी में हैं?

CASHIER: kaun sī *currency* mẽ hɛ̃?

| फ़िलिप: | अमेरिकन डालर। ऐक्सचेंज रेट क्या है? |
|---|---|
| PHILIP: | amrīkan *dollars. Exchange rate* kyā hɛ? |
| कैशियर: | एक अमेरिकन डालर चालीस रूपये का है। |
| CASHIER: | ek amrīkan dollar cālīs rupaye kā hɛ. |

*(Philip signs the cheques and the cashier gives him the equivalent amount in rupees)*

| कैशियर: | कुल दो सौ डालर्ज़। ये रहे आप के आठ हज़ार रूपये। गिन लीजिये। |
|---|---|
| CASHIER: | kul do sau *dollars*. ye rahe āpke āT<sup>h</sup> hazār rupaye. gin lījiye. |
| फ़िलिप: | ठीक है। धन्यवाद। |
| PHILIP: | T<sup>h</sup>īk hɛ. d<sup>h</sup>anyavād. |

| PHILIP: | *(There) is an American Express office nearby. Two days ago I went there. But today I cannot find (it).* |
|---|---|
| STRANGER: | *Do you know the address?* |
| PHILIP: | *I forgot the address.* |
| STRANGER: | *I think the American Express office is on the next* (i.e. **aglī**) *street.* |
| | (pointing to the street) |
| PHILIP: | (Seemingly puzzled) *That street is a beautiful one. Why do people call it 'ugly'?* |
| STRANGER: | *'aglī' is a Hindi word, not English. In English the meaning of 'aglī' is 'next'.* |
| PHILIP: | *(That's) great!* |

(Philip goes to the cashier's window at the American Express office)

| PHILIP: | *I need to get some traveller's cheques cashed.* |
|---|---|
| CASHIER: | *In which currency are they?* |
| PHILIP: | *In American dollars. What is the exchange rate?* |
| CASHIER: | *One American dollar to forty rupees.* |

(Philip signs the cheques and the cashier gives him the equivalent amount in rupees.)

| CASHIER: | *A total of two hundred dollars. Here are your eight thousand rupees. Please count it (for your own sake).* |
|---|---|
| PHILIP: | *That's fine* (lit. they are fine). *Thanks.* |

## शब्दावली  shabdāvalī  Vocabulary

| दफ़्तर | **daftar** (m.) | office |
|---|---|---|
| मिलना | **milnā** (+ko) | to find, to receive |
| अगला | **aglā** (m. adj.) | next |
| शब्द | **shabda** (m.) | word |

| अंग्रेज़ी | **angrezī** (f.) | the English language |
|---|---|---|
| अंग्रेज़ | **angrez** (m.) | an English man |
| मतलब | **matlab** (m.) | meaning |
| बहुत ख़ूब | **bahut xūb** | great! splendid! |
| कैश करना | *cash* **karnā** (+ne) | to cash |
| कैश करवाना | *cash* **karvānā** | to get someone to cash (+ne) |
| कुल | **kul** | total |
| सौ | **sau** | hundred |
| रहना | **<rɛhnā>** | to live |
| रहे | **rahe** | lived, are |
| हज़ार | **hazār** | thousand |
| गिनना | **ginnā** (+ne) | to count |
| गिन लेना | **gin lenā** (+ne) | to count (for one's benefit) |
| धन्यवाद | **dʰanyavād** | thanks |

## Notes

### नहीं मिल रहा **milnā** 'I cannot find it'

In the preceding units we came across three important usages of the verb मिलना **milnā** – namely 'to meet', 'to run into' and 'to be available'. Now observe another use of this verb in the following sentence from the dialogue. Also, note its word-for-word translation.

| लेकिन | आज | नहीं | मिल | रहा। |
|---|---|---|---|---|
| **lekin** | **āj** | **nahī̃** | **mil** | **rahā.** |
| but | today | not | find | ing |

But today (I) cannot find (it). (lit. but today I am not finding it)

When the verb मिलना **milnā** is used to express the meaning 'find', it takes the experiencer subject. If we insert the implied subject in the above sentence, the form of the Hindi subject will not be the nominative मैं **mɛ̃**, but the experiential subject मुझको **mujʰko** or मुझे **mujʰe**.

| लेकिन | आज | मुझे | दफ्तर | नहीं | मिल | रहा। |
|---|---|---|---|---|---|---|
| **lekin** | **āj** | **mujhe** | **daftar** (m.) | **nahī̃** | **mil** | **rahā.** |

Note that the verb does not agree with the subject. Instead it agrees with an object, which is दफ्तर **daftar** 'office' in the above sentence. The gender of दफ्तर **daftar** is masculine. Did you notice the missing element of the verb phrase?

## Negation and auxiliary verb deletion

Notice the missing element of the verb in the above sentence.

लेकिन आज मुझे दफ्तर नहीं मिल रहा है।
**lekin āj muj^he daftar nahī̃ mil rahā hɛ.**

The auxiliary verb है **hɛ** can be optionally deleted in negative sentences. Only the auxiliary verbs of the simple present and present progressive tenses are subject to this optional deletion. Note some examples:

| Positive sentences | Negative sentences |
|---|---|
| मैं जाता हूँ। **mɛ̃ jātā hū̃** I go | मैं नहीं जाता हूँ। **mɛ̃ nahī̃ jātā hū̃** I do not go |
| | मैं नहीं जाता। **mɛ̃ nahī̃ jātā** I do not go |
| मैं जा रहा हूँ। **mɛ̃ jā rahā hū̃** I am going | मैं नहीं जा रहा हूँ। **mɛ̃ nahī̃ jā rahā hū̃** I am not going |
| | मैं नहीं जा रहा। **mɛ̃ nahī̃ jā rahā** I am not going |
| तुम जाती हो। **tum jātī ho** you (f.) go | तुम नहीं जाती हो। **tum nahī̃ jātī ho** you (f.) do not go |
| | तुम नहीं जाती। **tum nahī̃ jātī** you (f.) do not go |
| तुम जा रही हो। **tum jā rahī ho** you (f.) are going | तुम नहीं जा रही हो। **tum nahī̃ jā rahī ho** you (f.) are not going |
| | तुम नहीं जा रही। **tum nahī̃ jā rahī** you (f.) are not going |

## Causative verbs

We came across the following related verbs in our earlier dialogues. Note the slight change in form and meaning.

| Verb | Causative-I | Causative-II |
|---|---|---|
| पढ़ **paR^h** study, read | पढ़ा **paR^hā** teach | पढ़वा **paR^hvā** have someone teach |
| कर **kar** do | —— | करवा **karvā** have someone do |
| लग **lag** seem | लगा **lagā** attach | लगवा **lagvā** cause to be attached |

You might already have observed the same base stem in the three verb forms. For the time being, we will omit the more intricate details of verb forms – such as the presence of the two verbs of करना **karnā** but three forms of the other two verbs – and proceed to the fundamental points. At first glance it becomes clear that the verb forms in columns two and three share the verb stem in column one, adding either the suffix आ **ā** or वा **vā** as in

| पढ़ | + | आ | = | पढ़ा | |
|------|---|----|---|--------|---|
| paR$^h$ | + | ā | = | paR$^h$ā | cause someone to read, teach |
| पढ़ | + | वा | = | पढ़वा | |
| paR$^h$ | + | vā | = | paR$^h$vā | to have x to teach y |

The two suffixes आ -**ā** and वा -**vā** form the causative verbs. The meaning they express can be translated as follows: आ -**ā** expresses 'make someone do something', whereas वा -**vā** means 'have x make y do something'. The English verb 'teach' is a causative verb in Hindi, but in most cases the causative verbs cannot be translated into English that easily. Note the following examples:

| में | कहानी | पढ़ता | हूँ। |
|------|---------|---------|------|
| **mẽ** | **kahānī** | **paR$^h$tā** | **hū̃.** |
| I | story | read-pres. | am |

I read a story.

| में | जॉन | को | कहानी | पढ़ाता | हूँ। |
|------|------|-----|---------|----------|------|
| **mẽ** | **John** | **ko** | **kahānī** | **paR$^h$ātā** | **hū̃** |
| I | John | to | story | read-caus. ā-pres. | am |

I make John read a story *or* I teach John a story

| में | जॉन | को | राम | से | कहानी | पढ़वाता | हूँ। |
|------|------|-----|------|-----|---------|-----------|------|
| **mẽ** | **John** | **ko** | **Rām** | **se** | **kahānī** | **paR$^h$vātā** | **hū̃** |
| I | John | to | Ram | by | story | read-caus. vā-pres. | am |

I have Ram make John read a story.

Notice that the causative verbs with वा -**vā** always have an indirect agent (e.g. राम से **Ram se** 'by Ram'). Did you notice the use of the causative verb in our dialogue? The following sentence contains a causative verb.

| मुझे | कुछ | ट्रैवलस | चैक्स | कैश | करवाने | हैं। |
|-------|------|-----------|--------|------|----------|------|
| **muj$^h$e** | **kuc$^h$** | *traveller's* | *cheques* | *cash* | **karvāne** | **hẽ.** |
| me | some | traveller's | cheques | cash | do-caus.vā-inf. | are |

I need to (have someone) get some traveller's cheques cashed.

In this sentence the indirect agent (by someone) is implied because of the causative verb with the suffix वा **-vā**.

## लेना **lenā as a helping verb**

When the cashier hands over the rupees to Philip, he says

| गिन | लीजिये |
|---|---|
| **gin** | **lījiye** |
| count | take-imp. |

Please (you) count (for your own benefit).

Had he used the simple verb form instead of the compound verb (i.e. गिनिए **giniye**), the beneficiary of the action of counting would have remained unspecified. The helping verb ले **le** indicates the subject as the beneficiary.

# पढ़ने का अभ्यास ९ **paRʰne kā abʰyās 1** Reading practice 1 (Audio 2:27)

## एक लोक-कथा *ek lok-katʰā A folk tale*

1 एक गाँव में चोर जेल से भाग गया।
   ek gā̃v mẽ ek cor jail se bʰāg gayā.
2 पुलिस वाला उसको पकड़ने के लिये दौड़ा।
   pulis (police) vālā usko pakaRne ke liye dauRā.
3 इतने में गाँव वालों ने भागते चोर को पकड़ लिया।
   itne mẽ gā̃v vālõ ne bʰāgte cor ko pakaR liyā.
4 पुलिस वाला ज़ोर ज़ोर से चिल्ला रहा था, 'पकड़ो, मत जाने दो।'
   pulis vālā zor zor se cillā rahā tʰā, 'pakRo, mat jāne do'.
5 ये सुनते ही गाँव वालों ने चोर को छोड़ दिया।
   ye sunte hī gā̃v vālõ ne cor ko cʰoR diyā.
6 जब पुलिस वाला गाँव वालों के पास पहुँचा।
   jab pulis vālā gā̃v vālõ ke pās pahũcā.
7 तो उसको बहुत गुस्सा आया।
   to usko bahut gussā āyā.
8 गुस्से में उसने गाँव वालों से पूछा।
   gusse mẽ usne gā̃v vālõ se pūcʰā,
9 'तुमने चोर को क्यों छोड़ दिया?'
   'tumne cor ko kyõ cʰoR diyā'
10 गाँव वालों ने जवाब दिया,
   gā̃v vālõ ne javāb diyā,

11 आपने ही कहा 'पकड़ो मत, जाने दो।'
   āpne hī kahā, 'pakRo mat, jāne do'.

1 *In a* (lit. one) *village, a thief ran away* (i.e. escaped) *from jail.*
2 *A policeman ran to catch him.* (lit. ran for catching)
3 *In the meanwhile the villagers caught the escaping* (lit. running)
   *thief.*
4 *The policeman was screaming very loudly, 'catch (him), do not let*
   *(him) go'.*
5 *As soon as the villagers heard this, they left the thief.*
6 *When the policeman reached the villagers* (lit. reached near the
   villagers)
7 *he became very angry.*
8 *Angrily* (lit. in anger) *he asked the villagers* (lit. asked from the
   villagers)
9 *'Why did you leave the thief?'* (i.e. why did you let the thief go?)
10 *The villagers answered.*
11 *You yourself said, 'Don't catch (him); let (him) go.'*

शब्दावली  **shabdāvalī   Vocabulary**

| लोक | **lok** | people |
|---|---|---|
| कथा | **katʰā** (f.) | story |
| लोक-कथा | **lok-katʰā** (f.) | folk tale |
| गाँव | **gāv** (m.) | village |
| भागना | **bʰāgnā** (–ne) | to run |
| भाग गया | **bʰāg gayā** (compound verb) | to run away |
| पुलिस वाला | **pulis vālā** (m.) | policeman |
| पकड़ना | **pakaRnā** (+ne) | to catch |
| दौड़ना | **dauRnā** (–ne) | to run |
| इतने में | **itne mẽ** | in the meanwhile |
| गाँव वाला | **gāv vālā** (m.) | villager |
| भागते | **bʰāgte** (present participle) | running |
| चोर | **cor** (m.) | thief |
| पकड़ना | **pakaRnā** (+ne) | to catch |
| पकड़ लिया | **pakaR liyā** (compound verb) | to catch (for one's benefit) |
| ज़ोर से | **zor se** | loudly |
| चिल्लाना | **cillānā** (–ne) | to scream |
| मत | **mat** | not (see notes) |
| जाने दो | **jāne do** (compound verb) | let (someone) go |
| सुनते ही | **sunte hī** (sun + te hī participle) | as soon as (someone) heard |
| छोड़ना | **cʰoRnā** (+ne) | to leave |

| | | |
|---|---|---|
| छोड़ दिया | c<sup>h</sup>oR diyā (compound verb) | left (for someone else's sake) |
| गुस्सा | gussā (m.) | anger |
| पूछना | pūc<sup>h</sup>nā (–ne) | to ask |
| जवाब | javāb (m.) | answer |
| जवाब देना | javāb denā (+ne) | to answer, to reply |

## Pronunciation

Compare the pronunciation of the stem पकड़ **pakaR** 'catch' in the following three verbal forms. Note the presence of the stem-final vowel अ **a** in the first two forms and its absence in the third form, which is written as पकड़ो **pakaRo** but is pronounced as पक्ड़ो **pakRo**. For further details about when the vowel अ **a** is retained and under what conditions it is dropped, see Script Unit 4 in this book.

| | | |
|---|---|---|
| **pakaRne ke liye** | पकड़ने के लिये | in order to catch |
| **pakaR liyā** | पकड़ लिया | caught (for their own benefit) |
| **pakRo** | पकड़ो | catch! |

## Notes

### Present participle

In the third line we came across the expression

| इतने | | में | गाँव | वालों | ने | भागते | चोर | को |
|---|---|---|---|---|---|---|---|---|
| **itne** | | **mẽ** | **gā̃v** | **vālõ** | **ne** | **b<sup>h</sup>āgte** | **cor** | **ko** |
| this much | | in | village-er | (agent) | | running | thief | to |
| पकड़ | लिया | | | | | | | |
| **pakaR** | **liyā.** | | | | | | | |
| catch | took | | | | | | | |

In the meantime (lit. in this much (time)), the villagers caught the thief.

The phrase **b<sup>h</sup>āgte cor ko** भागते चोर को is in the oblique form of the simple present participial phrase.

| भागता | (हुआ) | चोर |
|---|---|---|
| **b<sup>h</sup>āgtā** | **(huā)** | **cor** |
| run + present participle | happened | thief (m. sg.) |

The running thief *or* The thief who is/was/will be running.

The composition of the first element is as follows:

| भाग | + | त | + | ा |
|------|---|---------|---|------------------|
| bʰāg | + | t | + | ā |
| run | + | present | + | masculine singular |

You have probably guessed by now that this is the same form that we came across in the formation of the simple present tense. The only difference is that the auxiliary verb is absent.

The second element is the same form as the simple past tense form of the verb होना **honā**. Recall the forms हुआ **huā**, हुए **hue**, हुई **huī** and हुईं **huī̃**. The last form (i.e. the feminine plural हुईं **huī̃**) does not appear in the participial construction. Why? The reason is clarified by the explanation that this element is optional and it acts as an adjective. So it can easily be omitted in conversation. That is the case in our story.

Now compare the participial form with the present tense verb form.

| *Present participle* | *Simple present tense* |
|---|---|
| भागता  चोर | चोर  भागता  है |
| bʰāgtā  cor | cor  bʰāgtā  hɛ |
| The running thief. | The thief runs. |

In the present participial form the verb form ceases to function like a real verb and begins to behave like an adjective. Therefore, the verbal adjectives which are drawn from the simple present tense are called 'present participles'. In other words, they are like adjectives ending in आ -ā (i.e. participial adjective), the only difference being that they are derived from verbs.

Like the adjectives ending in आ -ā, these agree in number or gender with the following noun. For example:

| भागता | लड़का | bʰāgtā | laRkā | the running boy |
|---|---|---|---|---|
| भागती | लड़की | bʰāgtī | laRkī | the running girl |
| भागते | लड़के | bʰāgte | laRke | the running boys |
| भागती | लड़कियाँ | bʰāgtī | laRkiyā̃ | the running girls |

The main function of the present participial clause is to denote '*action in progress*'.

Note that, like adjectives, present participles do not have any inherent tense reference to time, as is clear from the English translation. The tense is usually supplied by the main verb form in the sentence. If in the third line the verb 'caught' is changed to the present or the future tense, the tense reference of the participial form 'running' will change to the present or the future correspondingly. That is why the alternative English translation of भागता चोर **bʰāgtā cor** contains three possible tense references.

## Ambiguity and pausing

| पकड़ो | मत | जाने | | दो। |
|-------|-----|------|---|-----|
| **pakRo** | **mat** | **jāne** | | **do** |
| catch | not | go-oblique infinitive | | give |

The translation of the verb phrase जाने दो **jāne do** is 'to allow to go' or 'to let go'. The familiar imperative form of the verb पकड़ना **pakaRnā** is पकड़ो **pakRo**, which means 'catch'. Depending upon the pause, the meaning changes. The pause is indicated by the comma.

| पकड़ो | मत, | जाने | | दो। |
|-------|------|------|---|-----|
| **pakRo** | **mat,** | **jāne** | | **do** |
| catch | not, | go-oblique infinitive | give | |

Don't catch (him); let (him) go.

But the pause is immediately after पकड़ो **pakRo**; then the negative particle मत **mat** negates the second verb, as in

| पकड़ो, | मत | जाने | | दो। |
|--------|-----|------|---|-----|
| **pakRo,** | **mat** | **jāne** | | **do.** |
| catch, | not | go-oblique infinitive | give | |

Catch, don't let (him) go.

## The negative particle मत **mat**

We encountered two negative particles – नहीं **nahī̃** and न **na** – in the earlier conversation. The third negative marker मत **mat** is primarily restricted to familiar and non-honorific imperatives. In prohibitives, the use of मत **mat** is particularly noteworthy.

## Word order and contrastive negation

We mentioned earlier that the negative particle is usually placed before the verb. So usually the Hindi equivalent of the English 'Do not catch' is

मत  पकड़ो ।
**mat  pakRo**
not  catch-imperative (familiar)
Don't catch.

However, the contrastive function is highlighted by the placement
of the negative particle in the postverbal position (i.e. after the
verb). This is the reason that मत **mat** is placed after पकड़ो **pakRo** in
the expression

पकड़ो    मत, जाने दो।
**pakRo    mat, jāne do**
Don't catch (him); let (him) go.

The other reading, 'Catch, do not let (him) go,' has conjunctive
rather than contrastive force. Therefore the negative particle
appears in its normal preverbal position.

## पढ़ने का अभ्यास २  **paR**ʰ**ne kā ab**ʰ**yās 2**
## Reading practice 2

### गाना  *gānā  Song*

*Here is a sample of the opening lines of an old Hindi romantic song. In
the song, the lover is imploring his beloved never to forget him. However, the approach is an indirect one (remember the politeness bug!).
Therefore, rather than asking directly not to forget him, he says:*

ये रातें, ये मौसम, ये हँसना, हँसाना
**ye rātē, ye mausam, ye hāsnā, hāsānā**
मुझे भूल जाना, इन्हें न भुलाना
**muj**ʰ**e b**ʰ**ūl jānā, inhē na b**ʰ**ulānā.**

These nights, this weather, this laughter and making (each
other) laugh,
(You may) forget me, but never make them forget.

### शब्दावली  **shabdāvalī  Vocabulary**

| | | |
|---|---|---|
| रात | **rāt** (f.) | night |
| मौसम | **mausam** (m.) | weather |

| हँसना | hãsnā (–ne) | to laugh |
| हँसाना | hãsānā (+ne) | to make someone laugh |
| भूलना | bʰūl (–ne) | to forget |
| भूल जाना | bʰūl jānā (compound verb) | to forget fully |
| भुलाना | bʰulānā (+ne) | to make someone forget |

## अभ्यास  abʰyās  Exercises

### Exercise 1

Match the words or phrases given in the following three columns to make appropriate Hindi sentences.

| आइये | की बात क्या | रखिए |
| तकलीफ | तशरीफ | है |
| शायद | आपका इंतजार | काम ज्यादा हो |
| वो | अर्ज | है |
| आदाब | आपको दफ़्तर में | कर रही थी |

| āiye | kī bāt kyā | rakʰiye |
| taklīf | tashrīf | hɛ |
| shāyad | āpkā intazār | kām zyādā ho |
| vo | arz | hɛ |
| ādāb | āpko dafter mẽ | kar rahī tʰī. |

### Exercise 2

Circle the appropriate form of the verb in each of the following sentences:

1  माफ कीजिये, मैं चैक भेजना (भूल लिया/भूल गया/भूल दिया)
   māf kījiye, mẽ cheque bʰejnā (bʰūl liyā/bʰūl gayā/bʰūl diyā).
2  मैंने खाना (खा लिया/खा पड़ा/खा दिया)
   mẽne kʰānā (kʰā liyā/kʰā paRā/kʰā diyā).
3  आपका बुखार (बढ़ लिया/बढ़ गया/बढ़ दिया)
   āpkā buxār (baRʰ liyā/baRh gayā/baRʰ diyā).
4  आपने कुछ ज़वाब नहीं (लिया/दिया/आया/गया)
   āpne kucʰ javāb nahī̃ (liyā/diyā/āyā/gayā).
5  आप मेरी सलाह मान (लीजिये/दीजिये/आइये)
   āp merī salāh mān (lījiye/dījiye/āiye).

## Exercise 3

Which job description matches the job?

| | | | |
|---|---|---|---|
| 1 | अध्यापक | इमारतें बनवाता है। | |
| | adʰyāpak | imāratẽ banvātā hɛ. | |
| 2 | डॉक्टर | कपड़े बनाता है। | |
| | DākTar (doctor) | kapRe banātā hɛ. | |
| 3 | कैशियर | खाना बनाता है। | |
| | cashier | kʰānā banātā hɛ. | |
| 4 | दर्जी | टीका लगाता है। | |
| | darzī 'tailor' | Tīkā lagātā hɛ. | |
| 5 | खानसामा | चैक कैश करता है। | |
| | kʰānsāmā 'cook' | *cheque cash* kartā hɛ. | |
| 6 | ड्राइवर | छात्रों को पढ़ाता है। | |
| | driver | cʰātrõ ko paRʰātā hɛ. | |
| 7 | सिविल इन्जीनियर | कार चलाता है। | |
| | civil engineer | kār calātā hɛ. | |

## Exercise 4

Ram and Shyam are brothers. Ram believes in self-help and does everything on his own. Shyam, on the other hand, gets someone to do his work. Write about Shyam according to the model given below:

राम ने अपना काम किया।
**rām ne apanā kām kiyā.**
Ram did his work.

शाम ने हिलडा से अपना काम करवाया।
**shyām ne hildā se apnā kām karvāyā.**
Shyam had Hildā do his work.

1 राम:    राम ने अपनी कार चलाई।
  श्याम:   _____
  Ram:   rām ne apnī kār calāī.
  Shyam: _____

2 राम:    राम अपना खत लिखेगा।
  श्याम:   _____
  Ram:   rām apnā xat likʰegā.
  Shyam: _____

3 राम: राम अपना घर बना रहा है।
  श्याम: _____
  Ram: rām apnā gʰar banā rahā hɛ.
  Shyam: _____

4 राम: राम अपनी कहानी सुना रहा था।
  श्याम: _____
  Ram: rām apnī kahānī sunā rahā tʰā.
  Shyam: _____

5 राम: राम अपनी लड़की को पढ़ाता है।
  श्याम: _____
  Ram: rām apnī laRkī ko paRʰātā hɛ.
  Shyam: _____

## Exercise 5

Fill out the appropriate present participial form according to the model given below:

| चलना: | मैं | चलती | गाड़ी | में | चढ़ा। |
|---|---|---|---|---|---|
| calnā: | mɛ̃ | caltī | gāRʰī | mẽ | caRʰā. |

| भागना: | मैंने | भागते | कुत्ते | को | देखा। |
|---|---|---|---|---|---|
| bʰāgnā: | mɛ̃ne | bʰāgte | kutte | ko | dekʰā. |

1 हँसना: मुझे वो —————— लड़की बहुत पसन्द है।
2 खेलना: —————— बच्चे बहुत सुन्दर लग रहे थे।
3 गाना: —————— चिड़िया उड़ रही थी।
4 सितार बजाना: —————— आदमी बहुत अच्छा है।
5 तैरना: —————— मछलियों को देखो।
6 रोना: डॉक्टर ने —————— बच्चे को टीका लगाया।

1 hāsnā: mujʰe vo _____ laRkī bahut pasand hɛ.
2 kʰelnā: _____ bacce bahut sundar lag rahe tʰe.
3 gānā: _____ ciRiyā uR rahī tʰī.
4 sitār bajānā: _____ ādmī bahut accʰā hɛ.
5 tɛrnā: _____ macʰaliyõ ko dekʰo.
6 ronā: DākTar ne _____ bacce ko Tīkā lagāyā.

## Exercise 6

Pac-Man has attacked the following text and, some elements have
been chewed up. Your task is to supply the postpositions or the
missing parts of the verb in those places where Pac-Man has left
three bullets behind.

मैं रेलवे स्टेशन पर अपने दोस्त • • • इंतज़ार कर रहा था। थोड़ी देर बाद गाड़ी आयी
और मेरा दोस्त गाड़ी से उतरा। हम बहुत खुश हो कर मिले। इस बार पाँच साल के बाद
हमारी मुलाकात • • •। थोड़ी देर बाद मैंने कहा, 'इस बार बहुत देर के बाद यहाँ आये
हो'। उसने जवाब • • •, अच्छी बात थी कि अगर गाड़ी देर से न • • •, तो मैं आज भी
न • • •।

mẽ *railway station* par apne dost • • • intzār kar rahā tʰā. tʰoRī
der bād gāRī āyī aur merā dost gāRī se utrā. ham bahut xush
ho kar mile. is bār pā̃c sāl ke bād hamārī mulākāt • • •. tʰoRī
der bād mẽne kahā, 'is bār bahut der ke bād yahā̃ āye ho.' usne
javāb • • •, 'accʰī bāt tʰī ki agar gāRī der se na • • •, to mẽ āj
bʰī na • • •.

# 9 फार्चून कुकी में क्या लिखा है?
## 'fortune cookies' mẽ kyā likʰā hɛ?
### What's written in the fortune cookie?

By the end of this unit you should be able to:

- use past participials
- understand how to say 'no' in socially sensitive situations
- use the participial forms as adverbials
- use the construction 'neither . . . nor'
- understand hidden assumptions
- form purpose clauses
- learn more about Indian and Chinese food (particularly curries).
- use the passive construction
- understand more on reduplication
- use idiomatic expressions

## पढ़ने का अभ्यास ९   **paR<sup>h</sup>ne kā ab<sup>h</sup>yās 1**
## Reading practice 1 🎧 (Audio 2:28)

### *जल्दी पैसा आने वाला है।*   ***jaldī pɛsā āne vālā hɛ***
### *Money will come soon*

सीन: अमरीका में एक चीनी रैस्टॉरैन्ट
**Scene: Chinese restaurant in the US**

1 एक दिन दो दोस्त खाना खाने एक चीनी रैस्टॉरैन्ट गये।
ek din do dost k<sup>h</sup>ānā k<sup>h</sup>āne ek cīnī *restaurant* gaye.
2 खाने के बाद बैरा 'फार्चून कुकीज़' लाया।
k<sup>h</sup>āne ke bād bɛrā *'fortune cookies'* lāyā.
3 दोनों ने अपनी-अपनी 'फार्चून कुकी' को खोला और अपनी-अपनी किस्मत के बारे में पढ़ा।
donõ ne apnī-apnī *'fortune cookie'* ko k<sup>h</sup>olā aur apnī-apnī kismat ke bāre mẽ paR<sup>h</sup>ā.
4 फिर एक दोस्त ने दूसरे से पूछा, 'कागज़ पर क्या लिखा है?'
p<sup>h</sup>ir ek dost ne dūsre se pūc<sup>h</sup>ā, 'kāgaz par kyā lik<sup>h</sup>ā hɛ?'
5 लिखा है – 'जल्दी पैसा आने वाला है।'
lik<sup>h</sup>ā hɛ – 'jaldī pɛsā āne vālā hɛ.'
6 यह तो बड़ी खुशी की बात है।
ye to baRī xushī kī bāt hɛ.
7 तो कोई लाटरी खरीदी है?
to koī lāTrī (*Lottery*) xarīdī hɛ?
8 नहीं, लेकिन कल अपना जीवन बीमा करवाया है।
nahī̃, lekin kal apnā jīvan bīmā karvāyā hɛ.

1 *One day two friends went to eat in a Chinese restaurant.*
2 *After eating (i.e. after they had finished eating), the waiter brought (them) fortune cookies.*
3 *(They) both opened their fortune cookie(s) and read about their fortune(s).*
4 *Then one friend asked the other, 'What is written on the paper?'*
5 *(It) is written – 'Money is about to come soon.'*
6 *This is a matter of great happiness.*
7 *Did (you) buy a lottery ticket?*
8 *No, but yesterday, I bought life-insurance.* (lit. I have caused the life insurance to be done)

## शब्दावली  shabdāvalī  Vocabulary

| दोस्त | dost (m.) | friend |
|---|---|---|
| खाना | kʰānā (m.) | food |
| खाना | kʰānā (+ne) | to eat |
| खाने (के लिये) | kʰane (ke liye) | (in order) to eat |
| चीन | cīn | China |
| चीनी | cīnī | Chinese |
| बैरा | bɛrā (m.) | waiter |
| लाना | lānā (–ne) | to bring |
| दोनों | donõ | both |
| खोलना | kʰolnā (+ne) | to open |
| किस्मत | kismat (f.) | fortune, fate |
| कागज़ | kāgaz (m.) | paper |
| लिखना | likʰnā (+ne) | to write |
| लिखा है | likʰā hɛ | is written |
| जल्दी | jaldī | quickly, hurry |
| पैसा | pɛsā (m.) | money; one hundredth of a rupee |
| आने वाला | āne vālā | about to come |
| जीवन | jīvan (m.) | life |
| बीमा | bīmā (m.) | insurance |

# Notes

## Cultural

Chinese food in India has a distinct Indian (spicy) taste and is very popular. However, Chinese restaurants in India don't usually offer fortune cookies.

## Purpose clauses and deletion

In the last chapter, we came across the following expression:

| पुलिस | वाला | उसको | <u>पकड़ने</u> | के लिये | दौड़ा। |
|---|---|---|---|---|---|
| **pulis** | **vālā** | **usko** | <u>**pakaRne**</u> | **ke liye** | **dauRā.** |
| police | one/man | him | to catch-obl. | for | ran |

The policeman ran <u>to catch</u> him.

Now compare this Hindi expression with the opening line:

| एक | दिन | दो | दोस्त | खाना | खाने | एक | चीनी |
|-----|-----|-----|-------|------|------|-----|------|
| **ek** | **din** | **do** | **dost** | **kʰānā** | **kʰāne** | **ek** | **cīnī** |
| one | day | two | friends | food | to eat-obl. | one | Chinese |

| रेस्टोरैन्ट | गये । |
|------------|-------|
| **restaurant** | **gaye.** |
| *restaurant* | went |

One day two friends went to a Chinese restaurant <u>to eat</u> food.

You must have observed by now that the underlined infinitive phrases in English, such as 'to catch' and 'to eat', are not translated as plain infinitives like पकड़ना **pakaRnā** and खाना **kʰānā**. The plain (simple) infinite phrase will yield an ungrammatical sentence in Hindi. As is clear from the Hindi expression पकड़ने के लिए **pakaRne ke liye** 'to catch', the Hindi equivalent of the English purpose clause 'to catch' is paraphrased as 'in order to catch', and therefore the postposition के लिए **ke liye** 'for, in order to' follows the infinitive phrase पकड़ना **pakaRnā**. Recall the peer pressure influence of the postposition on the noun that makes the noun oblique and, thus, पकड़ना **pakaRnā** changes to पकड़ने **pakaRne**. The postposition can be described as the ghost postposition – के लिए **ke liye**.

What determines the retention or deletion of the postposition in purpose clauses such as those discussed here? The answer lies in the main verb of each sentence, i.e. दौड़ा **dauRā** 'ran' and गए **gaye** 'went'. If the main verb is a motion verb, it is possible optionally to drop the postposition as खाने **kʰāne**. Similarly, it is possible to drop के लिए **ke liye** in the first sentence:

| पुलिस | वाला | उसको | <u>पकड़ने</u> | दौड़ा । |
|-------|------|------|---------------|---------|
| **pulis** (police) | **vālā** | **usko** | <u>**pakaRne**</u> | dauRā. |

If we replace the main verb in the above sentence with a stative (non-motion) verb, the postposition must be retained, as in

| पुलिस वाला | उसको | <u>पकड़ने के लिये</u> | है । |
|------------|------|----------------------|------|
| **pulis vālā** | **usko** | <u>**pakaRne ke liye**</u> | hε. |

The police are (there) to catch him.

The deletion of the postposition is ungrammatical; therefore, the following sentence is unacceptable:

| पुलिस | वाला | उसको | <u>पकड़ने</u> | है । |
|-------|------|------|---------------|------|
| **pulis** (police) | **vālā** | **usko** | <u>**pakaRne**</u> | hε. |

## Reduplication and distributive meaning

In Unit 4, we demonstrated that repetition expresses intensity. In sentence 3 the feminine form of the reflexive pronoun अपना **apnā** is repeated:

| दोनों ने | अपनी–अपनी | 'फ़ाचून कुकी' | को | खोला । |
|---|---|---|---|---|
| **donō ne** | **apnī-apnī** | **'fortune cookie'** | **ko** | **kʰolā** |
| both-agent | self self | fortune cookie | obj. | opened |

Both opened their fortune cookie(s).

अपनी **apnī** is repeated to convey that both opened their respective cookies.

## Past participle (expressing states): adjectival and adverbial use

In Unit 8 we introduced present participles. Compare the phrase भागते चोर को **bʰāgte cor ko** 'the running thief' with भागे चोर को **bʰāge cor ko**. The latter form is called the past participial form and can be translated into English as 'the escaped thief'.

Now compare the present forms with their corresponding past participial forms, and the difference in meaning rendered by the two forms:

| *Present participle* | *Past participle* |
|---|---|
| भागता चोर **bʰāgtā cor** the running thief | भागा चोर **bʰāgā cor** the escaped thief |
| बोलती लड़की **boltī laRkī** the speaking girl | बोली बात **bolī bāt** the spoken matter |
| लिखते लड़के **likʰte laRke** the writing boys (boys who are/were/will be writing) | लिखे शब्द **likʰe shabda** the written words |

Note the composition of the past participial form:

| *Stem* | | | + | *past participial marker* |
|---|---|---|---|---|
| भाग | **bʰāg** | run | + | आ **ā** past-masculine singular |
| बोल | **bol** | speak | + | ई **ī** past-feminine singular |
| लिख | **likʰ** | write | + | ए **e** past-masculine plural |

You have probably guessed by now that the past participle is the same form that we came across in the simple past tense formation.

The only difference is that the feminine singular form is used for both singular and plural forms.

The second element (optional) remains the same in both the present and past participial forms, i.e. हुआ **huā**, हुए **hue** and हुई **huī**.

As stated earlier, in the participle the verb form ceases to function like a real verb and begins to behave like an adjective, so the verbal adjectives which are drawn from the simple past tense are called 'past participles'. In other words, they are like adjectives ending in आ **ā** with the difference being that they are derived from verbs.

Like the adjectives ending in आ **ā**, they agree in number or gender with the following noun. Note the gender number agreement in the above examples.

Unlike the present participle which denotes '*action in progress*', the past participle indicates a *state*.

Note the difference in meaning between the present participle and its corresponding past participial form:

| *Present participle* | *Past participle* |
|---|---|
| बैठता लड़का **bɛTʰtā laRkā** | बैठा लड़का **bɛTʰā laRkā** |
| The boy who is (in the process of) sitting. | The seated boy. |
| सोती लड़कियाँ **sotī laRkiyā̃** | सोई लड़कियाँ **soī laRkiyā̃** |
| The girls who are in the process of sleeping. | The sleeping girls. (state) |

The present participial form सोती **sotī** indicates the dozing off stage prior to sound sleep whereas the corresponding past participle indicates the state of sound sleep.

## Adverbials

So far we have discussed the adjectival use of participles. Participial forms when placed before a verb mark adverbial usage. Note the translation of the quoted sentence given in sentence 4 of the reading passage.

| कागज़ | पर | क्या | लिखा | है? |
|---|---|---|---|---|
| **kāgaz** | **par** | **kyā** | **likʰā** | **hɛ?** |
| paper | on | what | written | is |

What is written on the paper?

Superficially it appears as if लिखा है **likʰā hɛ** is the present perfect form of the verb लिख **likʰ**, which should be translated as 'has written', but this is not the case. The main verb is है **hɛ**, while लिखा **likʰā** is the past participial form used as an adverb without the optional element हुआ **huā**. In short,

लिखा है। = लिखा (हुआ) है।
**likʰā hɛ** = **likʰā (huā) hɛ**

Since the main verb is है **hɛ** and लिखा **likʰā** is the past participle, the translation is 'is written' rather than 'has written'. The insertion of the optional element disambiguates it from the present perfect form of the verb लिख **likʰ**. In passing, it should be mentioned that the verb phrase in sentence 7 of the passage ख़रीदी **xarīdī hɛ** is a real present perfect form of the verb ख़रीद **xarīd** 'buy'; therefore, its literal translation is 'has bought'.

## बातचीत **bātcīt** Dialogue 1 🎧 (Audio 2:29)

## मेरा पेट भर गया है। *mera peT bʰar gayā hɛ*
## *I am full*

*Bill Hassett and his wife, who are visiting India for the first time, are invited to dinner by Bill's Indian partner. Bill's partner's wife, Jyotsna Singh, asks her guests about the type of food they would prefer. Bill suggests to his wife 'Honey, as is said in English: "Spice up your life." Why don't we both spice up our lives in the literal sense and try some spicy food?' So, with the intention of enjoying spicy food, he tells Jyotsna Singh:*

| | |
|---|---|
| बिल: | हिन्दुस्तानी 'करी' अभी तक हमने नहीं खायी। |
| BILL: | hindustānī *curry* abʰī tak hamne nahī̃ kʰāyī. |
| ज्योत्सना: | आपको मसालेदार खाना पसन्द है या 'करी'? |
| JYOTSNA: | āpko masāledār kʰānā pasand hɛ yā *curry*? |
| बिल: | दोनों में फ़र्क क्या है? |
| BILL: | donõ mẽ farka kyā hɛ? |
| ज्योत्सना: | अमरीका में करी एक डिश का नाम है लेकिन हिन्दुस्तान में ऐसी बात नहीं। |
| JYOTSNA: | amrīkā mẽ *curry* ek *dish* kā nām hɛ lekin hindustān mẽ ɛsī bāt nahī̃. |
| बिल: | हमारे यहाँ 'करी' का मतलब कोई मसालेदार हिन्दुस्तानी डिश है। |
| BILL: | hamāre yahā̃ *curry* kā matlab 'koī masāledār hindustānī dish' hɛ. |

ज्योत्सना: हिन्दुस्तान में न तो 'करी' हमेशा मसालेदार होती है और न ही 'करी पाउडर' अक्सर बिकता है। 'करी' अक्सर तरी वाली होती है और माँस, सब्जी, मछली या फल की बनी होती है।

JYOTSNA: hindustān mɛ̃ na to *curry* hameshā masāledār hotī hɛ aur na hī hindustān mɛ̃ *curry powder* aksar biktā hɛ. *curry* aksar tarī vālī hotī hɛ aur ye mãs, sabzī, macchlī yā phal kī banī hotī hɛ.

बिल: अरे! बिना मसाले की करी। यह तो हमने कभी नहीं सुना था।

BILL: are! binā masāle kī *curry*. ye to hamne kabʰī nahī̃ sunā tʰā.

ज्योत्सना: तो अब आपको कौन सी करी पसन्द है?

JYOTSNA: to ab āpko kaun sī *curry* pasand hɛ?

ज्योत्सना: आम के आम और गुठलियों के दाम। 'करी' के बारे में पता लग गया और असली 'करी' चखने का मौका भी मिल जायेगा। अच्छा, हमको तेज़ मसालेदार माँस की 'करी' बहुत पसन्द है।

BILL: ām ke ām aur guTʰlīyõ ke dām. *curry* ke bāre mɛ̃ patā lag gayā aur aslī curry cakʰne kā maukā bʰī mil jāyegā. acchā, hamko tez masāledār mãs kī curry bahut pasand hɛ.

*(They laugh at the unexpected turn of the conversation; the proverb has added a lighter touch to the conversation and they continue to talk . . . )*

ज्योत्सना: अरे, बात ही करेंगे या कुछ स्नैक्स भी खायेंगे।

JYOTSNA: are, bāt hī karɛ̃ge yā kuch snɛks bʰi kʰāyẽge

*(Even after Bill has eaten a couple of snacks, and he is full, she insists on giving him more. Bill puts his hands over his plate.)*

बिल: बस, और नहीं खा सकूँगा। मेरा पेट भर गया है।

BILL: bas, aur nahī̃ kʰā sakū̃ga, merā peT bʰar gayā hai.

बिल: बस, और बिल्कुल नहीं। बहुत खा लिया है। नहीं तो बीमार हो जाऊँगा।

BILL: bas, aur bilkul nahī̃. bahut kʰā liyā hai. nahī̃ to bimār ho jāū̃gā.

BILL: *So far, in India, we have not eaten curry.*

JYOTSNA: *Do you like spicy food or curry?*

BILL: *What is the difference between the two?*

JYOTSNA: *In America, curry is the name of a dish but this is not the case in India.*

BILL: *In our place (i.e. in America) curry is (called) a spicy Indian dish.*

JYOTSNA: *In India, curry is not always spicy nor is curry powder usually sold (commercially). Curry is usually liquified and (it) is made of meat, vegetables, fish or fruit.*

BILL: *Wow! Curry without spices. This we have* (lit. had) *never heard of (before).*

JYOTSNA: *So, which curry do you like?*

BILL: *(This is like) earth and heaven's joy combined. (Now) I have came to know about curry and will get an opportunity to taste a genuine curry. Well, we very much like the very spicy meat curry.*

(They laugh at the unexpected turn of the conversation; the proverb has added a lighter touch to the conversation and they continue to talk . . . )

JYOTSNA: *Hey, would you (like to) continue to talk or eat some (more) snacks?*

(Even after Bill has eaten a couple of snacks, and he is full, she insists on giving him more. Bill puts his hands over his plate.)

BILL: *Enough. (I) won't be able to eat more.*

BILL: *Enough, absolutely no more, otherwise I will get sick.*

## शब्दावली  shabdāvalī  Vocabulary

| | | |
|---|---|---|
| करी /कढ़ी | **curry** (f.) | curry (*see Notes) |
| मसाला | **masālā** (m.) | spice |
| मसालेदार | **masāledār** (adj.) | spicy |
| या | **yā** | or |
| फर्क | **farka** (m.) | difference |
| हमारे यहाँ | **hamāre yahā̃** | at our place (house, country, etc.) |
| न . . . न | **na . . . na** | neither . . . nor |
| मतलब | **matlab** (m.) | meaning |
| हमेशा | **hameshā** | always |
| अकसर | **aksar** | often, usually |
| तर | **tar** | wet |
| तरी | **tarī** (f.) | liquid |
| माँस | **mãs** (m.) | meat |
| सब्जी | **sabzī** (f.) | vegetable |
| मछली | **macchlī** (f.) | fish |
| फल | **phal** (m.) | fruit |
| बनना | **bannā** (–ne) | to be made |
| बनी | **banī** | made |
| बिना | **binā** | without |
| कभी | **kabhī** | ever |
| कभी नहीं | **kabhī nahī̃** | never |
| आम | **ām** (m. adj.) | mango (n.); common (adj.) |
| गुठली | **guThlī** (f.) | stone (of a fruit) |
| दाम | **dām** (m.) | price |
| आम के आम और . . . गुठलियों के दाम | **ām ke ām aur . . . guThilyõ ke dām** | earth's joy and heaven's combined |

| पता लगाना | **patā lagānā (+ko)** | to come to know |
|---|---|---|
| असली | **aslī** | real, genuine |
| चखना | **cak$^h$nā (+ne)** | to taste |
| मौका | **maukā** (m.) | opportunity |
| तेज़ | **tez** | fast, quick, sharp, strong |
| स्नैक्स | **snɛks** (m.) | snacks |
| बस | **bas** | enough |
| सकना | **saknā** | to be able to, can |
| खाना | **k$^h$ānā** | food, to eat |

## Pronunciation

The English word 'curry' is a derivative of the Hindi word कढ़ी **kaR$^h$ī**. Note the presence of the retroflex ढ़ **R$^h$** in the Hindi word.

## Notes

### Eating etiquette: how to say 'no'

Indians are very hospitable. One of the expressions of their hospitality is to insist on giving more food to their guests. This results in one of the most embarrassing situations that guests can encounter. In addition to the linguistic strategies given in the dialogue, here are some other important expressions to refuse food. Don't keep on eating more!

आपने तो पहले ही बहुत दे दिया है।
**āpne to pɛhle hī bahut de diyā hɛ**
You have already given so much food.

खाना तो बहुत अच्छा है, लेकिन मेरी तबियत ठीक नहीं है।
**k$^h$ānā to bahut acc$^h$ā hɛ, lekin merī tabiyat T$^h$īk nahī̃ hɛ.**
The food is very good, but I am not feeling well.

### Curry powder/curry

In the authentic Indian tradition, the English word 'curry' simply does not exist. It is part of the vocabulary of English-educated bilinguals. The Hindi word कढ़ी **kaR$^h$i** is restricted to a vegetarian curry which is made out from chick-pea flour. The chances are Hindi speakers will not use the term 'curry' to refer to the dishes mentioned in the dialogue, so, do not be surprised if this term is not understood in the native Indian context. Indians will express this concept by specifying the degree of spiciness and by qualifying a dish with words such as तरी वाली सब्जी **tarī vālī sabzī** or तरी वाला माँस/गोश्त **tarī vālā mās/goshta**. Curry is actually a blend of ground herbs and spices adapted by British settlers in India from the traditional spice mixtures of Indian cuisine. The basic ingredients of commercial curry powder are turmeric (which imparts the characteristic yellow colour), cumin, coriander, and cayenne pepper. Curry powder is primarily targeted at foreign consumption. English 'curry' is said to be derived from Tamil 'kari'.

## Focus and word order

The normal word order of the opening sentence of the above dialogue is as follows:

| हमने | हिन्दुस्तानी | 'करी' | अभी तक | नहीं | खायी। |
|------|------------|-------|--------|------|--------|
| hamne | hindustānī | curry | abʰī tak | nahī̃ | kʰāyī. |
| we-agent | Indian | curry | yet | not | ate |

We have not eaten Indian curry yet.

The two elements of the above sentence – time adverb and object – are placed in the sentence in the initial position as they are being singled out for emphasis.

| हिन्दुस्तानी | 'करी' | अभी तक | हमने | नहीं | खायी। |
|------------|-------|--------|------|------|--------|
| hindustānī | curry | abʰī tak | hamne | nahī̃ | kʰāyī. |
| Indian | curry | yet | we-agent | not | ate |

As yet, it is the Indian curry (that) we have not eaten.

## 'Neither . . . nor' न . . . न na . . . na and emphatic particles

Note the use of the emphatic particles with न . . . न **na . . . na** 'neither . . . nor'. Also, observe the placement of the phrase हिन्दुस्तान में **hindūstān mẽ** in the 'neither . . . nor' clause:

| हिन्दुस्तान | में | न | तो | 'करी' | हमेशा | मसालेदार |
|-----------|-----|---|-----|-------|-------|----------|
| hindustān | mẽ | na | to | curry | hameshā | masāledār |
| India | in | not | emp. part. | curry | always | spicy |
| होती | है |
| hotī | hɛ |
| be-present | is (aux.) |

| और | न | ही | हिन्दुस्तान | में | करी पाउडर | अकसर |
|---|---|---|---|---|---|---|
| **aur** | **na** | **hī** | **hindustān** | **mɛ̃** | *currypowder* | **aksar** |
| and | not | emp. part | India | in | curry powder | often |

| बिकता | है। |
|---|---|
| **biktā** | **hɛ.** |
| be sold-pres. | is |

As regards curry in India, it is neither always spicy nor is curry
powder often sold in India.

The emphatic particles तो **to** and ही **hī** are more intimately tied to
curry and curry powder, respectively, as shown:

| हिन्दुस्तान | में | न | करी | तो | हमेशा | मसालेदार |
|---|---|---|---|---|---|---|
| **hindustān** | **mɛ̃** | **na** | **curry** | **to** | **hameshā** | **masāledār** |
| India | in | not | curry | emp. part. | always | spicy |

| होती | है |
|---|---|
| **hotī** | **hɛ** |
| be-present | is (aux.) |

| और | न | हिन्दुस्तान | में | करी | पाउडर | ही | अकसर |
|---|---|---|---|---|---|---|---|
| **aur** | **na** | **hindustān** | **mɛ̃** | **curry** | **powder** | **hī** | **aksar** |
| and | not | India | in | curry | powder | emp. part. | often |

| बिकता | है। |
|---|---|
| **biktā** | **hɛ.** |
| be sold-pres. | is |

The movement of the emphatic particles from their original position
after the negative particle न **na** renders the emphatic counterpart of
the normal न . . . न **na . . . na** 'neither . . . nor' construction.

## Past participle: adverbial

The verb होती है **hotī hɛ** is the generic construction explained in Unit
4. Can you find the past participle in the following sentence?

| ये | माँस | सब्जी | मछली | या | फल | की | बनी |
|---|---|---|---|---|---|---|---|
| **ye** | **mā̃s** | **sabzī,** | **macchlī** | **yā** | **phal** | **kī** | **banī** |
| this | meat | vegetable | fish | or | fruit | of | make-past. ppl. |

| होती | है। |
|---|---|
| **hotī** | **hɛ.** |
| be-pres. | is (aux.) |

Yes, बनी **banī** is the past participial form of the verb बनना **bannā** 'to be made.' It can be followed by the optional element हुई **huī**. However, in the following sentence

| हमने | कभी | नहीं | सुना | था। |
|------|-----|------|------|-----|
| **hamne** | **kab<sup>h</sup>ī** | **nahī̃** | **sunā** | **t<sup>h</sup>ā.** |
| We-agent | ever | not | heard | was |

We had never heard of (it).

सुना **sunā** is not a past participle. In combination with the auxiliary था **t<sup>h</sup>ā**, it renders the past perfect form of the verb सुनना **sunnā** 'to hear/listen to'.

## Compound verbs with जाना **jānā** 'to go'

As explained in Unit 7, the helping verb जाना **jānā** expresses 'transformation' and/or 'finality or completeness'. Both semantic shades are reflected in the following conjunct sentence:

| करी | के बारे में | पता | लग | गया | और | असली | करी |
|-----|-------------|-----|-----|-----|-----|------|-----|
| **curry** | **ke bāre mẽ** | **patā** | **lag** | **gayā** | **aur** | **aslī** | **curry** |
| curry | about | address | strike | went | and | genuine | curry |

| चखने | का | मौका | भी | मिल | जायेगा। |
|------|-----|------|-----|-----|---------|
| **cak<sup>h</sup>ne** | **kā** | **maukā** | **b<sup>h</sup>ī** | **mil** | **jāyegā** |
| taste | of | opportunity | also | get | go-will |

The verbs पता लगना **patā lagnā** 'to come to know' and **milnā** मिलना 'to get' are subjected to the compound verb construction, and the helping verb जाना **jānā** 'to go' loses its literal meaning.

## The 'opportunity to . . .' x का मौका मिलना
## x kā maukā milnā

Note the word-for-word translation of the English expression, 'we will get the chance to taste the genuine curry'.

| हमको | असली | करी | चखने | का | मौका | मिल | जायेगा। |
|------|------|-----|------|-----|------|-----|---------|
| **hamko** | **aslī** | **curry** | **cak<sup>h</sup>ne** | **kā** | **maukā** | **mil** | **jāyegā** |
| we-to | genuine | curry | taste | of | opportunity | get | go-will |

The expression 'to get the opportunity to do x' requires the experiential subject; therefore, the subject हम **ham** 'we' is followed by the postposition को **ko**. Since the Hindi verb never agrees with the subject that is followed by a postposition, the verb in the above sentence agrees with मौका **maukā** 'opportunity', which is masculine singular. Also, the genitive का **kā** agrees with मौका **maukā**.

## बातचीत  **bātcīt**  Dialogue 2  🎧  (Audio 2:30)

### आग!आग!  **āg! āg!**  'Fire! Fire!'

*The next week, Mr and Mrs Bill Hassett come to the Singhs' residence for dinner. They converse with each other on a wide variety of subjects. Finally, the delicious smell of the food begins to overpower their conversation. In the meanwhile, the hostess announces that the dinner is served.*

बिल: वाह! वाह! शानदार खुशबू आ रही है, और इन्तज़ार करना मुश्किल है।

BILL: vāh! vāh! shāndār xushbū ā rahī hε, aur intazār karnā mushkil hε.

ज्योत्सना: आइये, तो खाना शुरु किया जाए। यह है आपकी पसन्द – तेज़ मिर्च वाली चिकन करी।

JYOTSNA: āiye, to kʰānā shuru kiyā jāye. ye hε, āpkī pasand – tez mirca vālī chicken curry.

*(Bill takes a lot of curry while Mrs Hassett takes only a little bit. After taking the first substantial bite)*

बिल: ओहहह! आग! आग!

BILL: (fanning his mouth) Ohhh . . . āg! . . . āg!

ज्योत्सना: क्यों क्या हुआ?

JYOTSNA: kyõ kyā huā?

बिल: ये तो 'करी' नहीं है! यह तो ज्वालामुखी है!! और मैं अपना आग बुझाने का सामान भी नहीं लाया।

BILL: ye to curry nahĩ hε! ye to jwālāmukʰī hε!! aur mẽ apnā āg bujʰāne kā sāmān bʰī nahĩ lāyā.

ज्योत्सना: आग बुझाने का सामान यह है – अगर बहुत मिर्च लग रही है तो दही लीजिए।

JYOTSNA: āg bujʰāne kā sāmān ye hε – agar bahut mirca lag rahī hε to dahī lījiye.

*(After a while Bill's mouth cools down)*

बिल: सच, अमरीका में तेज़ मसालेदार खाना इतना तेज़ नहीं होता।

BILL: sac, amrīkā (America) mẽ tez masāledār kʰānā itnā tez nahĩ hotā.

ज्योत्सना: हाँ, यह तो हिन्दुस्तान है।यहाँ 'तेज़' का मतलब 'बहुत तेज़' है। हम लोग बहुत तेज़ खाते हैं लेकिन हिन्दुस्तान में सब लोग इतना 'तेज़' नहीं खा सकते।

JYOTSNA:   hā̃, ye to hindustān hɛ. yahā̃ 'tez' kā matlab 'bahut tez'
           hɛ. ham log bahut tez kʰāte hɛ̃ lekin hindustān mɛ̃ sab
           log itnā tez kʰānā nahī̃ kʰā sakte.

बिल :      गलत–फ़हमी दूर करने के लिये शुक्रिया। मैं अब समझ गया कि 'तेज़'
           खतरनाक शब्द है।

BILL:      galat-fahamī dūr karne ke liye shukriyā. mɛ̃ ab samajʰ
           gayā ki 'tez' xatarnāk shabda hɛ.

BILL:      *Wow! Wow! the splendid fragrance (of food) is coming;
           (it) is difficult to wait any longer (i.e. I cannot wait more).*

JYOTSNA:   *Please come, let's start eating (lit. eating should be started).
           This is your favourite – hot chicken curry (lit. sharp pepper
           one chicken curry).*

(Bill takes a lot of curry while Mrs Hassett takes a little bit. After
taking the first substantial bite)

BILL:      *(fanning his mouth) Oh . . . h . . . h! Fire! Fire!*

JYOTSNA:   *Why? What happened?*

BILL:      *This is not curry! This is a volcano!! And I did not bring
           my fire extinguisher.*

JYOTSNA:   *This is (your) fire extinguisher – if (it) is very hot, then
           take some yoghurt. (lit. if very much pepper striking (you)).*

(After a while Bill's mouth cools down.)

BILL:      *Truly, in the US the spicy food is not so spicy.*

JYOTSNA:   *Yes, this is India. Here 'hot' means 'very hot.' We eat very
           hot food, but not all people can eat such hot (food) in India.*

BILL:      *Thanks for dispelling (my) misconception. Now I (fully)
           understand that 'tez' is a dangerous word.*

## शब्दावली  shabdāvalī  Vocabulary

| वाह! वाह! | **vāh! vāh!** | Wow! Wow! bravo! |
|---|---|---|
| शानदार | **shāndār** | grand, splendid |
| खुशबू | **xushbū** (f.) | fragrance (lit. happy smell) |
| शुरु करना | **shuru karnā** (+ne) | to begin |
| शुरु किया जाए/जाये | **shuru kiyā jāye** | should be started |
| मिर्च | **mirca** (f.) | chilli peppers |
| ओ | **oh** | exclamation of pain/sorrow |
| आग | **āg** (f.) | fire |
| ज्वालामुखी | **jwālāmukʰī** (m.) | volcano |
| बुझाना | **bujʰānā** (+ne) | to extinguish |
| सामान | **sāmān** (m.) | baggage, goods, stuff, tools |
| लाना | **lānā** (–ne) | to bring |
| दही | **dahī** (m./f.) | yoghurt |

| सच | sac (m.) | truth, true |
| इतना | <itnā> | this/so much/many |
| गलत | galat | wrong |
| गलतफ़हमी | galat-fahamī (f.) | misconception, misunderstanding |
| दूर | dūr | far, distant |
| दूर करना | dūr karnā (+ne) | to dispel, to eliminate |
| ख़तरा | <xatrā> (m.) | danger |
| ख़तरनाक | xatarnāk | dangerous |
| शब्द | shabda (m.) | word |

## Pronunciation

Words such as **xatrā** and **itnā** are written as ख़तरा **xatarā** and इतना **itanā**, respectively. The omitted vowel of ख़तरा **xatrā** surfaces in ख़तरनाक **xatarnāk**.

## Notes

### Ambiguity

The following expression from the opening line of Dialogue 2 is ambiguous:

| और | इंतजार | करना | मुश्किल | है । |
| **aur** | **intazār** | **karnā** | **mushkil** | **hɛ.** |
| and | wait | to do | difficult | is |

(It) is difficult to wait any longer *or* And, (it) is difficult to wait.

In other words, और **aur** can be interpreted either as a conjunction marker or as a modifier of इंतजार/इन्तजार **intazār**.

### Passive construction

The English expression 'Let's begin eating' is paraphrased as 'Eating should be done.'

| खाना | शुरु | किया | जाए/जाये । |
| **kʰānā** | **shuru** | **kiyā** | **jāye.** |
| eating | begin | did | go-subjunctive |

The verb phrase is in the passive subjunctive form. The passive construction in Hindi takes a compound verb construction in the sense that it involves a main verb and the helping verb. The only difference is that the main verb, rather than being in a stem form, is in the past form.

| Passive | | |
|---|---|---|
| *Main verb*<br>*(past form)* | *Helping verb*<br>(जाना *jānā* + *tense*) | |
| किया **kiyā** | जाए/जाये **jāye** | should be done |
| पढ़ा **paRʰā** | जाता है **jātā hɛ** | is read |
| पढ़ा **paRʰā** | गया **gayā** | was read |
| पढ़ा **paRʰā** | जाएगा/जायेगा **jāyegā** | will be read |
| बोला **bolā** | जा रहा है **jā rahā hɛ** | is being spoken/told |

In other words, the passive is formed by using the main verb in the past form. The helping verb is always जाना *jānā* 'to go', which undergoes tense conjugation like any other helping verb in a compound verb construction.

Like English passive subjects, which are appended with 'by', Hindi passive subjects are attached to the postposition से **se** 'from, by'. Here is the list of pronominal forms with the postposition से **se**:

मैं + से = मुझसे
**mɛ̃** + **se** = **mujʰse**     by me

तू + से = तुझसे
**tū** + **se** = **tujʰse**     by you

वह + से = उससे
**vo** + **se** = **usse**     by him/her

हम + से = हमसे
**ham** + **se** = **hamse**     by us

तुम + से = तुमसे
**tum** + **se** = **tum se**     by you

आप + से = आपसे
**āp** + **se** = **āpse**     by you (honorific)

वे + से = उनसे
**ve** + **se** = **unse**     by them

Since the passive subject is always followed by the postposition से **se**, the passive verb can never agree with it; instead it agrees with the object, as in

| मुझसे | किताब | पढ़ी | गई/गयी । |
|---|---|---|---|
| **mujʰse** | **kitāb** | **paRʰī** | **gayī.** |
| me-by | book (f.) | read-past-f. sg. | passive-go + past-f. sg. |

The book was read by me.

If the feminine object किताब **kitāb** 'book' is replaced by the masculine object ख़त **xat** 'letter', the passive verb form will be in the masculine singular form.

| मुझसे | खत | पढ़ा | गया। |
|---|---|---|---|
| **mujʰse** | **xat** | **paRʰā** | **gayā.** |
| me-by | letter (m.) | read-past-m. sg. | passive-go + past-f. sg. |

The letter was read by me.

One important difference between Hindi and English is that both transitive and intransitive verbs can be passivized in Hindi, while only transitive verbs can be passivized in English. See the Grammar section for more details.

## Omitted subject

| अगर | (आपको) | बहुत | मिर्च | लग | रही | है | तो | (आप) |
|---|---|---|---|---|---|---|---|---|
| **agar** | **(āp-ko)** | **bahut** | **mirca** | **lag** | **rahī** | **hɛ** | **to** | **(āp)** |
| If | (you-to) | very | pepper | strike | ing | is | then | (you) |

| कुछ | दही | लीजिये। |
|---|---|---|
| **kucʰ** | **dahī** | **lījiye.** |
| some | yoghurt | take |

The omitted subject of the first clause is experiential while it is simple nominative in the second clause.

## The past participle and the passive construction

You must have discovered by now that there is no neat correspondence between the English and Hindi passives. The English passive construction can be paraphrased in one of the following three ways. First, those instances where English and Hindi both use the passive construction to express the target idea. For example, English expressions such as 'it is said' and 'it is heard' are translated by means of the Hindi passive, as in:

| कहा | जाता | है। |
|---|---|---|
| **kahā** | **jātā** | **hɛ.** |
| say-past | passive-go-present | is |

(It) is said.

| सुना | जाता | है। |
|---|---|---|
| **sunā** | **jātā** | **hɛ.** |
| hear-past | passive-go-present | is |

(It) is heard.

As mentioned in Unit 2, Hindi is a 'pro-drop' language and the English dummy 'it' is not translated.

Second, English passives are sometimes translated as past participial forms in Hindi. Consider sentence 4 in Reading practice 1 at the start of this chapter:

| कागज़ | पर | क्या | लिखा | है? |
|-------|-----|------|------|-----|
| **kāgaz** | **par** | **kyā** | **likʰā** | **hɛ?** |
| paper | on | what | written (past. ppl.) | is |

What is written on the paper?

Compare the English sentence with its corresponding Hindi sentence. The Hindi sentence does not use the passive construction. Instead, the past participial form of the verb लिखना **likʰnā** is used in the corresponding Hindi sentence.

Third, Hindi intransitive verbs are translated as passive in English.

| Intransitive | | Transitive | |
|---|---|---|---|
| बिकना **biknā** | to be sold | बेचना **becnā** | to sell |
| बनना **bannā** | to be made | बनाना **banānā** | to make |
| खुलना **kʰulnā** | to be opened | खोलना **kʰolnā** | to open |

Since English does not have intransitive verbs corresponding to those in Hindi, the Hindi intransitive verbs are best translated by means of the English passive. For example, a common billboard sight in India is

| यहाँ | किताबें | बिकती | हैं | |
|------|---------|-------|------|--|
| **yahā̃** | **kitābẽ** | **biktī** | **hɛ̃** | |
| here | books | be sold-pres. | are | |

Books are sold here.

Notice that the English meaning does not correspond to the Hindi structure. In Hindi, the intransitive verb बिकना **biknā** is conjugated in the simple present tense form. Thus, the Hindi sentence is in its active form, as opposed to the passive form in English.

## Negation and auxiliary deletion

The present auxiliary verb is dropped with negative sentences in the following two sentences:

| अमेरिका | में | तेज़ | मसालेदार | खाना | इतना | तेज़। |
|---|---|---|---|---|---|---|
| amerikā | mẽ | tez | masāledār | kʰānā | itnā | tez |
| America | in | sharp | spicy | food | so much | sharp |

| नहीं | होता | है। |
|---|---|---|
| nahī̃ | hotā | hɛ |
| not | be-present | is[aux.] |

In America the hot food is not so hot.

and

| लेकिन | हिन्दुस्तान | में | सब | लोग | इतना | तेज़ | खाना |
|---|---|---|---|---|---|---|---|
| lekin | hindustān | mẽ | sab | log | itnā | tez | kʰānā |
| but | India | in | all | people | so much | sharp | food |

| नहीं | खा | सकते | (हैं)। |
|---|---|---|---|
| nahī̃ | kʰā | sakte | (hɛ̃). |
| not | eat | can-present | are |

But in India not everybody can eat such hot food.

## अभ्यास  **abʰyās   Exercises**

### Exercise 1

Match the places with the purpose for which people visit them. Then complete the sentence according to the model presented below:

| *Place* | *Purpose* | |
|---|---|---|
| पुस्तकालय | किताबें | पढ़ने |
| **pustakālaya** | **kitābẽ** | **paRʰne** |
| library | to read | books |

*Sentence*

| लोग | पुस्तकालय | किताब | पढ़ने | जाते | हैं। |
|---|---|---|---|---|---|
| **log** | **pustakālaya** | **kitābẽ** | **paRʰne** | **jāte** | **hɛ̃.** |

People go to the library to read books.

Do not attempt to translate the English place names into Hindi.

| | *Place* | *Purpose* | |
|---|---|---|---|
| 1 | laundromat | बियर पीने | *beer* **pīne** |
| 2 | restaurant | फिल्म देखने | *film* **dekʰne** |
| 3 | cinema | तैरने | **tɛrne** |

| | | |
|---|---|---|
| 4 college | पढ़ने | **paRʰne** |
| 5 swimming pool | खाना खाने | **kʰānā kʰāne** |
| 6 bar | दवाई लेने | **davāī lene** |
| 7 pharmacy | कपड़े धोने | **kapRe dʰone** |

## Exercise 2

Change the present participial phrase into its corresponding past participial form in the following sentences:

| | |
|---|---|
| 1 वो बैठते हुए बोला। | vo beTʰte hue bolā. |
| 2 जॉन सोते हुए हँस रहा था। | John sote hue hãs rahā tʰā. |
| 3 ये शहर सोता सा लगता है। | ye shɛhɛr sotā sā lagtā hɛ. |
| 4 लड़की रोती हुई घर आयी। | laRkī rotī huī gʰar āyī. |
| 5 औरत ने स्विमिंग पूल पर लेटते हुए कहा। | aurat ne *swimming pool* par leTte hue kahā. |

## Exercise 3

Which participial forms modify/match the noun.

| | | | |
|---|---|---|---|
| लिखा | likʰā | बात | bāt |
| सुनी | sunī | खत | xat |
| हँसता | hãstā | लड़का | laRkā |
| चलती | caltī | लोग | log |
| भूले | bʰūle | गाड़ी | gāRī |
| भागती | bʰāgtī | बिल्ली | billī |

## Exercise 4

Change the following sentences into their corresponding passive form:

| | |
|---|---|
| 1 जॉन ने एक कहानी पढ़ी। | John ne ek kahānī paRʰī. |
| 2 हम लोग खाना खा रहे हैं। | ham log kʰānā kʰā rahe hɛ̃. |
| 3 तुम क्या करोगे? | tum kyā karoge? |
| 4 मैंने चिकन करी बनाई। | mɛne *chicken curry* banāyī. |
| 5 बिल ये पढ़ेगा। | Bill ye paRʰegā. |
| 6 क्या आपने गाना गाया? | kyā āpne gānā gāyā? |

## Exercise 5

Underline the appropriate form of the subject, verb etc. given within the brackets in the following sentences:

1 (हमको/हम/हमने) वहाँ जाने का मौका (मिला/मिल) ।
   (hamko/ham/hamne) vahā̃ jane kā maukā (milā/mile).

2 (जॉन ने/जॉन/जॉन को) हिन्दुस्तान (जाना/जाने) का मौका अकसर मिलता है ।
   (John ne/John ko/John) hindustān (jānā/jāne) kā maukā aksar miltā hɛ.

3 ये सुनहरा मौका (था/थी) ।     सुनहरा 'golden'
   ye sunhɛrā maukā (tʰā/tʰī).

4 (आपको/आप) किताब लिखने का मौका कब (मिलेगी/मिलेगा) ।
   (āpko/āp) kitāb likʰne kā maukā kab (milegī/milegā).

5 इस कागज़ में क्या (लिखा/लिखी) है ।
   is kāgaz mẽ kyā (likʰā/likʰī) hɛ?

6 बिल्ली को मौका (मिला/मिली) और वो दूध पी गयी ।
   billī ko maukā (milā/milī) aur vo dudʰ pī gayī.

7 ये बहुत (अच्छा मौका/अच्छे मौके) की बात है ।
   ye bahut (acchā maukā/accʰe mauke) kī bāt hɛ.

# 10 भारतीय त्यौहार
# b<sup>h</sup>āratiya tyauhāra

## Indian festivals

**By the end of this unit you should be able to:**

- use various types of relative clauses
- use complex sentences
- understand more about Hindi passives
- get cultural information about the festivals of India
- distinguish between scholarly and formal Sanskritized style and informal Persianized style

**(Audio 2:32)**

In this unit we will describe some Indian festivals and other symbols which underlie the colourful mosaic of the culture and spirit of India. You will notice a slight shift in the style, which is more Sanskritized now. This style is preferred in formal, literary, scholarly and cultural endeavours. The Persianized style is preferred in informal and conversational situations.

## पढ़ने का अभ्यास ९   **paR$^h$ne kā ab$^h$yās 1**
## Reading practice 1

### दिवाली   *Dīvālī   The festival of lights*

1 दिवाली शब्द संस्कृत के दीपावली शब्द से आया है।
  'dīvālī' shabda sanskrit ke 'dīpāvalī' shabda se āyā hε.

2 दीपावली या दीवाली का अर्थ है – दीपकों की पंक्ति।
  dīpāvalī yā dīvālī kā art$^h$a hε – dīpakõ kī paŋkti.

3 यह भारत का सबसे प्रसिद्ध त्यौहार है।
  ye b$^h$ārat kā sab se prasidd$^h$a tyauhār hε.

4 दिवाली अक्तूबर या नवम्बर के महीने में आती है।
  divālī aktūbar (*October*) yā navambar (*November*) ke mahīne mẽ ātī hε.

5 यह त्यौहार अच्छाई की बुराई पर और प्रकाश की अंधकार पर विजय का प्रतीक है।
  ye tyauhāra acc$^h$āī kī burāī par aur prakāsha kī and$^h$kāra par vijaya kā pratīka hε.

6 ये राजा राम की राक्षस रावण पर विजय की खुशी में मनाया जाता है।
  ye rājā rām kī rākshasa rāvaN par vijaya kī xushī mẽ manāyā jātā hε.

7 कहा जाता है कि जब चौदह वर्ष के बनवास और रावण पर विजय पाने के बाद राजा राम अपने राज्य, अयोध्या, लौट रहे थे, तब हर घर ने खुशी में दिये जलाये।
  kahā jātā hε ki jab caudā varsha ke banvās aur rāvaN par vijay pāne ke bād rājā rāma apane rājya, Ayod$^h$yā, lauT rahe t$^h$e, tab har g$^h$ar ne xushī mẽ diye jalāye.

8 इसलिये दिवाली की रात को आज तक हर घर में दिये जलाये जाते हैं।
  isliye divālī kī rāt ko āj tak har g$^h$ar mẽ diye jalāye jāte hẽ.

9 आप इस त्यौहार को भारत का किसमस कह सकते हैं। यह त्यौहार भारत से बाहर – सिंगापुर, नेपाल, त्रिनिदाद, फीजी आदि कई देशों में मनाया जाता है।
  āp is tyauhār ko 'b$^h$ārata kā *Christmas*' kεh sakte hẽ. ye tyauhār b$^h$ārat se bāhar – Singapore, Nepal, Trinidad, Fiji ādi kaī deshõ mẽ b$^h$ī manāyā jātā hε.

10 दिवाली की रात को लोग पटाख़े और फुलझड़ियाँ चलाते हैं और हर घर में लक्ष्मी पूजन
 होता है |

 divālī kī rāt ko log paTāk$^h$e aur p$^h$ul-j$^h$aRiyā̃ calāte hɛ̃ aur har
 g$^h$ar mɛ̃ 'lakshmī pūjana' hotā hɛ.

11 जैसे किसमस सिर्फ़ ईसाई ही नहीं मनाते, वैसे दिवाली सिर्फ़ हिन्दुओं का त्यौहार नहीं है |
 आज–कल लगभग सभी धर्मों के लोग दिवाली मनाते हैं |

 jɛse *Christmas* sirf īsāī hī nahī̃ manāte, vɛse divālī sirf hinduõ
 kā tyauhār nahī̃ hɛ. āj-kal lagb$^h$ag sab$^h$ī d$^h$armõ ke log divālī
 manāte hɛ̃.

1 *The word 'dīvāli' originated* (lit. came from = originate) *the Sanskrit
 word 'dīpāvalī'.*
2 *The meaning of 'dīpāvalī' or 'dīvālī' is 'a row of lamps.'*
3 *This is the most famous festival of India.*
4 *Divali comes in the month of October or November.*
5 *This festival is a symbol of the victory of 'good' over 'evil', and
 'light' over 'darkness'.*
6 *This (festival) is celebrated in the glory* (lit. happiness) *of King
 Rama's victory over the demon (king) Ravana.*
7 *(It) is said that when, after fourteen years of exile and obtaining
 victory over Ravana, King Rama was returning to his kingdom,
 Ayodhya, then every house lit lamps in happiness (at his return).*
8 *Therefore, on Divali night until today, lamps are lit in every house.*
9 *You can call this festival 'the Christmas of India'. This festival
 is also celebrated in many countries outside India – Singapore,
 Nepal, Trinidad, Fiji, etc.*
10 *On Divali night, people light firecrackers and fireworks; and the
 goddess Lakshmi is worshipped* (lit. the worship of Lakshmi
 happens/occurs).
11 *(Just) as not only Christians celebrate Christmas, (similarly) Divali
 is not the festival of Hindus alone. Nowadays people of almost
 every religion celebrate Divali.*

## शब्दावली **shabdāvalī Vocabulary**

| दिवाली/दीवाली | **dīvālī** | the festival of lights/lamps |
|---|---|---|
| संस्कृत | **<sanskrita>** (f.) | Sanskrit |
| अर्थ | **art$^h$a** (m.) | meaning |
| दीपक/दिया | **dīpak/diyā** (m.) | an earthen lamp |
| पंक्ति | **paŋkti** (f.) | line, row |
| भारत | **<b$^h$ārata>** (m.) | the official name of India |
| प्रसिद्ध | **<prasidd$^h$a>** | famous |
| त्यौहार | **<tyauhāra>** (m.) | festival |

| अच्छाई | accʰāī (f.) | good (n.), quality, ideal |
| बुराई | burāī (f.) | evil |
| प्रकाश | \<prakāsha\> (m.) | light |
| अन्धकार | \<andʰkāra\> (m.) | darkness |
| विजय | \<vijaya\> (f.) | victory |
| प्रतीक | \<pratīka\> (m.) | symbol |
| राजा | rājā (m.) | king, emperor |
| राम | \<rāma\> (m.) | Lord Rama (proper name) |
| राक्षस | \<rākshasa\> (m.) | demon |
| रावण | \<rāvaNa\> (m.) | the demon king, Ravana |
| विजय | \<vijaya\> (f.) | victory |
| मनाना | manānā (+ne) | to celebrate (festival, holiday), persuade |
| चौदह | \<caudā\> | fourteen |
| वर्ष | varsha (m.) | year |
| बनवास | \<banvāsa\> (m.) | exile, residence in forest |
| पाना | pānā (+ne) | to find, obtain |
| राज्य | rājya (m.) | kingdom |
| अयोध्या | ayodʰyā (f.) | Ayodhya, a place name |
| लौटना | lauTnā (–ne) | to return |
| जलाना | jalānā (+ne) | to light, to burn; to kindle |
| आदि | ādi | etc. |
| कई | kaī | several |
| देश | \<desha\> (m.) | country |
| पटाखा | paTāxā (m.) | a firecracker |
| फुलझड़ी | pʰul-jʰaRī (f.) | a kind of firework that emits flower-like sparks |
| चलाना | calānā (+ne) | to drive, to manage (business), to light/play firecrackers |
| लक्ष्मी | lakshmī (f.) | Lakshmi, the goddess of wealth, fortune, prosperity |
| पूजन | \<pūjana\> (m.) | worship |
| जैसे (कि) | jɛse (ki) | as, as if |
| ईसाई | īsāī | a Christian |
| वैसे | vɛse | like that, similarly |
| हिन्दु | hindu | a Hindu |
| लगभग | \<lagbʰaga\> | about, approximately, almost |
| धर्म | \<dʰarma\> (m.) | religion |

## Pronunciation

With the exception of चौदह **caudā**, all the words enclosed in angle brackets < > are written with the word-final vowel अ **a**. However, in colloquial pronunciation, the final अ **a** is dropped. Since the above passage is written in high and formal style, the use of the word-final अ **a** is indicated.

The numeral **caudā** 'fourteen' is written चौदह **caudah**.

# Notes

## Sanskritized vs Perso-Arabic style

Style differences in Hindi primarily involve vocabulary. High or formal literary style is often equated with borrowing from Sanskrit, and colloquial style usually borrows from Arabic and Persian. The simple substitution of the Perso-Arabic words for the corresponding Sanskrit words will yield the informal colloquial style of Hindi.

| *Sanskrit* | | *Perso-Arabic* | | |
|---|---|---|---|---|
| अर्थ | **art$^h$a** | मतलब | **matlab** | *meaning* |
| भारत | **b$^h$ārata** | हिन्दुस्तान | **hindustān** | *India* |
| प्रसिद्ध | **prasidd$^h$a** | मशहूर | **mashhūr** | *famous* |
| वर्ष | **arsha** | साल | **sāl** | *year* |
| लगभग | **lagb$^h$aga** | करीब | **karīb** | *about, approximately* |

## Agentless passives

The Hindi equivalent of the English sentence 'this festival is celebrated' is:

| ये | त्यौहार | मनाया | जाता | है। |
|---|---|---|---|---|
| **ye** | **tyauhār** | **manāyā** | **jātā** | **hɛ.** |
| this | festival (m.) | celebrate-past | passive-go-pres. | is |

This festival is celebrated.

Hindi tends to omit the passive subject. The opening clause of sentence 7 of Reading practice 1 further exemplifies this point. Notice the omission of the passive subject ('by x') in the following paragraph:

| कहा | जाता | है। |
|---|---|---|
| **kahā** | **jātā** | **hɛ.** |
| say-past | passive-go-pres. | is |

(It) is said.

## पढ़ने का अभ्यास २   paR<sup>h</sup>ne kā ab<sup>h</sup>yās 2

## पढ़ने का अभ्यास २   paRʰne kā abʰyās 2
## Reading practice 2 🎧 (Audio 2:34)

### होली – एक और रंग-बिरंगा त्यौहार   *holī ek aur raŋga-biraŋgā tyauhār*   Holi, the festival of colours

1 होली भारत का एक और रंग-बिरंगा त्यौहार है।
holī bʰārat kā ek aur raŋga-biraŋgā tyauhār hɛ.

2 यह बसन्त ऋतु में आती है।
ye vasanta ritu mɛ̃ ātī hɛ.

3 इस समय गाँवों में फ़सल कटने के बाद हर घर में अनाज आ जाता है।
is samaya gãvõ mɛ̃ fasal kaTne ke bād har gʰar mɛ̃ bahut anāj ā jātā hɛ.

4 इसलिये ये त्यौहार ख़ुश-हाली का सन्देश लाता है।
isliye ye tyauhār xush-hālī kā sandesh lātā hɛ.

5 इस दिन लोग बहुत उत्साह से एक दूसरे पर रंग फेंकते हैं।
is din log bahut utsāha se ek dūsre par raŋga fɛ̃kte hɛ̃.

6 बच्चे पिचकारी से रंगीन पानी डालते हैं, जब कि बड़े लोग सूखे रंग से खेलते हैं, जिसको गुलाल कहते हैं।
bacce pickārī se raŋgīn pānī Dālte hɛ̃, jab ki baRe log sūkʰe raŋga se kʰelte hɛ̃ jis ko 'gulāl' kɛhte hɛ̃.

7 हालाँकि इस दिन हर तरह का रंग लगाया जाता है, लाल रंग सर्व—प्रिय है क्योंकि लाल रंग प्रेम का प्रतीक है।
hālā̃ki is din har tarā kā raŋga lagāyā jātā hɛ, lāl raŋga sarva-priya hɛ kyõki lāl raŋga 'prema' kā pratīk hɛ.

8 होली के दिन भारत में 'कार्नीवल' जैसा वातावरण होता है। यह बड़ी धूम-धाम से वृंदावन में मनाया जाता है जहाँ श्रीकृष्ण पले थे।
holī ke din bʰārat mɛ̃ 'Carnival' jesā vātāvaraNa hotā hɛ. ye baRī dʰūm-dʰām se brindāban mɛ̃ manāyā jātā hɛ jahã̄ shrī krishn pale tʰe.

9 होली के बारे में कई प्राचीन कहानियाँ प्रचलित हैं जो मन की पवित्रता पर ज़ोर देती है।
holī ke bāre mɛ̃ kaī prācīn kahāniyā̃ pracalit hɛ̃ jo mana kī pavitratā par zor detī hɛ̃.

10 इस दिन लोग बड़ी प्रसन्नता से एक–दूसरे को गले लगाते हैं और शत्रुता भूल कर शत्रु को भी मित्र बना लेते हैं।
is din log baRī prasannatā se ek-dūsre ko gale lagāte hɛ̃ aur shatrutā bʰūl kar shatru ko bʰī mitra banā lete hɛ̃.

1 *Holi is another colourful festival of India.*
2 *It falls during spring* (lit. it comes during the spring season).

3 *At this time after the harvest* (lit. cutting) *of the crop, every house is full of grain* (lit. in every house, a lot of grain comes).
4 *Therefore, this festival brings the message of prosperity.*
5 *On this day people throw colour on each other with great enthusiasm.*
6 *The children throw coloured water with a water-gun while the elders play with dry colour, which is called 'gulāl'.*
7 *Although on this day all kinds of colours are used, (the) red (colour) is the favourite because it is the symbol of 'love'.*
8 *On the day of Holi generally (there) is a carnival-like atmosphere in India. This (festival) is celebrated with great joy* (lit. pomp and show) *in Brindavan where Lord Krishna was brought up.*
9 *(There) are several stories prevalent about Holi which emphasize the purification of the mind.*
10 *On this day people embrace each other with great joy and, forgetting enmity* (lit. and having forgotten enmity) *(they) make even the enemy (their) friend.*

## शब्दावली   shabdāvalī   Vocabulary

| | | |
|---|---|---|
| होली | **holī** (f.) | the festival of colours |
| रंग | **raŋga** (m.) | colour |
| रंग–बिरंगा | **raŋga-biraŋgā** | colourful |
| बसन्त | <basanta> | spring |
| ऋतु | **ritu** (f.) | season |
| गाँव | **gā̃v** (m.) | village |
| फसल | **fasal** (f.) | crop |
| कटना | **kaTne** (–ne) | to be cut |
| के बाद | **(ke) bād** | after |
| अनाज | **anāj** (m.) | grain, corn |
| खुश–हाली | **xush-hālī** (f.) | prosperity |
| सन्देश | **sandesh** (m.) | message |
| लाना | **lānā** (–ne) | to bring |
| उत्साह | **utsāh** (m.) | enthusiasm, joy, zeal |
| एक दूसरे से | **ek dūsre se** | with one another/each other |
| फेंकना | **pʰēknā** (+ne) | to throw |
| पिचकारी | **pickārī** (f.) | a syringe-shaped water-gun made of wood or metal |
| रंगीन | **raŋgīna** | colourful |
| पानी | **pānī** (m.) | water |
| डालना | **Dālnā** (+ne) | to put in, throw |
| जबकि | **jabki** | while |
| सूखा | **sūkʰā** (m. adj.) | dry |

| खेलना | kʰelnā (+/–ne) | to play |
|---|---|---|
| कहते हैं | kɛhte hɛ̃ | is called/is said |
| हालाँकि | hālā̃ki | although |
| लगाना | lagānā (+ne) | to attach, to stick |
| लाल | lāl | red |
| सर्व-प्रिय | sarva-priya | loved by all, the most favourite |
| प्रेम | prema (m.) | love |
| जैसा | jɛsā | as |
| वातावरण | vātāvaraNa (m.) | atomosphere, environment |
| धूमधाम से | dʰūm-dʰām se | with pomp and show |
| बृंदावन | <brindāvan> | the place where Lord Krishna was brought up |
| श्रीकृष्ण | shrī krishna | Lord Krishna |
| पलना | palnā (–ne) | to be brought up |
| प्राचीन | prācīna | ancient |
| प्रचलित होना | pracalit honā (–ne) | to be prevalent |
| मन | mana (m.) | mind |
| पवित्रता | pavitratā (f.) | purification, holiness |
| ज़ोर देना | zor denā (+ne) | to emphasize |
| प्रसन्नता | prasannatā (f.) | happiness, joy |
| गले लगाना | gale lagānā | to embrace |
| शत्रु | shatru (m.) | enemy |
| शत्रुता | shatrutā (f.) | enmity, hostility |
| भूलना | bʰūlnā (+/–ne) | to forget |
| मित्र | mitra (m.) | friend |

## पढ़ने का अभ्यास ३  paRʰne kā abʰyās 3
## Reading practice 3 🎧 (Audio 2:35)

### रक्षा-बन्धन / राखी  *Rakshābandʰan or rākʰī*

### 'The festival of love and protection'

1. रक्षाबन्धन का दूसरा नाम राखी भी है।
   rakshābandʰban kā dūsrā nām rākʰī bʰī hɛ.
2. यह भाई-बहन के अटूट प्रेम को याद दिलाता है।
   ye bʰāī-bɛhɛn ke aTūT prem ko yād dilātā hɛ.
3. इस दिन हर बहन अपने भाई को सुनहरा धागा बाँधती हैं।
   is din har bɛhɛn apne bʰāī ko ek sunharā dʰāgā bã̄dʰtī hɛ̃.
4. इस धागे का अर्थ है कि भाई अपने बहन को वचन देता है कि वह हमेशा उसकी रक्षा करेगा।

is dʰāge kā artʰa hɛ ki bʰāī apnī bɛhɛn ko vacan detā hɛ ki vo hameshā uskī rakshā karegā.

5 यहाँ तक कि विदेशी भाई भी पुराने समय से इस वचन को पूरा करते रहे हैं ।

yahā̃ tak ki videshī bʰāī bʰī purāne samaya se is vacan ko pūrā karate rahe hɛ̃.

6 सोलहवीं शताब्दी में गुजरात के सुल्तान ने चित्तौड़ पर आक्रमण किया ।

saulvī shatābdī mɛ̃ gujarāt ke sultān ne cittauRa par ākramaNa kiyā.

7 चित्तौड़ की रानी कर्णवती ने पराजित होने से पहले दिल्ली के मुगल सम्राट हुमायूँ के पास राखी भेजी ।

cittauRa kī rānī karNavatī ne parājit hone se pɛhɛle dillī ke mugal samrāT hūmāyū̃ ke pās rākʰī bʰejī.

8 जब तक हुमायूँ अपनी अपनायी बहन को बचाने के लिये चित्तौड़ पहुँचा, तब तक रानी जौहर रचा चुकी थी ।

jab tak hūmāyū̃ apnī apnāyī bɛhɛn ko bacāne ke liye cittauRa pahũcā, tab tak rānī jauhar racā cukī tʰī.

9 लेकिन हुमायूँ ने फिर भी गुजरात के सुल्तान को हराया और रानी कर्णवती के बेटे को, जिसको लड़ाई के समय छिपाकर चित्तौड़ से बाहर भेज दिया गया था, राज्य का उत्तराधिकारी बनाया ।

lekin hūmāyū̃ ne pʰir bʰī gujrāt ke *sultān* ko harāya aur rānī karNavatī ke beTe ko, jisko laRāī ke samaya cʰipā kar cittauRa se bāhar bʰej diyā gayā tʰā, rājya kā uttarādʰikārī banāyā.

1 *Rakshabandan's other name is Rakhi.*
2 *This (festival) reminds (us) of the unbreakable love between brother and sister.*
3 *On this day every sister ties (bracelets of) golden thread (on) her brother('s wrist).*
4 *The meaning of this thread is that the brother vows to his sister that he will defend and always protect her.*
5 *Even foreign brothers have been fulfilling this vow since the olden times.*
6 *In the sixteenth century the Sultan of Gujarat attacked Chittaur.*
7 *The queen of Chittaur, Karnavati sent Rakhi to the Mogul king of Delhi before her defeat.*
8 *By the time Humayun reached Chittaur to save his (now) adopted sister, the queen Karnavati had immolated herself.*
9 *Still Humayun defeated the Sultan of Gujarat and made the son of the queen Karnavati the heir of the kingdom, who (had been) sent secretly out of Chittaur at the time of battle (with the Sultan of Gujarat).*

## शब्दावली   shabdāvalī   Vocabulary

| | | |
|---|---|---|
| रक्षा-बन्धन | raksha-bandʰan (m.) | 'the festival of love and protection' |
| अटूट | aTūT | unbreakable |
| याद दिलाना | yād dilānā (+ne) | to remind |
| सुनहरा | sunharā (m. adj.) | golden |
| धागा | dʰāgā (m.) | (bracelets of) thread |
| बाँधना | bā̃dʰnā (+ne) | to tie |
| अर्थ | artʰa (m.) | meaning |
| वचन | vacan (m.) | promise |
| रक्षा करना | raksha karnā (+ne) | to protect, to defend |
| यहाँ तक कि | yahā̃ tak ki | to the point, to the exent that |
| विदेशी | videshī (m.) | foreigner |
| पूरा | purā (m. adj.) | complete, whole, full |
| पूरा करना | pūrā karnā (+ne) | to complete |
| सोलहवीं | <solvī̃> | sixteenth |
| शताब्दी | shatābdī (m.) | century |
| गुजरात | gujarāt | the state of Gujarat |
| सुलतान | sultān (m.) | a Sultan, king, emperor |
| चित्तौड़ | cittauRa | a very famous historical place in Rajasthan |
| आक्रमण करना | ākramaNa karnā (+ne) | to attack |
| रानी | rānī (f.) | queen |
| पराजित होना | parājit honā (–ne) | to be defeated |
| मुग़ल | mugal | the Moguls |
| सम्राट | samrāT (m.) | king, emperor |
| भेजना | bʰejnā (+ne) | to send |
| अपनाना | apnānā (+ne) | to adopt |
| अपनायी | apnāyī | adopted |
| बचाना | bacānā (+ne) | to save |
| तब तक | tab tak | by then |
| जौहर रचाना | jauhar racānā | When defeat seemed certain, Rajput women immolated themselves while Rajput men used to perform a deliberate battle to the death, leaving the enemy with an empty victory. The Rajputs are from the colourful and glamorous desert state of Rajasthan in the north-west of India. |
| चूँकि | cū̃ki | because |
| हराना | harānā (+ne) | to defeat |

| | | |
|---|---|---|
| लड़ाई | **laRāī** (f.) | fight, battle, war |
| छिपा कर | **cʰipā kar** | secretly |
| राज्य | **rājya** (m.) | kingdom |
| उत्तराधिकारी | **uttarādʰikārī** (f.) | heir, inheritor |
| बनाना | **banānā** (+ne) | to make |

## *Cultural note*

उपहार देना और विनम्रता  **Gift-giving and politeness**

Gift-giving is a special art in India which requires linguistic finesse.
Most Indians don't open their gifts in the presence of their guests.
Don't come to a premature judgement about this behavior. They
express their gratitude indirectly using expressions such as:

| ये | तकलीफ़ | आपने | क्यों | की? |
|---|---|---|---|---|
| **ye** | **taklīf** | **āpne** | **kyõ** | **kī?** |
| This | trouble | you-agent | why | did |

Why did you go to this trouble?

Or

| इसकी | तो | कोई | ज़रूरत | नहीं | थी। |
|---|---|---|---|---|---|
| **iskī** | **to** | **koī** | **zarurat** | **nahī̃** | **tʰī.** |
| Its | to-part. | any | need | not | was |

As regards this, there was no need.

Your answer should be:

| तकलीफ़ | की | क्या | बात | है? |
|---|---|---|---|---|
| **taklīf** | **kī** | **kyā** | **bāt** | **hɛ?** |
| trouble | of | what | matter | is |

What's the trouble?

You, as a guest, can use the following expression while offering the
gift:

| एक | छोटी | सी | चीज़ | लाया/लायी | हूँ। | आशा | है | कि |
|---|---|---|---|---|---|---|---|---|
| **ek** | **cʰoTī** | **sī** | **cīz** | **lāyā/lāyī** | **hũ.** | **āshā** | **hɛ** | **ki** |
| one | little | -ish | thing | brought (m./f.) | am. | hope | is | that |
| आपको | पसन्द | आयेगी। | | | | | | |
| **āpko** | **pasand** | **āyegī.** | | | | | | |
| you-to | likeness | come-will | | | | | | |

(I) brought a very small(ish) gift. (I) hope you like it.

However, nowadays educated Indians are familiar with Western culture and both open gifts in the presence of their guests and openly express their gratitude.

## Observation exercise

भारतीय स्वास्तिक   b^hārtīya swāstika   'The Indian swastika'

Speaking of festivals, perhaps I should point out that one should not be frightened or draw the wrong conclusions if one sees a swastika sign on the occasion of a festivity, or even posted permanently on shops or products. In India, particularly among the Hindus, Buddhists and Jains, the symbol is an integrated aspect of spiritual, social and commercial life. The Nazis' symbol was borrowed from India and was twisted in meaning. The original Indian swastika is the symbol of universal prosperity and the well-being of humanity. The original Indian swastika is shown below.

You will have noticed that in the Indian swastika, the four lines point to the four directions and there is a point of cross-section in the middle. This cross-section point symbolizes an individual. The symbol states: 'Wherever I am there should be prosperity around me in all four directions.' Thus, this symbol is created and recreated in the spirit of world peace and prosperity in India every day. Never lose sight of its intrinsic symbolic meaning. If the word 'swastika' still creates shock waves in the West, then imagine the resentment of Indians whose most spiritual and auspicious symbol has been deformed in the West, to the extent that they feel totally betrayed. In short, the Indian swastika is not *twisted* but is straight. Furthermore, it is usually accompanied by an expression beginning with शुभ **shub<sup>h</sup>a**, which means 'auspicious'.

## अभ्यास  ab<sup>h</sup>yās  Exercises

### Exercise 1

Match the passive statements given in the right-hand column with the three festivals given on the left:

| दिवाली | divālī | शत्रुओं को भी मित्र बनाया जाता है। |
|--------|--------|-----------------------------------|
|        |        | shatruõ ko b<sup>h</sup>ī mitra banāyā jātā hε. |
| होली | holī | दिये जलाये जाते हैं। |
|      |      | diye jalāye jāte hε̃. |
| रक्षाबन्धन | rakshāband<sup>h</sup>an | धागा बाँधा जाता है। |
|           |                         | d<sup>h</sup>āgā bā̃d<sup>h</sup>ā jātā hε. |

पटाख़े चलाये जाते हैं।
paTāxe calāye jāte hε̃.

गुलाल लगाया जाता है।
gulāl lagāyā jātā hε.

रंग से खेला जाता है।
raŋga se k<sup>h</sup>elā jātā hε.

राजा राम के अपने राज्य लौटने की खुशी में
मनाया जाता है।
rājā rām ke apne rājya lauTne kī
xushī mε̃ manāyā jātā hε.

### Exercise 2

Translate into English the sentences given in the right-hand column in Exercise 1.

## Exercise 3

Read the following relative clause statements and then identify the festival associated with each statement:

1 वो त्यौहार जो अक्तूबर के महीने में आता है।
  vo tauhār jo aktūbar ke mahīne mẽ ātā hɛ.
2 वो त्यौहार जो भाई और बहन का है।
  vo tauhār jo bʰāī aur bɛhɛn kā hɛ.
3 वो त्यौहार जिसमें बहन भाई को धागा बाँधती है।
  vo tauhār jismẽ bɛhɛn bʰāī ko dʰāgā bā̃dʰtī hɛ.
4 वो त्यौहार जिस दिन लोग एक दूसरे पर रंग फेंकते हैं।
  vo tauhār jis din log ek-dūsre par raŋga pʰẽkte hɛ̃.
5 वो त्यौहार जिस दिन राजा राम अयोध्या लौटे थे।
  vo tauhār jis din rājā rām ayodʰyā lauTe tʰe.

# मूल व्याकरण
# mūl vyākaraNa
## Reference grammar

## Nouns

Nouns are inflected for gender, number and case.

## *Gender*

There are two genders in Hindi, masculine and feminine. The gender system is partly semantically based and partly phonologically based. The rule of thumb is that inflected nouns ending in आ -**ā** are usually assigned masculine gender whereas the nouns ending in ई -**ī** are feminine. The semantic criterion (logical sex) takes precedence over the phonological criterion. Overall, the gender is unpredictable. रास्ता **rāstā** 'path' is masculine but राह **rāh** 'path' is feminine. दाढ़ी **dāR**ʰ**ī** 'beard' is feminine and so is सेना **senā** 'army'. Although आदमी **ādmī** ends in ई -**ī**, it is masculine, and माता **mātā** ends in आ -**ā** but is feminine. The class of masculine nouns which *do not end* in आ -**ā** and the feminine nouns which do not end in ई -**ī** are affectionately called 'nerd' nouns.

People of the male sex take masculine gender while those of the female sex are assigned feminine gender. Therefore, nouns such as लड़का **laRkā** 'boy' and आदमी **ādmī** 'man' are masculine whereas लड़की **laRkī** 'girl' and औरत **aurat** 'woman' are feminine. The same is true of some non-human animate nouns. Nouns such as कुत्ता **kuttā** 'dog', घोड़ा **g**ʰ**oRā** 'horse', बंदर **bandar** 'monkey' and बैल **bel** 'ox' are masculine and कुतिया **kutiyā** 'bitch', घोड़ी **g**ʰ**oRī** 'mare', बंदरी **bandarī** 'female monkey' and गाय **gāy** 'cow' are feminine.

Nouns denoting professions are usually masculine, as भंगी **b**ʰ**aŋgī** 'sweeper'.

Some animate nouns (species of animals, birds, insects, etc.) exhibit unigender properties in the sense that they are either masculine or feminine. For example, मच्छर **macc<sup>h</sup>ar** 'mosquito', कीड़ा **kīRā** 'insect', चीता **cītā** 'leopard' and उल्लू **ullū** 'owl' are masculine in gender, and nouns such as चिड़िया **ciRiyā** 'bird', कोयल **koyal** 'cuckoo', तितली **titlī** 'butterfly', मक्खी **makk<sup>h</sup>ī** 'fly' and मछली **mac<sup>h</sup>lī** 'fish' are feminine. To specify the sex of animate nouns, words such as नर **nar** 'male' and मादा **mādā** 'female' are prefixed to create compound nouns such as मादा-मच्छर **mādā-macc<sup>h</sup>ar** 'female-mosquito' and नर-चिड़िया **nar-ciRiyā** 'male-bird'.

In the case of inanimate nouns, land, abstract, collective and material nouns gender is partly determined by form and partly by semantics. On many occasions both criteria fail to predict the gender. The names of the following classes of nouns are usually masculine:

trees – पीपल **pīpal** (the name of a tree), सागवान **sāgvān** 'teak', देवदार **devdār** 'cedar', चीड़ **cīR** 'pine', आम **ām** 'mango' (however, इमली **imlī** 'tamarind' is feminine);

minerals and jewels – लाल **lāl** 'ruby', सोना **sonā** 'gold', कोयला **koyalā** 'coal', हीरा **hīrā** 'diamond' (however, चाँदी **cãdī** 'silver' is feminine);

liquids – तेल **tel** 'oil', दूध **dūd<sup>h</sup>** 'milk', पानी **pānī** 'water' (however, शराब **sharab** 'wine/liquor' is feminine);

crops – धान **d<sup>h</sup>ān** 'rice', बाजरा **bājrā** 'millet', मटर **maTar** 'pea';

mountains and oceans – हिमालय **himālaya** 'Himalayas', हिन्दमहासागर **hindmahāsāgar** 'Indian Ocean';

countries – हिन्दुस्तान **hindustān** 'India', पाकिस्तान **pākistan** 'Pakistan', अमरीका **amrīkā** 'America';

Gods, demons, and heavenly bodies – ब्रह्मा **brahmā** 'Brahma', सूरज **sūraj** 'sun';

days and months (Native calendar) – सोमवार **somvār** 'Monday', वैसाख **vaisāk<sup>h</sup>** 'Vaisakh';

body parts – सिर **sir** 'head', कान **kān** 'ear', हाथ **hāt<sup>h</sup>** 'hand' (however, आँख **ãkh** 'eye', जबान **zabān** 'tongue' are feminine); and

abstract nouns – प्रेम **prem** 'love', गुस्सा **gussā** 'anger', सुख **suk<sup>h</sup>** 'comfort' (however, some abstract nouns, including a synonym of प्रेम **prem** 'love', i.e. मोहब्बत **mohabbat**, are feminine).

# Number

Like English, Hindi has two ways of indicating numbers: singular and plural. However, there are some differences between the Hindi and the English way of looking at the singularity or pluralrity of objects. Words such as पजामा **pajāmā** 'pyjamas', बाल **bāl** 'hair' and कैंची **kẽcī** 'scissors' are singular in Hindi but plural in English. Similarly, चावल **cāval** 'rice' is singular in English but is both singular and plural in Hindi.

Masculine nouns which end in आ -**ā** change to -**e** in their plural form. The other group (the 'nerd group') of masculine nouns that do not end in आ -**ā** remain unchanged. Therefore, they adopt they following patterns:

## Masculine nouns

## Pattern I: ending in ā → e

| बेटा | **beTā** | son | बेटे | **beTe** | sons |
| लड़का | **laRkā** | boy | लड़के | **laRke** | boys |

*Exceptions:* राजा **rājā** 'king', पिता **pitā** 'father' – remain unchanged.

## Pattern II ('nerd nouns'): not ending in ā → remain unchanged

| आदमी | **ādmī** | man | आदमी | **ādmī** | men |
| गुरु | **guru** | teacher | गुरु | **guru** | teachers |

## Feminine nouns

Similarly, feminine nouns also exhibit patterns. Singular feminine nouns ending in -**ī** (including those ending in **i** or **iyā**) change to **iyā** in their plural forms, while those feminine nouns not ending in -**ī** add **ẽ** in the plural.

## Pattern I: ending in ī → iyā̃

| बेटी | **beTī** | daughter | बेटियाँ | **beTiyā̃** | daughters |
| लड़की | **laRkī** | girl | लड़कियाँ | **laRkiyā̃** | girls |
| चिड़िया | **ciRiyā** | bird | चिड़ियाँ | **ciRiyā̃** | birds |

## Pattern II ('nerd nouns'): not ending in ī → add ẽ

| किताब | **kitāb** | book | किताबें | **kitābẽ** | books |
| माता | **mātā** | mother | माताएँ | **mātāẽ** | mothers |
| बहू | **bahū** | bride | बहुएँ | **bahuẽ** | brides |

Note that feminine nouns ending in a long **ū** shorten the vowel before the plural ending.

## *Direct and oblique case*

Some nouns or noun phrases reflect 'peer pressure' under the influence of a postposition, i.e. they change their shape when they appear before a postposition. The form of the noun which occurs before a postposition is called the *oblique* case. The regular non-oblique forms are called *direct* forms, as shown above.

Masculine singular nouns which follow pattern I change under the influence of postpositions. The word-final vowel आ **ā** changes to **e** in the oblique case. However, all plural nouns change and end in **õ** before postpositions. The following examples illustrate these rules.

### Masculine nouns

### Pattern I: ending in -ā

|            | *Direct*       |            | *Oblique case (before postpositions)* |            |                   |
|------------|----------------|------------|---------------------------------------|------------|-------------------|
| *Singular* | बेटा           | **beTā**   | son        | बेटेको    | **beTe ko**       | to the son        |
|            |                |            |            |           | (i.e. **ā → e**)  |                   |
| *Plural*   | बेटे           | **beTe**   | sons       | बेटोंसे   | **beTõ se**       | by the sons       |
|            |                |            |            |           | (i.e. **e → õ**)  |                   |

### Pattern II ('nerd nouns'): not ending in ā

|            | *Direct*       |            | *Oblique case (before postpositions)* |            |            |
|------------|----------------|------------|---------------------------------------|------------|------------|
| *Singular* | आदमी           | **ādmī**   | man        | आदमी में    | **ādmī mẽ**    | in the man    |
|            |                |            |            | (i.e. no change) |          |               |
| *Plural*   | आदमी           | **ādmī**   | man        | आदमियों में | **ādmiyõ mẽ**  | in the men    |
|            |                |            |            | (i.e. **õ** added; slight change in the vowel **ī** which becomes **i**, and the semivowel **y** intervenes.) | | |

## Feminine nouns

### Pattern I: ending in ī

|  | *Direct* | *Oblique case (before postpositions)* | |
|---|---|---|---|
| *Singular* | बेटी **beTī** daughter | बेटी पर **beTī par** (i.e. no change) | on the daughter |
| *Plural* | बेटियाँ **beTiyā̃** daughters | बेटियों पर **beTiyõ par** (i.e. ā̃ changes to õ) | on the daughters |

### Pattern II ('nerd nouns'): nouns not ending in ī

|  | *Direct* | | *Oblique case (before postpositions)* | |
|---|---|---|---|---|
| *Singular* | किताब | **kitāb** book | किताब में **kitāb mẽ** (i.e. no change) | in the book |
| *Plural* | किताबें | **kitābẽ** book | किताबों में **kitābõ mẽ** (i.e. ẽ changes to õ) | in the books |

## Articles

Hindi has no equivalents to the English articles 'a', 'an' and 'the'. This gap is filled by means of indirect devices such as the use of the numeral एक **ek** for the indefinite article, and the use of the postposition को **ko** with an object to fulfill the function of the definite article.

## Pronouns

Although the case system of pronouns is essentially the same as that of nouns, pronouns have more case forms in the oblique case than nouns, as exemplified below by the difference in pronominal form with different postpositions.

## *Personal: singular*

| Direct | Oblique | | | |
| --- | --- | --- | --- | --- |
| | *General Oblique* | *Oblique +* को *ko (e.g. me)* | *Oblique +* का *kā (e.g. my) possessives* | *Oblique +* ने *ne (agentive past)* |
| मैं **mɛ̃** I | मुझ **mujʰ** | मुझको = मुझे **mujʰko = mujʰe** me | मेरा **merā** my | मैंने **mɛ̃ne** I |
| तू **tū** you | तुझ **tujʰ** | तुझको = तुझे **tujʰko = tujʰe** (to) you | तेरा **terā** your | तूने **tūne** you |
| वह/वो **vo** he/she | उस **us** | उसको = उसे **usko = use** (to) him/her | उसका **uskā** his/her | उसने **usne** he/she |
| यह/ये **ye** this | इस **is** | इसको = इसे **isko = ise** | इसका **iskā** | इसने **isne** |

## *Personal: plural*

| Direct | Oblique | | | |
| --- | --- | --- | --- | --- |
| | *General Oblique* | *Oblique +* को *ko* | *Oblique +* का *kā (e.g. our) possessives* | *Oblique +* ने *ne (agentive past)* |
| हम **ham** we | हम **ham** | हमको = हमें **hamko = hamɛ̃** (to) us | हमारा **hamārā** our | हमने **hamne** we |
| तुम **tum** you (familiar) | तुम **tum** | तुमको = तुम्हें **tumko = tumhɛ̃** (to) you | तुम्हारा **tumhārā** your | तुमने **tumne** you |
| आप **āp** you (honorific) | आप **āp** | आपको **āpko** (to) you | आपका **āpkā** your | आपने **āpne** you |
| वे **ve** they | उन **un** | उनको = उन्हें **unko = unhɛ̃** (to) them | उनका **unkā** their | उन्होंने **unhõne** they |
| ये **ye** these | इन **in** | इनको = इन्हें **inko = unhɛ̃** | इनका **inkā** | इन्होंने **inhõne** |

## *Other Pronouns: singular*

| Direct | Oblique | | | |
|---|---|---|---|---|
| | *General Oblique* | *Oblique +* को *ko* | *Oblique +* का *kā* possessives | *Oblique +* ने *ne* (agentive past) |
| कौन **kaun** who? | किस **kis** | किसको = किसे **kisko = kise** (to) whom? | किसका **kiskā** whose? | किसने **kisne** who? |
| जो **jo** who (relative clause) | जिस **jis** | जिसको = जिसे **jisko = jise** (to) whom | जिसका **jiskā** whose | जिसने **jisne** who |
| क्या **kyā** what | किस **kis** | किसको = किसे **kisko = kise** | किसका **kiskā** | – |
| कोई **koī** someone | किसी **kisī** | किसीको **kisīko** (to) someone | किसीका **kisīkā** someone's | किसीने **kisīne** someone |

## *Other pronouns: plural*

| Direct | Oblique | | | |
|---|---|---|---|---|
| | *General oblique* | *Oblique +* को *ko* | *Oblique +* का *kā* possessives | *Oblique +* ने *ne* (agentive past) |
| कौन **kaun** who? | किन **kin** | किनको = किन्हें **kinko = kinhẽ** (to) whom? | किनका **kinkā** whose? | किन्होंने **kinhõne** who? |
| जो **jo** who (relative clause) | जिन **jin** who | जिनको = जिन्हें **jinko = jinhẽ** (to) whom | जिनका **jinkā** whose | जिन्होंने **jinhone** who |

## Adjectives

Adjectives can be classified into two groups: हरा **harā** 'green' (inflecting adjectives) and लाल **lāl** 'red' (non-inflecting adjectives). Like masculine nouns, green adjectives end in आ -ā. They change their form, or agree, with the following nouns in terms of number and gender and show the signs of 'peer pressure' before a postposition. Red adjectives which do not end in आ -ā remain invariable. The following endings are used with the green adjectives when they are inflected for number, gender and case.

## Pattern I: the हरा harā 'green' adjectives (inflecting)

|           | Direct case |        | Oblique case |        |
|-----------|-------------|--------|--------------|--------|
|           | Singular    | Plural | Singular     | Plural |
| Masculine | -ā          | -e     | -e           | -e     |
| Feminine  | -ī          | -ī     | -ī           | -ī     |

## Example:

| Direct | | | Oblique | |
|--------|--|--|---------|--|
| अच्छा लड़का | | | अच्छे लड़के से | |
| acchā laRkā | good boy | | acche laRke se | by a/the good boy |
| अच्छे लड़के | | | अच्छे लड़कों से | |
| acche laRke | good boys | | acche laRkõ se | by good boys |
| अच्छी लड़की | | | अच्छी लड़की से | |
| acchī laRkī | good girl | | acchī laRkī se | by a/the good girl |
| अच्छी लड़कियाँ | | | अच्छी लड़कियों से | |
| acchī laRkiyā̃ | good girls | | acchī laRkiyõ se | by good girls |

## Pattern II: the red (लाल lāl) adjectives (non-inflecting)

| Direct | | | Oblique | |
|--------|--|--|---------|--|
| सुन्दर लड़का | | | सुन्दर लड़के से | |
| sundar laRkā | handsome boy | | sundar laRke se | by a/the handsome boy |
| सुन्दर लड़के | | | सुन्दर लड़कों से | |
| sundar laRke | handsome boys | | sundar laRkõ se | by handsome boys |
| सुन्दर लड़की | | | सुन्दर लड़की से | |
| sundar laRkī | beautiful girl | | sundar laRkī se | by a/the beautiful girl |
| सुन्दर लड़कियाँ | | | सुन्दर लड़कियों से | |
| sundar laRkiyā̃ | beautiful girls | | sundar laRkiyõ se | by beautiful girls |

*Possessive pronouns* (listed under oblique pronouns + का **kā**), the *reflexive pronoun* अपना **apnā** 'self' and *participles* behave like green adjectives; therefore, they are inflected in number, gender and case.

# Postpositions

The Hindi equivalent of English prepositions such as 'to', 'in', 'at', 'on', etc. are called postpositions because they follow nouns and pronouns rather than precede them as in English.

## Simple postpositions

Simple postpositions consist of one word. Here is the list of some important simple postpositions.

| | | |
|---|---|---|
| का | **kā** | of (i.e. possessive marker) |
| को | **ko** | to; also object marker |
| तक | **tak** | up to, as far as |
| ने | **ne** | agent marker for transitive verbs in simple past, present perfect and past perfect tenses |
| पर | **par** | on, at |
| में | **mẽ** | in |
| से | **se** | from, by, object marker for some verbs. |
| वाला | **vālā** | -er (and wide range of meanings) |

Two postpositions, का **kā** and वाला **vālā**, also change like green adjectives; all others act like red adjectives.

## Compound postpositions

Compound postpositions consist of more than one word. They behave exactly the same way as the simple postposition, i.e. they are the source of peer pressure and thus require nouns or pronouns to be in the oblique case. Examples of some of the most frequent compound postpositions are given below:

| के **ke**-type | | | की **kī**-type | | |
|---|---|---|---|---|---|
| के बारे में | **ke bāre mẽ** | about | की तरफ | **kī taraf** | towards |
| के आगे | **ke āge** | in front of | की जगह | **kī jagah** | instead of |

| के सामने | ke sāmne | facing | की तरह | kī tarā | like |
| के पहले | ke pehle | before | की बजाय | kī bajāy | instead of |
| के बाद | ke bād | after | | | |
| के नीचे | ke nīce | below | | | |
| के ऊपर | ke ūpar | above | | | |

Notice that most compound postpositions begin with either के **ke** or की **kī** but *never* with का **kā**.

## Question words

In English, the question words such as 'who', 'when' and 'why' begin 'wh-' (exception 'how'); Hindi question words begin with the क **k-** sound. Some of the most common question words are listed below:

## *Pronouns*

| क्या | **kyā** | what | *see* pronouns for oblique forms |
| कौन | **kaun** | who | *see* pronouns for oblique forms |
| कौन-सा | **kaun-sā** | which | कौन **kaun** remains invariable but सा **sā** changes like the green adjectives |

## Possessive pronouns

See oblique + का **kā** forms of क्या **kyā** and कौन **kaun** in the section on pronouns.

## *Adverbs*

| कब | **kab** | when |
| कहाँ | **kahā̃** | where |
| क्यों | **kyõ** | why |
| कैसा | **kɛsā** | how, of what kind |
| कितना | **kitnā** | how much, how many |

The last two adverbs, कैसा **kɛsā** and कितना **kitnā**, are changeable and behave like the green adjectives.

## Question words and word order

In Hindi it is not usual to move question words such as 'what', 'how' and 'where' to the beginning of the sentence. The question words usually stay in their original position, i.e. somewhere in the middle of the sentence. The only exception is the yes–no question, where the Hindi question क्या **kyā** is placed at the beginning of the sentence.

## Verbs

The concept of time is quite different in Hindi from the 'unilinear' concept of time found in English. In other words, time is not viewed as smoothly flowing from the past through the present into the future. It is possible to find instances of the present or future within the past. For example, the English expression 'he said that he was going' will turn out to be 'he said that he is going' in Hindi. Similarly, the concept of habituality is also different in Hindi. It is possible to say in English 'I always went there'; however, in Hindi one has to use the past habitual instead of the English simple past to indicate a habitual act. Therefore, the translational equivalent of the English sentence 'I always go there' will be 'I always used to go there' in Hindi.

### Infinitive, gerundive or verbal nouns

ना **nā** is suffixed to the verbal stem to form the infinitive (or gerundive or verbal noun) form of the verb. ना **nā** follows the stem in Hindi rather than preceding it.

### Simple infinitive

| *Stem* | | *Stem* + ना *nā* | | |
|--------|--------|------------------|----------|------------------|
| पी | **pī** | पीना | **pīnā** | to drink, drinking |
| कर | **kar** | करना | **karnā** | to do, doing |
| जा | **jā** | जाना | **jānā** | to go, going |

The infinitive marker आ **ā** becomes ए **e** in the oblique case (e.g. पीने से **pīne se** 'by drinking').

## Causative verbs

Intransitive, transitive and detransitive verbs are made causative by
a very productive process of suffixation. Two suffixes, आ -ā (called
the 'first causative' suffix) and वा -vā (the 'second causative' suffix)
are attached to the stem of a verb, and are placed before the infinitive marker ना -nā. The process of causativization brings about some
changes in some stems (as in दे de 'to give'). Here are examples of
some causative verb types:

## Type 1

No changes occur in the verbal stem.

| Intransitive | Transitive | Causative |
|---|---|---|
| उड़ना uRnā | उड़ाना uRānā | उड़वाना uRvānā |
| to fly | to fly x | to cause y to fly x |
| पकना paknā | पकाना pakānā | पकवाना pakvnā |
| to be cooked | to cook x | to cause y to cook x |

## Type 2

The stem-vowel of the intransitive verb undergoes either a raising or
a shortening process (shown in *italics*) in its corresponding transitive
and causative forms.

| Intransitive | Transitive | Causative |
|---|---|---|
| जागना j*ā*gnā | जगाना j*a*gānā | जगवाना j*a*gvānā |
| to wake | to awaken x | to cause y to awaken x |
| लेटना l*e*Tnā | लिटाना l*i*Tānā | लिटवाना l*i*Tvānā |
| to lie down | to lay down | to cause y to lay down x |
| झूलना jʰ*ū*lnā | झुलाना jʰ*u*lānā | झुलवाना jʰ*u*lvānā |
| to swing | to swing x | to cause y to swing x |

## Type 3

The stem-vowel of the transitive verb undergoes either a raising or a
shortening process in its corresponding intransitive and causative
forms.

In cases where the stem is disyllabic, it is the second vowel that undergoes such changes. The distinction between the causative marker वा -vā and its corresponding transitive marker आ -ā is neutralized; the two causal suffixes occur in free variation.

## Type 3a

| Intransitive | Transitive | Transitive (with आ -ā)/causative |
|---|---|---|
| मरना **m***a***rnā**<br>to die | मारना **m***ā***rnā**<br>to kill | मराना/मरवाना **m***a***rānā/m***a***rvānā**<br>to cause y to kill x |
| पिसना **p***i***snā**<br>to be ground | पीसना **p***ī***snā**<br>to grind x | पिसाना/पिसवाना **p***i***sānā/p***i***svānā**<br>to cause y to grind x |
| पुजना **p***u***jnā**<br>to be worshipped | पूजना **p***ū***jnā**<br>to worship x | पुजाना/पुजवाना **p***u***jānā/p***u***jvānā**<br>to cause y to worship x |
| खुलना **k**ʰ***u***lnā**<br>to be/become opened | खोलना **k**ʰ***o***lnā**<br>to open x | खुलाना/खुलवाना **k**ʰ***u***lānā/k**ʰ***u***lvānā**<br>to cause y to open x |

## Type 3b

Transitive verbs show one of the following tendencies: a new semantic distinction between the derived and the base transitive forms is created, as shown by the gloss in set A; or derived transitive and causative verbs undergo one level of causativization, as is the case with the set B.

## Set A

| Transitive | Transitive (with आ -ā) | Causative |
|---|---|---|
| पढ़ना **paR**ʰ**nā**<br>to read | पढ़ाना **paR**ʰ**ānā**<br>to teach | पढ़वाना **paR**ʰ**vānā**<br>to cause y to teach x |
| बोलना **b***o***lnā**<br>to speak | बुलाना **b***u***lānā**<br>to call | बुलवाना **b***u***lvānā**<br>to cause y to call x |

## Set B

The causative marker वा -vā occurs in free variation with ला -lā. The verbal stem undergoes vowel changes, as in

| Transitive | | | Transitive (with आ -ā)/causative | | |
|---|---|---|---|---|---|
| देना | **denā** | to give | दिवाना/दिलाना | **d*i*vānā/d*i*lānā** | to cause y to give x |
| धोना | **dʰonā** | to wash | धुवाना/धुलाना | **dʰ*u*vānā/dʰ*u*lānā** | to cause y to wash x |

## Type 4

Some verbs show both consonantal and vowel changes in their corresponding transitive forms. The consonantal alternations are as follows: the intransitive stem-final क **k** becomes च **c**, and the intransitive stem-final ट **T** becomes retroflex ड़ **R**.

| Intransitive | Transitive | Causative |
|---|---|---|
| बिकना **b*i*knā** | बेचना **becnā** | बिकवाना **bikvānā** |
| to be sold | to sell x | to cause y to sell x |
| टूटना **T*ū*Tnā** | तोड़ना **t*o*Rnā** | तुड़ाना/तुड़वाना **t*u*RāNā/t*u*RvāNā** |
| to be broken | to break x | to cause y to break x |

## *Auxiliary/copula verb*

### Present

The present tense auxiliary/copular verb agrees in number and person with its subject.

### होना **honā** 'to be'

| | Singular | | | Plural | | |
|---|---|---|---|---|---|---|
| First person | हूँ | **hū̃** | I am | हैं | **hɛ̃** | we are |
| Second person | है | **hɛ** | you are | हो | **ho** | you (familiar तुम) are |
| | | | | हैं | **hɛ̃** | you (honorific आप) are |
| Third person | है | **hɛ** | he, she, it is | हैं | **hɛ̃** | they are |

## Past

The past tense auxiliary/copular verb agrees in number and gender with its subject.

# होना **honā** 'to be'

|  | Singular |  |  | Plural |  |  |
|---|---|---|---|---|---|---|
| *Masculine* | था | **tʰā** | was | थे | **tʰe** | were |
| *Feminine* | थी | **tʰī** | was | थीं | **tʰī̃** | were |

Another conjugation of होना **honā** is as follows:

|  | Singular |  |  | Plural |  |
|---|---|---|---|---|---|
| *Masculine* | हुआ | **huā** | happened | हुए | **hue** |
| *Feminine* | हुई | **huī** |  | हुईं | **huī̃** |

## Future

The future tense auxiliary/copular verb agrees in number, gender and person with its subject.

## होना **honā**: masculine

|  | Singular | Plural |
|---|---|---|
| *First person* | हूँगा **hū̃gā** | होंगे **hõge** |
|  | I will be | we will be |
| *Second person* | होगा **hogā** | होगे **hoge** |
|  | you will be | you (familiar) will be |
|  |  | होंगे **hõge** |
|  |  | you (आप **āp**, honorific) will be |
| *Third person* | होगा **hogā** | होंगे **hõge** |
|  | he/she/it will be | they will be |

## होना **honā**: feminine

For the feminine forms, replace the word-final vowel of the masculine forms with ई **ī**.

## Subjunctive

For the subjunctive forms of होना **honā**, simply drop the final syllable (i.e. गा **gā**, गे **ge**, गी **gī**) from the future tense forms.

## *Main Verb*

### Simple present/imperfective/present habitual

The simple present is formed by adding the following suffixes to the main verbal stem:

|           | Singular | Plural |
|-----------|----------|--------|
| Masculine | -ता  -tā | -ते  -te |
| Feminine  | -ती  -tī | -ती  -tī |

The main verb is followed by the present auxiliary forms.

### Example: verb stem लिख **lik^h** 'to write'

*Masculine*

| Singular | Plural |
|----------|--------|
| मैं लिखता हूँ   mɛ̃ lik^htā hū̃<br>I write | हम लिखते हैं   ham lik^hte hɛ̃<br>we write |
| तू लिखता है   tū lik^htā hɛ<br>you write | तुम लिखते हो   tum lik^hte ho<br>you (familiar) write<br>आप लिखते हैं   āp lik^hte hɛ̃<br>you (honorific) write |
| वह लिखता है   vo lik^htā hɛ<br>he writes | वे लिखते हैं   ve lik^hte hɛ̃<br>they write |

*Feminine*

Replace ता -tā and ते -te in the masculine paradigm with ती -tī.

### Past habitual

The past habitual is derived by substituting the past auxiliary forms for the present auxiliary forms in the simple present tense.

## Examples: verb stem लिख **lik$^h$** 'to write'

*Masculine*

| Singular | Plural |
|---|---|
| मैं लिखता था  **mɛ̃ lik$^h$tā t$^h$ā**<br>I used to write | हम लिखते थे  **ham lik$^h$te t$^h$e**<br>we used to write |
| तू लिखता था  **tū lik$^h$tā t$^h$ā**<br>you used to write | तुम लिखते थे  **tum lik$^h$te t$^h$e**<br>you (familiar) used to write<br>आप लिखते थे  **āp lik$^h$te t$^h$e**<br>you (honorific) used to write |
| वह लिखता था  **vo lik$^h$tā t$^h$ā**<br>he used to write | वे लिखते थे  **ve lik$^h$te t$^h$e**<br>they used to write |

*Feminine*

Replace ता **-tā** and ते **-te** in the masculine paradigm with ती **-tī**. Also substitute the auxiliaries थी **t$^h$ī** and थीं **t$^h$ī̃** for था **t$^h$ā** and थे **t$^h$e**, respectively.

## Simple past/perfective

The simple past is formed by adding the following suffixes to the verb stem. No auxiliary verb follows the main verb.

|  | Singular | Plural |
|---|---|---|
| *Masculine* | आ  **-ā** | ए  **-e** |
| *Feminine* | ई  **-ī** | ईं  **-ī̃** |

## Example: verb stem बैठ **bɛT$^h$** 'sit'

*Masculine*

| Singular | Plural |
|---|---|
| मैं बैठा  **mɛ̃ bɛT$^h$ā**<br>I sat | हम बैठे  **ham bɛT$^h$e**<br>we sat |
| तू बैठा  **tū bɛT$^h$ā**<br>you sat | तुम बैठे  **tum bɛT$^h$e**<br>you (familiar) sat<br>आप बैठे  **āp bɛT$^h$e**<br>you (honorific) sat |
| वह बैठा  **vo bɛT$^h$ā**<br>he sat | वे बैठे  **ve bɛT$^h$e**<br>they sat |

*Feminine*

The verb-final आ **ā** and ए **e** are replaced by ई **ī** and ईं **ī̃**, respectively.

## Transitive verb and the agentive postposition ने **ne**

Transitive verbs take the agentive postposition ने **ne** with the subject and the verb agreeing with the object instead of the subject. Observe the paradigm of the simple past tense with the transitive verb लिख **lik**[h] 'to write'.

## Example: verb stem लिख **lik**[h] 'to write'

*Masculine*

| Singular | | Plural | |
|---|---|---|---|
| मैंने चिट्ठी लिखी | **mɛ̃ne ciTT**[h]**ī lik**[h]**ī** | हमने चिट्ठी लिखी | **hamne ciTT**[h]**ī lik**[h]**ī** |
| I wrote a letter | | we wrote a letter | |
| तूने चिट्ठी लिखी | **tūne ciTT**[h]**ī lik**[h]**ī** | तुमने चिट्ठी लिखी | **tumne ciTT**[h]**ī lik**[h]**ī** |
| you wrote a letter | | you (familiar) wrote a letter | |
| | | आपने चिट्ठी लिखी | **āpne ciTT**[h]**ī lik**[h]**ī** |
| | | you (honorific) write a letter | |
| उसने चिट्ठी लिखी | **usne ciTT**[h]**ī lik**[h]**ī** | उन्होंने चिट्ठी लिखी | **unhɔ̃ne ciTT**[h]**ī lik**[h]**ī** |
| he wrote a letter | | they wrote a letter | |

The verb agrees with चिट्ठी **ciTT**[h]**ī** 'letter', which is a feminine singular noun. Therefore the verb stays the same regardless of the change in the subject.

Important transitive verbs which do *not* take the ने **ne** postposition are: मिलना **milnā** 'to meet', लाना **lānā** 'to bring' and बोलना **bolnā** 'to speak.'

*Default agreement*

The rule of thumb is that the verb does not agree with a constituent which is followed by a postposition. For example, if the object marker को **ko** is used with चिट्ठी **ciTT**[h]**ī**, the verb will agree with neither the subject nor the object. In such situations, the verb will stay in the *masculine singular* form.

## Present perfect

Present perfect verbs are formed by adding the present tense auxiliary forms to the simple past tense. Transitive verbs take the ने **ne** postposition with their subjects.

## Example: verb stem बैठ **bɛTʰ** 'to sit'

*Masculine*

| *Singular* | *Plural* |
|---|---|
| मैं बैठा हूँ  **mɛ̃ bɛTʰā hū̃** | हम बैठे हैं  **ham bɛTʰe hɛ̃** |
| I have sat (down) | we have sat (down) |
| तू बैठा है  **tū bɛTʰā hɛ** | तुम बैठे हो  **tum bɛTʰe ho** |
| you have sat (down) | you (familiar) have sat (down) |
| | आप बैठे हैं  **āp bɛTʰe hɛ̃** |
| | you (honorific) have sat (down) |
| वह बैठा है  **vo beTʰā hɛ** | वे बैठे हैं  **ve bɛTʰe hɛ̃** |
| he has sat (down) | they have sat (down) |

## Past perfect

Past perfect verbs are formed by adding the past tense auxiliary forms to the simple past tense. Transitive verbs take the ने **ne** postposition with their subjects.

## Example: verb stem बैठ **bɛTʰ** 'to sit'

*Masculine*

| *Singular* | *Plural* |
|---|---|
| मैं बैठा था  **mɛ̃ bɛTʰā tʰā** | हम बैठे थे  **ham bɛTʰe tʰe** |
| I had sat (down) | we had sat (down) |
| तू बैठा था।  **tū bɛTʰā tʰa** | तुम बैठे थे  **tum bɛTʰe tʰe** |
| You had sat (down) | you (familiar) had sat (down) |
| | आप बैठे थे  **āp bɛTʰe tʰe** |
| | you (honorific) had sat (down) |
| वह बैठा था  **vo beTʰā tʰā** | वे बैठे थे  **ve bɛTʰe tʰe** |
| he had sat (down) | they had sat (down) |

## Future

The following person-number-gender suffixes with a stem form the future tense.

| Pronouns | Singular | | | | Plural | | | |
|---|---|---|---|---|---|---|---|---|
| | Masculine | | Feminine | | Masculine | | Feminine | |
| First person | ऊँगा | -ū̃gā | ऊँगी | -ū̃gī | एँगे | -ẽge | एँगी | -ẽgī |
| Second person | एगा | -egā | एगी | -egī | ओगे | -oge | ओगी | -ogī |
| | | | | | एँगे | -ẽge | एँगी | -ẽgī |
| Third person | एगा | -egā | एगी | -egī | एँगे | -ẽge | एँगी | -ẽgī |

## Example: verb stem लिख **likʰ** 'to write'

*Masculine*

| *Singular* | *Plural* |
|---|---|
| मैं लिखूँगा   **mẽ likʰū̃gā** | हम लिखेंगे   **ham likʰẽge** |
| I will write | we will write |
| तू लिखेगा   **tū likʰegā** | तुम लिखोगे   **tum likʰoge** |
| you will write | You (familiar) will write |
| | आप लिखेंगे   **āp likʰẽge** |
| | you (honorific) will write |
| वह लिखेगा   **vo likʰegā** | वे लिखेंगे   **ve likʰẽge** |
| he will write | they will write |

*Feminine*

Replace the last syllable गा **-gā** and गे **-ge** in the masculine paradigm with गी **-gī**.

## Subjunctive/optative

The subjunctive (also called optative and hortative) is used to express suggestion, possibility, doubt, uncertainty, apprehension, wish, desire, encouragement, demand, requirement or potential. Subjunctive forms are not coded for gender. Drop the गा **gā**, गे **ge** and गी **gī** endings from the future form, and the remainder will constitute the subjunctive form.

## Imperative

The imperative is formed by adding the following endings to the stem:

| Intimate/impolite | Familiar | Polite | Extra polite | Future |
|---|---|---|---|---|
| no suffix | ओ **-o** | इए/इये **-iye** | इएगा **-iyegā** | ना **-nā** (=infinitive) |

## Examples

| *intimate/impolite* | तू जा | **tū jā** | Go |
|---|---|---|---|
| *familiar* | तुम जाओ | **tum jāo** | Go |
| *polite* | आप जाइए | **āp jāiye** | (Please) go |
| *extra polite* | आप जाइएगा | **āp jāiyegā** | (Please) go |
| *future* | आप जाना | **āp/tum jānā** | (Please) go |
| *(non-immediate)* | | | (sometime in future) |

## Negative particles and the imperative

नहीं **nahī̃** is not used with imperatives.
मत **mat** is usually used with intimate, familiar and future imperatives.
न **na** is usually used with polite, extra polite and future imperatives.

## Present progressive/continuous

The progressive aspect is expressed by means of the independent word रह **rah**, which is homophonous with the stem of the verb रहना **rahnā** 'to live'. The progressive marker agrees with the number and gender of the subject; therefore it can be realized in one of the following three forms:

## Progressive marker: रह **rah** '-ing'

| Singular | | Plural | |
|---|---|---|---|
| Masculine | Feminine | Masculine | Feminine |
| रहा **rahā** | रही **rahī** | रहे **rahe** | रहीं **rahī̃** |

## Examples: verb stem लिख **lik^h** 'to write'

*Masculine*

| *Singular* | *Plural* |
|---|---|
| मैं लिख रहा हूँ    **mɛ̃ lik^h rahā hũ**<br>I am writing | हम लिख रहे हैं    **ham lik^h rahe hɛ̃**<br>we are writing |
| तू लिख रहा है    **tū lik^h rahā hɛ**<br>you are writing | तुम लिख रहे हो    **tum lik^h rahe ho**<br>you (familiar) are writing |
| | आप लिख रहे हैं    **āp lik^h rahe hɛ̃**<br>you (honorific) are writing |
| वह लिख रहा है    **vo lik^h rahā hɛ**<br>he is writing | वे लिख रहे हैं    **ve lik^h rahe hɛ̃**<br>they are writing |

*Feminine*

Replace रहा **rahā** and रहे **rahe** in the masculine paradigm with रही **rahī**.

## Past progressive/continuous

The present auxiliary verb in the present progressive construction is replaced by the past auxiliary verb (था **t^hā** 'was'; थे **t^he** 'were'; feminine थी **t^hī**, थीं **t^hī̃**) in the past progressive forms.

## Irregular verbs

Here is a list of five Hindi irregular verbs in tense forms such as past, imperative and future:

| जाना | करना | लेना | देना | पीना |
|---|---|---|---|---|
| **jānā** | **karnā** | **lenā** | **denā** | **pīnā** |
| to go | to do | to take | to give | to drink |

## Simple past

| गया | किया | लिया | दिया | पिया |
|---|---|---|---|---|
| **gayā** | **kiyā** | **liyā** | **diyā** | **piyā** |
| went (m. sg.) | did (m. sg.) | took (m. sg.) | gave (m. sg.) | drank (m. sg.) |
| गये | किये | लिये | दिये | पिये |
| **gaye** (m. pl.) | **kiye** (m. pl.) | **liye** (m. pl.) | **diye** (m. pl.) | **piye** (m. pl.) |
| गयी | की | ली | दी | पी |
| **gayī** (f. sg.) | **kī** (f. sg.) | **lī** (f. sg.) | **dī** (f. sg.) | **pī** (f. sg.) |
| गयीं | कीं | लीं | दीं | पीं |
| **gayī̃** (f. pl.) | **kī̃** (f. pl.) | **lī̃** (f. pl.) | **dī̃** (f. pl.) | **pī̃** (f. pl.) |

## Imperative

|  |  |  |  |  |
|---|---|---|---|---|
| (polite) | कीजिए/कीजिये | लीजिए/लीजिये | दीजिए/दीजिये | पीजिए/पीजिये |
|  | **kījiye** | **lījiye** | **dījiye** | **pījiye** |
| (familiar) | regular | लो | दो | पियो |
|  |  | **lo** | **do** | **piyo** |

## Future

| लेना | लूँगा | लोगे | लेगा |
|---|---|---|---|
| **lenā** | **lū̃gā** | **loge** | **legā** |
| to take | I will take | you (तुम) will take | will take (m. sg.) |
|  | लेंगे |  |  |
|  | **lẽge** |  |  |
|  | will take (m. pl.) |  |  |
| देना | दूँगा | दोगे | देगा |
| **denā** | **dū̃gā** | **doge** | **degā** |
| to give | I will give | you (तुम) will give | will give (m. sg.) |
|  | देंगे |  |  |
|  | **dẽge** |  |  |
|  | will give (m. pl.) |  |  |

# *Participles*

## Present/imperfective participle

The present participial marker is **-t-** which immediately follows the verbal stem and is, in turn, followed by number and gender markers, as shown below:

| *Masculine* |  | *Feminine* |  |
|---|---|---|---|
| *Singular* | *Plural* | *Singular* | *Plural* |
| stem + ता | stem + ते | stem + ती | stem + ती |
| stem-**t-ā** | stem-**t-e** | stem-**t-ī** | stem-**t-ī** |

The present participle may be used as either adjective or adverb. The optional past participial form of the verb होना **honā** 'to be' may immediately follow the present participial form. The forms of the optional element are as follows:

| Masculine | | Feminine | |
|---|---|---|---|
| Singular | Plural | Singular | Plural |
| हुआ | हुए | हुई | हुईं |
| **huā** | **hue** | **huī** | **huī̃** |

## Examples

| चलता (हुआ) लड़का | **caltā (huā) laRkā** | walking boy |
|---|---|---|
| चलती (हुई) लड़की | **caltī (huī) laRkī** | walking girl |

The present participial form and the optional 'to be' form agree in number and gender with the following head noun. The retention of the optional form makes the participial phrase emphatic in nature. The present participle indicates an *ongoing action*.

## Past/perfective participle

The past participial form is derived by adding the following suffixes, declined for number and gender, to the verbal stem. Like the present participle, the optional past participial form of the verb होना **honā** 'to be' may immediately follow the past participial form.

| Masculine | | Feminine | |
|---|---|---|---|
| Singular | Plural | Singular | Plural |
| stem + ा | stem + े | stem + ी | stem + ीं |
| stem-**ā** | stem-**e** | stem-**ī** | stem-**ī** |

The past participle may be used as either adjective or adverb. The past participial form and the optional 'to be' form agree in number and gender with the following head noun. The retention of the optional form makes the participial phrase emphatic in nature. The past participle indicates a *state*, as in

| बैठी (हुआ) लड़का | **bɛTʰā (huā) laRkā** | a seated boy |
|---|---|---|
| बैठी (हुई) लड़की | **bɛTʰī (huī) laRkī** | a seated girl |

The irregular past participle is formed the same way as the past tense form.

## Absolutive/conjunctive participle

The absolutive/conjunctive participle is formed by adding the invariable कर **kar** to the verbal stem, as in

| Stem | | | Conjunctive participle | | |
|------|------|-------|------|------|------|
| लिख | **likʰ** | write | लिख कर | **likʰ kar** | having written |
| आ | **ā** | come | आ कर | **ā kar** | having come |
| पी | **pī** | drink | पी कर | **pī kar** | having drunk |

## ते ही -te hī participle 'as soon as'

This participle is formed by adding the invariable ते ही **-te hī** 'as soon as' to the verbal stem.

| Stem | | | 'as soon as' participle | | |
|------|------|-------|------|------|------|
| लिख | **likʰ** | write | लिखते ही | **likʰte hī** | as soon as (s/he) wrote |
| आ | **ā** | come | आते ही | **āte hī** | as soon as (s/he) came |
| पी | **pī** | drink | पीते ही | **pīte hī** | as soon as (s/he) drank |

## Agentive participle

The agentive participle is formed by adding the marker वाला **vālā** to the oblique infinitive form of the verb. वाला **vālā** agrees in number and gender with the following noun.

| Masculine | | Feminine | |
|-----------|--------|-----------|--------|
| Singular | Plural | Singular | Plural |
| वाला **vālā** | वाले **vāle** | वाली **vālī** | वाली **vālī** |

## Examples

| Stem | Oblique infinitive | Agentive participle | |
|------|--------------------|--------------------|---|
| लिख | लिखने | लिखने वाला लड़का | |
| **lik^h** | **lik^hne** | **lik^hne vālā laRkā** | the boy who writes. |
| write | | लिखने वाले लड़के | |
| | | **lik^hane vāle laRke** | the boys who write. |
| | | लिखने वाली लड़की | |
| | | **lik^hne vālī laRkī** | the girl who writes |
| | | लिखने वाली लड़कियाँ | |
| | | **lik^hne vālī laRkiyā̃** | the girls who write |

अभ्यास: कुंजी
# ab<sup>h</sup>yās: kuñjī

## Key to exercises

हिन्दी लेखन और उच्चारण   **hindī lek<sup>h</sup>an aur uccāraN**
## Hindi writing system and pronunciation

### Exercise 1

1 C   2 A   3 C   4 B   5 B

### Exercise 2

1 A, D   2 B, D   3 A, B   4 B, C   5 B, D

### Exercise 3

| | | |
|---|---|---|
| 1 टाक | Tāk | i.e. 1 B |
| 2 ठक | T<sup>h</sup>ak | i.e. 2 B |
| 3 डाग | Dāg | i.e. 3 B |
| 4 धक | d<sup>h</sup>ak | i.e. 4 A |
| 5 पड़ | paR | i.e. 5 B |
| 6 सर | sar | i.e. 6 A |
| 7 कढ़ी | kaR<sup>h</sup>ī | i.e. 7 B |
| 8 ठीक | T<sup>h</sup>īk | i.e. 8 B |

### Exercise 4

| | | |
|---|---|---|
| 1 काल | kāl | i.e. 1 A |
| 2 दिन | din | i.e. 2 A |
| 3 मिल | mil | i.e. 3 A |
| 4 चूक | cūk | i.e. 4 B |
| 5 मैल | mɛl | i.e. 5 B |

| 6 सेर | ser | i.e. 6 A |
|-------|-----|----------|
| 7 बिन | bin | i.e. 7 A |
| 8 बल | bal | i.e. 8 B |

## पहला पाठ – लिपि  **pɛhlā pāT$^h$ – lipi   Script unit 1**

### Exercise 1

| 1 aman | 2 asal | 3 jalan | 4 kalam | 5 kamal | 6 garam |
|--------|--------|---------|---------|---------|---------|
| 7 jab  | 8 kab  | 9 tab   | 10 sab  |         |         |

### Exercise 2

ka, ya, t$^h$a, ta, g$^h$a, d$^h$a, b$^h$a, ma, va, ba

### Exercise 3

1 ख, र, व    2 ठ, त, ठ, थ    3 द, ड, ध, ढ    4 प, फ, ब, य    5 र, ड, ढ़

### Exercise 4

| 1 कट  | 2 गल  | 3 चल   | 4 नमक  | 5 सबक | 6 परख | 7 सदर |
|-------|-------|--------|--------|-------|-------|-------|
| 8 चलन | 9 मन  | 10 पल  | 11 गरम |       |       |       |

## दूसरा पाठ – लिपि  **dūsrā pāT$^h$ – lipi   Script unit 2**

### Exercise 1

| 1 b$^h$ārī | 2 baRā | 3 kitanā | 4 kālā | 5 b$^h$ārat |
|-----------|--------|----------|--------|------------|
| 6 gāRī | 7 kinārā | 8 gīt | 9 gāyab | 10 cāval |
| 11 cāhnā | 12 ciRiyāg$^h$ar | 13 zarā | 14 jīvan | 15 jāpān |
| 16 cor | 17 mor | 18 p$^h$al | 19 b$^h$ūt | 20 caut$^h$āu |
| 21 Daul | 22 pulis | 23 hāt$^h$ī | 24 sitār | 25 shām |

(Note: व is transcribed as v above.)

### Exercise 2

| 1 जबकि | 2 की | 3 बाज़ार | 4 राजा | 5 रानी | 6 पहचान | 7 नई | 8 बनारस |
|--------|------|---------|--------|--------|---------|------|--------|
| 9 कानपुर | 10 माता | 11 पिता | 12 कभी | 13 मिलन | 14 ज़मीन | 15 कार | 16 महीना |
| 17 साल | 18 दिन | 19 चार | 20 सात | 21 सवेरा | 22 चाय | 23 पानी | 24 पति |
| 25 भालू | 26 रात | 27 दोपहर | 28 खोल | 29 सौ | 30 सोना | | |

## Exercise 3

1 रिचर्ड      2 बिल      3 सेयरा      4 जैनिफर      5 डॉन

## Exercise 4

| | |
|---|---|
| रुपया | डर |
| रूखा | नाम |
| कर | थान |
| कि | घर |
| और | डाल |

# तीसरा पाठ – लिपि   **tīsrā pāT$^h$ – lipi   Script unit 3**

## Exercises 1–2

1 थाना वहीं है।
2 आप मेरी मदद कर सकते हैं?
3 मैं वहाँ कैसे जाऊँ?
4 ये मेरी गलती नहीं।
5 यहाँ खतरा है।
6 बचाओ!
7 यह बहुत ज़रूरी है।
8 डाक-खाना कहाँ है?
9 किस खिड़की पर जाऊँ?
10 टिकट कितना लगेगा?
11 ई-मेल अमरीका भेजना चाहता हूँ।
12 मुझे चिन्ता/फ़िक है।

## Exercise 3

1 आइए      2 आओ      3 खाइए      4 खा लो      5 माइक

## Exercise 4

1 hā vs hā̃      2 hū vs hū̃      3 hɛ vs hɛ̃      4 me vs mẽ

# चौथा पाठ – लिपि   **caut$^h$ā pāT$^h$ – lipi   Script unit 4**

## Exercise 1

1 पूछ-ताछ का दफ़्तर।
2 मैं रास्ता भूल गयी हूँ।

3 मैं रास्ता भूल गया हूँ।
4 तंग मत करो।
5 मैं कुंजी ढूंढ रहा हूँ।
6 नहीं मिल रही।
7 चिट्ठी हवाई डाक से भेजिये।
8 क्या आप ये सामान सीधे बम्बई भेज सकते हैं?
9 समान के लिये रसीद दीजिये।
10 मेरा सामान नहीं आया।

## Exercise 2

1 ham ek haftā dillī mẽ rahẽge.
2 mẽ yahā̃ cʰuTTī par hū̃.
3 ham yahā̃ kām se āye hẽ.
4 ye merā pāsporT hɛ.
5 kyā is sāmān par DyūTī lagegī?
6 ye cīzẽ mere apne istemāl ke liye hẽ.
7 mere pās DyūTī vālā sāmān nahī̃ hɛ.
8 mere pās kucʰ gifTs hẽ.
9 is mẽ sirf kapRe aur kitābẽ hẽ.
10 is ke alāvā koī aur cīz nahī̃ hɛ.

## Exercise 4

nokiyā fon kī duniyā mẽ āpkā svāgat hɛ.

hindī mẽ TɛkT mɛsej bʰejie.

pāvar kuñjī            nevī  kuñjī
haTāẽ kuñjī            skrāl kuñjī
nambar kuñjiyā̃

पाँचवाँ पाठ – लिपि   **pā̃cvā̃ pāTʰ – lipi   Script unit 5**

## Exercise 1

1 ā # i # ye
2 aur # tẽ
3 paRʰ # tā
4 su # no
5 na # mas # te
6 mi # lẽ # ge
7 sun # kar
8 ād # mī

## Exercise 3

| mausam | dillī | mumbaī | kolkatā |
|--------|-------|--------|---------|
| tāpmān | das digrī sī | padrah digrī sī | solah digrī sī |
| barsāt | bārish | bādal | dʰūp |
| havā | tez | halkī | mand |

## पाठ ९   pāTʰ ek   Unit 1

## Exercise 1

1 नमस्ते। 2 ठीक है। 3 सलाम। 4 अल्लाह का शुक है। 5 अच्छा, नमस्ते।
6 सत् स्री अकाल है। 7 मेहरबानी है or अल्लाह का शुक है। 8 नमस्ते जी।
9 हुकम नहीं, विनती है।

1 namaste   2 Tʰīk hɛ.   3 salām   4 allāha kā shukra hɛ.   5 (accʰā),
namaste.   6 sat srī akāl jī.   7 meharbānī hɛ *or* (allāh kā) shukra hɛ.
8 namaste jī.   9 hukam nahī̃, vintī hɛ.

## Exercise 2

1 नमस्ते।                            नमस्ते।
2 क्या हाल है?                       ठीक है
3 आप के मिज़ाज कैसे हैं?        अल्लाह का शुक है।
4 खुदा हाफ़िज़                        खुदा हाफ़िज़।
5 सब खैरियत है?                    मेहरबानी है।
6 सलाम।                              सलाम

1 namaste.                          namaste.
2 kyā hāl hɛ?                        Tʰīk hɛ.
3 āp ke mizāj kaise hɛ̃?           allāh kā shukr hɛ.
4 xudā hāfiz                         xudā hāfiz.
5 sab xɛriyat hɛ?                    meharbānī hɛ.
6 salām                             salām.

## Exercise 3

## Conversation 1

A:  सलाम ।
B:  सलाम ।

B: सब ख़ैरियत है?
A: मेहरबानी है, और आपके मिज़ाज कैसे हैं?
B: अल्लाह का शुक्र है।

A: salām.
B: salām.
B: sab xɛriyat hɛ?
A: meharbānī hɛ, aur āp ke mizāj kɛse hɛ̃?
B: allāh kā shukr hɛ.

## Conversation 2

A: सत् स्री अकाल जी।
B: सत् स्री अकाल जी।
B: क्या हाल है?
A: ठीक है, और आप?
B: मैं भी ठीक हूँ।
A: अच्छा, सत् स्री अकाल।
B: सत् स्री अकाल।

A: sat srī akāl jī.
B: sat srī akāl jī.
B: kyā hāl hɛ?
A: Tʰīk hɛ, aur āp?
B: mɛ̃ bʰī Tʰīk hū̃.
A: acchā, sat srī akāl.
B: sat srī akāl.

## Exercise 4

1 सवाल: क्या हाल है?
  जवाब: ठीक है।
  सवाल: और आप?
  जवाब: मैं भी ठीक हूँ।
2 सवाल: आप कैसे हैं?
  जवाब: ठीक हूँ।

1 Question: kyā hāl hɛ?
  Answer: Tʰīk hɛ.
  Question: aur āp?
  Answer: mɛ̃ bʰī Tʰīk hū̃.
2 Question: āp kɛse hɛ̃?
  Answer: Tʰīk hū̃.

## Exercise 5

| | *Long sentences* | *Short sentences* |
|---|---|---|
| 1 | और आप कैसे हैं? | कैसे हैं? |
| 2 | मैं भी ठीक हूँ। | ठीक हूँ। |
| 3 | आपकी मेहरबानी है। | मेहरबानी है। |
| 4 | आपके मिज़ाज कैसे हैं? | मिज़ाज कैसे हैं? |

| | | |
|---|---|---|
| 1 | aur āp kɛse hɛ̃? | kɛse hɛ̃? |
| 2 | mɛ̃ bʰī Tʰīk hū̃. | Tʰīk hū̃. |
| 3 | āpkī meharbānī hɛ. | meharbānī hɛ̃. |
| 4 | āpke mizāj kɛse hɛ̃? | mizāj kɛse hɛ̃? |

## Exercise 6

Most probably both are Hindus. हिन्दू हैं। hirdū hɛ̃

## पाठ २ pāTʰ do Unit 2

## Exercise 1

मैं दिल्ली <u>का</u> हूँ। <u>मेरे</u> चार भाई हैं। मेरा छोटा भाई शिकागो में काम कर<u>ता</u> है। मेरे दो बड़े भाई इंग्लैंड में रह<u>ते</u> हैं। मेरा नाम अमर <u>है</u>। मैं स्कूल जा<u>ता</u> हूँ। मे<u>री</u> दो बहनें भी हैं। मे<u>रे</u> पिता जी भी काम कर<u>ते</u> हैं। आप कहाँ रहते हैं? आप<u>के</u> <u>कितने</u> भाई–बहनें हैं। आपकी माता जी <u>क्या</u> काम कर<u>ती</u> हैं।

mɛ̃ dillī <u>kā</u> hū̃. <u>mere</u> cār bʰāi hɛ̃. merā cʰoTā bʰāī *Chicago* mɛ̃ kām kar<u>tā</u> hɛ. mere do baRe bʰāī *England* mɛ̃ rɛhte hɛ̃. merā nām amar <u>hɛ</u>. mɛ̃ *school* jā<u>tā</u> hū̃. me<u>rī</u> do bɛhɛnẽ bʰī hɛ̃. me<u>re</u> pitā jī bʰī kām kar<u>te</u> hɛ̃. āp <u>kahā̃</u> rɛhte hɛ̃? āp<u>ke</u> kit<u>ne</u> bʰ āī-bɛhɛnẽ hɛ̃. āp<u>kī</u> mātā jī kyā <u>kām</u> kar<u>tī</u> hɛ̃?

## Exercise 2

| | | | |
|---|---|---|---|
| accʰa | burā | अच्छा | बुरा |
| baRā | cʰoTā | बड़ा | छोटा |
| bɛhɛn | bʰāī | बहन | भाई |
| laRkā | laRkī | लड़का | लड़की |
| ādmī | aurat | आदमी | औरत |
| hā̃ | nahī̃ | हाँ | नहीं |

## Exercise 3

| banāras | se | बनारस से |
| sheher | mẽ | शहर में |
| das | behenẽ | दस वहनें |
| cār | bʰāī | चार भाई |
| do | ādmī | दो आदमी |
| kitne | bʰāī | कितने भाई |
| pīlī | sāRī | पीली साड़ी |

## Exercise 4

| kahiye | कहिए |
| xushī | खुशी |
| baRī xushī huī | बड़ी खुशी हुई |
| pūrā nām | पूरा नाम |
| dūsrā | दूसरा |
| kitne bʰāī | कितने भाई |
| milẽge | मिलेंगे |

## Exercise 5

```
a d g a ⓑ a d z x ⓢ ⓤ ⓝ ⓘ ⓨ ⓔ z y x u f g
l l k j ⓐ z x c v b n m a s ⓟ q w e r t y
z x c v Ⓡ a d g a r t y f g h ⓐ s g h j o
r t y f ⓘ b g t ⓧ ⓤ ⓢ ⓗ ⓘ ⓘ z q ⓣ s k x p
c v b n ⓘ w s x e d v r a t g h t ⓐ h z c
q a z w c w s v f r y h n m h u i k ⓐ u c
```

## Exercise 6

Voices of two women: Abhilasha Pande and Meenu Bharati
Setting: A crowded shop

| अभिलाषा: | (bumps into Meenu) माफ़ कीजिये। |
| मीनू: | माफ़ी की बात नहीं। बहुत भीड़ है। |
| अभिलाषा: | सच। |
| मीनू: | मेरा नाम मीनू भारती है। |
| अभिलाषा: | और मेरा नाम अभिलाषा पाँडे है। |
| मीनू: | मैं यहाँ रोज़ आती हूँ। |
| अभिलाषा: | आप दिल्ली की हैं ना? |
| मीनू: | जी हाँ। |

ABHILASHA: (*bumps into Meenu*) māf kījiye.
MEENU: māf kī bāt nahī̃. bahut bʰīR hɛ.
ABHILASHA: sac.
MEENU: mera nām Meenu Bharati hɛ.
ABHILASHA: aur merā nām Abhilasha Pande hɛ.
MEENU: mɛ̃ yahā̃ roz ātī hū̃.
ABHILASHA: āp dillī kī hɛ̃ nā?
MEENU: jī hā̃.

## पाठ ३ pāTʰ tīn Unit 3

## Exercise 1

1 मुझको जयपुर की टिकट चाहिये/मुझको जयपुर के लिये टिकट चाहिये । *variation*: चाहिये = चाहिए
2 क्या आपको दवाई चाहिये?
3 मुझको दो घर चाहिये ।
4 मुझको *गराज* में कार चाहिये ।
5 आपको यह सुन्दर साड़ी चाहिये ।

1 mujʰko jaipur kī TikaT cāhiye/mujʰko jaipur ke liye TikaT cāhiye.
2 kyā āpko davāī cāhiye?
3 mujʰko do gʰar cāhiye.
4 mujʰko *garage* mɛ̃ kār cāhiye.
5 āpko ye sundar sāRī cāhiye.

## Exercise 2

1 मेरी एक बहन है ।   2 मेरे दो भाई हैं ।   3 मेरे पास एक कम्प्यूटर है ।
4 मेरा हाल ठीक है ।   5 मुझको सिर-दर्द है ।   6 मुझको काम चाहिये ।
7 मेरा लड़का घर लेता है ।

1 <u>merī</u> ek bɛhɛn hɛ.   2 <u>mere</u> do bʰāī hɛ̃.   3 <u>mere pās</u> ek kampyuTar hɛ.   4 <u>merā</u> hāl Tʰīk hɛ.   5 <u>mujʰko</u> sir-dard hɛ.   6 ~~mujʰko~~ kām cāhiye.   7 <u>merā</u> laRkā gʰar letā hɛ.

## Exercise 3

| मुझको | बुख़ार है । |
|---|---|
| मेरे पास | रुपये हैं । |

| | |
|---|---|
| आपके | घर में कितने आदमी हैं? |
| मेरा शहर | बहुत सुन्दर है। |
| इह फ्लाईट | आपके लिये है। |
| इसका दाम | क्या है? |

| | |
|---|---|
| mujʰko | buxār hε. |
| mere pās | rupiye hε̃. |
| āpke | ghar mε̃ kinte ādmī hε̃? |
| merā shεhεr | bahut sundar hε. |
| ye *flight* | āpke liye hε. |
| is kā dām | kyā hε? |

## Exercise 4

| | |
|---|---|
| WAITER: | नमस्ते। |
| YOU: | नमस्ते। |
| WAITER: | आप कैसे हैं? |
| YOU: | (मैं) ठीक हूँ। |
| WAITER: | आपको मैन्यू चाहिये? |
| YOU: | नहीं, लंच के लिये स्पेशल क्या है? |
| WAITER: | *लंच-स्पेशल* शाकाहारी *(i.e. vegetarian)* है। |
| YOU: | शाकाहारी-*स्पेशल* ठीक है। वह क्या है? *or* वैजीटेरियन-*स्पेशल* ठीक है। यह क्या है? |
| WAITER: | दाल, रोटी, रायता, सब्ज़ी और चावल। |
| YOU: | मुझको दाल ज़रा मसालेदार चाहिये। |
| WAITER: | ठीक है। |

| | |
|---|---|
| WAITER: | namaste. |
| YOU: | namaste. |
| WAITER: | āp kεse hε̃? |
| YOU: | (mε̃) Tʰīk hū̃. |
| WAITER: | āpko *menu* cāhiye? |
| YOU: | nahī̃, lunch ke liye *special* kyā hε? |
| WAITER: | *lunch-special* shākāhārī *(i.e. vegetarian)* hε. |
| YOU: | shākāhārī-*special* Tʰīk hε. vo kyā hε? *or vegetarian-special* Tʰīk hε. ye kyā hε? |
| WAITER: | dāl, roTī, rāytā, sabzī aur cāval. |
| YOU: | mujʰko dāl zarā masāledār cāhiye. |
| WAITER: | Tʰīk hε. |

## पाठ ४ **Unit 4**

### Exercise 1

मुझको पढ़ना पसन्द है। मुझको क्या पसन्द है? मुझको क्या–क्या पसन्द है। मुझको गाने का शौक है। मुझको तैरने का शौक है। मुझको खाने का शौक है।

muj^hko paR^hnā pasand hɛ. muj^hko kyā pasand hɛ? muj^hko kyā-kyā pasand hɛ? muj^hko gāne kā shauk hɛ. muj^hko tɛrne kā shauk hɛ. muj^hko k^hāne kā shauk hɛ.

By substituting आपको **āpko** for मुझको **muj^hko**, you can generate six more sentences.

### Exercise 2

1 जवाब:    गाने के अलावा जॉन को नाचना पसन्द है।
2 जवाब:    जूडी को कहानियाँ और कविताएँ लिखने के / का शौक हैं/ है ।
3 जवाब:    रमेश को मुर्गा खाना नापसन्द है।
          रमेश को माँसाहारी (*or चिकन*) खाना नापसन्द है।
          रमेश को कविताएँ नापसन्द हैं।
          रमेश को देशी–संगीत (*or कन्ट्री संगीत*) नापसन्द है।
4 जवाब:    रमेश को समोसा खाना पसन्द है।
          रमेश को शाकाहारी (*or वेजीटेरियन*) खाना पसन्द है।
          रमेश को कहानियाँ पसन्द हैं ।
          रमेश को भारतीय संगीत पसन्द है।
          रमेश को भारतीय (*or हिन्दुस्तानी*) संगीत पसन्द है।

1 gāne ke alāvā John ko nācnā pasand hɛ.
2 Judy ko kahāniyã aur kavitāẽ lik^hne kā shauk hɛ. *or*
  Judy ko kahāniyã aur kavitāẽ lik^hne ke shauk hɛ̃.
3 Ramesh ko murgā (or chicken) k^hānā nāpasand hɛ.
  Ramesh ko *non-vegetarian* (or mãsāhārī) k^hānā nāpasand hɛ.
  Ramesh ko kavitāẽ nāpasand hɛ̃.
  Ramesh ko deshī saŋgīt (or country music) nāpasand hɛ.
4 Ramesh ko samosā k^hānā pasand hɛ.
  Ramesh ko shākāhārī (or *vegetarian*) k^hānā pasand hɛ.
  Ramesh ko kahāniyã pasand hɛ̃.
  Ramesh ko b^hārtīya (or *hindustānī/Indian*) saŋgīt pasand hɛ.

### Exercise 3

1 John likes to eat/eating.        John likes food.
2 John likes to sing/singing.      John likes (the) song.

## Exercise 4 (examples)

x करने से मना करना। उन का कहना (कि) कमरा साफ़ करो।

x karne se manā karnā (to prohibit from doing x); unkā kɛhnā: kamrā sāf karo (their saying: clean your room).

## Exercise 5

मुझको तैरने का शौक है। मुझको तैरना पसन्द है। मुझको तैरना अच्छा लगता है।
Variation: मुझको = मुझे

mujʰko tɛrne kā shauk hɛ. mujʰko tɛrnā pasand hɛ. mujʰko tɛrnā accʰā lagtā hɛ.

## Exercise 6

| 1 | cats | बिल्लियाँ |
| 2 | dogs | कुत्ते |
| 3 | spicy foods | मसालेदार खाना |
| 4 | cricket (game) | किकेट |
| 5 | bʰaratnāTayam | भरतनाट्यम् |
| 6 | rock music | रॉक संगीत |

## पाठ ५   Unit 5

(If you are female, the final vowel of the verb forms given in italics needs to be replaced by the vowel ई ī.)

मेरा नाम x है।
(number) दिन आगरा रहूँ *गा*।
दिल्ली और आगरा जाऊँ *गा*।
यह दिल्ली (x शहर) का पता है।
*fill out the address.*
(number) दिनों के बाद।
(or x (number) तारीख़ को)।
जी नहीं।
merā nām x hɛ.
(number) din rahū̃*gā*.
dillī aur āgrā jāū̃*gā*.
ye dillī (x city) kā patā hɛ:
*(fill out the addresss)*

(number) dinõ ke bād.
(or x (number) tārīx ko).
jī nahī̃.

## Exercise 2

मैं आपके लिये क्या कर सकता हूँ? हम आगरा जाना चाहते हैं? आगरा कितनी दूर है? बहुत दूर नहीं, लेकिन आप कब जा रहे हैं? हम कल जाएँगे। गाड़ी सुबह दिल्ली से चलती है। आप गाड़ी से जाना चाहते हैं?

mɛ̃ āpke liye kyā kar saktā hū̃? ham āgrā jānā cāhte hɛ̃. āgrā kitnī dūr hɛ? bahut dūr nahī̃, lekin āp kab jā rahe hɛ̃? ham kal jāẽge. gāRī subā dillī se caltī hɛ. āp gāRī se jānā cāhte hɛ̃?

## Exercise 3

प्रिय राकेश

तुम्हारा ख़त मिला। पढ़ कर खुशी हुई। तुम कब आ रहे हो? कल मैं शिकागो जा रहा हूँ। शिकागो बहुत बड़ा शहर है। मैं शिकागो हवाई जहाज़ से जाऊँगा। लेकिन मैं हवाई जहाज़ से नहीं जाना चाहता हूँ। गाड़ी मुझे हवाई जहाज़ से ज़्यादा पसन्द है। बाकी सब ठीक है।

तुम्हारा दोस्त,
राजीव।

Priya Rakesh:

tumhārā xat milā. paRʰ kar xushī huī. tum kab ā rahe ho? kal mɛ̃ *Chicago* jā rahā hū̃. *Chicago* bahut baRā shɛher hɛ. mɛ̃ *Chicago* hawāī jahāz (airplane) se jāū̃gā. lekin mɛ̃ hawāī jahāz se nahī̃ jānā cāhtā hū̃. gāRī mujʰe hawāī jahāz se zyāda pasand hɛ. bākī sab Tʰīk hɛ.

tumhārā dost,
Rājīv

## Exercise 4

आप कहाँ जा रही हैं? आप यहाँ कितने दिन रहेंगी? आप किस का काम कर रही हैं? क्या आपको चाय बहुत पसन्द है? आपके कितने भाई हैं?

āp kahā̃ jā rahī hɛ̃. āp yahā̃ kitne din rahẽgī? āp kiskā kām kar rahī hɛ̃? kyā āpko cāy bahut pasand hɛ? āpke kitne bʰaī hɛ̃?

## Exercise 5

अगर मुझको एक मिलियन डॉलर मिलेंगे, तो मैं दुनिया का सफर करूँगा/ करूँगी । राजा/ रानी की तरह रहूँगा/ रहूँगी । अपने लिये एक नाव और रोल्स रॉयस ख़रीदूँगा/ ख़रीदूँगी । अपनी पत्नी / अपने पति के लिये हीरे ख़रीदूँगा /ख़रीदूँगी । लेकिन ख़ुशी से पागल नहीं हो जाऊँगा/ जाऊँगी । कुछ देर के बाद अपनी नौकरी करने ज़रूर जाऊँगा/ जाऊँगी ।

agar mujʰko ek *million dollars* milẽge, to mẽ duniyā kā safar karū̃gā/karū̃gī. rājā/rānī kī tarah rahū̃gā/rahū̃gī. apne liye ek nāv aur Rolls Royce xarīdū̃gā /xarīdū̃gī. apnī patnī/ apne pati ke liye hīre xarīdū̃gā/xarīdū̃gī. lekin xushī se pāgal nahī̃ ho jāū̃gā/jāū̃gī, kucʰ der ke bād apnī naukrī karne zarūr jāū̃gā/jāū̃gī.

## Exercise 6

हम *रोबात* हैं । हम *कैलिफ़ोर्निया* से हैं । हम हिन्दी बोल सकते हैं । हम हिन्दी समझ भी सकते हैं । हम हिन्दी गाने गा सकते हैं । हमारी *मैमोरी* बहुत बड़ी है । हम हर सवाल पूछ सकते हैं और हर जवाब दे सकते हैं । यानी हर काम कर सकते हैं । हम हमेशा काम कर सकते हैं । हम कभी नहीं थकते हैं । हमारे पास हर सवाल का जवाब है । लेकिन मसालेदार खाना नहीं खा सकते (हैं) ।

ham *Robot* hɛ̃. ham *California* se hɛ̃. ham hindī bol sakte hɛ̃. ham hindī samajʰ bʰī sakte hɛ̃. ham hindī gāne gā sakte hɛ̃. hamārī *memory* bahut baRī hɛ. ham har savāl pūcʰ sakte hɛ̃ aur har javāb de sakte hɛ̃. yānī har kām kar sakte hɛ̃. ham hameshā kām kar sakte hɛ̃. ham kabʰī nahī̃ tʰakte hɛ̃. hamāre pās har savāl kā javāb hɛ. lekin masāledār kʰānā nahī̃ kʰā sakte.

## Exercise 7

1 स्मिथ जि॰ *अमरीका* अगले महीने जाएँगे (जायेंगे) ।
2 वे *ब्रिटिश एयरवेज़ से न्यू यॉर्क* जाएँगे (जायेंगे) ।
3 जी नहीं ।
4 क्योंकि वे अपने बच्चों को *डिज़्नी वर्ड* दिखाना चाहते हैं ।
5 वे *डिज़्नी वर्ड* सात दिन (or एक हफ़्ता) रहेंगे ।

1 Smith jī *America* agle mahīne jāẽge.
2 ve *British Airways* se New York jāẽge.
3 jī nahī̃.
4 kyõki ve apne baccõ ko *Disney World* dikʰānā cāhte hɛ̃.
5 ve *Disney World* sāt din (*or* ek haftā) rahẽge.

## पाठ ६ Unit 6

### Exercise 1

मेरे दोस्त, वे दिन कितने अच्छे थे! मैंने सोचा वे दिन हमेशा रहेंगे। वे दिन बचपन के दिन थे। मैं हमेशा खेलता था और नाचता था । हर चीज़ सुन्दर थी। हर दिन नया था और हर रात का अन्दाज़ था। अब वे दिन नहीं रहे।

mere dost, ve din kitne acc$^h$e t$^h$e! mɛ̃ne socā ve din hameshā rahẽge. ve bacpan ke din t$^h$e. mɛ̃ hameshā k$^h$eltā t$^h$ā aur nāctā t$^h$ā. har cīz sundar t$^h$ī. har din nayā t$^h$ā aur har rāt kā andāz t$^h$ā. ab ve din nahī̃ din rahe.

### Exercise 2

1 मैं वहाँ <u>गयी</u>।
2 <u>उसने</u> मुझको <u>बताया</u>।
3 <u>हम</u> घर <u>आये</u>।
4 <u>तुम</u> घर देर से <u>पहुँचे</u>।
5 <u>उन्होंने</u> पुलिस को रिपोर्ट <u>की</u>।
6 <u>आपको</u> यह किताब कब <u>मिली</u>।

1 <u>mɛ̃</u> vahā̃ <u>gayī</u>.
2 <u>usne</u> muj$^h$ko <u>batāyā</u>.
3 <u>ham</u> g$^h$ar <u>āye</u>.
4 <u>tum</u> g$^h$ar der se <u>pahũce</u>.
5 <u>unhõne</u> *police* ko *report* <u>kī</u>.
6 <u>āpko</u> ye kitāb kab <u>milī</u>.

### Exercise 3

1 आपके माता-पिता का जन्म कहाँ हुआ?
2 आपके माता-पिता का जन्म कब हुआ?
3 क्या उनका परिवार अमीर था या ग़रीब था?
4 उनकी शादी कब हुई?
5 उनकी उमर कितनी थी जब उनकी शादी हुई?
6 उनकी अँरेंज्ड मैरिज हुई या लव मैरिज?
7 क्या आपकी माँ आपके पिता से छोटी हैं?

1 āpke mātā-pitā kā janma kahā̃ huā?
2 āpke mātā-pitā kā janma kab huā?
3 kyā unkā parivār amīr t$^h$ā yā garīb t$^h$ā?

4 unkī shādī kab huī?
5 unkī umar kitnī t<sup>h</sup>ī jab unkī shādī huī?
6 unkī *arranged marriage* huī yā *love marriage*?
7 kyā āpkī mā̃ āp ke pitā se choTī hɛ̃?

## Exercise 4

1 कल किसका जन्म दिन था?
2 किसके परिवार ने एक पार्टी की?
3 वह *पार्टी* कब हुई?
4 जान को किसके बारे में मालूम नहीं था?
5 यह कैसी *पार्टी* थी?
6 जॉन का जन्म दिन कब था?

1 kal kiskā janma din t<sup>h</sup>ā?
2 kiske parivār ne ek party kī?
3 vo *party* kab huī?
4 John ko kiske bāre mẽ mālūm nahī̃ t<sup>h</sup>ā?
5 ye kɛsī party t<sup>h</sup>ī?
6 John kā janma din kab t<sup>h</sup>ā?

## Exercise 5

| 1 सच | 2 झूठ | 3 झूठ | 4 झूठ | 5 सच | 6 सच | 7 सच |
|------|-------|-------|-------|------|------|------|
| 1 sac | 2 j<sup>h</sup>ūT | 3 j<sup>h</sup>ūT | 4 j<sup>h</sup>ūT | 5 sac | 6 sac | 7 sac |

1 पुराने ज़माने में आदमी घर में काम नहीं करते थे।
2 आज–कल सारा परिवार टीवी देखता है।
3 आज–कल आदमी और औरतें खाना बनाते हैं।

1 purāne zamāne mẽ ādmī g<sup>h</sup>ar mẽ kām nahī̃ karte t<sup>h</sup>e.
2 āj-kal sārā parivār *TV* dek<sup>h</sup>tā hɛ.
3 āj-kal ādmī aur auratẽ k<sup>h</sup>ānā banāte hɛ̃.

## पाठ ७   Unit 7

## Exercise 1

1 मुझको सितार आती है।
2 क्या आप तैर सकते हैं?
3 उसको कहाँ जाना पड़ता है।

4 उन्होंने संगीत कब सीखा?
5 वह *सेल्ज़मैन* है। उसको बाहर जाना पड़ता है।
6 जॉन को बहुत काम है। इसलिये उसको कुछ फ़ुरसत नहीं है।

1 muj<sup>h</sup>ko sitār ātī hε.
2 kyā āp tεr sakte hɛ̃?
3 usko kahā̃ jānā hε?
4 unhõne saŋgīt kab sīk<sup>h</sup>ā?
5 vo *salesman* hε. usko bāhar jānā paRtā hε.
6 John ko bahut kām hε. isliye usko kuc<sup>h</sup> fursat nahī̃ hε.

## Exercise 2

1 बिल को जल्दी है क्योंकि उसकी गाड़ी दस मिनट में <u>जाने वाली</u> है।
2 ड्राइवर जल्दी करो, मेरे दोस्त की फ़्लाइट <u>आने वाली</u> है।
3 सरदी का मौसम था, जल्दी बरफ़ <u>गिरने वाली</u> थी।
4 पार्टी के लिये मेहमान <u>पहुँचने वाले</u> हैं।
5 शाम का समय था, अन्धेरा <u>होने वाला</u> था।
6 आप कभी हिन्दुस्तान <u>गये</u> हैं?

1 Bill ko jaldī hε kyõki uskī gāRī das minute mẽ j<u>āne vālī</u> hε.
2 *Driver* jaldī karo, mere dost kī *flight* <u>āne vālī</u> hε.
3 sardī kā mausam t<sup>h</sup>ā, jaldī barf g<u>irne vālī</u> t<sup>h</sup>ī.
4 *party* ke liye mεhmān pahũc<u>ne vāle</u> hɛ̃.
5 s<sup>h</sup>ām kā samay t<sup>h</sup>ā, and<sup>h</sup>rā ho<u>ne vālā</u> t<sup>h</sup>ā.
6 āp kab<sup>h</sup>ī hindustān g<u>aye</u> hɛ̃?

## Exercise 3

1 अध्यापक — उसको पढ़ाना है।
2 डॉक्टर — उसको मरीज़ को देखना है।
3 गायक — उसको गाना है।
4 ड्राइवर — उसको कार चलानी है।
5 धोबी — उसको कपड़े धोने हैं।
6 लेखक — उसको लिखना है।

1 ad<sup>h</sup>yāpak — usko paR<sup>h</sup>ānā hε.
2 *Doctor* — usko marīz ko dek<sup>h</sup>nā hε.
3 gāyak — usko gānā hε.
4 *Driver* — usko kār calānī hε.
5 d<sup>h</sup>obī — usko kapRe d<sup>h</sup>one hɛ̃.
6 lek<sup>h</sup>ak — usko lik<sup>h</sup>nā hε.

## Exercise 4

1 क्या आप मेरे लिए *रिकोमेंडेशन लैटर* लिख <u>देंगे</u>?
2 रात आयी और अंधेरा हो <u>गया</u> था।
3 मैं हिन्दी नहीं पढ़ सकता, आप ये खत पढ़ <u>दीजिये</u> ।
4 वो थोड़ा थोड़ा तैर सकता/<u>लेता</u> है।
5 उसको बहुत अच्छा नाचना <u>आता</u> है।
6 मैं आपकी बात बिल्कुल भूल <u>गया</u>।

1 kyā āp mere liye *recommendation letter* likh <u>dẽge</u>?
2 rāt āyī aur and$^h$erā ho <u>gayā</u> t$^h$ā.
3 mẽ hindī nahĩ paR$^h$ saktā, āp ye xat paR$^h$ <u>dījiye</u>.
4 vo t$^h$oRā t$^h$oRā tɛr saktā/<u>letā</u> hɛ.
5 usko bahut acc$^h$ā nācnā <u>ātā</u> hɛ.
6 mẽ āp kī bāt bilkul b$^h$ūl <u>gayā</u>.

## Exercise 5

बचपन में मुझे दूध पीना पड़ता था। बचपन में *डॉक्टर* के पास जाना पड़ता था। बचपन में मुझे दवाई पीनी पड़ती थी। बचपन में मुझे टीका लगवाना पड़ता था। बचपन में मुझे माता–पिता के साथ चीज़ें खरीदने जाना पड़ता था।

bacpan mẽ muj$^h$e dūd$^h$ pinā paRtā t$^h$ā. bacpan mẽ muj$^h$e *doctor* ke pās jānā paRtā t$^h$ā. bacpan mẽ muj$^h$e davāī pīnī paRtī t$^h$ī. bacpan mẽ muj$^h$e Tikā lagvānā paRtā t$^h$ā. bacpan mẽ muj$^h$e mātā-pitā ke sāth cīzẽ xarīdne jānā paRtā t$^h$ā.

## Exercise 6

| 1 झूठ | 2 सच | 3 झूठ | 4 झूठ | 5 सच | 6 झूठ | 7 सच |
|-------|------|-------|-------|------|-------|------|
| 1 j$^h$ | 2 s | 3 j$^h$ | 4 j$^h$ | 5 s | 6 j$^h$ | 7 s |

# पाठ ८   Unit 8

## Exercise 1

आइये, तशरीफ़ रखिये। तकलीफ़ की बात क्या है? शायद आपको दफ़्तर में काम ज़्यादा हो। वह आपका इन्तज़ार कर रही थी। आदाब अर्ज़ है।

āiye, tashrīf rak$^h$iye. taklīf kī bāt kyā hɛ? shāyad āpko daftar mẽ kām zyādā ho. vo āpkā intazār kar rahī t$^h$ī. ādāb arz hɛ.

## Exercise 2

1 माफ़ कीजिये, मैं चैक भेजना <u>भूल गया</u> ।
2 मैंने खाना <u>खा लिया</u> ।
3 आपका बुखार <u>बढ़ गया</u> ।
4 आपने कुछ ज़वाब नहीं <u>दिया</u> ।
5 आप मेरी सलाह मान लीजिये ।

1 māf kījiye, mɛ̃ *cheque* bʰejnā <u>bʰūl gayā</u>.
2 mɛ̃ne kʰānā kʰā liyā.
3 āpkā buxār baRʰ gayā.
4 āpne kucʰ javāb nahī̃ diyā.
5 āp merī salāh mān <u>lījiye</u>.

## Exercise 3

| 1 अध्यापक | छात्रों को पढ़ाता है । |
| 2 डॉक्टर | टीका लगाता है । |
| 3 कैशियर | चैक कैश करता है । |
| 4 दर्जी | कपड़े बनाता है । |
| 5 खानसामा | खाना बनाता है । |
| 6 ड्राइवर | कार चलाता है । |
| 7 सिविल इंजिनियर | इमारतें बनवाता है । |

| 1 adʰyāpak | cʰātrõ ko paRʰātā hɛ. |
| 2 DākTar (doctor) | Tīkā lagātā hɛ. |
| 3 *cashier* | *cheque cash* kartā hɛ. |
| 4 darzī | kapRe banātā hɛ. |
| 5 kʰānsāmā | kʰānā banātā hɛ. |
| 6 *driver* | kār calātā hɛ. |
| 7 *civil engineer* | imāratẽ banvātā hɛ. |

## Exercise 4

1 श्याम ने हिल्डा से अपनी कार चलवायी ।
2 श्याम हिल्डा से अपना ख़त लिखवायेगा ।
3 श्याम हिल्डा से अपना घर बनवा रहा है ।
4 श्याम हिल्डा से अपनी कहानी सुनवा रहा है ।
5 श्याम हिल्डा से अपनी लड़की को पढ़वाता है ।

1 Shyam: shyām ne hilDā se apnī kār calvāyī.
2 Shyam: shyām hilDā se apnā xat likʰvāyegā.
3 Shyam: shyām hilDā se apnā gʰar banvā rahā hɛ.

4 Shyam:    shyām hilDā se apnī kahānī sunvā rahā tʰā.
5 Shyam:    shyām hilDā se apnī laRkī ko paRʰvātā hɛ.

## Exercise 5

1 हँसना:        मुझे वह हँसती लड़की बहुत पसन्द है।
2 खेलना:        खेलते बच्चे बहुत सुन्दर लग रहे थे।
3 गाना:         गाती चिड़िया उड़ रही थी।
4 सितार बजाना:   सितार बजाता आदमी बहुत अच्छा है।
5 तैरना:        तैरती मछलियों को देखो।
6 रोना:         डॉक्टर ने रोते बच्चे को टीका लगाया।

1 hãsnā:        mujʰe vo hãstī laRkī bahut pasand hɛ.
2 kʰelnā:       kʰelte bacce bahut sundar lag rahe tʰe.
3 gānā:         gātī ciRiyā uR rahī tʰī.
4 sitār bajānā:  sitār bajātā ādmī bahut accʰā hɛ.
5 tɛrnā:        tɛrtī macʰaliyõ ko dekʰo.
6 ronā:         *Doctor* ne rote bacce ko Tīkā lagāyā.

## Exercise 6

मैं *रेलवे स्टेशन* परअपने दोस्त का इंतज़ार कर रहा था। थोड़ी देर बाद गाड़ी आयी और मेरा दोस्त गाड़ी से उतरा। हम बहुत खुश हो कर मिले। इस बार पाँच साल के बाद हमारी मुलाकात हुई। थोड़ी देर बाद मैंने कहा, 'इस बार बहुत देर के बाद यहाँ आये हो'। उसने जवाब दिया, 'अच्छी बात थी कि अगर गाड़ी देर से न आती, तो मैं आज भी न आता'।

mɛ̃ *railway station* par apne dost kā intzār kar rahā tʰā. tʰoRī der bād gāRʰī āyī aur merā dost gāRʰī se utrā. ham bahut xush ho kar mile. is bār pãc sāl ke bād hamārī mulākāt huī. tʰoRī der bād mɛ̃ne kahā, 'is bār bahut der ke bād yahã̄ āye ho'. usne javāb diyā, 'accʰī bāt tʰī ki agar gāRhī der se na ātī, to mɛ̃ āj bʰī na ātā'.

## पाठ ६  Unit 9

1 लोग *लॉड्रीमैट* कपड़े धोने जाते हैं।
2 लोग *रेस्टोरेंट* खाना खाने जाते हैं।
3 लोग *मूवी थिएटर* फिल्म देखने जाते हैं।
4 लोग *कॉलिज* पढ़ने जाते हैं।
5 लोग *स्विमिंग पूल* तैरने जाते हैं।
6 लोग *बार* बियर पीने जाते हैं।
7 लोग *फार्मेसी* दवाई लेने जाते हैं।

1  log *laundrymat* kapRe dʰone jāte hɛ̃.
2  log *restaurant* kʰānā kʰāne jāte hɛ̃.
3  log *movie* theatre film dekʰne jāte hɛ̃.
4  log *college* paRʰne jāte hɛ̃.
5  log *swimming pool* tɛrne jāte hɛ̃.
6  log *bār beer* pīne jāte hɛ̃.
7  log *pharmacy* davāī lene jāte hɛ̃.

## Exercise 2

1  वह बैठे हुए बोला।
2  जॉन सोये हुए हँस रहा था।
3  यह शहर सोया सा लगता है।
4  लड़की रोयी हुई घर आयी ।
5  औरत ने *स्विमिंग पूल* पर लेटे हुए कहा।

1  vo bɛTʰe hue bolā.
2  John so(y)e hue has rahā tʰā.
3  ye shɛher sotyā sā lagtā hɛ.
4  laRkī royī huī gʰar āyī.
5  aurat ne *swimming pool* par leTe hue kahā.

## Exercise 3

| | |
|---|---|
| सुनी | बात |
| लिखा | खत |
| हँसता | लड़का |
| चलती | गाड़ी |
| भूले | लोग |
| भागते | बिल्ली |

| | |
|---|---|
| sunī | bāt |
| likʰā | xat |
| hɛ̃stā | laRkā |
| caltī | gāRī |
| bʰūle | log |
| bʰāgtī | billī |

## Exercise 4

1  जॉन से एक कहानी पढ़ी गयी ।
2  हम लोगों से खाना खाया जा रहा है।

3 तुमसे क्या किया जायेगा?
4 मुझसे *चिकन करी* बनायी गयी।
5 बिल से यह पढ़ा जायेगा।
6 क्या आपसे गाना गाया गया?

1 John se ek kahānī paR$^h$ī gayī.
2 ham logõ se k$^h$ānā k$^h$āyā jā rahā hɛ.
3 tumse kyā kiyā jāyegā?
4 muj$^h$ se *chicken curry* banāyī gayī.
5 Bill sẽ ye paR$^h$ā jāyegā.
6 kyā āpse gānā gāyā gayā?

## Exercise 5

1 हमको वहाँ जाने का मौका मिला।
2 जॉन को हिन्दुस्तान जाने का मौका अक्सर मिलता है।
3 यह सुनहरा मौका था।
4 आपको किताब लिखने का मौका कब मिलेगा?
5 इस कागज़ में क्या लिखा है?
6 बिल्ली को मौका मिला और वह दूध पी गयी।
7 यह बहुत अच्छे मौके की बात है।

1 hamko vahā̃ jāne kā maukā milā.
2 John ko hindustān jāne kā maukā aksar miltā hɛ.
3 ye sunhera maukā t$^h$ā.
4 āpko kitāb lik$^h$ne kā maukā kab milegā?
5 is kāgaz mẽ kyā lik$^h$ā hɛ?
6 billī ko maukā milā aur vo dud$^h$ pī gayī.
7 ye bahut acc$^h$e mauke kī bāt hɛ.

## पाठ १० Unit 10

## Exercise 1

दीवाली        दिये जलाये जाते हैं।
              पटाखे़ चलाये जाते हैं।
              राजा राम के अपने राज्य लौटने की खुशी में मनाया जाता है।
होली          शत्रुओं को भी मित्र बनाया जाता है।
              गुलाल लगाया जाता है।
              रंग से खेला जाता है।
रक्षाबन्धन     धागा बाँधा जाता है।

| dīvālī | diye jalāye jāte hɛ̃. |
| | paTāxe calāye jāte hɛ̃. |
| | rājā rām ke apne rājya lauTane kī xushī mɛ̃ manāyā jātā hɛ. |
| holī | shatruõ ko bʰī mitra banayā jātā hɛ. |
| | gulāl lagāyā jātā hɛ. |
| | raŋga se kʰelā jātā hɛ. |
| rakshābandʰan | dʰāgā bã̄dhā jātā hɛ. |

## Exercise 2

1 Enemies are also made friends.
2 Lamps are lit.
3 The thread is tied.
4 Fire crackers are lit.
5 Gulal is used.
6 (It) is played with colour.
7 (It) is celebrated in the happiness of the return of King Rama to his kingdom.

## Exercise 3

1 दीवाली       dīvālī
2 रक्षाबन्धन    rakshābandʰan
3 रक्षाबन्धन    rakshābandʰan
4 होली          holī
5 दीवाली        dīvālī

# शब्दकोष क्रम
# shabadkosh kram

## Dictionary order

The dictionary order of Devanagari script is given below, working vertically down the columns. The nasalized vowels precede the oral vowels. The conjunct forms of a consonant (non-syllabic) follow all the syllabic forms. Thus, आँ **ã** precedes आ **ā**, whereas the non-syllabic form क् **k** follows कौ **kau**. The Sanskrit letters क्ष **ksha**, त्र **tra** and ज्ञ **gya** follow क **k**, त **t** and ज **j**, respectively.

| | | | | | | | |
|---|---|---|---|---|---|---|---|
| अ | a | क/क़ | ka/qa | ठ | $T^h$a | ब | ba |
| आ | ā | ख/ख़ | $k^h$a/xa | ड/ड़ | Da/Ra | भ | $b^h$a |
| इ | i | ग/ग़ | ga/Ga | ढ/ढ़ | $D^h$a/$R^h$a | म | ma |
| ई | ī | घ | $g^h$a | ण | Na | य | ya |
| उ | u | ङ | ŋa | त | ta | र | ra |
| ऊ | ū | च | ca | थ | $t^h$a | ल | la |
| ऋ | ri | छ | $c^h$a | द | da | व | wa/va |
| ए | e | ज/ज़ | ja/za | ध | $d^h$a | श | sha |
| ऐ | ɛ | झ | $j^h$a | न | na | ष | SHa |
| ओ | o | ञ | ña | प | pa | स | sa |
| औ | au | ट | Ta | फ/फ़ | $p^h$a/fa | ह | ha |

# मूल शब्दावली
# aŋgrezī-hindī shabdāvalī
## English–Hindi glossary

Some basic vocabulary useful for everyday communication is given
below. The vocabulary is presented in the following groups:

- body, health and ailments
- colours
- family and relatives
- food and drink
- numbers
- time
- important verbs

The gender of the nouns is specified as masculine (m.) and feminine
(f.). Adjectives are given in their base masculine singular form. Since
the plural forms of the nouns are predictable from the gender, only
the singular forms are listed. Verbs are specified for the agentive
(+/–ने **ne**; in perfective tenses) and experiential subjects (+को **ko**) if
they fail to select the regular nominative subjects. Also, if the object
of a verb takes a specific postposition instead of the regular को **ko**
postposition, it is specified in the following way:

wait इंतज़ार करना      **x kā intzār karnā**      'to wait for x'

This shows that the verb इंतज़ार करना **intzār karnā** 'to wait' takes the
का **kā** 'of' postposition instead of को **ko** or the equivalent of the
English 'for'. Verbs are listed in the infinitive form.

# Body, health and ailments

## Parts of the body and appearance

| | | |
|---|---|---|
| ankle | एड़ी | eRī (f.) |
| back | पीठ | pīTʰ (f.) |
| bald | गंजा | ganjā (m.) |
| beard | दाढ़ी | dāRʰī (f.) |
| blood | लहू, खून | lahū (m.), xūn (m.) |
| body | शरीर, जिस्म | sharīr (m.), jisma (m.) |
| chest | छाती | cʰātī (f.) |
| ear | कान | kān (m.) |
| elbow | कोहनी | kohnī (f.) |
| eye | आँख | ãkʰ (f.) |
| face | चेहरा, मुँह | cehrā (m.), mũh (m.) |
| finger | उंगली | uŋglī (f.) |
| foot | पैर | pɛr (m.) |
| forehead | माथा | mātʰā (m.) |
| hair | बाल | bāl (m.) |
| hand | हाथ | hātʰ (m.) |
| head | सिर | sir (m.) |
| heart | दिल | dil (m.) |
| kidney | गुर्दा | gurdā (m.) |
| knee | घुटना | gʰuTnā (m.) |
| leg | लात, टाँग | lāt (f.), Tãg (f.) |
| lip | होंठ | hõTʰ (m.) |
| moustache | मूँछ | mũcʰ (f.) |
| mouth | मुँह | mũh (m.) |
| neck | गला | gardan (f.) |
| nose | नाक | nāk (f.) |
| shoulder | कंधा | kandʰā (m.) |
| stomach | पेट | peT (m.) |
| throat | गला | galā (m.) |
| thumb | अंगूठा | aŋgūTʰā (m.) |
| toe | पैर की उंगली | pɛr kī uŋglī (f.) |
| tongue | जीभ, ज़बान | jībʰ (f.), zabān (f.) |

## Health and ailments

| | | |
|---|---|---|
| ache, pain | दर्द | dard (m.) |
| ailment, sickness | बीमारी/बिमारी | bīmārī/bimārī (f.) |

| | | |
|---|---|---|
| appetite, hunger | भूख | bʰūkʰ (f.) |
| blind | अन्धा | andʰā (m.) |
| blister | छाला | cʰālā (m.) |
| boil | फोड़ा | pʰoRā (m.) |
| breath | साँस | sā̃s (f.) |
| burning sensation | जलन | jalan (f.) |
| cholera | हैज़ा | hɛzā (m.) |
| common cold | ज़ुकाम | zukām (m.) |
| cough | खाँसी | kʰā̃sī (f.) |
| deaf | बहरा | bɛhrā (m.) |
| defecation | टट्टी आना | TaTTī ānā (+ko) |
| dumb | गूँगा | gū̃gā (m.) |
| dysentry | पेचिश | pecish (f.) |
| feeling breathless | साँस चढ़ना | sā̃s caRʰnā (+kā) |
| feeling dizzy | सिर चकराना | sir cakrānā (+kā) |
| health | स्वास्थ्य, सेहत | svastʰya (m.), sehat (f.) |
| healthy | स्वस्थ, तन्दुरुस्त | svāstʰa, tandrust |
| ill | बीमार/बिमार | bīmār (m.) |
| indigestion | बद-हज़मी | bad-hazmī (f.) |
| injury | चोट | coT (f.) |
| itch | खुजली | kʰujlī (f.) |
| lame | लंगड़ा | laŋgRā (m.) |
| malaria | मलेरिया | maleriyā (m.) |
| rash | दाद | dād (m.) |
| sneeze | छींक | cʰī̃k (f.) |
| sprain | मोच | moc (f.) |
| swelling | सूजन | sūjan (f.) |
| temperature | बुख़ार | buxār (m.) |
| thirst | प्यास | pyās (f.) |
| typhoid | मियादी बुख़ार | miyādī buxār (m.) |
| tuberculosis | तपेदिक, क्षय | tapedik (m.), shaya (m.) |
| ulcer | नासूर | nāsūr (m.) |
| unconscious | बेहोश | behosh |

# Colours

| | | |
|---|---|---|
| black | काला | kālā |
| blue | नीला | nīlā |
| brown | भूरा | bʰūrā |
| colour | रंग | raŋga (m.) |
| green | हरा | harā |

| | | |
|---|---|---|
| orange | सन्तरी | santrī |
| pink | गुलाबी | gulābī |
| purple (dark) | बैंगनी | bæ̃gnī |
| purple (light) | जामनी | jāmnī |
| red | लाल | lāl |
| sky blue | आसमानी | āsmānī |
| saffron | केसरी | kesarī |
| white | सफेद | safed |
| white (skin) | गोरा | gorā |
| yellow | पीला | pīlā |

## Family and relatives

| | | |
|---|---|---|
| aunt | | |
| father's sister | बुआ | buā |
| father's older brother's wife | ताई | tāī |
| father's younger brother's wife | चाची | cācī |
| mother's brother's wife | मामी | māmī |
| mother's sister | मौसी | mausī |
| | ख़ाला | xālā (Muslim) |
| brother | भाई | bʰāī |
| brother-in-law | | |
| husband's older brother | जेठ | jeTʰ |
| husband's sister's husband | ननदोई | nandoī |
| husband's younger brother | देवर | devar |
| wife's brother | साला | sālā |
| wife's sister's husband | साँढू | sæ̃Dʰū |
| child | बच्चा, बच्ची | baccā (m.), baccī (f.) |
| daughter | बेटी | beTī |
| daughter-in-law | बहू | bahū |
| father | पिता | pitā (Hindu-Sikh) |
| | अब्बा | abbā (Muslim) |
| father-in-law | ससुर | sasur |
| granddaughter | | |
| daughter's daughter | दोहती | dohtī |
| son's daughter | पोती | potī |
| grandfather | | |
| father's father | दादा | dādā |
| mother's father | नाना | nānā |

grandmother

| | | |
|---|---|---|
| father's mother | दादी | **dādī** |
| mother's mother | नानी | **nānī** |

grandson

| | | |
|---|---|---|
| daughter's son | दोहता | **dohtā** |
| son's son | पोता | **potā** |

| | | |
|---|---|---|
| husband | पति | **pati** (Hindu, Sikh) |
| | ख़ाविन्द | **xāvind** (Muslim) |
| mother | माता, माँ | **mātā**, **mā̃** (Hindu, Sikh) |
| | अम्मी | **ammī** (Muslim) |
| mother-in-law | सास | **sās** |

nephew

| | | |
|---|---|---|
| brother's son | भतीजा | **bʰatījā** |
| sister's son | भाँजा | **bʰā̃jā** |

niece

| | | |
|---|---|---|
| brother's daughter | भतीजी | **bʰatījī** |
| sister's daughter | भाँजी | **bʰā̃jī** |

| | | |
|---|---|---|
| relative | रिश्तेदार | **rishtedār** |
| sister | बहन | **bɛhɛn** |

sister-in-law

| | | |
|---|---|---|
| brother's wife | भाभी | **bʰābʰī** |
| wife's sister | साली | **sālī** |
| husband's sister | ननद | **nanad** |

| | | |
|---|---|---|
| son | बेटा | **beTā** |
| son-in-law | जवाई | **javāī** |

uncle

| | | |
|---|---|---|
| father's older brother | ताऊ | **tāū** |
| father's sister's husband | फूफा | **pʰūpʰā** |
| father's younger brother | चाचा | **cācā** |
| mother's brother | मामा | **māmā** |
| mother's sister's husband | मौसा | **mausā** (Hindu, Sikh) |
| | ख़ालू | **xālū** (Muslim) |
| wife | पत्नी | **patnī** (Hindu, Sikh) |
| | बीबी | **bībī** (Muslim) |
| | घरवाली | **gʰarvālī** |

# Food and drink

## *Foodgrains and flours*

| | | |
|---|---|---|
| black beans | लोभिया | **lobʰiyā** (m.) |
| chickpea flour | बेसन | **besan** (m.) |

| chick peas | छोले | c<sup>h</sup>ole (m. pl.) |
| corn | मकई | makaī (f.) |
| flour | आटा | āTā (m.) |
| flour (refined) | मैदा | mɛdā (m.) |
| lentils | दाल | dāl (f.) |
| kidney beans | राजमाँह | rājmā̃h (f.) |
| moog beans/lentils | मूँग दाल | mũg dāl (f.) |
| rice | चावल | cāval (m.) |
| wheat | गेहूँ | gehũ (m.) |

## Fruits and nuts

| almond | बादाम | bādām (m.) |
| apple | सेब | sev (m.) |
| apricot | खुमानी | xumāni (f.) |
| banana | केला | kelā (m.) |
| cashew nuts | काजू | kājū (m.) |
| fruit; dry fruit | फल ; मेवा | p<sup>h</sup>al (m.); mevā (m.) |
| grapes | अंगूर | aŋgūr (m.) |
| guava | अमरूद | amrūd (m.) |
| lemon | नींबू/नीम्बू | nīmbū (m.) |
| mango | आम | ām (m.) |
| melon | खरबूजा | k<sup>h</sup>arbūjā (m.) |
| orange | संतरा/सन्तरा | santrā (m.) |
| peach | आड़ू | āRū (m.) |
| peanuts | मूँगफली | mũgp<sup>h</sup>alī (f.) |
| pear | नाशपती | nāshpātī (f.) |
| pistachio | पिस्ता | pistā (m.) |
| plum | आलूबुख़ारा | ālūbuxārā (m.) |
| tangerine | नारंगी | nāraŋgī (f.) |
| walnut | अखरोट | ak<sup>h</sup>roT (m.) |
| watermelon | तरबूज | tarbūj (m.) |

## Vegetables

| beetroot | चुकन्दर | cukandar (m.) |
| bittergourd | करेला | karelā (m.) |
| cabbage | बन्दगोभी | bandgob<sup>h</sup>ī (f.) |
| courgette | तोरी | torī (f.) |
| cucumber | खीरा | k<sup>h</sup>īrā (m.) |

| | | |
|---|---|---|
| fenugreek | मेथी | **met$^h$ī** (f.) |
| garlic | लहसुन | **lɛhsun** (m.) |
| ginger (fresh) | अदरक | **adrak** (f.) |
| mustard | सरसों | **sarsõ** (m.) |
| okra | भिंडी | **b$^h$iNDī** (f.) |
| onion | प्याज़ | **pyāz** (m.) |
| peas | मटर | **maTar** (m.) |
| potatoes | आलू | **ālū** (m.) |
| pumpkin | कद्दू | **kaddū** (m.) |
| radish | मूली | **mūlī** (f.) |
| spinach | पालक | **pālak** (f.) |
| tomato | टमाटर | **TamāTar** (m.) |
| vegetable | सब्ज़ी | **sabzī** (f.) |

## Herbs and spices

| | | |
|---|---|---|
| aniseed | सौंफ़ | **sãũf** (m.) |
| asafoetida | हींग | **hĩg** (f.) |
| bay leaves | तेज़ पत्ता | **tez pattā** (m.) |
| black cardamom | बड़ी इलायची | **baRī ilāyacī** (f.) |
| black pepper (black) | काली मिर्च | **kālī mirca** (f.) |
| cardamom | इलायची | **ilāyacī** (f.) |
| chilli | मिर्च, लाल मिर्च | **mirca** (f.), **lāl mirca** (f.) |
| cinnamon | दालचीनी | **dālcīnī** (f.) |
| cloves | लौंग | **lãũg** (m.) |
| coriander | धनिया | **d$^h$aniyā** (m.) |
| cumin | जीरा | **jīrā** (m.) |
| curry powder | करी पाउडर | **karī pāuDar** (m.) |
| ginger (dry) | सौंठ | **sãũT$^h$** (f.) |
| mango powder | अमचूर | **amcūr** (m.) |
| mint | पौदीना | **paudīnā** (m.) |
| mixed spices | गरम मसाला | **garam masālā** (m.) |
| mustard seeds | राई | **rāī** (f.) |
| nutmeg | जायफल | **jāyp$^h$al** (m.) |
| saffron | केसर | **kesar** (m.) |
| salt | नमक | **namak** (m.) |
| spices | मसाला/मसाले | **masālā/masāle** (m.) |
| tamarind | इमली | **imlī** (f.) |
| turmeric | हल्दी | **haldī** (f.) |

## Food items (dishes), etc.

| | | |
|---|---|---|
| alcoholic drinks | शराब | **sharāb** (f.) |
| betel leaf | पान | **pān** (m.) |
| betel nut | सुपारी | **supārī** (f.) |
| bread (Indian) | रोटी, चपाती | **roTī** (f.), **capatī** (f.) |
| | फुल्का, नान, | **pʰulkā** (m.), **nān** (m.) |
| | पूरी, पराठा | **pūrī** (f.), **parāTʰā** (m.) |
| | कुल्चा, भटूरा | **kulcā** (m.), **bʰaTūrā** (m.) |
| bread (Western) | डबल रोटी | **Dabal roTī** (f.) |
| butter | मक्खन | **makkʰan** (m.) |
| buttermilk | लस्सी | **lassī** (f.) |
| cheese | पनीर | **panīr** (m.) |
| coffee | काफ़ी | **kāfī** (f.) |
| curry (Indian) | कढ़ी | **kaRʰī** (f.) |
| egg | अंडा | **aNDā** (m.) |
| food | खाना | **kʰānā** (m.) |
|    non-vegetarian | माँसाहारी | **mā̃sāhārī** |
|    vegetarian | शाकाहारी | **shākāhārī** |
| juice | रस | **ras** (m.) |
| lentils | दाल | **dāl** (f.) |
| meat | माँस, गोश्त | **mā̃s** (m.), **goshta** (m.) |
| milk | दूध | **dūdʰ** (m.) |
| oil | तेल | **tel** (m.) |
| purified butter | घी | **gʰī** (m.) |
| sugar (white) | चीनी | **cīnī** (f.) |
| sugar (brown) | शक्कर | **shakkar** (f.) |
| sweets | मिठाई | **miTʰāī** (f.) |
| tea | चाय | **cāy** (f.) |
| tobacco | तम्बाकू | **tambākū** (m.) |
| vinegar | सिरका | **sirkā** (m.) |
| water | पानी | **pānī** (m.), **jal** (m.) |
| yoghurt | दही | **dahī** (m./f.) |

## Cooking processes

| | | |
|---|---|---|
| baking (oven cooking) | तन्दूरी | **tandūrī** |
| boiling | उबालना | **ubālnā** (+ne) |
| cooking | पकाना | **pakānā** (+ne) |
| cutting | काटना | **kāTnā** (+ne) |
| frying | तलना | **talnā** (+ne) |

| | | |
|---|---|---|
| grilling | सेंकना | **sēknā (+ne)** |
| grinding | पिसना | **pīsnā (+ne)** |
| kneading | गूँदना | **gūdnā (+ne)** |
| mixing | मिलाना | **milānā (+ne)** |
| peeling | छीलना | **c<sup>h</sup>īlnā (+ne)** |
| roasting | भूनना | **b<sup>h</sup>ūnnā (+ne)** |
| rolling | बेलना | **belnā (+ne)** |
| seasoning | तड़का लगाना | **taRkā lagānā (+ne)** |
| sieving | छानना | **c<sup>h</sup>ānnā (+ne)** |
| slicing | चीरना | **cīrnā (+ne)** |

## Tastes

| | | |
|---|---|---|
| bitter | कड़वा | **kaRvā** |
| delicious/tasty | मज़ेदार | **mazedār** |
| savoury/salty | नमकीन | **namkīn** |
| sour | खट्टा | **k<sup>h</sup>aTTā** |
| spicy | मसालेदार, मिर्चदार | **masāledār, mircavālā** |
| | चटपटा | **caTpaTā** |
| sweet | मीठा | **mīT<sup>h</sup>ā** |
| taste | स्वाद | **svād** |
| tasteless | फीका, बेस्वाद | **p<sup>h</sup>īkā, besvād** |

# Numbers

## Cardinal

| | | | | | |
|---|---|---|---|---|---|
| 1 | एक | **ek** | 14 | चौदह | **caudah** |
| 2 | दो | **do** | 15 | पन्द्रह | **pandrah** |
| 3 | तीन | **tīn** | 16 | सोलह | **solah** |
| 4 | चार | **cār** | 17 | सत्तरह, सत्रह | **sattrāh** |
| 5 | पाँच | **pãc** | 18 | अठारह | **aThārah** |
| 6 | छह | **che** | 19 | उन्नीस | **unnīs** |
| 7 | सात | **sāt** | 20 | बीस | **bīs** |
| 8 | आठ | **āT<sup>h</sup>** | 21 | इक्कीस | **ikkīs** |
| 9 | नौ | **nau** | 22 | बाईस | **bāīs** |
| 10 | दस | **das** | 23 | तेईस | **teīs** |
| 11 | ग्यारह | **gyārah** | 24 | चौबीस | **caubīs** |
| 12 | बारह | **bārah** | 25 | पच्चीस | **pacc<sup>h</sup>īs** |
| 13 | तेरह | **terah** | 26 | छब्बीस | **c<sup>h</sup>abbīs** |

| | | | | | | |
|---|---|---|---|---|---|---|
| 27 | सत्ताईस | sattāīs | | 64 | चौंसठ | cãūsaT$^h$ |
| 28 | अठाईस | aT$^h$āīs | | 65 | पैंसठ | pẽsaT$^h$ |
| 29 | उनतीस | untīs | | 66 | छियासठ | c$^h$iyāsaT$^h$ |
| 30 | तीस | tīs | | 67 | सरसठ | sarsaT$^h$ |
| 31 | इकत्तीस | ikattīs | | 68 | अड़सठ | aRsaT$^h$ |
| 32 | बत्तीस | battīs | | 69 | उनहत्तर | unhattar |
| 33 | तैंतीस | tẽtīs | | 70 | सत्तर | sattar |
| 34 | चौंतीस | cãūtīs | | 71 | इकहत्तर | ikhattar |
| 35 | पैंतीस | pẽtīs | | 72 | बहत्तर | bahattar |
| 36 | छत्तीस | c$^h$attīs | | 73 | तिहत्तर | tihattar |
| 37 | सैंतीस | sẽtīs | | 74 | चौहत्तर | cauhattar |
| 38 | अड़तीस | aRatīs | | 75 | पचहत्तर | pac$^h$attar |
| 39 | उनतालीस | untālīs | | 76 | छिहत्तर | c$^h$ihattar |
| 40 | चालीस | cālīs | | 77 | सतहत्तर | satahatta |
| 41 | इकतालीस | iktālīs | | 78 | अठहत्तर | aT$^h$hattar |
| 42 | ब्यालीस | byālīs | | 79 | उनासी | unāsī |
| 43 | तैंतालीस | tẽtālīs | | 80 | अस्सी | assī |
| 44 | चौवालीस | cauvālīs | | 81 | इकासी | ikāsī |
| 45 | पैंतालीस | pẽtālīs | | 82 | बयासी | bayāsī |
| 46 | छियालीस | c$^h$iyālīs | | 83 | तिरासी | tirāsī |
| 47 | सैंतालीस | sẽtālīs | | 84 | चौरासी | caurāsī |
| 48 | अड़तालीस | aRtālīs | | 85 | पच्चासी | paccāsī |
| 49 | उनचास | uncās | | 86 | छियासी | c$^h$iyāsī |
| 50 | पचास | pacās | | 87 | सत्तासी | sattāsī |
| 51 | इक्यावन | ikyāvan | | 88 | अट्ठासी | aTT$^h$āsī |
| 52 | बावन | bāvan | | 89 | नवासी | navāsī |
| 53 | तिरपन | tirpan | | 90 | नब्बे | nabbe |
| 54 | चौबन | cauvan | | 91 | इक्यानवे | ikyānve |
| 55 | पचपन | pacpan | | 92 | बयानवे | bayānve |
| 56 | छप्पन | c$^h$appan | | 93 | तिरानवे | tirānve |
| 57 | सत्तावन | sattāvan | | 94 | चौरानवे | caurānve |
| 58 | अट्ठावन | aTT$^h$āvan | | 95 | पचानवे | pacānve |
| 59 | उनसठ | unsaT$^h$ | | 96 | छियानवे | c$^h$iyānve |
| 60 | साठ | sāT$^h$ | | 97 | सतानवे | satānve |
| 61 | इकसठ | iksaT$^h$ | | 98 | अठानवे | aTT$^h$ānve |
| 62 | बासठ | bāsaT$^h$ | | 99 | निन्यानवे | ninyānve |
| 63 | तिरेसठ | tiresaT$^h$ | | 100 | सौ | sau |

| | | |
|---|---|---|
| 0 | शून्य, सिफ़र | shūnya, sifar |
| 150 | एक सौ पचास | ek sau pacās |
| 1,000 | हज़ार | hazār |
| 10,000 | दस हज़ार | das hazār |

| | | |
|---|---|---|
| 100,000 (a hundred thousand) | एक लाख | **ek lāk$^h$** |
| 1,000,000 (a million) | दस लाख | **das lāk$^h$** |
| 10,000,000 (ten million) | एक करोड़ | **ek karoR** |
| 1,000,000,000 (a billion) | दस करोड़ | **das karoR** |
| 10,000,000,000 (ten billion) | अरब | **arab** |
| 100,000,000,000 (a hundred billion) | दस खरब | **das arab** |
| 1,000,000,000,000 (a trillion) | खरब | **k$^h$arab** |

## Ordinal

| | | |
|---|---|---|
| first | पहला | **pehlā** |
| second | दूसरा | **dūsrā** |
| third | तीसरा | **tīsrā** |
| fourth | चौथा | **cauthā** |
| fifth | पाँचवाँ | **pãcvā** |

(Afterwards just add the suffix वाँ **-vā** to the cardinal numbers.)

## Fractions

| | | |
|---|---|---|
| ¹/₄ (a quarter) | (एक) चौथाई | **ek chaut$^h$āī** |
| ¹/₂ (a half) | आधा | **ād$^h$ā** |
| ³/₄ (three-quarters) | पौना | **paunā** |
| 1¹/₄ (one and a quarter) | सवा | **savā (ek)** |
| 1¹/₂ (one and a half) | डेढ़ | **DeR$^h$** |
| 1³/₄ (one and three-quarters) | पौने दो | **paune do** (i.e. the next number) |
| 2¹/₄ | सवा दो | **savā do** |
| 2¹/₂ | ढाई | **D$^h$āī** (the numeral two is incorporated in the word) |
| 2³/₄ | पौने तीन | **paune tīn** (i.e. the next number) |
| 3¹/₄ | सवा तीन | **savā tīn** |
| 3¹/₂ | साढ़े तीन | **sāR$^h$e tīn** |
| 3³/₄ | पौने चार | **paune cār** |

Then follow the pattern given below to derive the other fractional numbers.

| | |
|---|---|
| number + ¹/₄ | **savā** + number |
| number + ¹/₂ | **sāR$^h$e** + number |
| number + ³/₄ | **paune** + *next* number |

## Decimal point

| decimal | दशमलव | dashamlav |
|---|---|---|
| (*Example*: 1.5 | एक दशमलव पाँच | ek dashamlav pãc) |

## Percentages

| Percentage | प्रतिशत, फ़ीसदी | pratishat, fīsdī |
|---|---|---|
| (*Example*: 50% | पचास प्रतिशत | pacās pratishat) |

# Time

## Hours

| o'clock | बजे | baje |
|---|---|---|
| 1:15 | सवा (एक) | savā (ek) |
| 1:30 | डेढ़ | DeR<sup>h</sup> |
| 1:45 | पौने दो | paune do (i.e. the next number) |
| 2:15 | सवा दो | savā do |
| 2:30 | ढाई | D<sup>h</sup>āī (the numeral two is incorporated in the word) |
| 2:45 | पौने तीन | paune tīn (i.e. the next number) |
| 3:15 | सवा तीन | savā tīn |
| 3:30 | साढ़े तीन | sāR<sup>h</sup>e tīn |
| 3:45 | पौने चार | paune cār |

---

### Examples

| कितने | बजे | हैं? | वक़्त | क्या | है? |
|---|---|---|---|---|---|
| **kitne** | **baje** | **hɛ̃?** *or* | **vakta** | **kyā** | **hɛ?** |
| how many | o'clock | are | time | what | is |

What time is it?

| एक बजा है। | **ek bajā hɛ.** | It is 1 o'clock. |
|---|---|---|
| डेढ़ बजे हैं। | **deR<sup>h</sup> baje hɛ̃.** | It is 1:30. |
| पौने तीन बजे हैं। | **paune tīn baje hɛ̃.** | It is 2:45. |

---

| 9:00 am | सवेरे/सुबह के नौ | **savere/subā ke nau** |
|---|---|---|
| 9:00 pm | रात के नौ | **rāt ke nau** |
| 4:20 | चार बजकर बीस मिनट | **cār <u>bajkar</u> bīs minaT** |

| | | |
|---|---|---|
| 6:50 | सात बजने में दस मिनट | sāt **bajne mē** das minaT |
| year | साल | sāl (m.) |
| month | महीना | mahīnā (m.) |
| day | दिन | din (m.) |
| hour | घन्टा | gʰanTā (m.) |
| minute | मिनट | minaT (m.) |
| second | सैकिन्ड, पल | sɛkinD (m.), pal (m.) |

## Days of the week

| | | |
|---|---|---|
| Monday | सोमवार | somvār (Hindu-Sikh), pīr (Muslim) |
| Tuesday | मंगलवार | maŋgalvār |
| Wednesday | बुधवार | budʰvār |
| Thursday | गुरूवार, बृहस्पति | guruvār, brihaspativār (Hindu–Sikh) |
| | जुम्मेरात | jummerāt (Muslim) |
| Friday | शुक्रवार | shukravār (Hindu–Sikh), |
| | जुम्मा | jummā (Muslim) |
| Saturday | शनिवार | shanivār (Hindu–Sikh), |
| | हफ़्ता | haftā (Muslim) |
| Sunday | रविवार, इतवार | ravivār, itvār |

## Months

The names of the months of the Hindu and Muslim calendar are different from the Christian calendar. However, the Christian calendar is officially used, so the Indian pronunciation of the months is given below:

| | | |
|---|---|---|
| January | जनवरी | janvarī |
| February | फ़रवरी | farvarī |
| March | मार्च | mārca |
| April | अप्रैल | aprɛl |
| May | मई | maī |
| June | जून | jūn |
| July | जुलाई | julāī |
| August | अगस्त | agasta |
| September | सितम्बर | sitambar |
| October | अक्तूबर/अक्टूबर | aktūbar, akTūbar |
| November | नवम्बर | navambar |
| December | दिसम्बर | disambar |

## Years

The word 'year' when used as part of a date is translated as सन् **san**. For instance, 1995 (the year) is सन् उन्नीस सौ पचानवे **san unnīs sau pacānve** but one can *not* say एक हज़ार नौ सौ पचानवे **ek hazār nau sau pacānve**.

## Professions

| doctor | डॉक्टर | *Doctor* |
|---|---|---|
| driver | ड्राइवर | *Driver* |
| hero | नायक | **nāyak** |
| heroine | नायिका | **nāyikā** |
| lawyer | वकील | **vakīl** |
| policeman | पुलिस वाला | **pulis vālā** |
| singer | गायक | **gāyak** |
| teacher | अध्यापक | **ad$^h$yāpak** |
| washerman | धोबी | **D$^h$obī** |
| writer | लेखक | **lek$^h$ak** |

## Important verbs

Hindi verbs are listed in the infinitive form.

## Abbreviations

| (intr.) | intransitive verb; does not take the ने **ne** postposition in the perfect tenses |
|---|---|
| (tr.) | transitive verb; takes the ने **ne** postposition in the perfect tenses |
| (+ने **ne**) | takes the ने **ne** postposition in the perfect tenses |
| (–ने **ne**) | does not take the ने **ne** postposition in the perfect tenses |
| (+/–ने **ne**) | may or may not take the ने **ne** postposition in the perfect tenses |
| (+को **ko**) | takes the को **ko** postposition with its subject; indicates non-volitional action |

| | | |
|---|---|---|
| accept, agree | मानना | **mānnā** (+ने ne) |
| ache | दर्द होना | **dard honā** (+को ko) |
| afraid | डर लगना | **Dar lagnā** (+को ko) |
| agree | मानना | **mānnā** (+ने ne) |
| (be) angry | गुस्सा होना | **gussā honā** |
| | गुस्सा करना | **gussā karnā** (+ने ne) |
| become angry | गुस्सा आना | **gussā ānā** (+को ko) |
| appear | लगना, नज़र आना | **lagnā, nazar ānā** (+को ko) |
| be able to/can | सकना | **saknā** (–ने ne) |
| be | होना | **honā** (–ने ne) |
| beat | मारना | **mārnā** (+ने ne) |
| be born | x का जन्म होना | **x kā janma honā** (–ने ne) |
| begin, start | शुरु होना | **shuru honā** (intr.) (–ने ne) |
| | शुरु करना | **shuru karnā** (tr.) (+ने ne) |
| break | तोड़ना | **toRnā** (+ने ne) |
| bring | लाना | **lānā** (–ने ne) |
| burn | जलना, जलाना | **jalnā** (intr.), **jalānā** (tr.) |
| buy | ख़रीदना | **xarīdnā** (+ने ne) |
| call | बुलाना | **bulānā** (+ने ne) |
| catch | पकड़ना | **pakaRnā** (+ने ne) |
| celebrate | मनाना | **manānā** (+ने ne) |
| change | बदलना | **badalnā** (+/–ने ne) |
| choose | चुनना | **cunnā** (+ने ne) |
| climb | चढ़ना | **caRhnā** (–ने ne) |
| collide | x से टकराना | **x se Takrānā** (+ने ne) |
| come | आना | **ānā** (–ने ne) |
| compare | x की y से तुलना करना | **x kī y se tulnā karnā** (+ने ne) |
| complain | x की y से शिकायत करना | **x se y kī shikāyat karnā** (+ने ne) |
| complete | पूरा करना | **pūrā karnā** (+ने ne) |
| converse | x से बात करना | **x se bāt karnā** (+ने ne) |
| cost | लगना | **x (amount) lagnā** (–ने ne) |
| count | गिनना | **ginnā** (+ने ne) |
| cover | ढकना | **Dhaknā** (+ने ne) |
| cry | रोना, चिल्लाना | **ronā, cillānā** (–ने ne) |
| cut | कटना, काटना | **kaTnā** (intr.), **kāTnā** (tr.) |
| dance | नाचना | **nācnā** (+ने ne) |
| desire | x की इच्छा होना | **x kī icchā honā** (–ने ne) |
| die | मरना | **marnā** (–ने ne) |
| disappear | गायब होना | **gāyab honā** (intr.) (–ने ne) |
| | गायब करना | **gāyab karnā** (tr.) (+ने ne) |
| dislike | नापसन्द होना | **nāpasand honā** (+को ko) |

| | | |
|---|---|---|
| | नापसन्द करना | **nāpasand karnā** (+ने ne) |
| do | करना | **karnā** (+ने ne) |
| drink | पीना | **pīnā** (+ने ne) |
| drink (alcohol) | शराब पीना | **sharāb pīnā** (+ने ne) |
| drive | (कार) चलाना | **[kār] calānā** (+ने ne) |
| earn | कमाना | **kamānā** (+ने ne) |
| enjoy | मज़ा होना | **mazā honā** (intr.) (–ने ne) |
| | मज़ा करना | **mazā karnā** (tr.) (+ने ne) |
| | मज़ा लेना | **mazā lenā** (tr.) (+ने ne) |
| eat/dine | खाना खाना | **kʰānā kʰānā** (+ने ne) |
| eat breakfast | नाश्ता करना | **nāshtā karnā** (+ने ne) |
| enter | घुसना | **gʰusnā** (–ने ne) |
| fall | गिरना | **girnā** (–ने ne) |
| feed | खिलाना | **kʰilānā** (+ने ne) |
| feel sick | x की तबीयत ख़राब होना | **x kī tabīyat xarāb honā** (–ने ne) |
| feel happy | खुश होना | **xush honā** (–ने ne) |
| feel sad | उदास होना | **udās honā** (–ने ne) |
| fight | लड़ना | **laRnā** (–ने ne) |
| finish | ख़त्म होना | **xatam honā** (intr.) (–ने ne) |
| | ख़त्म करना | **xatam karnā** (tr.) (+ने ne) |
| fix, recover, repair | ठीक होना | **Tʰīk honā** (intr.) (–ने ne) |
| | ठीक करना | **Tʰīk karnā** (tr.) (+ने ne) |
| fly | उड़ना, उड़ाना | **uRnā** (intr.), **uRānā** (tr.) |
| forgive, pardon | माफ करना | **māf karnā** (+ने ne) |
| get down, descend | उतरना | **utarnā** (–ने ne) |
| give | देना | **denā** (+ने ne) |
| go | जाना | **jānā** (–ने ne) |
| go back | वापस जाना | **vāpas jānā** (–ने ne) |
| grind | पीसना | **pīsnā** (+ने ne) |
| hate | x से नफ़रत करना | **x se nafrat karnā** (+ने ne) |
| hear | सुनना | **sunnā** (+ने ne) |
| | सुनाई देना | **sunāī denā** (+को ko) |
| hire | किराये पर लेना | **kirāye par lenā** (+ने ne) |
| hope | x की आशा होना | **x kī āshā honā** (–ने ne) |
| (get) hot | गरमी पड़ना | **garmī paRnā** (–ने ne) |
| (get) hurt | चोट लगना | **coT lagnā** (+को ko) |
| inquire | पूछताछ करना | **pūcʰtācʰ karnā** (+ने ne) |
| invite | x के घर आना | **x ke gʰar ānā** (–ने ne) |
| | x को न्यौता देना | **x ko nyautā denā** (+ने ne) |
| jump | कूदना | **kūdnā** (–ने ne) |
| kill | मारना | **mārnā** (+ने ne) |

| knock at | खटखटाना | $k^h aTk^h aTānā$ (+ने ne) |
| know | जानना | jānnā (+ने ne) |
| | मालूम होना | mālūm honā (+को ko) |
| | पता होना | patā honā (+को ko) |
| (come to) know | पता लगना | patā lagnā (+को ko) |
| laugh | हँसना | hāsnā (–ने ne) |
| learn | सीखना | $sīk^h nā$ (+ने ne) |
| like | पसन्द होना | pasand honā (+ko) |
| | पसन्द करना | pasand karnā (+ने ne) |
| | अच्छा लगना | $acc^h ā$ lagnā (+को ko) |
| love | x से प्रेम होना | x se prem honā (+को ko) |
| | x से प्रेम करना | x se prem karnā (+ने ne) |
| live | रहना | rɛhnā (–ने ne) |
| look | देखना | $dek^h nā$ (+ने ne) |
| make | बनाना | banānā (+ने ne) |
| meet | मिलना | milnā (–ने ne) |
| melt | पिघलना | $pig^h alnā$ (–ने ne) |
| mix | मिलाना | milānā (+ने ne) |
| need, want | चाहिये, चाहना, | $cā^h iye$ (+को ko), cāhnā (+ने ne) |
| | x की ज़रूरत होना | x kī zarūrat honā (+को ko) |
| (be) nervous | घबराना | $g^h abrānā$ (–ने ne) |
| object | x पर ऐतराज़ करना | x par ɛtrāz karnā (+ने ne) |
| open | खुलना, खोलना | $k^h ulnā$ (intr.), $k^h olnā$ (tr.) |
| order (someone; | आज्ञा देना, | āgyā denā (+ने ne) |
| but not something) | हुक्म करना | huxam karnā (+ने ne) |
| peel | छीलना | $c^h īlnā$ (+ने ne) |
| permit | इजाज़त देना | ijāzat denā (+ने ne) |
| persuade | मनाना | manānā (+ने ne) |
| place | रखना | $rak^h nā$ (+ने ne) |
| play | खेलना | $k^h elnā$ (+ने ne) |
| play (instrument) | बजाना | bajānā (+ने ne) |
| praise | x की तारीफ़ करना | x kī tārīf karnā (+ne) |
| prepare | तैयार होना | taiyār honā (intr.) (–ने ne) |
| | तैयार करना | taiyār karnā (tr.) (+ने ne) |
| pour | डालना | Dālnā (+ने ne) |
| press | दबाना | dabānā (+ने ne) |
| push | धकेलना | $d^h akelnā$ (+ने ne) |
| put off | टालना | Tālnā (+ने ne) |
| put | रखना, डालना | $rak^h nā$ (+ने ne), Dālnā (+ने ne) |
| quarrel | लड़ना | laRnā (–ने ne) |
| rain | बारिश होना | bārish honā (–ने ne) |
| reach | पहुँचना | pahũcnā (–ने ne) |

| | | |
|---|---|---|
| read | पढ़ना | pa**R**ʰnā (+ने ne) |
| recognize | पहचानना | pεhcānnā (+ने ne) |
| refuse, prohibit | x से मना करना | x se manā karnā (+ने ne) |
| remember | याद होना | yād honā (intr. +को ko) |
| remember, memorize | याद करना | yād karnā (+ने ne) |
| respect | x की इज़्ज़त करना | x kī izzat karnā (+ने ne) |
| rest | आराम करना | ārām karnā (+ने ne) |
| return, come back | वापस आना, लौटना | vāpas ānā (–ने ne), lauTnā (–ने ne) |
| return (something) | वापस करना, लौटाना | vāpas karnā (+ने ne), lauTānā (+ने ne) |
| ripe | पकना | paknā (–ने ne) |
| rise | उठना, चढ़ना | uTʰnā (–ने ne), caRʰnā (–ने ne) |
| run | दौड़ना, भागना | dauRnā (–ने ne), bʰāgnā (–ने ne) |
| say | कहना | kεhnā (+ने ne) |
| seem | लगना | lagnā (+को ko) |
| sell | बेचना | becnā (+ने ne) |
| send | भेजना | bʰejnā (+ने ne) |
| show | दिखाना | dikʰānā (+ने ne) |
| (take) shower | नहाना | nahānā (+/–ने ne) |
| sing | गाना | gānā (+ने ne) |
| sit | बैठना | bεTʰnā (–ने ne) |
| sleep | सोना | sonā (–ने ne) |
| slip | फिसलना | pʰisalnā (–ने ne) |
| sneeze | छींकना | cʰĩknā (+/–ने ne) |
| snow | बर्फ़ गिरना | barf girnā (–ने ne) |
| speak | बोलना | bolnā (+/–ने ne) |
| spend (money) | खर्च करना | xarca karnā (+ने ne) |
| spend (time) | बिताना, काटना | bitānā (+ने ne), kāTnā (+ने ne) |
| spill | गिराना | girānā (+ने ne) |
| spread | बिछाना | bicʰānā (+ने ne) |
| stand | खड़ा होना | kʰaRā honā (–ने ne) |
| stay | रहना, ठहरना | rεhnā (–ने ne), Tʰεhεrnā (–ने ne) |
| steal | चोरी करना | corī karnā (+ने ne) |
| stop | रुकना, रोकना | ruknā (intr.), roknā (tr.) |
| study | पढ़ना | paRʰnā (+/–ने ne) |
| (be) surprised | हैरान होना | hεrān honā (–ने ne) |
| swim | तैरना | tεrnā (–ने ne) |
| take care of | देख–भाल करना | dekʰ-bʰāl karnā (+ने ne) |
| take | लेना | lenā (+ने ne) |
| taste | चखना | cakʰnā (+ने ne) |

| teach | पढ़ाना | **paRʰānā** (+ने ne) |
| telephone | टेलीफ़ोन करना | **Tɛlīfon karnā** (+ने ne) |
| tell, mention | बताना | **batānā** (+ने ne) |
| think | x का ख़्याल होना | **x kā xyāl honā** (–ने ne) |
| | सोचना | **socnā** (+ने ne) |
| throw | फेंकना | **pʰɛ̃knā** (+ने ne) |
| tired | थकना | **tʰaknā** (–ने ne) |
| touch | छूना | **cʰūnā** (+ने ne) |
| try | x की कोशिश करना | **x kī koshish karnā** (+ने ne) |
| turn | मुड़ना, मोड़ना | **muRnā** (intr.) **moRnā** (tr.) |
| turn over | पलटना | **palaTnā** (+ने ne) |
| understand | समझना | **samajʰnā** (+/–ने ne) |
| use | x का इस्तेमाल करना | **x kā istemāl karnā** (+ने ne) |
| uproot | उखाड़ना | **ukʰāRnā** (+ने ne) |
| wait | x का इंतज़ार करना | **x kā intzār karnā** (+ने ne) |
| wake up | उठना | **uTʰnā** (–ने ne) |
| walk | चलना | **calnā** (–ने ne) |
| want, need | चाहिये, चाहना | **cāhiye** (+को ko), **cāhnā** (+ने ne) |
| wash | धोना | **dʰonā** (+ने ne) |
| waste | गवाँना | **gavā̃nā** (+ने ne) |
| wear | पहनना | **pɛhɛnnā** (+ने ne) |
| weep | रोना | **ronā** (–ने ne) |
| win | जीतना | **jītnā** (+/–ने ne) |
| worry | x की चिन्ता करना | **x kī cintā karnā** (+ने ne) |
| worship | x की पूजा करना | **x kī pūjā karnā** (+ने ne) |
| write | लिखना | **likʰnā** (+ने ne) |

---

### Web resource

The following link is useful for translating English words into Hindi:

http://shabdkosh.com/

# हिन्दी-अंग्रेज़ी शब्दावली
# hindī-aŋgrezī shabdāvalī

## Hindi–English glossary

The Hindi vocabulary used in the dialogues and reading practice pieces is presented below in roman alphabetical order. However, it should be pointed out that the vowel symbol ɛ follows y, whereas the nasalized vowels (with ~) and short vowels precede their corresponding oral long vowels, respectively.

| | | |
|---|---|---|
| अभी | ab<sup>h</sup>ī | right now |
| अभी भी | ab<sup>h</sup>ī b<sup>h</sup>ī | even now |
| अच्छा | acc<sup>h</sup>ā | good, Okay |
| अच्छाई | acc<sup>h</sup>āī (f.) | good (n.), quality, ideal |
| अच्छा लगना | acc<sup>h</sup>ā lagnā (+ko) | to like |
| अफ़सोस | afsos (m.) | sorrow (m.) |
| अगला | aglā | next |
| अकाल पड़ना | akāl paRnā (–ne) | famine to occur |
| अकेला | akelā | alone |
| अकसर | aksar | often, usually |
| अमीर | amīr | rich |
| अनाज | anāj (m.) | grain, corn |
| अन्दाज | andāz (m.) | style |
| अन्धकार | and<sup>h</sup>kāra (m.) | darkness |
| अंगेज़ | aŋgrez (m.) | the English |
| अंगेज़ी | aŋgrezī (f.) | the English language |
| अपना | apnā | one's own |
| अपनाना | apnānā (+ne) | to adopt |

| | | |
|---|---|---|
| अर्थ | art<sup>h</sup>a (m.) | meaning |
| अर्ज़ | arz (f.) | request |
| असल में | asal mẽ | in fact, in reality |
| असली | aslī | real, genuine |
| अटूट | aTūT | unbreakable |
| और | aur | and, more, other, else |
| और भी | aur b<sup>h</sup>ī | even more |
| औरत | aurat (f.) | woman |
| अयोध्या | ayod<sup>h</sup>yā (f.) | Ayodhya (place name) |
| आँख | ā̃k<sup>h</sup> | eye |
| आदाब | ādāb | salutation, greetings |
| आदि | ādi | etc. |
| आदत | ādat | habit |
| आदमी | ādmī | man |
| आग | āg | fire |
| आज–कल | āj-kal | nowadays |
| आक्रमण करना | ākramaNa karnā (+ne) | to attack |
| आम | ām | mango (n.); common (adj.), general |
| आना | ānā (–ne) | to come |
| आने वाला | āne vālā | about to come |
| आप | āp | you (honorific) |
| आपके | āpke | your |
| आपको | āpko | to you |
| आराम | ārām (m.) | comfort, rest |
| आराम करना | ārām karnā (+ne) | to rest |
| आटा | āTā (m.) | flour |
| | | |
| बचाना | bacānā (+ne) | to save |
| बच्चा | baccā (m.) | child |
| बचपन | bacpan (m.) | childhood |
| बहुत | bahut | very |
| बहुत खूब | bahut xūb | great! splendid! |
| बजे | baje | o'clock |
| बनाना | banānā (+ne) | to make |
| बनारस | banāras | Banaras (one of the oldest cities of India) |
| बन्द | banda | closed |
| बन्द होना | banda honā (–ne) | to be closed |
| बन्द करना | banda karnā (+ne) | to close |
| बनना | bannā (–ne) | to be made |

| | | |
|---|---|---|
| बनवास | banvāsa (m.) | exile, residence in forest |
| बड़ा | baRā | big |
| बढ़ना | baRʰnā (–ne) | to increase, advance |
| बताना | batānā (+ne) | to tell |
| बाँधना | bā̃dʰnā (+ne) | to tie |
| बाहर | bāhar | outside, out |
| बार | bār (f.) | time |
| बारह | bārah | twelve |
| बात | bāt (f.) | matter, conversation, topic |
| बेचना | becnā (+ne) | to sell |
| बेकार | bekār | useless |
| बेटा | beTā (m.) | son |
| बेटी | beTī (f.) | daughter |
| भई | bʰaī | hey, well (excl.) |
| भरना | bʰarna (+ne) | to fill |
| भागना | bʰāgnā (–ne) | to run |
| भागते | bʰāgte (present participle) | running |
| भाई | bʰāī (m.) | brother/brothers |
| भारत | bʰārat (m.) | India |
| भारतीय | bʰāratīya | Indian |
| भेज देना | bʰej denā (+ne) | to send (compound verb) |
| भेजना | bʰejnā (+ne) | to send |
| भेंट | bʰɛ̃T | gift |
| भी | bʰī | also |
| भूलना | bʰūlnā (+/–ne) | to forget |
| भूत | bʰūt (m.) | ghost, past |
| बिजली | bijlī (f.) | electricity, lightning |
| बिमारी/बीमारी | bimārī (f.) | illness |
| बिना | binā | without |
| बिंदी | bindī (f.) | dot |
| बीबी | bībī (f.) | wife |
| बीमा | bīmā (m.) | insurance |
| बोलना | bolanā (+/–ne) | to speak |
| बृन्दावन | brindāvan | Brindavan (the place where Lord Krishna was brought up) |
| बुझाना | bujʰānā (+ne) | to extinguish |
| बुरा | burā | bad |
| बुराई | burāī (f.) | evil |
| बुखार | buxār (m.) | fever |
| बहन | bɛhɛn (f.) | sister |
| बैरा | bɛrā (m.) | waiter |

| | | |
|---|---|---|
| चखना | cak<sup>h</sup>nā (+ne) | to taste |
| चलाना | calānā (+ne) | to drive, to manage (business), to light /play firecrackers |
| चलना | calnā (–ne) | walk |
| चौदह | caudā | fourteen |
| चाँद | cā̃d (m.) | moon |
| चाँदनी | cā̃dnī | moonlit |
| चाहिये/चाहिए | cāhiye (+ko) | desire, want |
| चाहना | cāhnā (+ne) | to want |
| चार | cār | four |
| चाय | cāy (f.) | tea |
| छाता | c<sup>h</sup>ātā (m.) | umbrella |
| छिपा कर | c<sup>h</sup>ipā kar | secretly |
| छोड़ना | c<sup>h</sup>oRnā (+ne) | to leave |
| छोटा | c<sup>h</sup>oTā | small |
| चीन | cīn (m.) | China |
| चीनी | cīnī | Chinese, sugar |
| चिल्लाना | cillānā (–ne) | to scream |
| चित्तौड़ | cittauRa (m.) | Chitaur (a very famous historical place in Rajasthan) |
| चोर | cor (m.) | thief |
| चोरी करना | corī karnā (+ne) | to steal |
| करी/कढ़ी | curry (f.) | curry |
| चूँकि | cū̃ki | because |
| दफ़्तर/दफ़तर | daftar (m.) | office |
| दही | dahī (m./f.) | yoghurt |
| दर्द | dard (m.) | pain, ache |
| दरवाज़ा | darvāzā (m.) | door |
| दस | das | ten |
| दस्त | dasta (m.) | diarrhoea |
| दौड़ना | dauRnā (–ne) | to run |
| दवाई | davāī/davā (f.) | medicine |
| डॉक्टर | DākTar (m.) | doctor |
| डालना | Dālnā (+ne) | to put in, throw, pour |
| दाम | dām (m.) | price |
| देखना | dek<sup>h</sup>nā (+ne) | to see, to look at, to notice |
| देर | der (f.) | delay, time (period of, slot of) |
| देश | desh (m.) | country |
| धन्यवाद | d<sup>h</sup>anyavād | thanks |
| धर्म | d<sup>h</sup>arma (m.) | religion |
| धागा | d<sup>h</sup>āgā (m.) | (bracelets of) thread |

| धूम-धाम से | dʰūm-dʰām se | with pomp and show |
|---|---|---|
| दिखाना | dikʰānā (+ne) | to show |
| दिल्ली | dillī (f.) | Delhi (the capital city) |
| दिमाग़ | dimāg (m.) | brain |
| दिन | din (m.) | day |
| दो | do | two |
| दोनों | donõ | both |
| दीपक/दिया | dīpak/diyā (m.) | an earthen lamp |
| दीवाली | dīvālī | the festival of lights/lamps |
| दोस्त | dost (m.) | friend |
| दुनिया | duniyā (f.) | world |
| दूर | dūr | far, distant |
| दूर करना | dūr karnā (+ne) | to dispel, to eliminate |
| दूसरा | dūsrā | second, other, another |
| एक | ek | one |
| एक दो | ek-do | one or two |
| एक दूसरे से | ek dūsre se | with one another, each other |
| एक–सा | ek-sā | alike |
| फ़रिश्ता | farishtā (m.) | angel |
| फ़र्क | farka (m.) | difference |
| फर्ज़ | farz (m.) | duty |
| फसल | fasal (f.) | crop |
| फुरसत | furasat (f.) | free time, spare time, leisure |
| गलत | galat | wrong |
| गलत–फ़हमी | galat-fahamī (f.) | misconception, misunderstanding |
| गले लगाना | gale lagānā (+ne) | to embrace |
| गये/गए | gaye | went |
| गाँव | gā̃v (m.) | village |
| गाँव वाला | gā̃v vālā (m.) | villager |
| गाना | gānā (m.), v. (+ne) | song (n.), to sing (v.) |
| गाड़ी | gāRī (f.) | train, vehicle, cart |
| घन्टा/घंटा | gʰanTā (m.) | hour |
| घर | gʰar (m.) | house |
| घोड़ा | gʰoRā (m.) | horse |
| घोड़ी | gʰoRī (f.) | mare |
| गिनना | ginnā (+ne) | to count |
| गोली | golī (f.) | tablet, pill; bullet |
| गुजरात | gujarāt (m.) | the State of Gujarat |
| गुमना | gumnā (–ne) | to be lost |

| गुस्सा | **gussā** (m.) | anger |
|---|---|---|
| गुठली | **guThlī** (f.) | stone (of a fruit) |
| ग्यारह | **gyārah** | eleven |
| | | |
| हमारे यहाँ | **hamāre yahã** | at our place (house, country, etc.) |
| हमेशा | **hameshā** | always |
| हराना | **harānā** (+ne) | to defeat |
| हवा | **havā** (f.) | air, wind |
| हवाई अड्डा | **havāī aDDā** (m.) | airport |
| हज़ार | **hazār** | thousand |
| हाँ | **hã** | yes |
| हाल | **hāl** (m.) | condition |
| हालाँकि | **hālãki** | although |
| हाथ | **hāt**ʰ (m.) | hand |
| हिन्दु/हिन्दू | **hindu/hindū** | a Hindu |
| हिन्दुस्तान | **hindustān** (m.) | India |
| हिन्दुस्तानी | **hindustānī** | Indian |
| हो | **ho** | are (you; तुम) |
| होली | **holī** (f.) | the festival of colours |
| होना | **honā** (–ne) | to be |
| हुकम | **hukam** (m.) | order |
| हूँ | **hũ** | am |
| हैं | **hẽ** | are |
| है | **hɛ** | is |
| | | |
| इंतजार/इन्तज़ार | **intzār** (m./f.) | wait |
| इंतजार करना | **intzār karnā** (+ne) | to wait |
| इसलिये | **isliye** | therefore, so, thus, because of this |
| इतना | **itnā** (m. adj.) | so much/many, this much/many |
| इतने में | **itne mẽ** | in the meantime |
| ईसाई | **īsāī** | a Christian |
| | | |
| जब | **jab** (relative pronoun) | when |
| जब कि | **jab ki** | while |
| जहाज़ | **jahāz** (m.) | a ship, vessel, plane |
| जलाना | **jalānā** (+ne) | to light, to burn; to kindle |
| जल्दी | **jaldī** (f.) | quickly, hurry |
| जन्म | **janma** (m.) | birth |
| जवाब | **javāb** (m.) | answer |
| जवाब देना | **javāb denā** (+ne) | to answer, reply |
| जाना | **jānā** (–ne) | to go |
| जाने वाले | **jāne vāle** | going, about to go |

| | | |
|---|---|---|
| जाने दो | jāne do | let (someone) go |
| जानवर | jānvar (m.) | animal |
| जेब | jeb (f.) | pocket |
| जेब काटना | jeb kāTnā (+ne) | to pick-pocket |
| जी | jī | honorific word |
| जीवन | jīvan (m.) | life |
| जैसा | jɛsā | as |
| जैसे कि | jɛse (ki) | as, as if |
| ज्वालामुखी | jwālāmukʰī (m.) | volcano |
| | | |
| कब | kab | when |
| कभी | kabʰī | ever |
| कभी-कभी | kabʰī kabʰī | sometimes |
| कभी नहीं | kabʰī nahī̃ | never |
| कहाँ | kahā̃ | where |
| कहानी | kahānī (f.) | story |
| कई | kaī | several |
| कल | kal | yesterday, tomorrow |
| कम | kam | less |
| कमरा | kamrā (m.) | room |
| करीब | karīb | about, approximately |
| करना | karnā (+ne) | to do |
| कथा | katʰā (f.) | story |
| कटना | kaTnā (–ne) | to be cut |
| कौन | kaun | who |
| कौन सा | kaun sā | which one |
| का | kā | of |
| काफी | kāfī | enough, sufficient |
| कागज़ | kāgaz (m.) | paper |
| काम होना | kām honā (+ko) | to have work |
| काटना | kāTnā (+ne) | to cut |
| के बाद | (ke) bād | after, later |
| के बारे में | ke bāre mẽ | about, concerning |
| के बिना | (ke) binā | without |
| के लिये | ke liye | for |
| के साथ | ke sātʰ | with, together |
| के अलावा | ke alāvā | besides, in addition to |
| खाना | kʰānā (m.), v (+ne) | food (n.), to eat (v.) |
| खलनायक | kʰalnāyak (m.) | villain |
| खेलना | kʰelnā (+/–ne) | to play |
| खिड़की | kʰiRkī (f.) | window |
| खोलना | kʰolnā (+ne) | to open |

| | | |
|---|---|---|
| कीजिए/कीजिये | **kījie** | please do |
| किस | **kis** | which |
| किसी | **kisī** | someone |
| किस्मत | **kismat** (f.) | fortune, fate |
| किताब | **kitāb** (f.) | book |
| कितना | **kitnā** | how much/many? |
| कोई | **koī** | some, any, someone, anyone |
| कुछ | **kuc<sup>h</sup>** | some |
| कुल | **kul** | total |
| कुरसी | **kursī** (f.) | chair |
| क्या | **kyā** | what |
| क्या | **kyā!** | what! I do not believe it! |
| क्यों | **kyõ** | why |
| क्योंकि | **kyõki** | because |
| कहना | **kɛhnā** (+ne) | to say |
| कहते हैं | **kɛhte hɛ̃** | is called, is said |
| कैसे | **kɛse** | how |
| | | |
| लाल | **lāl** | red |
| लाना | **lānā** (–ne) | to bring |
| लगाना | **lagānā** (+ne) | to attach, to stick, to fix, apply |
| लगभग | **lagb<sup>h</sup>ag** | about, approximately, almost |
| लगना | **lagnā** (+ko) | to seem, to be applied, to appear |
| लगना | **lagnā** (–ne) | to cost, to take (time) |
| लक्ष्मी | **lakshmī** (f.) | Lakshmi, the goddess of wealth, fortune, prosperity |
| लंदन | **landan** | London |
| लड़ाई | **laRāī** (f.) | fight, battle, war |
| लड़का | **laRkā** (m.) | boy |
| लड़की | **laRkī** (f.) | girl |
| लौटना | **lauTanā** (–ne) | to return, to come |
| लेकिन | **lekin** | but |
| लेना | **lenā** (+ne) | to take |
| लिखना | **lik<sup>h</sup>nā** (+ne) | to write |
| लोग | **log** (m.) | people |
| लोक कथा | **lok kat<sup>h</sup>ā** (f.) | folk tale |
| | | |
| मछली | **mac<sup>h</sup>lī** (f.) | fish |
| महा | **mahā** | great |
| महाभारत | **mahāb<sup>h</sup>ārat** (f.) | one of the two greatest epics from Sanskrit |
| महीना | **mahīnā** (m.) | month |

| | | |
|---|---|---|
| मन | **man** (m.) | mind |
| मनपसन्द | **man-pasand** (f.) | favourite |
| मनाना | **manānā** (+ne) | to celebrate (festival, holiday), to persuade |
| मर्द | **mard** (m.) | man |
| मरीज़ | **marīz** (m.) | patient |
| मरना | **marnā** (–ne) | to die |
| मसाला | **masālā** (m.) | spice |
| मसालेदार | **masāledār** | spicy |
| मत | **mat** | not |
| मतलब | **matlab** (m.) | meaning |
| मौका | **maukā** (m.) | opportunity |
| मज़ा करना | **mazā karnā** (+ne) | to enjoy |
| माँस | **mā̃s** (m.) | meat |
| मालूम होना | **mālūm honā** (+ko) | to know, to be known |
| माता | **mātā** (f.) | mother |
| में | **mẽ** | in, during |
| मेहरबानी | **meharbānī** (f.) | kindness |
| मिलना | **milnā** (–ne) | to meet, to be available |
| मिलना | **milnā** (+ko) | to find, to receive, to get |
| मिर्च | **mirca** (f.) | chilli peppers |
| मित्र | **mitra** (m.) | friend |
| मिज़ाज | **mizāj** (m.) | temperament, nature |
| मुगल | **mugal** | the Moguls |
| मुझे | **mujʰe** | (to) me |
| मुलाकात | **mulākāt** (f.) | meeting |
| मुलाकात होना | **mulākāt honā** (–ne) | to meet |
| मुश्किल | **mushkil** | difficult, difficulty (f.) |
| मैं | **mẽ** | I |
| महँगा | **mɛhɛ̃gā** | expensive |
| महल | **mɛhɛl** (m.) | palace |
| | | |
| न . . . न | **na . . . na** | neither . . . nor |
| न? | **na?** | isn't it? |
| नहीं | **nahī̃** | not |
| नहीं तो | **nahī̃ to** | otherwise |
| नकल | **nakal** (f.) | copy, fake, imitation |
| नमक | **namak** (m.) | salt |
| नमस्ते | **namaste** | Hindu greeting and replies to the greeting (may be used by other religions too) |
| नया | **nayā** | new |

| नज़र | **nazar** (f.) | vision |
|------|------|------|
| नाम | **nām** (m.) | name |
| नापसन्द | **nāpasand** (f.) | dislike |
| नाश्ता | **nāshtā** (m.) | breakfast |
| ने | **ne** | agent marker in the perfective tenses |
| ओह | **oh** | exclamation of pain/sorrow |
| पहुँचना | **pahũcnā** (–ne) | to reach, arrive |
| पकड़ना | **pakaRnā** (+ne) | to catch |
| पलना | **palnā** (–ne) | to be brought up |
| पंक्ति/पंक्ति | **paŋkti** (f.) | line, row |
| पर | **par** | on, at |
| पराजित होना | **parājit honā** (–ne) | to be defeated |
| परेशान | **pareshān** | troubled |
| परहेज़ | **parhez** (m.) | abstinence |
| परहेज़ करना | **parhez karnā** (+ne) | to abstain, avoid |
| पढ़ना | **paRʰnā** (–ne) | to study |
| पढ़ना | **paRʰnā** (+ne) | to read |
| परिवार | **parivār** (m.) | family |
| पड़ना | **paRnā** (–ne) | to fall, to lie down, |
| पसन्द | **pasand** (f.) | choice, liking |
| पश्चिम | **pashcim** (m.) | west |
| पश्चिमी | **pashcimī** | western |
| पता | **patā** (m.) | address |
| पता लगना | **patā lagnā** (+ko) | to come to know |
| पटाखा | **paTāxā** (m.) | a firecracker |
| पत्रा | **patrā** (m.) | astrological chart |
| पवित्रता | **pavitratā** (f.) | purification, holiness |
| पाना | **pānā** (+ne) | to find, obtain |
| पानी | **pānī** (m.) | water |
| पास | **pās** | near |
| फल | **pʰal** (m.) | fruit |
| फेंकना | **pʰẽknā** (+ne) | to throw |
| फिर | **pʰir** | again, then |
| फुलझड़ी | **pʰul-jʰaRī** (f.) | a kind of firework which emits flower-like sparks |
| पिचकारी | **pickārī** (f.) | a syringe-shaped water-gun made of wood or metal |
| पीला | **pīlā** | yellow |
| पीना | **pīnā** (+ne) | to drink |
| प्रचलित होना | **pracalit honā** (–ne) | to be prevalent |

| प्राचीन | prācīn | ancient |
|---|---|---|
| प्रकाश | prakāsha (m.) | light |
| प्रसन्नता | prasanntā (f.) | happiness, joy |
| प्रसिद्ध | prasidd<sup>h</sup>a | famous |
| प्रतीक | pratīka (m.) | symbol |
| प्रेम | prema (m.) | love |
| पुलिस वाला | pulis vālā (m.) | policeman |
| पुराना | purānā | old (inanimate) |
| पुस्तकालय | pustakālaya | library |
| पूछना | pūc<sup>h</sup>nā (–ne) | to ask |
| पूजन | pūjana (n.) | worship |
| पूरा | pūrā | complete, whole, full |
| पूरा करना | pūrā karnā (+ne) | to complete |
| प्यार | pyār (m.) | love |
| पहला | pɛhlā | first |
| पहले | pɛhle | (at) first, ago, previously |
| पैसा | pɛsā (m.) | money (one hundredth of a rupee) |
| रक्षा-बन्धन | rakshā-band<sup>h</sup>ban (m.) | the festival of love |
| रक्षा करना | rakshā karnā (+ne) | to protect, to defend |
| रंग | raŋga (m.) | colour |
| रंग बिरंगा | raŋga-biraŋgā | colourful |
| रंगीन | raŋgīn | colourful |
| राजा | rājā (m.) | king, emperor |
| राज्य | rājya (m.) | kingdom |
| राक्षस | rākshasa (m.) | demon |
| राम | rāma (m.) | Lord Rama (proper name) |
| रानी | rānī (f.) | queen |
| रात | rāt (f.) | night |
| रावण | rāvaNa (m.) | the demon king, Ravana |
| रेशम | resham (m.) | silk |
| रेशमी | reshmī | silken |
| ऋतु | ritu (f.) | season |
| रिवाज | rivāj (m.) | custom |
| रुकना | ruknā (–ne) | to stop |
| रुपया | rupayā (m.) | rupees (Indian currency) |
| रहना | rɛhnā (–ne) | live |
| सब | sab | all |
| सब्ज़ी | sabzī (f.) | vegetable |
| सच | sac (m.) | truth, true |
| सच | sac! | truth! It can't be true! |

| सकना | saknā (–ne) | can, be able to |
|---|---|---|
| सलाह | salāh (f.) | advice |
| सलाह लेना | salāh lenā (+ne) | to seek/take advice |
| सलाह मानना | salāh mānnā (+ne) | to accept/take advice |
| सलाम | salām (m.) | Muslim greeting and reply to the greeting |
| समझना | samajʰnā (+/–ne) | to understand |
| समय | samaya (m.) | time |
| सम्राट | samrāT (m.) | king, emperor |
| संदेश | sandesh (m.) | message |
| संगीत | saŋgīt (m.) | music |
| संस्कृत | sanskrita (f.) | Sanskrit |
| सर्व-प्रिय | sarva-priya | loved by all, the most favourite |
| सौ | sau | hundred |
| सवाल | savāl (m.) | question |
| सवेरा | saverā (m.) | morning |
| साहिब | sāhib (m.) | sir |
| साल | sāl (m.) | year |
| सामान | sāmān (m.) | baggage, goods, stuff, tools |
| साड़ी | sāRī (f.) | saree |
| सात बजे | sāt baje | seven o'clock |
| से | se | from, with, by, than |
| सेवा | sevā (f.) | service |
| शादी | shādī (f.) | marriage |
| शादी-शुदा | shādī-shudā | married |
| शाम | shām (f.) | evening |
| शानदार | shāndār | splendid, great |
| शायद | shāyad | perhaps |
| शब्द | shabda (m.) | word |
| शरीर | sharīr (m.) | body |
| शताब्दी | shatābdī (m.) | century |
| शत्रु | shatru (m.) | enemy |
| शत्रुता | shatrutā (f.) | enmity, hostility |
| शौक | shauk (m.) | hobby, fondness, interest |
| श्रीकृष्ण | shrī krishna | Lord Krishna |
| शुभ | shubʰa | auspicious |
| शुक्रिया | shukriyā (m.) | thanks |
| शुरु करना | shuru karnā (+ne) | to begin |
| शहर | sheher (m.) | city |
| सीखना | sīkʰnā (+ne) | to learn |
| सिंगार | siŋgār (m.) | make up |
| सिर | sir (m.) | head |

| | | |
|---|---|---|
| सिर्फ़ | sirf | only |
| सोचना | socnā (+ne) | to think |
| सोलहवीं | solvī̃ | sixteenth |
| सुबह | subā (f.) | morning |
| सुलतान | sultān (m.) | a Sultan, king, emperor |
| सुनहरा | sunharā (m. adj.) | golden |
| सुनते ही | sunte hī | as soon as (someone) heard |
| सूखा | sūkʰā (m. adj.) | dry |
| सूत | sūt (m.) | cotton |
| सूती | sūtī | cotton (adj.) |
| सैनिक | sɛnik (m.) | soldier |
| | | |
| ताज | tāj (m.) | crown |
| ताजमहल | tāj mɛhɛl (m.) | the Taj Mahal |
| तब तक | tab tak | by then |
| तबीयत | tabīyat (f.) | health, disposition |
| तकलीफ | taklīf (f.) | trouble, bother |
| तकलीफ देना | taklīf denā (+ne) | to bother |
| तलाक | talāk (m.) | divorce |
| तर | tar | wet |
| तरी | tarī (f.) | liquid |
| तशरीफ़ | tashrīf (f.) | (a term signifying respect) |
| तशरीफ़ लाना | tashrīf lānā (–ne) | to grace one's place, welcome, come |
| तशरीफ़ रखना | tashrīf rakʰnā (+ne) | to be seated |
| तेज़ | tez | fast, quick, sharp, strong |
| था | tʰā | was |
| ठीक | Tʰīk | fine, okay |
| ठीक-ठाक | Tʰīk-Tʰāk | fine, hale and hearty |
| टीका लगाना | Tīkā lagānā (+ne) | to give an injection/a shot |
| तोहफा | tohfā | gift |
| थोड़ा | tʰoRā | little, few |
| तो | to (particle) | to, then, as regards |
| त्यौहार | tyauhāra (m.) | festival |
| तैरना | tɛrnā (–ne) | to swim |
| | | |
| उम्र | umar (f.) | age |
| उपहार | uphār | gift |
| उत्साह | utsāh (m.) | enthusiam, joy, zeal |
| उत्तराधिकारी | uttarādʰikārī (m.) | heir, inheritor |
| | | |
| वचन | vacan (m.) | promise |
| वह/वो | vah/vo | that, he, she |

| वही | **vahī (vah+hī)** | same, that very |
|---|---|---|
| वर्ष | **varsha** (m.) | year |
| वसन्त | **vasanta** (m.) | spring |
| वाह | **vāh** | ah! excellent! bravo! |
| वाह! वाह! | **vāh! vāh!** | wow! wow! bravo! |
| वापस | **vāpas** | back |
| वापस आना | **vāpas ānā** (–ne) | to come back |
| वातावरण | **vātāvaraNa** (m.) | atmosphere, environment |
| विदेशी | **videshī** (m.) | foreigner |
| विजय | **vijaya** (f.) | victory |
| विनती | **vintī** (f.) | request |
| वह कैसे | **vo kɛse** | how come? |
| वैसे | **vɛse** | otherwise, in addition, like that, similarly |
| ख़राब | **xarāb** | bad |
| ख़रीदना | **xarīdna** (+ne) | to buy |
| ख़तरनाक | **xatarnāk** | dangerous |
| ख़तरा | **xatrā** (m.) | danger |
| ख़्याल | **xayāl** | opinion, view |
| ख़ासकर | **xāskar** | especially, particularly |
| ख़ुद | **xud** | oneself |
| ख़ुदा हाफ़िज़ | **xudā hāfiz** | goodbye |
| ख़ुश-हाली | **xush-hālī** (f.) | prosperity |
| ख़ुशबू | **xushbū** | fragrance (lit. happy smell) |
| ख़ुशी | **xushī** | happiness |
| ख़ैरियत | **xɛriyat** (f.) | safety, welfare |
| यहाँ | **yahā̃** | here |
| यहाँ तक कि | **yahā̃ tak ki** | to the point, to the extent that |
| या | **yā** | or |
| याद दिलाना | **yād dilānā** (+ne) | to remind |
| यानी | **yānī** | that is, in other words |
| ज़रा | **zarā** | little, somewhat |
| ज़रूर | **zarūr** | of course, certainly |
| ज़रूरत | **zarūrat** (f.) | need, necessity |
| ज़रूरी | **zarūrī** | important, urgent, necessary |
| ज़ोर से | **zor se** | loudly |
| ज़ोर देना | **zor denā** (+ne) | to emphasize |
| ज़्यादा | **zyādā** (invariable) | more |

**Web resource**

The following link is useful for translating Hindi into English:

http://shabdkosh.com/

# Index

# Hindi: An Essential Grammar

### Rama Kant Agnihotri

This text provides a reader-friendly guide to the structural patterns of modern standard Hindi. Ideal for both independent learners and classroom students alike, this book covers the essentials of Hindi grammar in readable, jargon-free sections.

This edition includes:

- sections on the speech sounds of Hindi
- detailed analysis of Hindi sentence structure
- full examples throughout.

ISBN13: 978-0-415-35670-1 (hbk)
ISBN13: 978-0-415-35671-8 (pbk)
ISBN13: 978-0-203-00282-7 (ebook)